VERLAINE

VERLAINE

PRINCE OF POETS

By

Lawrence & Elisabeth
Hanson

CHATTO & WINDUS
WITH SECKER & WARBURG
LONDON

PUBLISHED BY
CHATTO & WINDUS LTD
42 WILLIAM IV STREET
LONDON WC 2

*

CLARKE, IRWIN & CO. LTD
TORONTO

PRINTED IN GREAT BRITAIN
© LAWRENCE AND ELISABETH HANSON, 1958

Preface

ALMOST all biographies of Paul Verlaine have praised the work and condemned the man. We find this attitude incomprehensible; we do not understand how a biographer can write a book on a man he despises; still less do we understand how, if Verlaine is the kind of man these biographers would have their readers believe, he could have written the poems they admire so much. We believe that good can only come from good, greatness from greatness; good or great work from a man neither good nor great seems to us, whose purpose is to relate work we admire to the man who created it, a contradiction in terms. We have common English usage to support us; the double meaning of the word "good" suggests that English-speaking peoples have tacitly recognised a connection between virtue and work well done.

As a result, this study of Verlaine is one of the very few to approach the work as an inevitable expression of the man and the man as an inevitable begetter of the work, self-evident though the proposition may seem to most readers. Verlaine does not cut an heroic figure in the usual sense of the words and we have not attempted to make him appear so; remembering, however, that the great man is larger than life in every direction, in faults, virtues, talents, temptations; remembering too that if ordinary men have no great faults they have no outstanding virtues and that the lives of very few would come out well from the kind of scrutiny we have given Verlaine.

We have been greatly helped during the writing of this book. Our dedication indicates one of the chief sources of indebtedness, with whom we gratefully join that kindest and most stimulating of hostesses, Madame Roland de Margerie. We also owe much to our friend Frédéric de Heeckeren's magnificent readings of Verlaine, Rimbaud and Baudelaire and to his promptness in answering difficult questions; to Madame Renée Modot, who first introduced us to the nineteenth-century French poets; to Madame Joly-Segalen; to Mademoiselle J. Gallagher; to Madame Marie Dornoy; to Monsieur Jean Adhémar; to Monsieur Bernard Dorival; to Mr and Mrs J. Baljeu; to Miss

5

B. Carpenter; to Monsieur Jean Loize; to Councillor W. J. Whitelock, J.P., Mayor, and to Mr Francis Pepin, Librarian, of Bournemouth; to Mr C. L. Hoffrock Griffiths, Town Clerk of Boston; to the Town Clerk of Nottingham; and to Monsieur Henri Matarasso, who put his magnificent collection at our disposal.

We have another and very pleasant sort of acknowledgment to make, to all those relatives of Verlaine, descendants of his friends and others who have helped us during our visits to the Verlaine-Rimbaud country. These kind people have not merely given us photographs and letters rarely and in some cases never before printed, they have more importantly provided direct evidence of Verlaine's movements and behaviour at certain periods of his life. This has often enabled us to correct inaccuracies and malicious gossip which have been repeated in book after book these last sixty years. It is not possible to include the name of every interested and helpful person in these districts, since this would involve printing the names of half the inhabitants in tiny villages and small towns, but certain acknowledgments must be made in addition to our general indebtedness to those in the Gendarmerie Nationale and the various Mairies: Mme Veuve Prévost and M. Jean Imbert of Juniville; M. Jules Rigot and M. and Mme Décloux of Coulommes; Mme Veuve Fricoteau of Roche; Professor Verdelot and M. Charles Namur of Rethel; Mme Veuve and Mlle Evrard of Jehonville; M. Grandjean and M. Charles Péture of Bertrix; M. Jean Barras of Paliseul; M. Taute and M. Deshayes of Charleville; and M. Prunis of Reims.

Finally, among those who have written about Verlaine, we are especially indebted to V. P. Underwood for his indispensable work on Verlaine in England; Harold Nicolson, for his account of Verlaine's place in French poetry; and Y.-G. le Dantec, whose edition of Verlaine is a biographer's dream.

The bibliography of Verlaine is enormous and some kind of selection has been essential. In our bibliography we have therefore omitted all articles, which run into hundreds, and have confined as far as possible our list of books to those written by Verlaine's contemporaries.

It is customary for a biography of Verlaine to include a fairly full account of Rimbaud's life after he and Verlaine parted. We

PREFACE

have not done so; partly because it is largely irrelevant to Verlaine's later life, partly because we hope in due course to complete our study of Rimbaud.

We have made no attempt to translate the poems scattered throughout the book because we believe Verlaine to be untranslatable. It is a curious fact that all the virtues of this most English of French poets are lost in translation and we would advise readers neither to judge him nor to confuse their impression of his work by translated versions. It is in any case possible, Verlaine being essentially the poet of sound and feeling, even for the reader with little French, by reading a poem often, preferably every night, to obtain from it much of what it has to offer the French reader; indeed in some respects even more, since the Frenchman is unfortunate enough never to be able to hear, as the foreigner hears, the French language superbly used.

Our thanks for permission to reproduce illustrations are due to the Louvre, the Bibliothèque Nationale, the *London Illustrated News*, *Mercure de France*, Bibliothèque Jacques Doucet, Musée Rimbaud, British Museum, La Direction de l'Architecture, Libraire Giraud-Badin, S.P.A.D.E.M., Mme Veuve Evrard, M. H. Matarasso, and to the owner of the Picasso portrait.

L. H.
E. M. H.

Tourrettes-sur-Loup
1958

TO
ROLAND DE MARGERIE
*in gratitude for his
help and encouragement*

Contents

List of Illustrations

LIST OF ILLUSTRATIONS

"I've loved much in my life. Much too much? Oh no! decidedly not! For love, you must understand—and believe me rather than condemning me outright—love is if not everything, ah! at least almost everything and practically the sole motive for all actions worthy of the name. Don't speak to me of other things, ambition, money, fame! At the very most, perhaps, one might except Art. And yet, and yet, Art, by itself . . . ?"

Chapter One

THE CHILD

1844-1851

IN what is now the Belgian Luxembourg is a village named
Verlaine, sometimes written Villane, Verlane or Verlée. In
the centuries before the French Revolution the village was a
part of northern France. In it lived a family of the same name.
The family was not, so far as can be known, a part of the small
but noble family which occupied the château in the hilly woods
surrounding the village. It may have been connected with the
Sieurs de Verlaine by way of the privilege soon to be attacked
by Beaumarchais, but the probability is that the name came
into common use when the family moved from the village and
the father, living for the first time near strangers with the same
Christian name, discovered the necessity of a surname.

At all events, when this particular family enters the period
of firm records in the late eighteenth century it had settled in
and about the village of Arville, still in present-day Belgian
Luxembourg. It was an unremarkable family, with its counter-
part by the thousand in every province of France, of peasant
farmers and small shopkeepers, pious, hard-working, close,
neither rich nor poor, respectable if at times given to heavy
drinking, but so insignificant that one forgets that if these people
never made history they allowed history to be made, since
without them there would have been no France.

Insignificant the Verlaines indubitably were. There is a
mention of one as student in the University of Luxembourg,
then silence. Over them rolled wars, revolts, revolutions, but
imperturbable, hard-faced, sparing of speech except in their
cups, they cultivated their land, built and re-built their houses
and shops, married, gave birth, sowed and harvested, sold their
wares, saved every sou, attended mass and above all remained
unshakably ordinary, their small ambitions driving them imperceptibly to form an unthinking inarticulate part of the *petite
bourgeoisie*. One Verlaine fought in the army but went back to
the land, and it was left to his son Henri to be the first Verlaine

to make a small name for himself as a character. He moved away from family tradition by setting up a lawyer's office in the large village of Bertrix, some miles south of Arville, but for the rest he seems to have been a somewhat shifty (or politic) individual blowing hot and cold before the years of the Revolution much as he alternated between bouts of drinking and religionism. In the last years of his life, however, Henri Verlaine revealed, besides an ability to butter his bread, an unexpected sense of principle. The success of the Revolution swung him once and for all to the side of the people. When Napoleon seized power, the notaire of Bertrix denounced him as a traitor; at first in the family circle, then, in 1804, indignation overwhelming caution, publicly. Critics, however obscure, of the new Emperor were marked men. Henri Verlaine was haled summarily to Luxembourg, but died before he could be brought to trial.

His father's defiant end did not impress his one son, Nicolas. In due course (he was only six when his father died) he was put into the office at Bertrix, but in company with most of the lads of France he worshipped the all-conquering Emperor, and in 1814, before his seventeenth birthday, he abandoned the law, ran away and enlisted. The moment was scarcely propitious, for within a year Napoleon had been finally beaten at Waterloo, the French Army humbled, Louis XVIII thrust uncertainly on the throne, and the entire Verlaine family found itself on foreign soil when the canton of Bouillon, which included all the villages into which they had settled or married—Arville, Bertrix, Paliseul and Jehonville—was taken into the newly formed Kingdom of the Netherlands.

But Nicolas, like his father, was ambitious and could rise to occasions. He opted for French nationality and decided to make his career in the army, defeated and disorganised though it was. So well did he acquit himself that by 1828 he had won a commission in the Engineers. He was one of the first of the "rankers" whose appearance formed an early symptom of the social revolution of the century.

By this time Charles X was in the last stages of his brief inglorious reign. Two years later came the mild revolution and France was once again "respectable" under the innocuous Louis Philippe, being governed by and for the upper middle class, few in numbers but making money with a scarcely decent speed, and the least reputable remnant of the aristocracy. It was an age of factories, more and larger shops, experimental railways and, by natural reaction, of excessively romantic poets and novelists; of a Paris given over on the surface (if the behaviour of the élite was to be taken as guide) to gossip about the latest amours, clothes and manners, and to another kind of vulgarity, amassing and ostentatious spending of fortunes by the business men; whilst underneath were heard the mutters of the "Reds", as they were called, making and collecting arms and biding their time. Not perhaps a France so respectable as the other European powers persisted in seeing her, and certainly not "safe", but on the whole dull and undistinguished—a combination which can be mistaken easily enough for respectability. Her army, outwardly respectable too, had accepted its new rôle of keeper of order within the reduced frontiers; it did not forget Napoleon, but Nicolas was in a fair way to forgetting his origins; he did not precisely state that he had gone through the Ecole Polytechnique, but he did not discourage the impression.

He did in truth cut an excellent figure—he was an upright man in every sense, well turned out and with an air—he was an efficient if not brilliant soldier, and at the soirées and balls of the garrison towns he must have seemed to admiring girls far removed from the popular idea of the ranker as a coarse upstart. Though ambitious and more than a trifle snobbish, he was governed in many things by native caution; when, after serving with credit under Cavaignac in Algeria and at the regular garrison towns and reaching the rank of Captain Adjutant-Major, he finally married, the match was in every way sensible; indeed it was more, it was happy. He did not go outside his class, but chose from the most prosperous part of it, the small manufacturers then springing up all over the north of France. The family of Dehée had originated, like the Verlaines, as peasant proprietors, but round about Fampoux in the Pas de Calais, that flat bare country known too well to the Englishmen of the 1914 war and which with its dead-straight roads lined with poplars, its wide and windy skies, is so different from the woods and hills and streams of the Verlaine country. Their advance was slightly the more practical as they had preferred hard cash to the social advantages of the law; they made the land work for them, setting up sugar-beet factories to serve their great centre of Arras.

Arras was one of the regular garrison towns, and there Nicolas Verlaine met Stéphanie Dehée. They made not a striking but an eminently suitable couple. He, then in his thirties, was tall, rigid, clean-shaven but for the small moustache then in military fashion, a notable figure in the brave colours of that day, with clipped speech and two clear blue eyes looking out of a hard, closely cut oval head. "Every inch a soldier" perfectly describes him; he was almost as stupid as most, as brave, quite as conventional, rather more honest and perhaps a shade kindlier. He may even have concealed unsuspected depths, as they are called, beneath that impassive exterior, but if so they remained concealed for the rest of his life.

Altogether he was a more impressive personality than his wife. Elisa Stéphanie was far from beauty; her brown eyes were set at too acute a slant, her face was too long, her chin too heavy and her black hair unremarkable. She was above medium height, slim to the point of scragginess and would scarcely earn a second look in any company: not an obvious catch. But Captain Verlaine was in essence, whatever his trappings, a peasant; plain Stéphanie might be and apparently insignificant too, but she cared for him, and if her expression of emotion was inclined to excess she remained respectable, she had manners which were almost too good and she brought with her a substantial dowry, very substantial for her position in life. And as he too had been careful, the pair began life together with more than a sufficiency of money.

Appearances are not everything; one wonders whether the Captain realised what lay behind the demure exterior of his wife. His marriage to Stéphanie at the end of 1831 was, affection apart, a good piece of business; her marriage to him was a step in the dark, a delightful adventure. For she was some way from the respectable norm that her birth, upbringing and appearance seemed to guarantee; stuffed with the romantic novels sprung up to counteract prosaic reality, she had lived one long dream in the big house at Fampoux, and with a little more daring, a little less conscience and much more sexual attraction she could have become another Madame Bovary. As it was, true product of her not very happy age, she dreamed of romance, seized it when it appeared to have come miraculously her way, and then spent much of her time inventing explanations for its habit of

Verlaine at 21

Verlaine the Schoolboy, 1857

Captain Verlaine

Elisa Moncomble

slipping through her fingers. Her husband in his regimentals was no doubt a cut above poor dingy Charles Bovary, and the frequent moves from one garrison town of France to another, the colour and romance of parades and displays, not to speak of the occasional rumour and the ever living possibility of real action, all provided the adventurous element that this over-nourished soul craved for and that the Captain, brought down to essentials, was incapable of satisfying.

On the surface all was well, all exemplary. If beneath her gentility a certain restlessness persisted, Stéphanie was too much a creature of her station to reveal it except in sudden surprising bursts of excitability. But these could be and were put down to a natural volubility; she remained a loving and dutiful wife, a good hostess in a somewhat embarrassingly ladylike way—a manner which did her no disservice in an age of parvenus and the bourgeois virtues. In such a world the Verlaines in their small and limited way moved in an aura of approval; their teas and soirées were impeccably dull, their quarters filled with the appropriate knick-knacks; they represented that most stable and satisfying of sights, the domesticated soldier. Behind that bourgeois façade of the 'thirties and 'forties stirred all the dissatisfactions from hunger to intellectual disgust, but the Verlaines and the circle in which they moved ostrich-like were oblivious to the inevitable; mild gossip and flirtation, incessant speculation about promotion, the regular bustle of transfer from one station to another every year or so made up a life that they and all about them found good, useful and indeed indispensable.

Yet all was not well in this domesticated paradise. Stéphanie's husband was eleven years her senior and physically almost inarticulate. Her son tells the story, which could be true, of Captain Verlaine (who did not always enjoy the best of tempers) opening the window of their dining-room and ejecting an omelette as unfit to be eaten. His wife chose to think, dared not think otherwise for fear of dullness, that this was an unconventional signal to another woman. The thought and her consequent agitation made her almost happy for a time. Thus her true passion (vocation it cannot be called) necessarily rose elsewhere. Passion would seem an incongruous word to use of this mild if pleasing nobody, this weak though amiable woman looking up to her ramrod of a husband, delighting in insipidities. Nevertheless she was ruled by passion; denied romance in her husband, she hungered for children with an intensity, a single-mindedness that can rarely have been equalled. Maternity, like all that runs to excess, can be a disease, and in this Stéphanie was diseased.

It would be reassuring to think that she had intimations of greatness, but in truth the poor woman simply wanted children, as many as possible and as soon as possible. They would, of course, all of them be unusual, but their mere existence was the thing. This she had persuaded herself was her life's adventure, to bear them and to live her dreams through them. There were, as there must always be, chinks in this self-protective armour. To satisfy oneself vicariously is no true answer to the demands that rise in every living being. Stéphanie was to "break out" from time to time in her own limited fashion. But as long as she had no children she could always believe that children were the answer.

And she had none. She conceived, but she could not bear. Three times she miscarried. Frantic in her mild way, she preserved the foeta in spirits and with them always before her in her room enjoyed as best she could the unsubstantial relationship of mother and three children. Sterile she was not, and that thin consolation she hugged to herself as she gazed ardently at the bottles ranged in order of birth.

By this time she was thirty. Hope dwindled. Some live child she must have. She looked about. She had not far to seek; a sister had died leaving a boy and girl to the care of a drunken indifferent father. Madame Verlaine adopted her little niece Elisa Moncomble.

This was in 1842. Elisa, eight years old, settled down happily and the family seemed at last complete. Madame Verlaine did not precisely lose hope of a child of her own, but she for the first time felt something approaching the resignation that the Church had so long enjoined on her. Not unexpectedly it was at this moment that she conceived for the fourth time. And on March 30, 1844, she gave birth to her first and only live child, a boy who was christened Paul Marie.

The Verlaine family was then in Metz. It might just as well have been in Montpellier, Arras or any other of the garrison towns. Nevertheless it was of Metz that the grown man was to think, talk and write with a fervour which has often been criticised as insincere. Verlaine was to invite such criticisms by

THE CHILD

wilful though good-natured exaggerations to please an audience, but this feeling for his birthplace was neither excessive nor unbelievable; he spent his first two years in Metz and also the years from five to seven, two vital periods for a child as observant and as affectionate as he; there he had his first love affair, there he first made friends, there he was something of a regimental pet; of this place he was to have nothing but happy memories.

The other years of childhood, from three to four, were spent at Montpellier in the south, and were brought to an end by the flight of Louis Philippe, the proclamation of the Second Republic and the three-day massacre of May when Cavaignac and his troops killed three thousand "Reds". The regiment was recalled to Metz, where the small boy enjoyed three blissful years before his father abruptly left the service—blissful not only for the reasons given above but because the young Paul enjoyed absolutely uninhibited admiration and love at home. His mother inevitably worshipped him, this abused word being here strictly relevant, but with a whole-heartedness and abandon that must have surprised even her husband: Paul was perfect, Paul could do no wrong, he was to be sheltered from every unpleasantness.

The innocent Elisa was not on the side of the angels. This little girl who had enjoyed two years as the darling of the family might well have resented the newcomer. But she was an exceptionally nice child and a loving one, though not perhaps very wise, and she abetted Madame Verlaine in spoiling the child with a thoroughness that ought to have proved disastrous. She welcomed a playmate who could also be treated as a living doll and she took up the rôle of second mother in a spirit of self-dedication and fervent love.

One would expect the victim of this two-fold maternal assault to show early and unfavourable signs of it; we have all met spoiled children. Yet the truth is that the child Paul, doted on and protected to a near maniacal degree, was decidedly and deservedly popular. He did not take this popularity at second hand; his father had always been too reserved to be really well liked, his mother too insignificant. He did not owe it to his beauty, for he had none, but he was outstandingly good-natured, had next to no pride, was never puffed up and for all his lack of obvious good looks (to a point because of it) he possessed what has always over-ridden the powers of physical

19

beauty—a potent charm. No one has yet satisfactorily defined charm, but in Paul Verlaine, child, boy and man, it came explicably from a finely made body, an intriguing face, a lively sense of humour, a remarkable absence of conceit (which means the showing of a true interest in the affairs of others), an impish disregard of ceremony and at times even decency, and from a warm and generous nature; all this, and even more from a something on which one cannot lay a finger—a personality, a soul, call it what you will.

So there, in the years 1848 to 1851, was this small boy, lording it lovingly over his mother and cousin, a little restrained by the occasional awe with which he regarded that undemonstrative man his father, but essentially no prig, not precocious, not anything in particular but a nice playful child. Yet even in these early years the man is to be seen plainly in the manner of the child's reception of devotion. For there are ways and ways: one can accept demonstrations of love without thought, with gratitude, in humility, as one's right, and one can return it or not as the case may be in a hundred different styles all indicative of the future. Paul revelled in the caresses he was freely offered and returned them with a blend all his own of a softly rapturous, dedicated yet curiously detached air. He relished caresses as he relished food and could scarcely have enough of either. This could be dismissed as greed, and no doubt there was something of that in his raptures; but what must strike anyone who examines the records of his childhood is the evidence of a strongly sensuous nature; even so early he had begun consciously to distinguish degrees of sensation and to respond to each with the appropriate alacrity.

In this can be distinguished clearly the seeds of the future; yet poetry and the life that the poet was eventually to lead seem far removed from that pampered, adored yet apparently ordinary child taking the air day after day on the fashionable Esplanade of Metz with the Rhine flowing below, a child made much of, at ease even in first love, conscious of popularity but unspoiled by it. No wonder that he was to look back to that time with nostalgia.

Chapter Two

THE BOY

1851-1862

I

CAPTAIN VERLAINE's retirement from the army, though apparently sudden, was inevitable, the man being what he was, from the moment in December 1848 when Louis Napoleon was elected President of the Republic. By 1851 the whole of France and many outside France had come to realise that Louis Napoleon had no intention of giving up the presidency at the end of his four-year term; that, on the contrary, he would almost certainly try to establish himself as Emperor. Though the countries surrounding France regarded such a possibility with alarm and anger, most of the French people, disappointed with the vacillating and unspectacular record of the Republican government and still nourishing its memories of Napoleonic triumphs and grandeurs, were willing, were even anxious for the great man's nephew to try to restore greatness as they saw it to their country. But there were exceptions, distinguished ones. Cavaignac was such a man; he distrusted Louis Napoleon as a politician and despised him as a soldier; an old-fashioned patriot, he could see nothing but disaster for France if either the common man (epitomised by the Reds) or the careerist (in the person of Louis Napoleon) held power. He had tried to prevent Louis Napoleon from re-entering France after the abdication of Louis Philippe, and when this failed he fought him in the Assembly and stood against him as rival candidate for the presidency. But Cavaignac had a bad record; the "May massacre" had earned him the hatred of every Parisian working man and woman, every Communist throughout the large towns; he was rejected.

Captain Verlaine's retirement has been explained as pique on account of being passed over in the most recent batch of promotions. This certainly explains a part of the man: the ranker's touchy pride taking offence. But the true interest lies not so much in his reaction to the slight as in the reason for it. He was not passed over because of any failing as a soldier or as patriot, but simply because he was a Cavaignac man and would not declare for Louis Napoleon. Captain Verlaine's superior officer, Major Niel, thought much of him and urged him to change his mind; but Niel, like most of the army, was solidly for Louis and was years later to become War Minister under him. The Captain refused; he had worshipped Napoleon as a boy, he had admired and served under Cavaignac as a man; he could not or would not transfer his allegiance a third time even for a Napoleon. So at fifty-three, abandoning the prospect of several years' profitable service, he retired to Paris; he had money, he had health and a small but devoted family; his principles would seem to have let him off more lightly than most.

A few months later, towards the end of November 1851, the young Paul heard indignant mutters of "coup d'état" coming from the room in which his father entertained his friends, and soon afterwards the long-anticipated stroke took place and France once more had a Napoleon as Emperor. The event seemed at first to have left the Verlaine household unmoved; Captain Verlaine was not among the few, exhorted by Victor Hugo, who raised the barricades again in the name of liberty; he confined his opposition to verbal fireworks with like-minded army men who had settled near him. But Madame Verlaine, caught in a moment of dissatisfaction which she was obliged to smother under any distraction near to hand, had read and listened with increasing excitement; increasing frustration too, because this moment of history with all its blood and splendour appeared only too likely to be passed by the Verlaines in their drawing-room. It became clear that her husband would not move a step and was blind to adventure on his very doorstep. So Madame Verlaine "broke out"; early in the afternoon of December 4, the day of the barricades, she left the peace and security of her house in Batignolles, that suburb of high respectability stuffed with retired army men, and began to walk eagerly downhill.

She was not alone; she took with her the eight-year-old Paul. They reached Boulevard des Italiens just before three o'clock. From there or from one of the neighbouring boulevards Madame Verlaine hoped that they might obtain a view of the fighting at the barricades to the south. Many others had had a similar thought; the street was crowded, the shop doors and apartment windows looking south were a mass of eager faces. Parading the street too were Canrobert's troops, but peacefully in this middle-class district of good repute. The one sign of troop-baiting was the occasional cry of *"Ratapoil!"* from some politically minded member of the crowd. Paul took up the cry—he had no idea of its meaning but liked the sound of the word—and his mother laughed at the childish treble piping out sedition. But she was a little alarmed too, and took him as quickly as she could into Boulevard Montmartre, where the crowds were thick. Too thick for comfort, in fact, and they moved on again, threading a way through the people massed in street and on pavement alike, but had not gone more than a few paces down Boulevard Poissonière when Paul, a timid child, took fright; the character of the crowd was changing as they moved eastward, it was rougher and sang the Marseillaise and other revolutionary songs.

Paul had heard the Marseillaise sung in the streets once before, at Montpellier when the Republic was proclaimed, but this second outburst sounded threatening and alarmed him. He and his mother retreated hand in hand as quickly as they were able to the respectable watchers of Boulevard des Italiens. But no sooner had they returned than shots suddenly rang out. One or two soldiers fell. In an instant the street became a battleground; the soldiers returned the fire and killed outright some fifty civilians—the famous massacre of December 4.

Paul, too small even to see a soldier, shared the panic which seized all the survivors. The street was black with a struggling mass trying to escape in all directions, men, horses and carriages mixed inextricably in a shouting, screaming mob. At last the mother and child, carried on a wave of people, were sucked through the open doorway of a large shop and into the half darkness beyond. There they remained willy-nilly, listening to the shouts and the galloping of horses as the troops cleared the street. Then all was quiet and they walked the long way home, shaken but, being what they were, cheerful too. Paul at an early age was thus given a view of politics which, happy-go-lucky though he was, he was not likely to forget. More importantly, the adventure demonstrated that the "protected" life of this child had its limitations; he was indulged in food, in caresses and, when his father was not about, in behaviour, but he was always at the mercy of that despotic and disconcerting master, the romantic temperament. Here it had led his doting mother to subject her darling to obvious physical danger; in the future the danger was to be less obvious and he was not to escape so easily.

The greyness of Paris at first depressed the boy's spirits as it has depressed many; then, again in conformity with the majority, he saw its beauty and felt its charm. It was a Paris on the eve of considerable and beneficial change. Within two years of Paul's arrival Haussmann was appointed Préfet of the Seine and forthwith began the extensive pulling down and rebuilding that changed the face of Paris. By 1855, the year of the first Louis Napoleon Exposition, when Paul was a schoolboy of eleven, the grand new boulevards were already taking shape before the admiring eyes of visiting foreigners, Notre Dame and the Hôtel de Ville had been set free from clustering houses (whose narrow streets had been an invitation to the throwing up of barricades by the dissatisfied), the Bois laid out, the Louvre, the Palais de Justice and the Sainte Chapelle completed and restored. On his walks with his parents—he and his mother in particular were great walkers—the boy must often have seen the fine new Boulevard de Strasbourg which drove, wide and straight and handsome, through the old streets from Gare de l'Est to Châtelet.

He nowhere comments on the work of Haussmann (as a good bourgeois he could be expected to approve of it), but the romantic spirit fostered by his mother retained, contrary to common sense and even safety, a fondness for the old, narrow, twisty streets and ramshackle houses that at first had depressed him. The difference between his vision and the vision of a thousand other boys lay in this, that what he saw and felt did not slip into the usual oblivion. The images were conventional enough up to a point, as he was to show—mist over the river, crowded roof-tops, glaring gas-lit cafés and the like—but the most lasting and most typical invariably concerned the look and behaviour of the people. He was building up an intensely personal and poetic response to life.

But no one except his infatuated parents and cousin would have believed such a thing to be possible. He was to all appearances an ordinary boy who leaned literally and metaphorically on the bosoms of his womenfolk, lapped the cosiness, adored the calm and the raptures alike and snuggled happily against the comforting sense of security. He was in many respects another Oblomov, possessing all that engaging man's good nature and some of his sloth, and the Verlaine home was a Parisian Oblomovka.

This sheltered, respectable existence was barely touched when with many a sigh from his mother and Elisa he was sent to school. The ordeal, which began early in the year following the December *coup d'état* at the insistence of Captain Verlaine (the boy's perpetual questions wearied him, he said), was in truth not severe since the school was no further from home than rue Hélène and its single unpleasantness was the startling sight of the master in tears after the death of his daughter. The round of Verlaine life continued: the rush home to the last stages of the afternoon receptions, with Madame Verlaine in her invariable black dispensing cakes and emotional but meaningless conversation; the long, substantial meals decorously devoured, the scent of cigar smoke floating up to his bedroom at nights with the occasional male laugh, and not least the visits to the many relatives of his mother at Fampoux and neighbouring villages and of his father at Paliseul and Bouillon. He loved every moment of it, the petting, the rich food, the airless over-furnished rooms, even (for he was no country child) the heavy scent of the hay under the spare sun of the Pas de Calais, the sough of the trees in the Ardennes.

Scarcely a cloud disturbed the sunshine under which he lived; the nearest he ever came to a rebuff was his father's occasional sharp petulance when he still tried to acquire knowledge at home, his mother's hastily offered cake or confection if he turned to her, and Elisa's pained face after he had been caught in some petty deceit. He had therefore to think his own thoughts and conceal his little peccadilloes the more carefully. All else was a sheer and mostly sensuous joy which extended uncritically to his regard for the outside world. All men, his mother held with an optimism that verged on the inane, were good and were to be treated as such. And to him as a child this must have seemed no more than obvious truth; it was to become second nature, this lovable, ineradicable fallacy.

But he was growing in every sense, and quickly. Within little more than a year he had grown out of the school in rue Hélène;

his capacity for understanding and assimilating what he heard and his promise of a prodigious memory made him, very ready to rest on his oars if given half a chance, an outstanding pupil despite himself.

There were further family consultations. Captain Verlaine announced his decision to a shocked and unbelieving circle of which he was one: Paul must go to a boarding-school, prepare himself for a career. What shape the career was to take remained vague, Madame Verlaine inclining to the engineering profession, the Captain favouring the civil service and the boy wanting, so little did he know himself, to follow his father.

Paul started off in character, gaily, proud of his new cap, filled with optimism; he would love all, all would love him. He was escorted by the family—hand in hand an imaginative biographer declares. The Captain would hardly have lent himself to such an embarrassing demonstration, but in spirit the boy was un-questionably borne on the sad journey by three pairs of hands, even perhaps by four, since Elisa's brother Victor was then staying with the Verlaines. The walk was familiar to all, being one of Paul's favourites, along Boulevard des Batignolles to Place de Clichy, down rue Ballu with a right and left turn—no more than fifteen minutes from rue Saint-Louis; and the house they entered was familiar too, at least as to the ornate gold lettering on large black boards outside announcing the presence behind the high wall of the Institution Landry, which prepared pupils for courses at the Lycée Bonaparte, for the *baccalauréat* and so on. Paul, chatting away on these earlier walks, had, in effect, sealed his own doom, for, impressed by the "pompous façade", he declared that if ever he had to go to school it must be to that one. His parents took him at his word. Again, however, his lot was less hard than it might have been; he was not only comfort-ably close to his home, he was granted the unusual privilege of being allowed to spend every Sunday there.

Rue Chaptal was to have other claims to fame—to the Goupil gallery there, managed by Theo van Gogh, was to come a few years later that message from the Louvre scrawled in chalk "I'm here. Vincent."—but it is unlikely that M. Landry would have conceded them; the Institution Landry was in effect its *raison d'être*; he proudly indicated the roll of honour with Saint-Beuve heading the list of distinguished past pupils. The roll remained incomplete; why should not the name of this latest little boy be added in due course? The good man did not know—how could he?—how woefully his polite gesture was to fall short of the truth, but his visitors were no doubt pleased and two at least would not have accused him of exaggeration.

But the partings had to be made and the boy—very small by then—left to face the disadvantages of an arrival at school in mid-term and halfway through the day. He was put temporarily in a class of older boys. The boys were not pleased and made their displeasure plain as boys do. By supper-time Paul was in tears, every illusion shattered for the moment. The supper, which was neither better nor worse than a thousand such, was so far removed from the repasts of rue Saint-Louis both in content and presentation that his wretchedness reached the pitch of action. The day boys trooped out after the meal was done. He joined himself to them as casually as he was able, then ran for home, hatless, breathless, beside himself.

There were no reproaches—one suspects that the Paul-less family was experiencing too much guilt and sorrow of its own to feel anything but joyful surprise. His mother flung her arms round him (the escapade was after her own heart), Elisa petted him and he was set down at table, where they were sitting, to a meal of special delicacy with an extra glass of good wine to round it off.

After the meal his father (restrained until then by an unusually dominant Madame Verlaine) had his say. It was mild, its burden being the call of duty, but it was adequate, and the boy, aflare with optimism again, was led back willingly the next morning by his cousin Victor, who symbolised all the military virtues in his spotless uniform and erect bearing.

2

From this moment the Verlaine family passed into the background of Paul's life. It formed an important background, from the ever-present awareness of its existence to the tangible Sunday reunions, from the loving letters of the women to the daily appearance of the Captain at school, producing invariably from a capacious pocket some tempting or solid titbit saved from the previous night's dinner to supplement a school diet which he

feared was insufficient for a rapidly growing boy; but a background it remained. Paul, put into a class of boys of his own
age, quickly flourished—he was, astonishingly, neither a cry-
baby nor bumptious—and, as man can acknowledge only one
good at a time, unconsciously allowed his home to recede to
second place; that nightmare of a false beginning at school did
not so much vanish from his mind (he forgot little) as drift
equably into memory; he could laugh at it whilst retaining an
authentic vision of unhappiness.

In a boy so enviably gifted as to nature, failings were bound
to show themselves; it soon appeared that he could be swayed
easily from almost any purpose—one had only to appeal to his
good nature; he also had, as might be expected, a longing for
general good-will and could be made instantly and desperately
wretched by a cold shoulder. Fortunately for him that rare
combination, charm and a good heart, carried him almost un-
scathed through the first year or so. After that, all was joy: he
was consistently cheerful, laughed easily and without malice,
was only too malleable and, a certain physical timidity apart,
a "good sport". He was also refreshingly generous, showing not
the faintest awareness of the value of money (or could it be that
he had stumbled on its true value?), which prime preoccupation
of the French nation had never asserted itself more vigorously
than in those palmy days of the mid-nineteenth century. And if
his credulity and good nature were frequently taken advantage
of, he reacted so amicably that he soon escaped the attentions
of the bully. He was in any case a big boy and strong even if he
had no idea how to use his strength, and was not quite the
guileless child he appeared to be and sometimes liked to make
out.

Despite a ready yielding to every available distraction, Paul
at twelve found himself walking twice every weekday except
Thursdays in the long line of uniformed senior boys down rue
Blanche, round the as yet unfinished church of the Trinité, along
rue St-Lazare to rue Caumartin, through a "monumental"
doorway, between "not less monumental" fountains into the
Lycée Bonaparte (as it then was), where he listened, not always
with rapt attention (he had discovered amongst other things the
charms of the sketch and the caricature), to lectures on the
classics, on history, geography, physics, mathematics and philo-

sophy. His companion on these walks was more often than not a certain Edmond Lepelletier. No two boys could have differed more profoundly, hence their friendship; outwardly Lepelletier was one of those people who exist everywhere, changeless from cradle to grave, without a face; it could not be called pleasant or unpleasant, being nothing and forgotten as soon as out of sight, and the emotions that registered themselves on it were no deeper than the reflection of light on a rock; inwardly he was cold, vain, ambitious, masterful and was as little poetical as anyone could be. His attraction for a Paul Verlaine, dreamy, warm-hearted and indecisive, is obvious; add the facts that his parents lived in rue Lécluse, which Paul could see from his bedroom window at home, and that Lepelletier's maternal grandfather and paternal uncle were both army men, and the intimacy was inevitable. Inevitable and for a time much to Paul's benefit; he needed a strong hand and a sense of direction, his own enthusiasms veering madly to every breeze; he had affection enough for two, though it must be said that Lepelletier was a good friend according to his lights. Paul's charm worked its usual magic, no doubt; nevertheless Lepelletier, a youth and man of almost insufferable rectitude, withstood admirably the many shocks that Paul was to give him.

Lepelletier had no face to speak of; Paul had so much face that Madame Lepelletier, dispensing tea with thankful glances from his face to that of her son, declared afterwards in the quiet of the family circle that she thought when Paul first entered the room that an ape had escaped from the zoo. Paul's face became an obsession of the Lepelletiers, and Lepelletier himself, writing as an old man, was to describe with eloquent inaccuracy the embarrassments and limitations his dead friend's hideousness had brought on him. Expecting a monster, the reader regards the photographs with some bewilderment; he sees a massive forehead and beautifully shaped head, thick black eyebrows curving comically at the far end, long slanting eyes separated by a broad short nose, high and wide cheekbones, a sensuous mouth, a prominent chin, fine black hair waving with a zest that is not long for this world. No beauty, no horror either. Faunesque, Silenic, Socratic—the similes have often been made. Is a faun, was Socrates or even Silenus repulsive? Paul Verlaine we know, having other and better witnesses than Lepelletier as well as our own eyes, was decidedly not so. On the contrary he was, the first shock over, engaging; naturally enough, since as always, in men at least, the expression is the thing, and Paul's expression was essentially attractive. His schoolfellows did not run from him or avoid him any more than his grown friends were to do. They drew spirited caricatures of him fish-faced, as a turk, as a pig-tailed Chinese, as a nightcapped philosopher stargazing with eyes so oblivious of worldly matters that he ignores the open drain at his feet; for the rest, they clustered round him, laughing at and with him, and took him for granted. What was a face but a heaven-sent invention to inspire caricatures and to differentiate a Faure minor from a Faure major? Mothers of course compared his looks gratefully with their sons', but men and boys did not give them a second thought. What women were to do can be left for the moment.

Lepelletier bases his theory on Paul's visits to the brothels. Paul was a month or six weeks from his seventeenth or sixteenth birthday (the date is not clear) when, having collected the sum of ten francs, he invented a summons home one Saturday and was granted an *exeat*. Some time earlier (he is naturally not precise) he had been broken in to the sexual underlife of the school; but—and this is the only point that matters—with so little lasting satisfaction that one May evening he is found timidly but determinedly knocking at the discreetly closed door of a house recommended by an older pupil, sitting in the red salon and choosing with what sangfroid he could muster his partner for the night. Others whispered of it, handed thumbed books under the desk, but he . . . ! He was anything but a bold creature, but in this matter then and hereafter he was a veritable lion.

It is difficult to imagine where Lepelletier thought that Paul was to satisfy himself if not at the brothels; it was not, as he implies, that nice girls were so appalled by the Mongol face that the wretched young Verlaine was driven to the sordid. There was never any possibility that nice girls of that day would be allowed to grant such a favour even to an Adonis, let alone a schoolboy of sixteen. Lepelletier, as cold as a fish, could and did meet these girls freely. When Paul excused himself, he thought the worst. Yet given Paul's initiation into sex, his discovery of an enormous appetite in this direction, and his upbringing, the brothels were inevitable.

If Verlaine is to be understood, his exhaustless enthusiasm for a life of sensation, of which this was merely an inevitable stage, must be accepted. Every form of bodily pleasure pleased him, preferably but not necessarily when he could share in it, the feeling, imagined or experienced, being the main point. And one form of pleasure led to another. The Frenchman is sexually a connoisseur as he is a connoisseur of good food and wine; Verlaine received all sensation like the good wine that partly at least had induced it; he had begun early and was to end only with death. He spoke about copulation as an Englishman might speak about the fragrance of his roses. He would in any case see only a difference of degree in physical pleasure. He was later to adopt from time to time the "naughty boy" attitude because he understood that it was expected of him, but he was not truly conscious of doing anything but obeying a dominant law of life. He has often been called a child of impulse, and so he was if it be remembered that the child was in some respects more adult than any adult of his time.

He was to become a poet of life as it is lived; to condemn his life and praise his work is to ignore the reality that the one depends absolutely on the other; had Verlaine been, as we say, a less self-indulgent man, had he not savoured the flesh (which with him ranged impartially from a well-spread table to a companioned bed, from a scent to a sigh, from touch to sound) with a fresh and perceptive joy, he could not have written the poems famed and loved throughout the world, for they spring from the same source.

By the time he was eighteen the young man was a regular visitor to the brothels, and loved it. He looked forward to a more respectable method of enjoying himself in due course, but for the moment he was contented. What, after all, were brothels for if not for such as he?

In another direction he had also progressed fast by the age of eighteen. Here Lepelletier was a strong influence for good. Not Lepelletier alone—Paul was far too convivial a soul to be satisfied with a solitary friend—but he chiefly because bent on knowledge and, through knowledge, advancement. Verlaine sat at the feet of the great preachers and revelled in their oratory, dispassionately feeding himself concurrently with the atheistic *Force et Matière* of Buchner, and he toured the museums and churches—

these last chiefly to study the Delacroix frescoes. But books were the obvious highway to knowledge, and the two boys read ravenously and discussed their reading without end. In his fifteenth and sixteenth years, haunting the Bibliothèque Sainte-Geneviève, Paul raced through a great medley of French and foreign literature and ephemeral rubbish. The compulsory classics apart, he devoured the novels from Balzac to Dumas, the books of travel, the macabre stories then in vogue from Hoffmann to Poe, the historians, the philosophers, the literary critics, translations from English, Spanish and German, the religious books of the East and anything else he could lay hands on. And every week he called at the bookshop to collect the latest part of *Les Misérables*. A rite, this, as much as an enjoyment, for Hugo had become his god as he was the god of practically the whole of literary and republican France. His first poem, following custom, was sent to the hero in exile; he was then in his fifteenth year and prayed judgment on "this first step on the stormy path of poetry".

It is unlikely—Verlaine in later life supports the theory—that even the schoolboy Paul truly sympathised with the writings of Hugo, their romantic blustering was so much the antithesis of his own quietly personal vision. But Hugo was then much more than the *grand maître* of French letters, he stood as a voluble symbol of freedom. From his exile in Jersey the little man, when he was not sleeping with every woman he could find or who could find him (for he was the most famous lover of the age), directed a stream of words into France: abuse of "Napoleon le Petit", novels, poems, plays, invocations to the people to rise and destroy the tyrant, approval at once patronising, pompous and fulsome of literary productions by the younger writers at home. Marine Terrace was the Mecca to which almost all rebels looked; and when a man could not make the pilgrimage in person he sent his latest poem, book, play, whatever it might be, to obtain the sanction of the master. Not all, perhaps not many, were whole-hearted in this admiration; Hugo, though he tried his hand at everything, was in truth gradually becoming *passé*, a relic of the romanticism of the eighteen-thirties; but all or almost all trod the path whatever they might privately think or do. A symbol, a centre was necessary, and Hugo with a curious but not unknown mixture of greatness, adroitness, bull-headed sincerity and barefaced volte-face had planted himself on a pedestal from which no one dared try to pull him down.

The young Paul eagerly followed the general example. In a schoolboy this was understandable, in grown men less so unless the state of intellectual France is borne in mind. By 1860, when Paul was sixteen and reading for dear life, Louis Napoleon had established himself firmly, as it seemed, in his uncle's seat; the victory of the Crimea (for as such it was then widely seen) followed by his success, to his own secret surprise for he was no general, of 1859 against the Austrians had enabled him to make a triumphal ride through Paris when he was for once widely acclaimed. Men walked and drove along the noble new boulevards spanning and encircling the city, their wives shopped at the grand new stores, men and women talked of and travelled in the new railways covering France, attended sumptuous performances of opera and ballet, gazed admiringly at the beginnings of the ornate Opéra rising close to Boulevard des Italiens to take the place of its humbler and more tasteful predecessor, watched the crowds of foreigners sight-seeing with gaping reverence and pocketed their share of the money the visitors lavishly expended. Paris was great again, the centre of the world.

But there was another side to the picture. The beautification of the city, the popularisation of France cost money. Prices rose, the masses were sweated, many starved. In 1860, the year of Louis' triumphal ride through Paris, the number of arrondissements was increased from twelve to twenty; the workers displaced by the Haussmann clearances of the centre who had made new homes on the outskirts automatically became liable to municipal taxation—the main reason for the extension—although sharing none of the benefits. This caused an outcry which the government ignored and made new enemies of the régime by the thousand. There was altogether too much gold watch-chain; the vulgar display of wealth in the capital and chief towns was a constant offence to the tasteful, the hungry and the envious, and rumours not without foundation of corruption in high places roused bitterness. Orsini's attempt to assassinate Louis outside the Opéra in 1858 had even then expressed the hatred of thousands, and the victimisation of the revolutionaries that followed it increased the already widespread detestation of the Emperor. Nor did art escape: painters and writers of a kind were patronised but the forward-looking were frowned on and from time to time persecuted. The year before the assassination attempt Flaubert had been prosecuted for publishing an immoral work, *Madame Bovary*: Baudelaire's *Fleurs du Mal* was proscribed and the author fined; Renan was soon to arouse the enmity of the Church with his *La Vie de Jésus* and to be driven from his post. There followed naturally an alliance between the artist and the revolutionary; numerous anti-Louis pamphlets and underground newspapers appeared; journalists (including young writers of distinction) were thrown into prison year after year. The spirit of dissatisfaction, disgust and revolt grew; the political prominence of a France represented by fat shopkeepers, over-dressed manufacturers and a debased section of aristocracy was, in the eyes of the intellectual patriot, a poor exchange for the intellectual leadership she was throwing away.

In an English school all but the pageantry and the battles would have passed over the heads of the boys. In a French school such blindness, or innocence if one prefers the term, is impossible. The Institution Landry seethed with revolutionary fervour and the well-worn sheets handed surreptitiously about the school were not often the "smut" so beloved of the adolescent but free-thinking pamphlets, calls, as violent as they were ineffectual, to political action, abuse of Louis and the Church which bolstered him, glorification of the depressed workers and the persecuted *élite* of art.

To this last all the school intellectuals instinctively attached themselves. To be a modern reader and writer was to be a revolutionary; it was as simple and as attractive as that. Lepelletier was one of the most voluble of the band, but the leader was another schoolfriend of Paul's, Raoul Rigault, an alarming representative of the revolutionary leader in embryo, single-minded to the point of insanity, blind to compassion, stupid, cold to all and everything but an impracticable idea, caring neither for his own life nor for the lives of others.

To find Paul in this galley is not without its amusing side. Had he followed his inclination he would have concentrated on the "smut", for he was developing an absolute passion for the obscene, with this difference from the other boys, that he would shout not whisper the words which gave him increasing delight. Unlike Lepelletier and Rigault, who as their lives showed were

politically minded, he lived simply for and in his particular
sensation of the moment; and, lazy and easily led as he was, the
sensation originated more often than not in other minds. The
appeal of the Church to such a nature is obvious; the ritual
pleases the senses, the discipline soothes and fascinates the mind,
the infallibility relieves the conscience from the distressing
necessity of making a decision. To be anti-religious, to be at all
politically serious was for him to mock himself. Nevertheless,
spurred on by a fanatical Rigault, a purposeful Lepelletier and a
longing to agree with those he loved, he did so with a will: none
hotter than he, none wilder in speech and writing. He enjoyed
himself immensely playing at revolution with these rather
frightening young men who called themselves his friends. And
in this spirit he read the blustering prose and verse of Victor
Hugo; to this extent and no further Hugo was his "god".

3

Paul's true gods were very different from Hugo, whose verse
he had read only, like those of other poets, in "chosen morsels"—
the choice being that of the master or compiler of the textbooks
used at school. One day, however, he saw lying on a chair,
forgotten by its owner, a first edition of *Fleurs du Mal*. He read
and re-read the poems with astonishment; it was a measure of
Baudelaire's obscurity at that time that to the bookworm Paul
his name conveyed nothing. The meaning of the poems for the
most part escaped him—an interesting commentary on his
persistent innocence—but two characteristics at once impressed,
the sonorous music of the lines and their austerity. The appeal
of the first was inevitable to one who was to become the most
musical of poets, but that it was possible to combine this
musicality with a monastic condensation, that the sensuous could
at the same moment be ascetical amazed him; how much so can
be imagined when one remembers that the work of the popular
poets of the day and the whole conception of poetry praised in
school and discussed by the boys was of highly romantic not to
say sentimental ideas expressed either in florid, excessively
"poetic" language or in a lifeless classical style.

The schoolboy of sixteen knew no more than that he had
discovered something exquisitely pleasurable and a something

that he longed to imitate. But the immediate and more important effect of *Fleurs du Mal* was to fix part of his mind on poetry and send him in search of other modern poets. He was, thanks to his mother, a good though leisurely walker accustomed to the drop down to the centre of Paris and the return upward pull—a good hour or more—as all in the day's work. He now extended his range, exploring the islands and the left bank until the city was known to him, and he began, with Lepelletier, what he called his "booksearchings" whenever he had an afternoon off, tirelessly tramping the lanes and river bank, dipping into all the stalls and bargain boxes outside bookshops. It was at a shop on Quai Voltaire that he found, on his first "booksearching", a copy of Théodore de Banville's youthful *Cariatides*. Paul's excitement at this discovery greatly exceeded his reception of *Fleurs du Mal*, and this accurately places the two poets, for *Cariatides* presented no miracle to the boy beyond the miracle of its appearance at that time and place. It was wonderful to him naturally, but, as he read and read until he knew the poems by heart, an entirely explicable wonder; the technical devices which made the merit of the book, skilful though they were, were visible to an acute eye, and Paul's eye even at sixteen was in this matter acuity itself. Hence his excitement as he plumbed the not very great depths and made the book his own, whereas with *Fleurs du Mal* the much that was above his head tempted him for self-respect's sake to underrate it.

To *Cariatides* he added during later journeys but at the same shop the *Vignes Folles* of Albert Glatigny and the *Philoméla* of Catulle Mendès, and began to get a reasonably accurate picture of the work of the younger generation of poets. He was enchanted. Not much of that enchantment is felt today, but in the early 'sixties Mendès and Glatigny seemed advanced, charming, spirited rebels with all manner of comprehensible merits to a boy who loved to admire, yearned to write and who had had intimations that there was more in poetry than met the eye in school books.

He built himself a small library of "moderns" as his walks ended more and more often at the quayside, moderns which included the *Poèmes Antiques* and *Poèmes Barbares* of Leconte de Lisle, the *Ensorcelée* of Barbey d'Aurevilly and the *Emaux et Camées* of Gautier, and, inspired by his many heroes, wrote passable imitations of all in bursts of poetic industry which carried him pleasantly to his nineteenth year. He did other things, plenty of them; he planned and perhaps began to write (few fragments exist today) a series of historical dramas impassioned and bloodthirsty, on the "Wise" and "Mad" Charles V and VI and on the two Louis XV and XVII, a fairy play and, with Lepelletier, he really did complete the first act of a fierily republican tragedy the *Forgerons*, with a working-man hero. In all it could be said with fair accuracy that he spent the greater part of these days, weeks, months and years in pleasing himself, and that of his pleasures the reading and writing of poetry on the whole most satisfied him. Yet this poetry cannot convey to the reader the raptures that it presumably gave him. He early discovered a facility for the writing of verse, he was clever in catching the tone of a particular hero when composing, but not a suggestion of the great or even the good poet can be found. Here was no born genius breaking out of insignificance, but a charming, decidedly lazy and quite remarkably sensuous young man sipping honey from a variety of flowers.

4

He was, however, at school with an aim in which poetry played next to no part—to obtain in due course the *baccalauréat* without which in his father's eyes and in the eyes of all good Frenchmen the long years of schooling would be so much money thrown away. In that elaborately written parchment with its great seal and flowing signatures, its gold leaf and grandiose wording, were the order, tradition, rectitude, respectability so dear to the French heart and, almost as though the examination had been created for this, the entry to the civil service.

How reconcile the *baccalauréat* and all that was supposed to follow with Paul Verlaine reading and writing poetry with a languorous fury? It is not difficult. He was above all things suggestible; the line of least resistance (provided only that it promised no unpleasantness) was the line he favoured. If asked why he gave so much time to poetry he would probably have replied that it pleased him. He would be a poet if he did not become playwright first, but that did not exclude a safe job, a snug home and all the amenities; in the Paris of that time the combination would be considered *de rigueur*. On the other side was the ugly vision of poverty, mean living, strife, even starvation, from which he averted his eyes with an incredulous shudder. Everything had become respectable—that was Louis Napoleon's achievement—the "moderns" not least. Had one suggested to Paul that he read or wrote poetry because he must, that it was as essential to him as the food and the embraces he loved, and that he would suffer for it he would have laughed with that rather gruff engaging laugh of his.

The *baccalauréat* therefore appeared a boring but essential stage towards security, the preservation of respectability and the perpetuation of all the pleasures including the composition of poetry, drama and anything else that came into the head in one's spare moments. There would be plenty of these moments, of course, because whoever's will prevailed as to the exact nature of his future—his father, mother or himself—the result would be a sinecure. And on August 16, 1862, having submitted himself to examination, he was duly granted the status of a Bachelor of Letters and, having to wait for some months for the official diploma and being in any case wishful to rest after unprecedented labours, withdrew himself, as soon as he had secured M. Landry's consent, to the supposed peace and quiet of his relatives in the north.

In later years Verlaine, following custom, made light of his passage through the examination; if he is to be believed, a mixture of luck and cheek pulled him through at the first time of asking. In fact he is not to be believed; every statement he makes about himself has to be taken with a large grain of salt. His sense of humour and his modesty are both more English than French; the truth is there often enough, but not often the truth he would have the reader or listener believe. The joke if carried to extremes can become a disease and Verlaine's passion for self-denigration was not far removed from this; it was a childish trait he never threw off. In this case, though there is a considerable element of luck in every form of examination, a study of the questions and of the fate of many of his companions including Lepelletier and the "cramming" they found necessary before sitting again make clear that merit played its part, and no mean part, in his success. In a letter of the time he tells a cousin that he is working "like a nigger", and there is no reason to doubt it. Lucky he may have been, lazy he certainly was, but only to the extent that he was sufficiently clever to afford to be so; a fact borne out by the certificate from Landry which shows him to have been one of the most promising pupils in the school.

These questions, needless to say, did not concern him in the least; he was conscious of virtue and of the reward that should follow it; he was not averse from acting the successful city nephew and cousin before admiring relatives; and by the late summer he was in the north.

Chapter Three

THE YOUNG MAN

1862-1865

I

THE boy who was soon lounging about the fields and farms and small factories of the Pas de Calais, reclining in the woods and fishing in the streams of the Ardennes (the general name for all that romantic country on both sides of the frontier), was not far short of six feet and, for one so indolent, robust with an upright and beautifully proportioned body. He could have stood as symbol of ten thousand other boys of his kind; more amiable than most, perhaps, certainly gentler, but in essence a true product of his time and class and upbringing— the perfect young *petit bourgeois* with all the virtues and limita- tions of the species. His one ambition was to enjoy a good time; he was conventional, impractical, emotional and, if his words were to be accepted literally, hopelessly sentimental. He seemed bound for a blameless and utterly useless life.

Yet he was not all he appeared and wished to be, and his future, could he have foreseen it, would have appalled him. The bourgeois in him, fostered so sedulously by his mother and father and by every recognisable desire in himself, was to be countered by the peasant heritage. Apparently he was his mother's son; actually he was to look back more and more, for good and ill, to his paternal grandfather and his forebears.

This did not mean, however, that he was a countryman *manqué* as Lepelletier afterwards claimed on the strength of a few sentimental passages in letters of this time. Verlaine was a city man from birth, and his occasional raptures over the country and plans to settle there were the raptures and plans that most city men, and especially the self-deceivers, indulge in from time to time. He enjoyed himself in the north-country strongholds of his relatives because he took care never to stay at any place long enough to wear the pleasure thin. When he found himself temporarily trapped in the country, his true feelings soon showed themselves. For the moment he extracted a sensuous delight from scenes, sights, smells, sounds, as only a poet and a city poet could do, but even this was incidental to his main pleasures. He could tickle the trout in the Semois at Bouillon, lie in the fields at Fampoux, laze through the woods of Bertrix, take pot shots at rabbits across the marshes of Lécluse, but he was twice the man if he had company and could talk out his emotions.

And never more so than in this summer of 1862 when a new friend, the young Dujardin, was at his side. Dujardin was the son of a widowed sugar manufacturer who had just married Elisa; the Verlaines stayed with the Dujardins at Lécluse, near Douai, for some weeks, and the friendship between the young men ripened with a speed and ardour that was to be characteristic of all Verlaine's relationships; he could do nothing by halves and his friends had to be the soul of perfection. His extravagant praise of Dujardin and his hints years afterwards that this and other male friendships were not all that they might have been have led naturally to suspicions of his relationships with men. For this last Verlaine has only himself to blame; he loved to shock and to mystify. But beyond the juvenile wish to baffle others and blacken himself the truth is that he loved men and women indiscriminately as the Greeks did and could never reconcile himself to the distinction drawn between the sexes by the society of his time. If he were to be judged by the language in which he spoke of Dujardin, then every man-jack of the literati of his time and tens of thousands besides would stand self-confessed homosexuals. Hear, for instance, Leconte de Lisle: "You know my love too well for me to tell you that it will never be extinguished. Oh! may memory bridge as best it can the vast space that parts us and may it assuage the bitterness of our sorrow and the tears of absence! I see you, speak to you, hold you in my arms!" These passionate words were addressed to a young man, but Leconte de Lisle was a notorious womaniser; it was a fashion of speech merely, a legacy of the romantics. The young Paul Verlaine was or would be the romantic of romantics; if he could not quite succeed in going the whole romantic way, not he consciously but the unconscious saving grace, the peasant kernel, forbade. But he could and did protest his loves with the best.

When facts are examined he and Dujardin are found to have shot together, fished together and danced not together but with every pretty village, town and city girl (for Parisiennes were on holiday there) they could find. They danced six nights running, they were for the time mad about dancing and their partners, they talk and write about them incessantly as boys do. No mention is made of Verlaine shunned, only of him dancing until he could have dropped.

Innocuous indeed. Then he and Dujardin found another way of passing their evenings and Verlaine was soon complaining not only of his legs but of his stomach. His complaints were not serious; he felt rather a dog: women and wine! Unfortunately he did not confine himself to wine, in fact scarcely tasted it. Young Dujardin was of course no more than a cipher; anybody would have done; the thing was inescapable. A later friend, Ernest Delahaye, has explained what happened. Delahaye knew his people—he too was from the Ardennes—and he knew Verlaine. The countryfolk were hard drinkers with good heads; hard workers too and shrewd; they kept their serious potations for special occasions, the birthday, fête day, first communion, marriage. And what better occasion than the arrival in their midst of the great Paul Verlaine, Bachelor of Letters at eighteen and with a future of such brilliance shining before him that the entire family (which in France extends endlessly through the realms of second, third and fourth cousins) was anxious to acclaim him; that is to eat heavily and at length and to drink deep into the small hours; to drink not the, in their eyes, insipid wines of the centre and south, but beer and spirits swallowed with grim relish and in alarming quantities.

It is not difficult to see the young Verlaine, the hero of hour after hour, tall, dark and dressed for the part in his borrowed rustic blouse and cap, small eyes glinting with mischievous good humour under their heavy brows, long arms waving, large mouth opening to emit a stream of words in the deep and rather husky voice. He would be a countryman! He would dress like one, smoke like one, puffing a clay pipe, and drink like one, tossing down one stiff potion after another nonchalantly; he would, he declared, have worked like one did not common politeness insist on the round of "thank you" calls which demanded a drink or two and usually ended in another carousal. And then there was more stomach trouble; head trouble too, for Verlaine was not then of the calibre of his hosts nor was he given their chance of recuperation. They were in their fields the next morning none the worse for the night before unless to be a shade more short of speech, but he was continuing his triumphal tour of "calls" when he would "clear his throat" and his head with eggs swallowed raw, a row of *p'tits cafés* which with the lightest of pressure by his host became the less innocuous *bistoules* (half coffee, half spirits), rounded off by several *gn'niefs* (gins) or the most potent and soon most beloved *trois couleurs* composed of a cup of black coffee and glasses of rum, cognac and kirsch from which he drank in turn. The point came soon enough when the remedy was overtaken by the malady it had set out to cure. He would lie down for an hour or two. Having rested, he would be too late in decency to leave and was persuaded without difficulty to sit down to another huge meal washed down with pots of *breune* and *chl'blinque*, the dark and light beers of northern France, and followed by a repetition of the morning drinks.

For he was not only naturally gregarious, he had discovered a taste for liquor. The two things, he happily discovered, formed the perfect combination. During a night of drinking he felt god-like, his words golden, his thoughts wonderfully illumined. And if his stomach troubled him the next day, well, what better remedy than more of the hair of the dog that bit him?

His parents did nothing to stop him. His father, who might have exercised a restraining influence, was in his own way being quite as foolish as his son and with less excuse; succumbing to the passion of the day for speculation, he had begun to "play the markets". He had no need of extra money, but boredom and vanity led him to do his best to dissipate what he had. He did not see it like that, naturally, he saw himself as in a small way a financial Napoleon, but such was the effect; every speculation went wrong, the comfortable Verlaine fortune was dwindling and it was becoming a question whether Paul would inherit anything but debts. Immediately after his latest reverse some hint of this would dawn on the Captain and he would grow pre-occupied and unwell. He was so then; his son's long absences were excused and the curious moods of elevation followed by biliousness were overlooked.

Elisa was also preoccupied by this first official visit of her beloved trio and thought more of making her new home fit for them than of the curious behaviour of the adored Paul outside the home. Mme Verlaine, fluttered by the festivities and enjoying her rôle as mother of the man of the moment (for although Paul's triumphs were as sure as day following night she did not disdain the world's acknowledgments), also had more of her time filled than was usual. However, she had eyes for her son as always and could observe what escaped her husband and Elisa, that the soul of perfection had begun to sow quite a few wild oats. That was how the romantic woman saw it; when she worried (and she was always worrying about something), she could tell herself that not only was Paul virtually immune from the common weaknesses, the one weakness that he now patronised was the one most forgivable, natural and looked at in a certain light even a matter for pride. To drink on equal terms with hard-drinking men and at such an age to carry his drink (more often than not) with an air—that was the thing! No serious reproof was to be looked for from that quarter; the doting Mme Verlaine could scarcely be expected to realise that her darling was not sowing his own oats but reaping the oats of another.

2

He returned to Paris late that autumn with an appetite for drink, but it is just possible that had circumstances been different he might have remained one of those who "take a drop too much" only when life does not run smoothly. At all events, to drink for the sake of it seemed a far cry from the young man who came back to Paris and a career—a young man with devoted parents, a sufficiency of money (his father's efforts notwithstanding) and, if his headmaster was to be believed, with a fine future.

There was some delay before this future materialised, and it was not until he had tried a snatch of law study, a few months' clerking in an insurance office and the marriage registry department of the ninth arrondissement, that soon after his twentieth birthday and to the general family delight he is found sitting at his desk in the Hôtel de Ville, a fully fledged civil servant with a good salary, excellent prospects and the promise of a pension.

These delays did not in the least perturb Verlaine; the one cloud in his sky, the possibility of military service (so far had he moved from his plan to follow his father), was happily blown away when he drew a good number and spared his parents the search for a substitute. For the rest he was so easy-going that nothing mattered to him so long as he was enjoying himself; this included some drinking in company but depended more on the company than the drinking. If he could be with a crowd, making music, making rhymes, talking the wildest politics or the most romantic nonsense, he was happy; and happy he was without serious interruption between that autumn of 1862 and the winter of 1865—three years of "having a good time". Café lights blazing, the buzz or to be exact the blare of argument on every hand, the bustle of waiters, the comforting clink of glasses on marble-topped tables, these were accessories to that good time. Like all intellectual Frenchmen his set found intoxication in words and had no need of another kind though they sometimes took it in passing. Some, such as Lepelletier, were practically non-drinkers; almost all the others, including Verlaine for most of this period, contented themselves with what, in comparison with northern habits, were mild stimulants, wines and apéritifs for the most part.

There was nothing Bohemian about the Paul Verlaine of 1862 to 1865 and especially in his first years as civil servant. One must imagine a smartly dressed young man in frock-coat, striped trousers, light waistcoat, shining boots, tall hat and splendid cravat who every weekday morning arrived not too early at the entrance to the great building close to the river jauntily swinging a cane and surveying the world with sprightly benevolence.

3

His duties and behaviour at the Hôtel de Ville have been, like his youthful drinking, the subject of many inaccurate comments. Verlaine can so easily be made a figure of fun—he is the first to play that game—that it is not easy to resist temptation. The facts are that by normal standards, which admittedly were not high, he had plenty of work. To him after the shortest of intervals this work was insufficient to occupy his time, far less his talents. He did not ask for more—he was the most human of beings—but either despatched what he had quickly and efficiently or tried to spin it out through the day. His spare hours, which grew every month, he devoted to more congenial subjects than the salary of priests (one of his official jobs): to the reading of newspapers without which no Frenchman's day would be complete, to the writing of poems, scenes for plays and anything else that came into his head and, as he came to know the staff, to rewarding conversations with like-minded members.

There were quite a few of these; as the practice of practically no form of the arts paid its way, would-be painters, musicians and writers sought the safety of the civil service; every branch of it was sprinkled with them. In the Hôtel de Ville Verlaine was soon hobnobbing with Léon Valade, Albert Mérat, Armand Renaud and Georges Lafenestre, would-be poets all, who gained their bread and butter at the expense of the State, and to a lesser extent with the older one-eyed Jules Andrieu, author of a book on the Middle Ages and an anthology of famous love songs, and, what was to be more to the point, a fervid revolutionary.

Verlaine quickly became intimate with the first two. Indeed, to become attached to one was to be attached to both, for the young men were inseparable, so much so that Valade was quickly Albert to his companions and Mérat Léon, the little group having a penchant for the juggling of names. Verlaine was particularly attracted to Valade, three years his senior, and a gentle soul too. Valade was shy, however, as Verlaine was not, preferring quiet corners and walking noiselessly so that he should not draw undue attention to himself. He said little and that in a high fluting voice, but his rare contributions to the conversation were listened to with some respect, not only because his silence was so extra-ordinary amidst the hubbub but because his ironical little asides were considered worth hearing. His pale bearded face set off by black hair brushed over the forehead soon became a dim but essential part of the mid-morning gatherings which were even known to pause for his opinion. His poems faithfully echoed himself: "I am a milk drinker", he would say, speaking of his fear of excess. He was translating some Heine lyrics and writing with Mérat a selection of poems in which his contributions were sad little songs of Paris and the Parisians, love lyrics from which passion or even a hint of it was carefully excluded.

The big broken-nosed Mérat, as would be expected, was his friend's opposite. He was nicknamed "the disdainful cigar" because he was rarely without one, walking slowly and majestically, head held high, cigar tilted, eyes raised and with an expression which suggested that he was determined not to acknowledge the existence of a world filled with stupid people. Like Valade he spoke little, but what he said in his quiet, rather tired voice, rasped and stung. He threw explosive comments into conversation, smiling sardonically at the resultant clamour, and told delightful stories of a certain Hôtel de Pérou where he and Valade had huddled penniless, homeless but with plenty of spirit amongst a little group of would-be poets until they were snatched into the security of the civil service. He had a flaw, a serious one; he was envious. His envy of the slightest success of a comrade (no more than the acceptance of a poem by some non-paying magazine) burst out in recriminations so naïve as to raise laughter, no one except Valade taking them seriously. Like so many young writers of these years Mérat had talent, but it was neither original nor powerful. He was a city nature poet as his *Poèmes de Paris* was to show, but a derivative one, melancholy and sentimental. Eventually an unbearable sense of failure and the success of so many of his companions were to drive him to suicide after false reports. But this was far ahead; in the 'sixties he was a stimulating young man though not always a popular one.

Their discussions in the Hôtel de Ville were sometimes interrupted by those who, having no more work than the talkative poets but less ability to despatch it, were irritated by this display of superiority, and Verlaine, leaving his hat on its peg to vouch for his presence, grew into the habit of adjourning bareheaded to the nearby Café du Gaz to continue the conversation. He relates this with the self-depreciatory gusto common to all his confessions: "See what a naughty boy I was—and am", his tone implies. But because it would spoil the story he omits to mention (as he always omits to mention commonplaces) the damping fact that to leave one's hat on its peg was a widespread custom throughout the building, as indeed it was and is in every civil service building in the world. Valade for one, and Mérat of course, would be found at his table in the café (that is, when the three young men had not sauntered out arm in arm) with others from similar sinecures. The Treasury, for instance, had to make its way as best it could for half an hour or so whilst its clerk Armand Silvestre discussed his poems with his comrades. The burly Silvestre, older than *"Les Trois"* as Verlaine, Valade and

Mérat came to be known, was accorded a certain respect because he was an occasional drinking companion of Baudelaire. The respect would have been awe had Silvestre been another man; as it was, his gross laugh riding high over the room is sufficient description of him, and for that matter of the poet, long forgotten except for an odd comic song or nonsense rhyme. He was addicted to the risqué joke more than most and Verlaine laughed with him, his sensuality tickled, but Silvestre was not to become one of his intimates.

The Café du Gaz was one of the centres of the arts that Verlaine was to know so well; respectable as some of his later haunts were not; jammed with frock-coated young men apparently dithering unresolvedly between displays of childishness and the deadly earnest. The first fitted Verlaine like a glove, the last is not a word that sits easily on him at any time; his type of earnestness is better known to the English than to his own countrymen. Yet in these years, for all his fatuities and careful clinging to convention, he became aware that he was a writer and he thought, in quite the wrong direction, that he had something to say. That this would ever conflict with jokes and arguments in respectable cafés, with large and regular meals and top-hats on pegs and frock-coats and a comfortable home in the suburbs, never occurred to him; he would have been dismayed not to say terrified at the mere thought of it. All he knew and cared to know was that he had a gift and that he was living at a moment when the gift could in the pleasantest manner conceivable bring him excitement and happiness. His idea of exercising the gift was modest indeed, no more than the writing of an occasional poem and the beginnings of bloodthirsty social dramas and broad farces more planned than written, but no matter, he was an author even if an unpublished one and—this was more than half the attraction—in excellent company. He had as co-authors Lepelletier and a melancholy youth, Lucien Viotti, first met at the Lycée Bonaparte, and as audience, whenever he could get a word in, the young hopefuls of the Café du Gaz. Even the death of Captain Verlaine at the end of 1865, though it roused him for a moment to a most uncharacteristic display of assertiveness (he forced reluctant authorities to give his father a military escort on a public holiday), could not deflect him for long from following with lazy ardour what appeared as a most delightful

Verlaine at about 23

Verlaine the Dandy, 1869

Top left   Théodore de Banville

Above   Charles Cros

Left   Leconte de Lisle

Below left   François Coppée

Below   Catulle Mendès

destiny, to be one of a crowd, a gay, sometimes elegant sometimes raffish but always convivial crowd which collected round the tables of the Café du Gaz and, when the day's work was nominally done, at the Café de Bobino in rue de Fleurus.

Even when the French have nothing to say they say it at length and make it more interesting than would seem credible; and when, as with the young intellectuals of Verlaine's day, they have something to say the result in sheer sound is deafening, bewildering, exhilarating too, and not merely because of the magnificent music of the language. History is for ever repeating itself. Today the huge American cars of the B.O.F. aimlessly café-crawling, the gaping arrogant tourists, the swarm of beggars, the grasping shopkeepers, the torrent of useless oratory at the Palais de Bourbon, the endless talk of money, the whole sense of waste, decay, nothingness in a setting of superb loveliness, merely serve to whet the intellectual appetite. In one of the largest Paris theatres a full orchestra can be heard enthusiastically performing Monsieur X's variations on some themes of Monsieur Y; in France the composer is a dance-band leader, in England he would still be chiefly concerned by the newness of his gown in some Oxford or Cambridge college; the "maître" from whose work the themes have been extracted is well on the tender side of thirty, but the themes are original and excellent, the variations extremely clever. So in the closing years of Louis Napoleon the vulgarity, the corruption, the false morality, the emphasis on wealth, the atmosphere of uncertainty and dissatisfaction provoked in the young a particular enthusiasm for the arts. Many of the antics of these very young men, their rowdy fooling, their assumption of titles not their own, their extravagances in speech, clothes and behaviour appear pretentious, juvenile, absurd, as they often were; but related to their day they can be seen also as not unadmirable protests against the stifling régime of "Monsieur Prudhomme", a régime which was eventually to stifle many of the protestants. But that was in the future; in the present they reacted violently in act and in thought. Paris was intellectually alive and hopeful, and amidst all the talk there was talent and more than talent. The stimulus of political discussion had much to do with it, since to be revolutionary in one thing was to be revolutionary in all, music, poetry, politics appearing then as manifestations of a single spirit.

The ambitions of Verlaine's friends reached no higher—though seeming to them height enough—than the publication of the verses all were pouring profusely on to paper. Mérat excepted, they felt little envy; a merit due in Verlaine to laziness and to the unpretentiousness which made him such a popular companion. He did not see himself as specially gifted and the idea of genius never crossed his mind. There were, in any case, geniuses enough. The conversation was thick with names reverently pronounced; one would have thought, listening to them, that Paris was alive with poets.

The most frequently recurring of these names, apart from the inevitable Hugo—*"le Père est là-bas dans l'île"*, they would cry after Théodore de Banville—were those of Baudelaire, who was spoken of as a man at once mysterious and, the proscription of *Fleurs du Mal* being awesomely fresh in mind, a martyr, a man somehow withdrawn from life, immersed in the creation of his *frisson nouveau* as Hugo had well described the Baudelairean verse; of Leconte de Lisle, mysterious too but in the sense of the formidable rather than the inaccessible; and finally of Banville, who one could guess by the tone of these young men was a very different kind of hero, Théo to them although they counted themselves lucky to catch a glimpse of him. All these heroes were the elders by twenty years or more of the café crowd. Other names shouted across the table were those of true contemporaries, Glatigny and Mendès foremost. These names were pronounced with a special intonation, compact of familiarity, envy, affection, jest and pride.

The one genius amongst this talkative and imitative company shone, if at all, by virtue of nothing more imposing than a genius for absurdity. Who could dream that the would-be dandy with his buttonholed and velvet-collared frock-coat, his flowing spotted cravat, lazily twinkling deep-set eye, cane twirling idly, was anything but an innocuous addition to the band, a useful listener who at times had begun to show a certain flair for the telling of questionable tales and who in expansive moments was given to the confession of improbable misdeeds? Not his companions, and certainly not he. To look at the long and languid figure sprawled as much as one can sprawl in the chair of a Paris café, to hear the queer gruff voice tell a doubtful anecdote, praise in wildly exaggerated terms some poet of the day, or to answer the ready smile of the large loose mouth and respond to the infectious good-natured laugh, was to think, when his companions bothered to think at all, what a nice chap the young Verlaine was: a bit of an ass, perhaps, rather a weakling maybe, but definitely a good fellow.

One day not far in the future this amiable nonentity was to astonish the little coterie by appearing somewhat self-consciously with a large square monocle jammed uncomfortably into his right eye, a thick black silken cord dropping down the long face to a decidedly florid bow in the buttonhole. That ridiculous monocle was a sign and a symbol; a sign of his adherence to a poetic school, even of a measure of seriousness and, if one proceeds sufficiently far ahead, of the poet himself. But that is another story, a story which began when the monocled one was still at school.

Chapter Four

THE PARNASSIAN

I

CATULLE MENDÈS

1861

AT the beginning of 1861 a youth, Catulle Mendès, came up to Paris from Bordeaux. He was just eighteen, one year older than the schoolboy Verlaine, and had the intention in good provincial style of taking the capital by storm. He had much in common with Verlaine besides nearness of age; he possessed considerable charm, he was gregarious, excellent company of a kind, and was to become an omnivorous lover of women and strong drink. He also had that which Verlaine was utterly without, the wish and the will to "get on". He had Jewish blood in him, which may explain the pushing element; he was of Spanish extraction, which seems to explain nothing; but his appearance showed no trace of Jew or Spaniard: fresh-faced, blue-eyed, with a cloud of fair hair—much like the mane of Hugo when young—that he had an engaging way of tossing off his forehead when making a point. "Apollo in person!", Louis Ménard was to say; a vulgar Apollo, on occasion obscene, but with undeniable vivacity and force of manner.

Perhaps his attractive looks proved irresistible, perhaps his "drive", for he had a tireless tongue, a hide as tough as steel and a broad sense of humour that laughed off the occasional rebuff. He had taken his first steps in poetry at the feet of Valade and possibly the decision to assault Paris, for both came from the same city, but was soon off on his own in a manner that Valade could not and did not wish to imitate. Within a month the boy, regally splashing the entire *dot* his fond parents had sent with him, was sitting in the editor's chair of the *Revue fantaisiste* in an opulent room in Passage de Mirès receiving celebrities as nonchalantly as possible. His taste in decoration was imperfect, the office being hung with Persian tapestries in green and rose, cluttered with mahogany desks and tables, a leather armchair

52

and a gaudy couch—"a room trying hard to be a boudoir"—
but in another and more important respect his instinct was
correct for he founded the revue "to tilt against the two great
failings of the literature still revered by most Frenchmen—
elegiac sentimentalism and defective French". Hugo, ignoring
with Olympian blindness the presence in much of his own work
of these failings and eager as always to proclaim his eternal
youth, encouraged the venture with the customary flourish of
eloquence.

Hugo's support was of symbolic value only; Mendès was
merely taking the obvious precaution of the opportunist; the
most regular visitor to the office and the most important by
contemporary judgment was Théodore de Banville. In fact,
allowance made for Mendès' self-assurance, the existence of the
office and of the *Revue fantaisiste* was due to Banville. He looked
neither important nor a poet. He came from the beautiful capital
of the Bourbons and was a typical Bourbonnais: chubby, round-
cheeked hairless face, plump and insignificant body, indeter-
minate nose, sharp but empty blue eyes, and he spoke between
his teeth, clipping his words in a manner which had become the
fashion in all advanced literary circles. For this man, just twice
the age of his young protégé and looking like an unprosperous
commercial traveller, was the most successful and most highly
regarded poet of his time. He was unquestionably one of the
nicest men of his day, generous without envy or pride, good-
natured and, allowing for contemporary taste, witty. No young
man called on him in vain; he found them work, lent them
money, introduced them to editors and, as with Mendès, even
helped to set them up on their own. His Thursday soirées were
famous, and unlike some others—for every evening of the week
was open house at the home of some leader of the arts—
considered the stomachs of the struggling poets, painters and
musicians, who were free to drop in at rue de Buci and to step
from the salon to the salle à manger where food was spread on
the tables. Yet hungry though they might be, not a man would
move when Banville was talking in his high-pitched voice. He
had a gift of speech remarkable even for a Frenchman, bright
with clever paradoxes, brilliant with caricatures of the famous
and not so famous men and women in the Parisian art world,
particularly of those in the theatre. He exaggerated wildly,

53

discovering a new genius weekly and having a fresh scandal or two up his sleeve for every occasion, but his manner was so joyous and so inoffensive that his hearers merely laughed and enjoyed the game of trying to spot the grain of truth. All the Paris salons and cafés had laughed at and loved the young Banville, who at the end of an evening years earlier had said to the amorous Hugo, then the darling of society, that it was ridiculous for a man to play the lover after the age of seventeen— a typically provocative remark which put new life into the gathering, the great man replying with raised eyebrows and reddened face, "I should like to hear that extraordinary theory explained"; which Banville did for a twenty minutes so sparkling that the entire party began afresh.

Banville was not respected, having no dignity of person, but was immensely and understandably popular. "Clown étonnant", Verlaine was to call him, but contortionist would be nearer the mark. He was far too good a Frenchman even to think of breaking the strict rules which had governed French poetry for centuries; he employed his exceptionally agile mind in the playing of verbal games within the limits convention assigned to him; and certainly if verbal dexterity is the criterion he was a wizard and deserves all the admiration he received. Cleverness appealed to the French intellectual then as now, and from the moment when he published his first book of verse Banville was a made man; the fact that he had nothing to say was overlooked in admiration for the manner, or rather manners, in which he said it; the banality of his thought was overlooked for the optimism, facile but attractive, that sweetened it.

Here, then, was Banville, affable, successful, kind, coming day after day to Passage de Mirès to see how his latest young follower was getting on, allowing him to print new verses and introducing him to his friends. Mendès soon took the measure of his master. He genuinely admired Banville's technical virtuosity—a natural pasticheur, he was to become just such another poet-journalist— and having an eye to the main chance as most of his contemporaries had not, he saw not only how his goodness and popularity could be put to the use of Catulle Mendès but, more important, he saw that from Banville's attitude towards his work a theory of poetry might be extracted. And there was nothing quite so advancing to a man in Paris as the putting forward of a theory which was, or at least sounded, new.

But this last was to come later; the germ of it can be seen in Mendès' description of the aims of the *Revue fantaisiste*. Being firstly a practical youth, he concerned himself light-heartedly and with a fervour (the blend being fairly common then) with the question of filling his columns advantageously. In this Banville's patronage was all-important; Gautier and Daudet permitted extracts from their work to be printed and one after another of the friends of Banville came into the office with contributions. The first of these was Baudelaire, "slim, elegant, a little furtive, almost alarming because of his attitude of one with a secret fear which could be discerned from time to time beneath an hauteur of manner softened by a grave courtesy. He had the irresistible charm of beauty in distress and carried himself with the air of a fastidious bishop somewhat fallen from grace who had donned an elaborate lay costume to go on his travels— His Eminence Monseigneur Beau Brummel."

The description is by Mendès, who describes even more of himself; if offensive, it accurately places the manner in which the great poet was regarded. Baudelaire was then forty years of age, a disappointed man conscious of greatness denied, and a haunted man, haunted physically by his creditors from one mean lodging to another and by the disease that was to kill him, haunted spiritually by his consciousness of sin, and physically and spiritually by the dreadful attacks of despairing *ennui* that his loneliness induced. His dandyism, slightly decayed, and his perfect manners sat eerily on the ravaged face with its great burning eyes and majestic forehead, the most obvious face of genius ever seen, but Mendès was more concerned to place his guest within a neat phrase than to comprehend his tragedy. If the spectacle of Baudelaire carrying his wares from one petty magazine to another, humbling himself before a youngster not out of his teens, was painful, Mendès was not the man to feel it; he was absorbed by pleasure in the prose poems that Baudelaire brought with him and by elation at his capture. His attitude towards Baudelaire's work fairly expressed the man, freely criticising, amending and rejecting—all done under cover of a genuine appreciation: "I have violently admired your verses", he was to write in the act of cutting them. Like the young

Verlaine, Mendès' admiration for Baudelaire's work was confused by the poet's "martyrdom", but unlike Verlaine his self-
importance was unpuncturable even by close contact with genius.

This inability to gauge Baudelaire's true standing was shared
by many, including the next visitor, the twenty-three-year-old
Villiers de l'Isle-Adam. Like others in Paris this young man had
no claim to the aristocratic name and birth he advertised in and
out of season, but remarkable in his own right he was, having
a flair for the horror story with the ironic twist and loving
"ferocious and funereal pleasantries". Again like other young
hopefuls in Paris he had devoted parents who, believing him a
genius, sold all they had and moved to a single furnished room
in the capital so that their son should come into his own. This
was two years earlier, and Villiers, to give him the only name
remotely his, had acquired neither fame nor fortune by the time
he arrived in Passage de Mirès his pockets stuffed with manuscripts, but a gift for picturesque speech and the twists of a
strange imagination had brought him a certain notoriety, one
critic even describing him as "the most magnificently gifted
young man of his generation". He had already written two un-
actable dramas and a philosophical novel so obscure that the
few who glanced through it were persuaded without difficulty
that his genius was too profound for words.

He brought a story which Mendès quickly agreed to print,
and a fiery enthusiasm for Wagner, whose *Tannhäuser* had recently
been damned at the Paris Opéra. Hero worship of Wagner was
to become a *sine qua non* amongst the young intellectuals, attach-
ing itself naturally enough to the revolutionary fulminations of
the cafés. Mendès, who had already determined to use the pages
of the *Revue fantaisiste* to propagate the Wagnerian gospel,
greeted this fellow-spirit rapturously.

Villiers was followed by a tall young man "thin to the point
of transparency" who bounded into the office a few days later.
His entrance was too dramatic to be real; without a word he
plumped into a chair, threw a manuscript on the desk and
followed it with two large and tattered boots protruding from
patched nankeen trousers which in turn merged into the remnants of a shirt covered halfway up his chest by a small red
waistcoat shining out of a shrunken metal-buttoned blue jacket.
From a tie flapping wide rose a long thin neck on the top of

which perched a small round head covered with fair hair falling straight to the open collar. The face, worn and hollow, contained two heavy-lidded eyes glinting humorously under heavy eyebrows and a gash of a mouth which opened to announce in the hoarse voice of the heavy drinker: "Glatigny". This was superfluous, Banville having warned Mendès of his approach and given "with his enchanting mixture of Orpheus and Balzac" an outline of this protégé's career. Albert Glatigny looked the strolling player who had spent his teens acting small parts throughout the provinces; particularly so at this moment as he was wearing his stage clothes, having none of his own. And a strolling player he would have remained had he not one night, dossing down as usual in a barn, found an old volume of Ronsard. He instantly adored and read every book of poetry he could buy or borrow. At eighteen he discovered *Cariatides* and determined immediately that he must be a poet.

A little later the schoolboy Verlaine, wandering along the quays, made a similar discovery, but his reaction was less violent; for Glatigny not only began feverishly to write poems but the moment he had saved a few sous made his way on foot to Paris. Paris took no notice of him. The next year he tried again, encouraged by Banville, who found him a room and occasional journalistic work and showed his poems to Hugo and Sainte-Beuve. Again he was forced to go on tour, leaving his manuscript poems with Banville, who finally arranged their publication. This was *Vignes Folles* of 1860, which, like the Banville, Verlaine came across on a riverside bookstall, learned by heart and proclaimed to his schoolfellows as a modern masterpiece.

The young Verlaine was not alone; in contemporary poetic circles Glatigny was hailed as a latter-day Villon. He had a gift; like Banville (and like Mendès for that matter) he displayed a verbal facility and juggled dexterously with rhymes; he even, in one or two fantastic pieces, showed a certain originality; but like Banville and Mendès he had nothing to say; he wrote because he loved words, and thanks to a prodigious memory had acquired an enormous vocabulary, and because he panted to imitate his chosen master. This he did sufficiently well to confuse a critical sense then generally distrait.

He was besides, to further bedevil the critics, a "character". Whenever he had a sou to his name he took root in his favourite

Buffet Germanique and there would hold spellbound two formidable habitués in Baudelaire and Silvestre. Both men, no mean talkers, would listen by the hour to one fantastic tale following another, punctuated by the teller's bull-like roar of laughter, the impish gleam in the bright eyes until, having drunk heavily on an empty stomach, Glatigny would stretch his legs on the table and instantly sleep. His largeness of heart was prodigious. His customary food in Paris was raw carrots, but he would give half, and the best half, to any hungry poet, actor, painter, musician he happened to meet. Although he had never handled a pistol in his life outside the stage dummy, he called out the critic Albert Wolff for daring to speak slightingly of Banville and escaped miraculously with a graze. One cold autumn, when he could not pay the toll to cross one of the Paris bridges, he swam the Seine to borrow money for a friend in distress.

To think hardly of such a man was difficult, to mistake him for another Villon too easy. Superficially he was like Mendès, who sat facing him for the first time; both were loud, boisterous, vulgar, both possessed charm to a high degree. But in another direction Glatigny was the antithesis of Mendès and a fore-runner of Verlaine, a modest man thinking little of his achievement, without ambition to dominate, to acquire money or fame. He asked for nothing but company, absinthe if it could be had, conversation, laughter and more absinthe.

Hearing from Banville of the enthusiastic reception given to *Vignes Folles*, he had hurried back to Paris as soon as he could raise the fare and precipitated himself into the office of the *Revue fantaisiste*. Mendès astutely took in this fellow-spirit at a glance. He read a few lines of the manuscript on the desk, then exclaimed excitedly, "You are a poet!" "You too!" replied Glatigny ingenuously, and a bargain was quickly struck between the two boys—one can hardly call them men. Glatigny was not only to contribute to the magazine—he began at once with a laudatory article on Hugo—but to act as assistant editor. The question of salary was not raised, Glatigny typically overlooking it, Mendès typically forgetting to remind him.

But this job, like all the others he had taken in his brief life, did not occupy Glatigny for long. The eighteen-year-old editor was not content to "tilt against" the romantic writers of the first decades of the century by printing neo-romantic poems and articles and preaching the gospel of form, he wished to expose the stuffy rules of the Second Empire regulating right conduct in contemporary literature, an equally admirable aim but which he mistakenly tried to attain by printing in instalments from the second number onwards his own sultry play *Le Roman d'une Nuit*.

The challenge was taken up by the police with some relish; in November the *Revue* was fined five hundred francs for publishing indecent material, and as Mendès was unable to pay he was imprisoned for a month in the Sainte-Pélagie and the *Revue* came to an end. Released and in disgrace with his respectable parents, he joined Valade and Mérat at a fifth-rate hotel in a sunless passage off rue Dauphine. This hotel (by name the Pérou but known to posterity as the Dragon Bleu) had become the temporary stronghold of a few young poets existing on next to nothing. They were writing hard—almost as hard as they talked —but it was a red letter day when anything appeared in print and they trooped out to eat a decent meal and, if they could find fifteen sous apiece, to invade a Pasdeloup concert and applaud the rare Wagner overture or aria. As the months passed, a meal of any kind became a luxury: they often went thirty-six hours without food. "One dined on a page of Ronsard", said Mendès, a remark with more truth in it than such remarks generally have.

From time to time an outsider visited the band of forgotten ones, possibly leaving a little cash behind and almost certainly treating them to a meal. One winter day as Mendès, huddled in a blanket, was trying to urge his chilled fingers across a sheet of paper, the door burst open and a hairy young poet named Glaser threw himself into the room with a crash. Behind him advanced timidly the neat Napoleonic figure of a small, plumpish young man with the eye and the nose worn by ten thousand Frenchmen. "François Coppée", announced Glaser in his customary voice of thunder: "He has read your poetry." He added that his friend was a clerk in the War Office but that he repented of his ways and wished to become a poet.

Mendès looked at the impeccable black suit and overcoat of the newcomer, his soft hands and clean nails, and began to bridle: the War Office! But before he could let loose one of the caustic remarks for which he was becoming notorious Coppée, who had been gazing about him wonderingly, exclaimed in a queer deep voice and with naïve and irresistible ecstasy, "Oh, Mendès, how I envy you your room!" Mendès, melting at this, motioned the visitor into his only chair, a dilapidated cane affair, Glaser stretched himself on the bed and Mendès sat on the floor. There was a moment's silence, the three looking round at the room Coppée envied so much; then all simultaneously broke into laughter. "We were friends at once", said Mendès, and wished at once to celebrate the friendship. Then he remembered that he had no coat. "That's nothing", airily remarked Glaser, who had just collected a fee for an article in the *Dictionnaire Bouillot*; he scrambled off the bed, was gone for a few minutes, returned with an overcoat from a nearby second-hand clothes shop, and out they went to dine and talk.

To talk; and when all allowance is made for the nonsense habitual to the high-spirited young men there remained the serious purpose which Mendès, faced with a new disciple, developed with florid emphasis. He outlined the theory which was to lead Verlaine, just about to leave school, to his first book of poems and to settle him in his career as poet.

2

BEGINNINGS OF THE SCHOOL

1862

The regeneration of French poetry; that, with various excursions into less impersonal matters, was the grand theme of the discussions in the Hôtel de Pérou: away with the sickly romanticists prating nauseatingly of the state of their heart, debasing a great language for unworthy personal ends.

Neither Mendès nor those who sat on the hard bed with him, leaned their backs to the dirty wall or paced the bare boards gesturing were original thinkers; they expressed views heard in any advanced writers' café and they followed the lead of their seniors. They were original only in that, disciplined by their forceful young leader, they attempted to put into practice on a large scale a theory so far restricted to a few individuals. Mendès used the dreary months in the hotel, womanless, drinkless months which covered the whole year of 1862, to try to reason and work out what he considered poetry should be and do. Much of the day and well into the night he and his followers read all the great poets, studied the practice of metre and rhyme and declaimed poems based on their study. Often enough they barely heard one another speak; all had something to say, some observation that could never wait to be said even if it had to be shouted, and each believed with a fervency invariably overcoming modesty that the poem he had just written contained the imperishable germ of the doctrine all burned to express.

This doctrine did not take the form, as one might have expected, of a reversion to realism—that was far ahead. It consisted simply of an effort to express pure as against personal romanticism: created art was greater than its creator—this was their view or rather, for all were exceedingly human young men, this was the view that for one reason or another they were determined to hold.

When Mendès a year earlier had explained the purpose of his *Revue fantaisiste*, he was echoing the pronouncements of greater men, but he sensed correctly the prevailing mood of the young intellectual of the day and that his own advancement was best linked with the advancement of this cause, which in turn was dependent on publicity; in a city where all talked, only the loudest, most persistent voice would be heard. He had failed once, but, ever the opportunist, used the material to his hand to propagate the gospel in the only way now open to him, by a band of disciples.

The first man to express the new creed had been, curiously enough, one of the young hopefuls of the 1830 school of romantics—Théophile Gautier; in 1835 his preface to his novel *Mademoiselle de Maupin* contained the first mention of art for art's sake. At the time the preface fell flat, most of those who noticed it commenting acidly that Gautier deprecated subjective poetry merely because he had difficulty in writing it. Seventeen years later he published his *Emaux et Camées*, one of the schoolboy Verlaine's favourites, the poems of a travelled man, exotic descriptive verses written with great care and in which both personal feeling and references to contemporary events are absent. This book brought him the devotion of Baudelaire, who declared, "there is no good and no bad in the ethereal regions of true poetry" (a conclusion which must have given Gautier some uneasy moments) and who dedicated to him the *Fleurs du Mal* of 1857. In the same year Gautier marched red-waistcoated into the offices of *L'Artiste* shouting, "The idea is born of the form", a phrase which he had caught from Flaubert that morning, Flaubert declaring that "the artist should not express opinions, which change, but should confine himself to art, which is for all time; let him be in his work like God in his creation, felt but not seen". The result of this conversation was seen in Gautier's *L'Art*, published in *L'Artiste* late that year, in which he called for "impassibility" in the poet "so that truth and feeling shall be conveyed through perfection of form".

Of more importance to Mendès and his young men was the attitude of Banville and Leconte de Lisle. A year before *L'Art* appeared, Banville had entered the lists with an ode to Gautier and went about declaring joyously, "Art is my religion!" Leconte de Lisle began even earlier; in 1852, the year of Gautier's *Emaux et Camées*, he published his own *Poèmes Antiques*, which exalted the past ages of man and his pagan gods and included a nostalgic evocation of the author's native island of Réunion. His descriptions, particularly of wild life, were highly coloured to the point of caricature but had an impersonal grandeur carried on lines which read like an incantation and in stanzas marked by impeccable form and a strong rhythm. This, coming from a man reputedly difficult to meet, earned him a mysterious reputation with the young intelligentsia in the Hôtel de Pérou—a reputation enhanced by his preface, which said bleakly, "There must be no trace of personal emotions in a book", and deplored the vanity of parading the feelings in public. The romantics, he declared brusquely, were "without ideas because without a philosophy, weaklings who can express nothing but their own inanity". These plain words were repeated with delight through the cafés, to be followed by recitations of extensive quotations from his *Poèmes Barbares* of 1862, which leaned backwards as far as the Eastern mythologies in the determination to be impersonal. Soon afterwards, the book having been criticised in the more reactionary journals, he wrote a letter expressing the utmost contempt for critic and public. This letter, of which the gist soon spread from café to café, settled the eventual ascendancy of Leconte de Lisle. To all the young writers who could not get published, to all who were published but criticised, to all who were published but not sold (that is, to virtually everyone), this open defiance of public opinion appeared godlike and, in lieu of success, to be immediately imitated.

Gautier, Banville and Leconte de Lisle, poets of substantial reputations, had therefore been preaching for years, each in his own fashion, and demonstrating in his work that the writer must be impersonal, reason controlling feeling, devoted to impeccable form, and should look for inspiration at least as far back as the great days of Greece and Rome. And the man whose knowledge of France and the French is limited may well wonder why with this volume of sanction behind them Mendès and his followers should do more than quietly follow their masters' example. But this is to ignore both the ambition of Mendès and the peculiarities of the French character. It is a paradox that the Frenchman, the most independent of men, to whom for instance the notice *Défense d'entrer* reads as a challenge to go in at once, is nevertheless the slave of method. For him to receive an idea is not, as it would be with, say, an American or an Englishman, simply to possess a subject for discussion; to him it appears an immediate and even agonising demand to disseminate by organisation. He must if humanly possible collect and convert a group, give this group a name, acquire a journal and propagate the idea. Until the idea is thus pigeon-holed and advertised, no young Frenchman worth his salt could enjoy a moment's peace.

In the eyes of Mendès and his youths the new movement, if it could be called so, was no more than a series of isolated statements over the years by men who for one reason or another had been sufficiently un-French to let these straws blow in the wind instead of collecting them neatly into an unmistakable haystack. It had no name, no organised body of adherents, no journal and so no future. It was, in brief, unregulated, than which no more damning judgment could be found in the whole of France. The work, the discussion, the agitation in the Hôtel de Pérou thus becomes understandable and, particularly in the eyes of Mendès, essential. But read, talk, write though they might, they had no conceivable chance, even if they discovered and agreed on a name, of purchasing a paper to exploit it. All they could do was to bide their time, which they used to compose and recite poems increasingly "impassible" and remote from the slightest slur of

63

topicality. And leaving the hungry, high-spirited, moneyless, nameless and paperless group in the hotel, this narrative crosses the river to visit another and very different milieu in the respectable suburb of Batignolles, where another young man was in process of striking out for himself and as a result of which Verlaine was to appear for the first time in print.

3

LOUIS-XAVIER DE RICARD

1863

In Boulevard des Batignolles, a few steps from the homes of Verlaine and Lepelletier, lived a distinguished old soldier, the Marquis de Ricard, former aide-de-camp to Prince Jérôme. He had one son, Louis-Xavier, a young man who could without difficulty have been mistaken for a thousand others of his type, long-faced with straggly black beard, pince-nez sitting on the bridge of a strong nose, long black hair brushed back smoothly to a long thin neck correctly cravated, long thin body attired elegantly *à la mode* of the 'sixties. As he resembled the common picture of the young intellectual in appearance, so in mind he was on a par with a thousand others then talking, gesturing, writing in the four corners of Paris. He had, however, an opinion of his talents which was considerable even in days when genius by general consent flowered on every other bush; and as his parents had money, a good name and plenty of room in their house, young De Ricard had every possibility of surrounding himself with a company which for one reason or another accepted his pretensions.

And if allowance is made for a vanity impossible to justify, for more than a touch of envy and pigheadedness, he made a tolerably good companion as long as he could somehow be prevented from undue speech, this not being his forte. Some— Mendès for example, and Leconte de Lisle—were to wonder, not silently, precisely what his forte was; perhaps it consisted in optimism, for although only in his early twenties he had tried his hand without trace of originality at poetry, criticism, novels, journalism, plays, history, philosophy, theology, politics, this last with a certain ferocity. Only memoirs were to come, as in time they did. Meanwhile he had yet to edit a journal and in the beginning of 1863 he made this gesture which was obligatory to every young Parisian with intellectual pretensions and the requisite financial backing. His *Revue du Progrès* ran for a year thanks to his parents and to a (for those days) curiously lax censorship or one reluctant to notice a De Ricard; but it was notable finally only for a contribution by Verlaine which he was to regret.

Not that the *Revue* lacked fire; it was predominantly political and regularly tore the government to shreds, proposed Utopian remedies for all social problems (these were the days of Fourier and Comte) and published much unpublishable prose and verse. The running of a journal called for a weekly soirée, nominally a gathering of contributors but in practice including their friends and, soon, the friends' friends. For the guests were entertained luxuriously. The Marquis, partially paralysed, remained upstairs writing indiscreet memoirs, but his wife, some years his junior and with a passion for young people, made a hostess of much charm, encouraging the shy and treating the far from shy with an admirable tact; a good violinist and with a taste for amateur dramatics, she and not her rather stiff son was at the heart of the entertainment.

Lepelletier was soon in the thick of the fray, all caution leaving him when he turned revolutionary but remaining intrinsically dull, and with him came a Verlaine at first somewhat timid, a Verlaine of nineteen who had barely thrown off the last traces of the schoolboy but who quickly became an habitué with no more than a growl from a father unable to resolve the dilemma of admiration of the Marquis and disapproval of the young De Ricard.

Verlaine had only to be let loose amidst well-disposed men and pretty girls, plenty of talk, music, food and drink, to be in bliss. Privately he was a little shocked by De Ricard's militant atheism, considered his anti-Church diatribes in indifferent taste and his political rhodomontades excessive: understood, that one disapproved of the corrupt and effete Church, the government of the vulgar and the reign of Louis Napoleon, but . . . However, he was far too unsure of himself, too amiable and too anxious to stand well with present company to do more than smile uneasily. Moreover, the soirées were eminently respectable despite the occasional hot words, all present being dressed well, reciting their poems to a reasonably silent audience, listening with commendable patience to piano solos and to ballads, a patience that turned to rapture if Wagner was the composer, and flirting harmlessly, inspired by an innocuous lemonade punch, with the demure young ladies invited from neighbouring houses. There was nothing to disquiet the bourgeois in Verlaine and almost everything to please the gregarious youth, including the ever-popular charades. Nevertheless, conscious of a reprehensible political apathy, he grasped the chance to atone when De Ricard asked him later in the year for a contribution. He wrote a sonnet on Monsieur Prudhomme, the mythical archetype of the bourgeois provincial Frenchman who since the advent of Louis and the industrial revolution had invaded Paris. This display of satirical fireworks, the satire borrowed out of sheer good-fellowship (the author having much in common with the type he attacked), appeared in the August number.

Until the end of the year the *Revue* miraculously survived; then De Ricard, desperate perhaps for the distinction of martyrdom, made an attack on Christianity too violent to be ignored, and was duly sent to prison. His parents did not, like those of Mendès, withdraw support from him. Moreover, his sentence was for three months, which ensured a larger halo. He emerged in the spring of 1864 the man of the moment in advanced literary circles and for the next year or two held something of the position he had dreamed of.

The change was quickly reflected in the attendance at his soirées, which, although the *Revue* had been suppressed, flourished as never before. The big names were seen in the De Ricard salon approvingly watching an amateur performance of *Marion de Lorme*—Flaubert, the Goncourts, Gautier and other eminent gods in evening-dress. More important, Banville was to be seen there occasionally, ever-amiable, talkative, the plump centre of a circle in which his round smooth head of fine fair hair could just be made out through the listening wall of frock-coats; and following his example the young men of promise began to drop in.

Of the musicians, Emmanuel Chabrier's work alone is still played, but at that time, a boyhood friend of Manet, he was wavering between music and painting. His small body could be distinguished from afar since whatever the weather he wore a mustard-coloured ulster, and on a closer view his cravat was seen to be set at precisely the crooked angle then the height of fashion. Although he was only in his early twenties, the fair hair was already beginning to recede from the round face notable for its large forehead, protruding, heavy-lidded eyes and lips perpetually thrust forward in a childish pout; but when he laughed with a mouth all teeth his plainness was forgotten for his good nature. The wide hands and short thick pianist's fingers were at the disposal of all, to accompany, to improvise by the hour. Even his restlessness, one agitated expression chasing another across his face, quick abrupt gestures of the short arms, foot-tapping whenever he was obliged to stand still for a moment, and a formidable range of sudden humours from petulant to jovial, made him an excellent if at times embarrassing party man.

Villiers made one sensational entry after another, a genius if looks and behaviour were to be believed; one evening he would come into the room like a somnambulist, eyes glazed, alternately muttering and giving a high-pitched laugh as at some private joke. When a bold guest summoned courage to address him, he did not answer for a minute or two, gazing at the speaker with startled blue eyes; then in a profound voice and as if terrified by his own words said: "It isn't necessary to have a great idea of God", a remark which would strike the company into temporary silence through incomprehension and the uneasy suspicion that in that simple statement lay some tremendously important key to life. Another time he would declaim Poe's *Raven*, acting it out with wild gestures and staring eyes and—for these were refreshingly unsophisticated days—leaving jangled nerves and chilled blood behind him.

A different kind of blood-chilling was practised by a nebulous-faced young man attired after the manner of an undertaker's assistant who would glide discreetly into the room, giving occasional circumspect glances from cool, keen eyes, shake hands distantly then stand aside and regard the crowd with a slight sneer. He always carried one or more large books under his arm. He too could scarcely be other than a genius. His name was difficult to come by, but gradually he became known and slightly feared as Anatole France.

4

RUE DE DOUAI

1864

Then came Coppée, came and conquered. There was a some-thing about Coppée, perhaps nothing more than a sparrow-like ordinariness, that endeared him to people; he was so obviously not out of one's reach that he came as a distinct relief after a run of geniuses. He was good-natured too, modest, yet showed a refreshing tinge of delicate malice when telling a story. He read one or two distinctly poor poems so unaffectedly that he became a general favourite. Verlaine loved him practically at sight and immediately besought him to join the civil service group at the Café du Gaz, but then Verlaine was also highly taken by Chabrier and liked everyone else with a broad and indiscriminate good nature.

And with Coppée came the beautiful Mendès, a Mendès at last released from the Hôtel de Pérou, a Mendès whose first book of poems had been published. *Philoméla* showed promise and like *Vignes Folles* brought its author much praise in his own circle. It earned next to no money, but its existence convinced his parents that he would be a poet and presumably (since volumes of new poetry were scarce in Bordeaux) was one already. They relented, sent money, and Mendès soon established himself in rue de Douai in an apartment which he measured by the number of fellow-poets it would hold; eight to ten, he reckoned.

This Mendès of the De Ricard soirées was curiously subdued, a young man who could almost have been described as ordinary were it not that he was incapable of passing unnoticed. But he seemed out of place and in due course explained why, as he explained everything. "At the De Ricards'", he said, "we narrowly escaped being fashionable, having to appear in black and looking for all the world like lawyers reciting sonnets."

At rue de Douai the atmosphere was otherwise. There an afternoon, Tuesday, was set aside each week for a literary tea-party commonly all-male; if a woman were seen there she was not of a kind that would be admitted to Boulevard des Batignolles. The key to the tone of those Tuesdays was given by the reception of each guest. After he had knocked the door was opened an inch or two, a sharp eye peered through the crack and a hoarse voice whispered, "Qui est là?" If the answer was anything but "Tragaldabus", the door slammed before a creditor's foot could be thrust into the opening. If the visitor gave the correct password, the door swung wide to reveal Mendès' valet, a Parisian gamin with the typical cockney face, sharp, thin, droll, whom Mendès had first seen selling rabbits and geese at a fair in Montmartre. Covielle was a cool customer, more than a match for the creditors who hung about (Mendès being no respecter of his own or anybody else's money) and for the occasional obstreperous guest. "One brought champagne instead of tea if one could afford it", says Mendès; none the less these Tuesdays were not orgies though they might occasionally end rowdily; they were informal, as the De Ricard soirées were not, and they had, riding all the jokes and abuse and high spirits, a purpose lacking in Boulevard des Batignolles once the *Revue du Progrès* had collapsed.

At first sight the onlooker would see little but oddities. Villiers would make one of his famous entrances, walking unsteadily, chewing a cigarette, throwing back his fair hair with a shake of the head, twining his small fair moustache with nervous fingers, and after a wild glance about the room with pale blue eyes, shaking hands all round with a distracted air. "Villiers! Here's Villiers!" all would cry with delight. Then, noticing that the piano was open, he would sit himself at it and begin to play, singing in a quavering voice a song that he had improvised on his walk to rue de Douai, a setting of one of the sonnets of Baudelaire. He was no singer and no pianist, but he silenced the talkative roomful until before the song had ended he would strum the notes with an impatient hand, get up, close the piano, walk into the darkest corner of the room, and rolling another cigarette agitatedly, would regard the stupefied audience with a suspicious stare, "the kind of look Ophelia received from the Hamlet sitting at her feet".

The artist André Gill, "a fine-looking fair-haired young man with an all-conquering moustache", was by comparison ordinary, his one peculiarity being the pleasant habit of laughing at his own vanity. Glatigny had been in and out of Paris as funds permitted, usually out, and in 1864 reappeared momentarily with the publication of his second book of poems, *Flèches d'or*, was photographed by Etienne Carjat, who had more genius than most of his poetical companions put together, then was not seen again for two years. His coming was announced by a thunderous beat at the door and a head-first entrance, the door being insufficiently high to let him pass freely. His stage clothes were as short as ever and his hunger as insatiable—he had been living, he explained, on the biscuits he was supposed to nibble in the second act. As a two-book man he was regarded with respect for a few moments, but respect could not live long with his "*folle causerie*", which, lewd, cynical, gay, foolish, suggested "a Panurge in his naïve sensuality but honest as Panurge was not". Most of the company felt the better for his zest for life, untouched by privations which made the Hôtel de Pérou seem paradisal. Verlaine, meeting him for the first time, liked him altogether too well.

De Ricard looked askance at the tattered giant, but then De Ricard enjoyed the teas only when they were teas; when they moved into something stronger and the talk grew broad he was a fish out of water, having little capacity for liquor or fun and his one idea of originality being to choose a grotesque subject. Mendès, cultivating him with some care, succeeded with difficulty in preserving the dignity of the dedicated spirit against the assaults of Glatigny humour and the general free speech and behaviour as afternoon turned to night.

Another visitor out of his element was Stéphane Mallarmé, at twenty-two one of the youngest men present. He taught English in a provincial school, but even had he lived in Paris it may be doubted whether he would have been seen at Mendès' more often. He was small, quiet, with calm and sacerdotal gestures, and had a habit when speaking "of lowering his silky eyelids on the eyes of a sentimental goat". Not a picture of one likely to be at home in rue de Douai, yet Mallarmé had more in common with Mendès than met the eye. He was to bring to one kind of finality a development of the poetry his host was striving to define and had already begun *Hérodiade*, the poem symbolising virginity which was to occupy him at intervals for the rest of his life, an effort to rinse a poem of every imperfection, every obviousness, that Mendès would heartily approve.

For although the rowdy company at rue de Douai was mixed

to a degree unknown at the De Ricards', it was, paradoxically, more serious than the well-behaved, well-dressed visitors to Boulevard des Batignolles; it says much for Mendès that he not only kept it together but, in the intervals between fooling, with its head pointed roughly in the direction which he hoped would exploit his talent for literature and leadership. As at the Hôtel de Pérou, he and his friends read together, studied, discussed, theorised, experimented, not endlessly but with a persistence that went strangely with their outward irresponsibility. But their leader was of this nature: "he was", admitted one who had no cause to love him, "a great trainer of men, and directed on them all his irresponsible charm in the guise of an apostle of belles lettres—a charm from which I have never seen anyone escape".

Coppée provides a good example. One Tuesday soon after the meetings began, Mendès recited an unsigned poem. Who was the author? all clamoured to know; the manuscript had been put on the table unobserved. Coppée, sitting quietly as usual in the background, made a sign to Mendès to come outside. The poem was his, he explained. Mendès returned, announced the author, and there was vigorous handclapping. Mendès remained cautious: "But are you just a one-poem man?" he asked. "Have you written others?" "Six thousand lines," replied Coppée calmly. "Show them to me tomorrow," said Mendès. He was shown the poems next day, read some, then pushed the pile aside with a brief "Execrable!" Coppée, still calm, put the whole into the fire. This heroic gesture so much impressed Mendès that he took Coppée in hand and, as the latter afterwards freely admitted, made a successful poet of him.

"Seductive but imperious", said Verlaine of Mendès, which from him was positively harsh. For Verlaine was there, a minor figure, the youngest of the company, still in process of adjusting himself to the Hôtel de Ville, which he had recently joined, and a little alarmed as well as charmed by what he heard and saw of his host. He asked for a quiet life but had an uneasy feeling that he would not get it if Mendès had his way. The Mendès programme was too much like work. He therefore lay low. He was drawn to the quietly affable Mallarmé and had begun to plan joint efforts with Coppée, whom he had already persuaded to leave his hat on a peg at the War Office and join the Café du Gaz group for their mid-morning refreshment. He relished the sentimental suburban outlook, spiced by a quiet irony, of this new friend, and had been introduced to the Coppée home with its Balzacian mother and sister convinced that their beloved François was a genius and—a faith which unlike most of this kind was to be handsomely confirmed—would make a name for himself. But one suspects that he yearned after the De Ricard charades, in which, suitably disguised, he could make an ass of himself, and for company he leaned towards the mercurial Chabrier, a youthful violinist, Ernest Boutier, and the yellow-haired and yellow-bearded giant, Ernest Cabaner, who kept life in himself by playing the piano in a third-rate left-bank café and whose awareness of the outside world was so slight that Verlaine, a voracious reader of newspapers and periodicals, for some time suspected a hoax behind the sublime ignorance. Verlaine began to see in the musical comedy stage a pleasant and not too strenuous field for his talents, and he discussed plots in vague terms with everybody who had a musical score to his name. He contributed no more than a dutiful enthusiasm to the Mendèsian hue and cry after verses in which the form should be all, yet despite himself he learned much of his trade at rue de Douai and was to be given by Mendès and company his first chance to display his true gift publicly. He was later to pay his tribute to the effect on him of *Philoméla*:

> Lorsque j'étais un tout petit poète en herbe,
> En herbe bien plutôt et perdu dans l'espace,
> "Je t'aime! dit l'essaim des colombes qui passe"
> Et ce vers fut vraiment ma colombe de l'arche.

quoting, significantly, from a poem that Mendès had dedicated to Baudelaire.

5

LECONTE DE LISLE

1864-1866

The most convincing sign of Mendès' acuity was his realisation that the movement which he was trying to bring to life needed a leader and that this leader could not ostensibly be himself. Who then? Banville would not do for all his popularity; he was not serious, he was too approachable and not at all impressive. Gautier at first sight appeared an obvious choice since the movement sprang from him, but he was handicapped by his public reputation as a romantic of the old school, he travelled often and had never become a Paris "figure". There was another objection; Gautier was beginning to look askance at this pushing young provincial and Mendès' relations with him were to become singularly unfortunate. As also with the next man, Hugo, who disqualified himself by his exile, by his insistence on standing full in the limelight and by the fact, though no one would so much as breathe a hint of it, that his sincerity was suspect. Baudelaire, whom Mendès would have preferred, was a lone wolf, he was not respectable, and that would never do: so Mendès, far from respectable himself, was obliged to reason.

This left Leconte de Lisle; his reputation, though restricted, stood high; he was difficult of access, very much a man with a gospel which he was too proud to propagate in person, he was by all accounts dignified to the point of disagreeableness, his hauteur was a byword at the De Ricards' and rue de Douai. Glatigny had dedicated his second volume to him (his first had been dedicated to Banville), a dedication claiming him firmly as the inspiration of all that was "impassible" in the poems, and Mendès took this to be a sign of the times. He exerted his charm to obtain an introduction. Banville obligingly contributed to his own displacement; he introduced Mendès to Louis Ménard, one of the select visitors to Boulevard des Invalides and the strangest. Ménard had met Marx in England, became a Communist and fought at the barricades in 1848; he was also poet, painter, philosopher, scientist and a naturalist devoted particularly to the study of snakes, coming home day after day with his pockets stuffed with these reptiles gathered from the country surrounding Paris. Above all he was a Hellenist, practising a kind of mystic stoicism which he expressed in poems anticipating the Symbolists and which had contributed to the formation of Leconte de Lisle's outlook and style. In person he was a thin middle-aged man, brown hair springing irrepressibly from a large head, a wispy brown beard that looked as if it had been stuck on to the bony chin, kind blue eyes, a pinched nose. He never had a sou to bless himself with, but seemed not to notice the lack. His clothes were all but falling off his back, but this detail also escaped him.

This queer but attractive figure worshipping the gods as he did was naturally much taken with Mendès: "Apollo in person!" an exclamation that has already been heard. He sought and obtained the master's permission to introduce Mendès and his friends, and one Saturday evening the little cavalcade—Ménard, Mendès, Coppée, De Ricard and Villiers—climbed to the fifth floor of the house in Boulevard des Invalides where the great man and his satellites awaited them.

The contrast between Leconte de Lisle and Ménard was extreme, Ménard all affability and rags, Leconte de Lisle stiff, correct, impeccably clothed, sitting in a salon which had the air of a museum. However, he was gracious; though not admitting the fact, he knew the writings of Mendès and had privately determined that he could use the objectionable but undeniably go-ahead young man to forward his own intention of becoming the foremost figure in the literary world of Paris. Each imagining himself the spider to the other man's fly, the meeting was cordial, that is to say Mendès poured out all his not inconsiderable powers of flattery ("Here is our Mecca!" was one of his first remarks), which Leconte de Lisle accepted imperturbably but with an expression that in another could have been described as benign.

It was in fact not possible for Leconte de Lisle to look benign. How one regarded him depended on the angle from which one did so, for he had a blind eye in which he wore the famous square monocle. He was also on the short side and rather stout (he was then verging on fifty), and it was freely and correctly said that he could tell friends from enemies from the position they took up, facing him or content with a side view. He helped his friends by sitting sideface, and stationed thus he formed an arresting figure, decidedly Lisztian, with strong profile and long hair to the collar. "His brow has the mystery of a temple!" cried Silvestre, a somewhat unexpected devotee. "His eyes are those of an eagle!"

Leconte de Lisle was a strong poet and the effect of his work on the young poets is understandable. Nevertheless his work, like the man of the Saturday soirées and like the name he had assumed, was primarily a pose. He was in origin a Le Conte, a Norman family of no particular account (father a doctor, grandfather a chemist) who had allied themselves at several removes with a noble house. He would speak occasionally of his descent

74

from the Vikings. As a young man he was politician rather than poet, pressing for the freeing of the slaves on which his family, who had become sugar planters in Réunion, depended, and, after his father had cut off his money, leaving the island and the quadroon cousin he had adored since boyhood to become one of the many anti-Christian republicans in the Paris of Louis Philippe. There he met Ménard and founded a club which had as its guiding principle the theory of the transmigration of the soul from star to star. From this to the socialism of George Sand and Fourier was no great step, and the young Le Conte was soon preaching civil war and the inalienable right of the poor to happiness, an exemplary aim but coming strangely from a man fundamentally unfriendly and who could not bear contact with the multitude—strange, that is, were this not the case in nine social reformers out of ten. His family disowned him. He joined the Central Republican Club and was given the mission, in 1848, of "opening the eyes of Brittany". But Brittany preferred to keep its eyes closed and gave the missionary, busily preaching against the evils of religion, such a hot reception that he barely escaped to Paris with his life. He took part in the Revolution, but as a matter of form only; like all idealists unblessed with a sense of humour, he had become disgusted with politics and people; he arrived inevitably at a disillusioned middle age, a disillusion which he covered, effectively one must admit, by setting himself up as Leconte de Lisle the poet-priest of the cult of impassivity, a mixture of the Hindu, Buddhist and Confucian philosophies.

Actually he remained a romantic, sentimental and bad-tempered man, but had successfully imposed the veneer of "impassibility" on all but his young wife (in company "my child") and his several women friends. He was in truth a cold man and unsociable, and to this extent was able to believe in the person he presented to the public, but he did not deceive the envious De Ricard, who said acidly, "he always had a tinge of the barbarian in him". Mendès, his "Mecca" notwithstanding, was simply bored: "We had a pretty dull time of it; not one good story."

In the presence, however, Mendès played up to his company and launched into a dissertation on the difference between the chaste pagans and the licentious early Christians. He backed his argument by several Mendèsian examples, and one of the women present complained of such stories being told before her daughter. Whereupon the master, "glaring at her through his terrible monocle", replied coldly that "in my house friends are in their own home, and in any case the elevation of their thoughts places them above all worldly conventions".

Such was Leconte de Lisle. He has long since been relegated to histories of French literature, being notable now for a single fact, that he was the only poet and almost the only person to arouse Verlaine's dislike, a feat which explains him better than many words.

Two of his disciples had distinction. Léon Dierx, also a creole from Réunion, was a tall fair young man given to the writing of melancholy poems. Pale-faced, sad-faced, quiet to the point of non-utterance, his devotion to the master was embittered by Leconte de Lisle's immoderate passion for women and by what he saw as unfaithfulness, for he too had been separated from his first love in the island. Dierx had published his first volume of poems, *Les Aspirations*, five years earlier and was on the eve of his second. He was to become well known, but at the time his talent remained unacknowledged. Nevertheless his sombre black clothes, grave voice, tranquil but pensive expression, slow and hesitant gestures, exquisite politeness and even his distant manner, as though his thoughts were for ever elsewhere, were being accepted at the various soirées of poets, painters and musicians as a necessary part of the atmosphere. "One of our saints. Never has he sinned against the dream and the ideal", declared Mendès unctuously. And even De Ricard could say no worse of him that that "he always seemed to be in a dream". He was a romantic writer persuaded by Leconte de Lisle into "impassibility". To connect this eminently poetical figure with railways would seem a sacrilege, yet such was his fate. His poems did not pay, his family was ruined by the failure of the sugar crop, and, helped by Mendès "so that he could develop his talent in peace", he followed so many of his kind into a civil service clerkship, which in his case was to lead him incongruously to the baggage office of a provincial railway station.

He and the other staunch disciple, J. M. de Heredia, shared a common faith, both firmly remaining Catholic in spite of Leconte de Lisle's bitter anti-clericalism, and a common courtesy. But Heredia's manners were the pseudo-ceremonious ones of a

Spanish grandee turned parvenu—he was from Cuba—and they did not always include consideration for the feelings of others. He was rich, for instance, and was apt to forget the poverty of the poets he consorted with. Even the master, to whom he had begun to lend money, was to be affronted by him; complaining one day that actors were taking liberties with a play he had written and would not listen to his criticisms, Heredia replied in his loud confident voice: "Let *me* go to the theatre with you. These curs will soon see that you are with a man of the world and that will impress them. Then they'll listen to you." Man of the world was Heredia's favourite expression, and he lived up to it; he was big and handsome and spent a small fortune on his clothes, parading the streets and, less happily, marching importantly into the mean rooms of other poets with perfectly cut trousers and frock-coat, swinging a gold-headed malacca cane and fingering negligently the silk cravat, different every day, that shone with splendour on his thick neck.

On this particular evening he differed with Ménard, who, his easily inflamed enthusiasm aroused by Mendès' defence of paganism, suggested impetuously that they make a ceremonial sacrifice of pigeons to Venus. Heredia, after a prolonged stare through his monocle (all disciples wore the square monocle as a tribute to the master), said coldly, "I don't care for pigeon pie." The subject was dropped.

Heredia was understandably not popular with the young poets of his age and there was much mockery of his mannerisms the moment he left the room, and some spiteful remarks while he was still in it. Even Mendès, anxious to impress Leconte de Lisle and constitutionally unable to be downright disrespectful to a wealthy man, could not force himself to more than an over-smiling shadow of cordiality. Yet of all the poets of his time this loud, vain, over-dressed creature was to write poems with a polished and at times exquisite craftsmanship which demonstrated to perfection the theory and the absurdity of Art for Art's sake.

Happily unaware of this irony in store, Mendès hurried back to rue de Douai, where a conclave headed by himself, Coppée and Villiers decided, with the blessings of Dierx and Heredia, that Leconte de Lisle be acknowledged the head of the forward movement in poetry—or the return to essentials as they would have it. Leconte de Lisle, the picture of gratified dignity, received his new disciples Saturday by Saturday at Boulevard des Invalides. He even in mellow moments permitted young aspirants such as Paul Verlaine to be brought before him and to sit in goggling silence in a far corner; which gesture led to the immediate though hesitant sprouting of a square monocle in the Hôtel de Ville and at the Café du Gaz after preliminary essays before the bedroom mirror in rue Saint-Louis. He did more; acceding to Mendès' importunities, he gave his patronage to the "Lectures Poétiques", regular readings of poetry in a large hired room by young poets unable to get their work published, the poets carefully sifted by Mendès and the room filled with as many influential people as could be scraped together.

So far so good; this gave satisfaction and hope to the talented young men who then as now struggled vainly for a hearing; Mendès as a publisher-poet was genuinely concerned about their plight, remembering his own frustrations at the Hôtel de Pérou. But to that other Mendès, the Napoleonic Mendès, a journal it was not, a movement it was not, and nameless and paperless he looked about him hungrily once more; looked and, such is the reward of persistence, eventually found.

6

NINACUM

1864-1865

Twenty-one years before this first visit of Mendès to Leconte de Lisle a girl, Marie Anne Gaillard de Villard, was born in Paris, daughter and granddaughter of well-to-do solicitors; and as their wives brought each of them a handsome dowry she grew up a wealthy woman. Nina, as she was always known, was an only child and an unwanted one; her hardship was to be given her own way in everything. By the time she reached her twenty-first year her father, "a phlegmatic and nonchalant Lyonnais", had retired permanently to the third floor of their house in rue Chaptal, where Verlaine had spent so many years at school. The mother's interests in life were cats, dogs and a monkey, which, pampered to the point of idiocy, reigned over the second floor; but, being indulgent as well as indifferent, she presided nominally at her daughter's soirées, "following her about like a shadow without ever risking the least observation".

For Nina had begun the soirées which were to become the most notorious in Paris. Late in 1864 she married the Comte Hector de Callias, a handsome, charming and penniless journalist and, unknown to her, a dipsomaniac. He married for money, she for a mixture of affection, kindness and ambition; family love being denied her, she had thirsted after fame since her teens and hoped to win it by proxy. But the only genius this young man possessed was for the bottle, and although the marriage lingered on in law for three years, it ended, except for silent hopes on Nina's part, within a few months, early in 1865.

Unhappy and bored, Nina sought distraction; ambitious, talented (she was a good pianist) and generous, she yearned to reign over and encourage young and gifted men. The answer to everything was plainly an artistic salon; but not for lions: differing in this from other hostesses of her time, to her the important people of Paris were the struggling artists: "Sculptor, musician, poet are her guests", Verlaine was to write.

The soirées began as musical afternoons, then, reports spreading of Nina's brilliance on the pianoforte and of the sumptuous refreshments, blossomed into musical evenings. The star of afternoon and evening alike, the hostess excepted, was Charles de Sivry, a small black-haired young man with long drooping black moustaches that gave him a slightly oriental air. He was popular for several reasons: for his rank (he was a Marquis, a fact to which he never referred); for his talent (he had arranged many folk-songs and composed light music with contemptuous ease); but specially for his high spirits and affability. He used never to leave his bed until early afternoon, which may partly explain his increasing brightness as evening succeeded afternoon and night evening. By the small hours he was the life and soul of the party—any party, he was not particular so long as he was at one. At Nina's musical gatherings he would begin soberly enough, accompanying the singers, singing himself, and improvising dutifully, but as time went on and tea was followed by apéritifs the mischievous in him bubbled out and practical jokes became the order of the evening. The decorous disappeared and the rest gave themselves over to fun with the lively little De Sivry as ringleader.

So opened the soirées at rue Chaptal. But the name soirée was soon to lose its meaning; there were no Tuesdays, Thursdays, Saturdays as at Mendès', Banville's, Leconte de Lisle's and elsewhere; from time to time as Nina's fame spread formal receptions were held, but essentially the house became open house to all young, deserving, interesting and hard-working artists: "No one needs fine clothes to be received by me," she said, "a sonnet is enough." Such could come at any hour, leave at any time, and if they had no bed—and Villiers, Cabaner, Dierx and Glatigny of the company we know were often homeless—were welcome to sleep on the sofa, the great rug by the fire, the hammock in the garden. Even on the nights of formal receptions the night truly began when the distinguished guests had gone leaving Nina with her circle of intimates sprawled on the floor, declaiming from the hearthrug, perched on the piano. None had any notion of time; there were newly written poems to be read, newly composed songs to be sung, plans to be hatched against the government and, that standard form of *jeu d'esprit* despatched, the work of their great predecessors to be studied, analysed and emulated. "All loved Nina's because they obtained there not only food and wine but enthusiasm and encouragement for the most wretched and broken. Rich and poor they came to bewail the misery of their failures, to be consoled, to argue, to quarrel and above all to express their ideas, always having in common the supremacy of art."

The lines were Mendès', for of course Mendès was soon there. De Sivry knew Chabrier, Chabrier knew Mendès, it was simple in the Paris of those days. In no time at all Mendès and his assorted company had virtually taken possession of Nina's house, and the preponderantly musical element of the gatherings changed as Nina discovered the charms of poetry and poets. Soon Banville, Leconte de Lisle, Gautier and other celebrities were to be seen at the occasional dinner, and Nina had been launched as a literary hostess. The memoir writers have found it difficult to take her seriously, indeed have not tried very hard; many stories have been told about Nina and her poets and musicians, and almost all leave the impression of a bedlam. "The studio of cerebral disorder", reported the Goncourts: "My private Charenton", said Nina once, and such sanction from the ringleader has been too great a temptation to resist. There was much fooling, some of it stupid, but there was also in these early days a sense of a mission.

There was none the less something in Nina's face even then, in her eyes particularly, which foretold her end and the end of her soirées. But no one troubled to see the unpleasant, obvious though it was, the present being altogether too attractive. Only one man, and he surely the last one would expect, not merely had an inkling of the truth but wrote it down at the time. The young Verlaine first came into his own in the "Quartier Nina-cum" as he called it; that is to say Nina drew him out. What she drew was not particularly impressive; he showed himself a good second or third to De Sivry, Chabrier and the other bright sparks, he was loud in the condemnation of Offenbach, Delibes, Halévy, Lecocq and Hervé, which was compulsory in that company. Nevertheless the book for an operetta which he was soon enthusiastically planning called for music of precisely that nature. Yet something else was stirring, for Verlaine's sonnet to his hostess shows observation and ability. His opening line "Des yeux tout autour de la tête" puts a finger on her one beauty, the enormous black eyes, intelligent, emotional, with their alarming glint of irresponsible playfulness, of the wilful, the reckless glowing from an excessively pale face and set off by

> Ses cheveux, noir tas sauvage où
> scintille un barbare bijou.

As for the person behind those exciting, disturbing eyes:

> Point très bonne. Un esprit d'enfer
> Avec des rires d'alouette.

a picture that needs no bush. "Ange perverse", Verlaine sums up, for there was little peace and no certainty where she was except the delightful-horrific knowledge that there could be no boredom and would probably be trouble. He also uses the nickname by which she came to be known: *La Pétroleuse*; and this characterises her accurately, the incendiary revelling in the stirring of revolt against the smug, the satisfied, the established. Verlaine does not mention her gift of putting the most disparate people at their ease, yet, admirable hostess though she was, apparently shaping the company to her wishes, there was another and less obvious aspect of her that he saw through the glamour:

La font reine et la font fantoche

he says truly; for Mendès, whilst giving good value for his entertainment, was using her for his own ends. They were her ends too, regarded in the large, but this was incidental; she had money, she had influence, she could help the movement of modern poetry to its feet; to this extent she was the queen acquiescent in her puppetdom.

Mendès liked to describe himself as Porthos to Glatigny's D'Artagnan, the Aramis of Coppée and the grave Athos of Dierx, but his charm roused in Nina nothing more lethal than a mixture of admiration and amusement. In her house Othello was preferred to Apollo. Othello was Charles, the most remarkable of the Cros brothers. Henri Cros had just sketched Verlaine, a long-haired Verlaine with a slight Mongol moustache—a faint effort to imitate the more luxuriant growth of his "Sivrot"—but Charles was to be the chief glory of the family, a glory that Nina clearly perceived. In appearance he showed a negroid origin, woolly hair parted in the middle, flat-nosed, tiny moustache ornamenting a long upper lip, but with clear blue eyes contrasting oddly with swarthy skin. Not in repose a particularly attractive young man, but he was rarely seen in repose. He spent his life searching after the unknown, said an admirer, beginning the search as a small boy—"Father, I've discovered how to raise the dead. I'm beginning after breakfast." "Oh please don't, Charles, they would be so unhappy"—and continuing to search for the rest of his short life. He invented colour photography, the telephone and the gramophone amongst other things, but, hurrying on to the next discovery, forgot or could not raise the money to put his inventions to commercial use, a fact which still fills many Frenchmen with patriotic bitterness; and as poet he anticipated the later Rimbaud and the Symbolist school with his surrealistic prose poems and fantastic, macabre verses. An original in his butterfly way, he was not a member of the Mendès-Leconte de Lisle school; he was to form his own group, from which many of the lesser Symbolists emerged. His interest in the house was in Nina and later in Verlaine, who even then regarded his mental and physical busyness with the admiration of the lazy; and it may be that Cros' imitations of Leconte de Lisle and mockery of his mystical pretensions did more than merely shock the younger man and that his penchant for plain speech and un-loaded verses struck, dimly and half heard, an answering chord in the one who was destined eventually "to wring the neck of eloquence".

Dierx was, next to Cros, Nina's favourite; desperately poor, he took to sleeping there every night; he regarded with wonder, being a perfectionist, a very youthful poet, Jean Richepin, successfully carrying out his wager that he would speak in verse throughout dinner; and neatly put one of the rare notoriety hunters in his place: "Do you write your verses to be read or to be heard?" "To be smelt," returned the melancholy Dierx. For the rest he remained quiet, statuesque, seen but never heard.

After Cros and Dierx the most regular visitor was the ubiquitous Villiers, who since the year of the *Revue fantaisiste* had been led to strange shifts to keep his head above water, teaching boxing in a suburban gymnasium, begging loans at the gates of the Benedictine monasteries in Paris and at last feigning madness so that he could get food and a bed in an asylum. By the time of Nina the monks had lost patience, the asylum doctors had decided that insanity could be overdone, and Villiers joined Dierx, Cabaner and Glatigny when in Paris as one of the perma-nent guests at rue Chaptal.

As clown in chief he did his duty. In worn black trousers, chimney-pot hat, loose grey overcoat trimmed with fur, pockets bulging with manuscripts, he would enter the salon with his customary chamois-like bounds, legs meeting the ground un-steadily, chewed cigarette jerking between his lips, every feature of his face working, and never failed to provide the expected sensation. Howling with hysterical laughter, he would tell how he had seen an acquaintance reading Hoeckel's *History of the Creation*, had asked its price, and when told ten francs had replied, "The catechism costs only two sous." Having related the story, he immediately retold it in a falsetto voice, again in a voice of deepest bass, and yet again in a series of yodels. Then he would spring to the organ and sing it to his own refrain; and from the organ to the piano, where it would be sung again to a different accompaniment, all performances punctuated by bursts of high-pitched laughter. In another mood he would bound shamblingly to the organ, pull out every stop and play the

Tannhäuser overture, after which—if he did not, as at Mendès', subside into a corner—he would stand in the centre of the room and say mysteriously: "Plot for my next story. Scene, a room with a bed, on the bed a woman, round about the bed everything needed for an accouchement, doctor, midwife, bottles, jars, phials, everywhere the atmosphere stale, stale. Then appears feebly the head of a newborn child; he opens his eyes, looks round about, sniffs, then cries: 'So this is it—life! Oh!' And he hurriedly dives back into the womb." Or having heard during the day some praise of a realistic novelist, probably of Zola himself, a harsh critic of Mendès and company, he would say impressively before he was well through the door: "Monsieur so and so? Very good. Excellent. I'm going to write an analytical novel too. I have already studied my subject deeply. A rentier goes into the country one Sunday but forgets to take his purse." Silence, everyone looking at him expectantly. "Well?" a listener asks at last as he remains silent, his eyes rapt. "That's all," he replies absently. "If anything else happens in his life, which I doubt, I'll write a second volume." Someone, changing the subject, speaks of Vitu, the theatrical critic before whom the contemporary theatre trembled. Villiers raises an imperious hand, says in the tone of Lady Bracknell: "Vitu? No!" and Vitu is exterminated. Like everybody at Nina's he read his poems, and once, reciting to a large and fashionable audience, the guest of honour an Austrian Countess, he felt a twinge at his heart, dropped his manuscript and, obeying his doctor's orders to the letter, undid his trousers, lay flat on the floor and rested his feet on the keyboard of the piano, reciting soulfully. On the few occasions when Leconte de Lisle attended a dinner at Nina's, Villiers was liable to take him up on some abstruse reference to the Hindu scriptures; though whether this queer poseur, who would discuss Hegel, Kant and the Eastern mystics with impartial passion, was truly well read or whether the master had skimmed the surface too is a question.

The exuberant Heredia, as unwelcome as Villiers was welcome, would stride imposingly into Nina's of an evening patting his latest sartorial creation with a loud "Well, my friends! and what do you think of this thick pearl-grey cloth I'm wearing for the first time today in your honour? Admire it; thirty-one francs seventy-five sous at the Trois-Quartiers!" And the friends, most of whom would have been glad to put their hands on the odd seventy-five sous, would look hungrily and growl beneath their breath when he launched for the thousandth time on an anecdote of his grandfather, bosom companion, he assured them, of the great Pizarro. But when, later, he faced them from the fireplace resonantly reading his latest sonnet, the admiration was as genuine as the envy. One or two succumbed to the malice of the quiet individual who stood about, book under arm, in but not of the company, the man of whispers: "Didn't you know? Leconte de Lisle writes them all for him." Anatole France, one felt, was surely destined to be a power in the land; Leconte de Lisle, it was known, thought much of him, even listened to him; he was tolerated with the kind of regretful respect one gives to a cat with a mouse.

For the rest the young men flocked to Nina's as they had flocked to De Ricard's and Mendès'; her soirées had all the comforts of the one without its formality and all the freedom of the other without its discomforts. Coppée was a favourite as ever, Valade obscure as usual, Mérat threw the expected stones into the pool. Cabaner, swathed in a long and hairy cloak, bright yellow in strange contrast to his brick-red face, drifted in absent-mindedly after midnight to discuss the setting to music of poems by Cros and Dierx and was occasionally persuaded to sing in an unmusical broken voice some of his own songs or to play a part of the oratorio he was writing. He was always good for a laugh: at the funeral of his father—"a man", he explained, "of the same type as the first Napoleon but less beastly"—he gazed wonderingly at the forest of raised hats with a "I should never have believed I was so well known!"

Manet headed the painters, the hero of the scandalised reception of *Déjeuner sur l'Herbe* at the Salon des Refusés before Nina's soirées had begun and of *Olympia* soon after they were in full swing; he made a portrait of his hostess which re-creates her alarming black eyes. Revolutionaries of another kind were there too: Lepelletier reading blistering articles against the "tottering régime" as he prematurely described it, and Rigault, whose sinister suavity made the other hotheads appear somewhat childish, specially Nina and her friend, the fiery cigarette-smoking Augusta Holmes in her symbolical red velvet dress. Augusta, unlike her friend, was one of the "modern" women with close-cropped hair and curt masculine manner. She gave her own soirées, musical ones at which the presiding god was Wagner. Later, on the centenary of the Revolution, she was to publish a triumphant ode; for the present she played Wagner with a fervour and meditated a Wagnerian opera of her own.

But the hot speeches, like the fooling of De Sivry and his henchmen, did not give a true picture of Nina's in these years; for that one had to wait until most of the guests had gone and the select gathered in the walled crescent garden of the kind to be made famous by Proust. There, by a magnificent magnolia giving off thick night fragrance, Nina, wearing the Japanese dressing-gown just coming into fashion with eastern pots, paintings and fans, moved gently in a rocking-chair, head back, meditatively blowing smoke rings as she listened to Charles Cros, who stood under the great plane tree discussing magic with Villiers; for magic, like Japanese art, was then, thanks mainly to Levi, an obligatory stage in the intellectual grand tour of the young Frenchman. The dark Spanish beauty Manoel de Grand-fort lay prone on a couch working out the next of the "fantasies" she was contributing to *La Vie Parisienne* or the next chapter of *La Cousine d'André*, by which she was soon to make a slender name. Augusta swung in the hammock, its faint creaks drowned by the splash of the ornamental fountain in the centre of the paved walk; she was picking snatches of the conversation between Mendès and Mallarmé, who walked up and down trying to thresh out the latter's creed: "Poetry must be an enigma; the charm of it must lie in the attempt to divine the meaning. Describe things only by their reminiscence. Suggest, never state." Mallarmé had explained his theory at a Leconte de Lisle soirée, to be met at once by a cry of "Do you know where this leads, this abuse of the indirect and abstract? It leads to madness!" The timid young man, veiling his eyes, had tried to appear as though he had heard nothing, whilst the master pinched his thick lips joyfully to witness the snub of a disciple who dared to think for himself. Mendès did not officially take this view; on the contrary, he told Mallarmé that his poems were "miracles of dream, sensibility and charm"; his "horrible vision of a pure work in trying to decipher which I have nearly lost my reason and have entirely lost the meaning of the most familiar words" was in the future; in Nina's garden in the summer of 1865 he saw in this mild little spinner of words, this careful avoider of the obvious, this fastidious shrinker from unclad emotion, a disciple beyond price. But he was on safer ground when they moved to the familiar question, what name should the Art for Art's sake movement bear, and was even more at home when, pausing by the table on which stood glasses of champagne, he raised one in toast to the other three musketeers, Coppée, Dierx and the absent Glatigny. Dierx, hearing his name spoken, shrank deeper into the shade of the wall against which he leaned pensively eyeing the stars; but Nina, noticing his movement, begged him to read poetry appropriate to the night and the company. He rarely refused her; after some moments of reflection he inclined his head and recited in his grave, sad voice:

> Le soir fait palpiter plus mollement les plantes
> Autour d'un groupe assis de femmes indolentes.

7

L'ART

1865-1866

Verlaine was not often of this select company on Nina's lawn night by night. His devotion to poetry had progressed little further than the enjoyment of hearing it discussed. It was not that he had lost interest, it was not even that his attention was given largely to lighter matters, it was simply that he did little about his enthusiasms but enthuse. There was a reason for this beyond an inveterate laziness. If ever the suspicion flitted into his head that the Art for Art's sake doctrine was opposed to his nature and talent he allowed it to flit out again because his mind did not work thus; in a sense it scarcely worked at all; friendliness was its driving force and friendliness is not the most inspiring or clear-sighted of muses. The few poems he had actually written were mediocre and a less promising member of the group could scarcely have come under the bright but calculating glance of Mendès.

Fortunately for him, Mendès was human too. None more so. Verlaine, drawn out by Nina, made a companion very much to the leader's mind; and when, towards the end of 1865, with

Nina's help and encouragement, another journal was launched with De Ricard skilfully placated as editor and Mendès his all-powerful assistant, Verlaine was asked to contribute.

The new journal was called *L'Art* after Gautier and devoted itself to the popularisation of impassibility; poems by Leconte de Lisle, Coppée, Mendès, Dierx and De Ricard demonstrated the strict application of art for art's sake; articles explained why the personal must be cut out of poetry, castigated the emotionalism of Lamartine, the sensibility of De Musset and the lyricism of the Lake poets in England, and praised the importance of the form and the sovereign rights of art. "The new generation of poets," the editors stated, "convinced that reverie and the neglect of form are the characteristic signs of infancy in art, devote themselves above all to the inflexible cult of this so greatly despised form and to the mathematical precision of ideas." And Villiers, doing the utmost violence to his nature, declared solemnly: "Poetry consists solely in the choice and juxtaposition of certain unusual words, bizarre sounds and suggestive assonances. The perfect sonnet is one in which the poet makes the most possible use of ingenious and exceptional epithets without the slightest hint of emotion or idea. When a so-called poet objects that I produce works of a glacial coldness and gives me a look of disdainful pity, I reply with an hieratical solemnity, 'Monsieur, marble is cold also!'"

After digesting this barrage of statement and example on the objective and intellectual approach to poetry, one reads with a certain stupefaction the two poems that Verlaine was permitted to print: one begins:

> Souvenir, souvenir, que me veux-tu?

and continues:

> Nous étions seul à seule et marchions en rêvant,
> Elle et moi,

whilst the second launches itself with a

> J'ai peur dans les bois.

Both poems, indifferently good, are characteristic to this extent, that they are unrepentantly personal. He to some extent redeemed himself by an article attacking a tiresome romantic of the old school, Barbey d'Aurevilly, who lived and dressed after the manner of the eighteen-thirties and had fostered the usual high-sounding appendage to the too plebeian Barbey. Verlaine's stock rose still higher with an article on Baudelaire which Mendès thought so well of that (with apologies for the faulty spelling) he sent the three numbers in which it appeared to Brussels, where Baudelaire had embarked on his tragic series of lectures. Baudelaire, though speaking of the "talent in the younger men, but how much folly", was sufficiently pleased to forward the article to his mother with a "it seems there is now a *school of Baudelaire*".

So Verlaine lived to fight another day in the ranks of the moderns, and perhaps because of his narrow escape became excessively impassible, wearing his square monocle with a defiant and even haughty air in so far as he was able to assume an attitude so wildly out of character, and beginning at last to write poems with a will and a direction. One of these, the now famous epilogue, he recited in Nina's drawing-room. The last two lines (which owe something to Villiers it would seem),

> L'Art n'est pas d'éparpiller son âme.
> Est-elle en marbre ou non, la Vénus de Milo?

brought him tumultuous applause.

8

LE PARNASSE CONTEMPORAIN

1866

For a moment the young Verlaine (he was still only twenty-two) seemed to have won a modicum of attention to no purpose. Early in 1866 *L'Art* stopped publication; it had been bought only by enemies and by friends who had not succeeded in obtaining a free copy. The public uninterest in modern poetry, as in painting, remained abysmal. Only Gautier, Banville and Leconte de Lisle were being published; the wretched Baudelaire, now near his end, had spent the last twenty years in one demoralising attempt after another to beg, cajole and flatter editors and publishers into printing his verses; the younger and lesser poets faced the dismal prospect of writing endlessly for an audience of friends who would praise but not pay. The readings organised by Mendès and Leconte de Lisle had failed to spread their name beyond a small fashionable circle; no periodical could live for more than a few months; at Nina's, De Ricard's, Mendès' and the rest they were preaching to the converted, in no way did they seem able to reach the general reader.

At this depressing moment light appeared from an unexpected quarter. *L'Art*, all agreed, had been yet another failure. Yet it was not so; its readers had been few, but one of them, the least regarded of all, strode into the disconsolate circle like a god and saved the day. Preoccupied by the fortunes of the periodical, they had overlooked the publisher, but it was he who, actually reading what he printed and liking it, gave the movement a new and this time lasting lease of life. Alphonse Lemerre, a big autocratic Breton with fine grey eyes, friendly smile and great yellow beard, a blend of Viking and proconsul Mendès and company thought, had taken over the business of Percepied in Passage Choiseul. Percepied had specialised in the lucrative printing and sale of Première Communion manuals and other religious books but Lemerre had different ideas; he was ambitious and kind, he wished to make himself famous through literature and to help the pleasant and talented young men he had met through *L'Art*. "Let the little poets come unto me!" he cried with his famous roar of laughter, large blond head thrown back. And the little poets came; came to lunches in his apartment in rue Claudin, flocked to his shop every afternoon, where from five to seven he held open house as Theo van Gogh was to do with his young painters twenty years later. Eating good food and watching their host at the head of the table, a benevolent despot, the poor poets felt themselves to be in an earthly paradise. And not only watching but listening, for this curious publisher was not interested simply in making a name from his connection with promising poets, he knew and appreciated their poems; he learned by heart all the sonnets of Heredia, which he declaimed in stentorian voice between mouthfuls, he spoke the verses of Leconte de Lisle with florid gusto. His generosity became proverbial; no poet of any reasonable pretensions should go hungry, he declared; all should eat and all should see their poems in print. Eat they did at his expense, and plans were soon under way for the printing.

THE PARNASSIAN

The small office and shop in Passage Choiseul became the headquarters of every progressive poet in Paris. Every afternoon the office on the first floor was jammed with gesticulating young men declaiming, arguing at the tops of their voices; the entresol where books were stored and sold was packed by a kind of overflow meeting and the iron corkscrew staircase connecting the two was cluttered with poets trying to thrust themselves into the heaven of the upstairs room where the great men were to be seen and heard. Gautier looked in from time to time and received the plaudits for his every scarce word with a sleepy benignity— a benignity that did not extend itself to Mendès, who had had the temerity to glance admiringly at his beautiful young daughter Judith, still less to Villiers, whose parents, when they heard of his engagement to another of Gautier's daughters, promptly forbade it on the grounds that Gautier, master or no master, was a commoner.

Banville bounded rotundly up the corridor cleared for him on the staircase and immediately began to bandy words with Lemerre. Leconte de Lisle made no such error; he paid short visits two or three times a week, aloof, majestic and on occasion "acrimoniously olympian". A dozen square monocles flashed in his honour before eyes having no need of their assistance; his slightest word was greeted with acclamations from poets astride the corners of the desk, balancing on piles of books, sitting tailorwise on the floor, propping up the door, occupying every step of the staircase; even the silent Dierx was once heard to exclaim in a voice broken with emotion after someone had attempted to praise him, "I am only a lover of poetry, a humble disciple of him who will carry the sceptre so majestically when Hugo passes it on."

The masters gone, the meetings grew noisier and the atmosphere more stifling. Across the room Silvestre's indecent laugh would burst out in contrast to the delicate chuckle of Emile Blémont, a coming light who had recently been introduced to Verlaine at a Banville soirée with that slight hush in the voice which indicated a man with a book of poems soon to be published. Mérat entered puffing the inevitable cigar and, if he thought the atmosphere too peaceful, would interject a "Surely a little passion wouldn't hurt?" or, even more effectively, "The *Prunes* of Daudet are admittedly infantile but there are one or two pleasant lines", a saying which brought imprecations about his head, Daudet having declared himself an enemy. Painters led by Manet formed their own little group within a group of which only the floatingly fair-haired Fantin-Latour, painter of attractive flower pieces, is now remembered. Even Nina (then busily composing passionless poems) was once seen there supported by Charles Cros.

All but one had to be thrust out of doors after seven o'clock had struck. This one was De Ricard. He was the kind of man who hugs a grievance, and he had found a good one. Had he not begun the soirées three years earlier, edited two of the three periodicals and, finally, discovered Lemerre? This last was a little wide of the mark, since Lemerre had actually been introduced to Lepelletier and Verlaine by the ephemeral Boutier, then playing second violin in a theatre orchestra, but De Ricard had made the first approaches. Yet where was the hush when he spoke, the deference to his opinions? Through his pince-nez he observed with increasing rancour that Lemerre was undisputed King of Passage Choiseul except when he made way for Leconte de Lisle, and that of the younger group, much swollen, which had first come together in his father's house, Mendès was now foremost, having finally thrown off the fiction of leading-reins.

No doubt this rebuff sharpened the revolutionary in De Ricard; in this (Rigault not attending) he remained unchallenged leader and, supported by Lepelletier and Verlaine, made bloodthirsty speeches which produced roars of laughter from Lemerre. Lemerre might well laugh; anything less formidable than this fierceness would be hard to imagine. De Ricard looked like a Museum Curator imitating one of his livelier exhibits, and sure enough this was what he was to come to; Lepelletier presented the ludicrous spectacle of a suburbanite conscientiously writing "Red" plays, poems and articles; Verlaine in tub-thumping mood had little to recommend him but disarming enthusiasm. All three seemed booked for a comfortable maisonette and, if lucky, a ribbon across the chest.

Verlaine had come out of his shell with a vengeance, Nina, Mendès and the monocle all having had their effect, not to speak of the two published poems. Lepelletier or De Ricard about, and he preached revolution; absent, and he preached Leconte de Lisle with loud assurance, swallowing against every instinct the general worship and imitation from monocle to Buddhism. "Pa Indra!" he exclaimed one day. "How beautiful! And how it disgusts one with the Bible, Evangelists and all the *vomissements* of the Fathers of the Church!" For which he was given a resounding cheer. And he was soon declaiming with enormous emphasis a jingle he had just completed of which two lines are enough:

> Ils marchaient droit dans la stricte observance,
> Les chers, les bons, les braves Parnassiens!

Parnassians: for at long last they had a name. Lemerre had proposed that, periodicals being unprofitable and unable to popularise a poetic theory, the theory should be made public by an anthology of poems, the anthology to be published in parts week by week. The offer, joyfully accepted, reopened the battle for a title; the chief runners were Fantaisistes, Stylistes, Formistes and Impassibles as opposed to the abhorred Passionistes. Of these Impassibles was most favoured, Glatigny having written a much admired poem to Gautier, *L'Impassible*, and it being widely known that Leconte de Lisle liked to be referred to in similar terms. Yet the debate continued, the years having possibly given the subject such glamour that no one had the heart to end it, and all showed signs of enjoying perpetual indecision when a chance visitor blowing into the midst of the discussion and no doubt becoming bored by it said hastily, "Why not Parnasse Contemporain?" a suggestion which Lemerre instantly adopted.

The number of contributors and the order in which they should appear was an even more ticklish decision to take, and Mendès, throwing a sop to De Ricard and giving himself one by the way, took over the job without so much as a by your leave. "L.-X. de Ricard, that absurd but divine man, has founded with me *Le Parnasse Contemporain*", he wrote to Baudelaire in a letter seeking contributions; and, the business man, "I have put all useless people outside and hope to conduct the Parnasse in a serious way".

And to a point he did so. De Ricard wished the editors' contributions to be published first; Mendès' vanity, though it had the better excuse, was neither so tactless nor so unbusiness-like. Gautier opened the first part at the beginning of March in company with Banville and Heredia, Leconte de Lisle occupied the second and Baudelaire the next. Then, having leaned back so far in abnegation, the editors let themselves go; each had a part to himself, printing sixteen pages of poems, twice the space given to Leconte de Lisle, Banville and Coppée, four times as much as Gautier and Heredia and many times more than the selections of the remaining thirty contributors, which were thrust into thirteen issues. The series finished at the end of June. It brought no money to thirty-five of the contributors—only Baudelaire and Leconte de Lisle were paid—but it justified Mendès' hopes, put the Parnassians on the map and, perhaps somewhat to the astonishment of that easy-going young gentleman, made a poet of Paul Verlaine.

Chapter Five

THE POET PUBLISHED

I

POÈMES SATURNIENS

1866

CONSIDERING the obscurity in which the Parnassians had lived for the past five years, if one dates the movement no further back than the *Revue fantaisiste*, the stir caused by *Le Parnasse Contemporain* is astonishing. True they had formerly walked in the darkness of no name, and certainly the name when it came provided a temptation that no comedian worth his salt could ignore; nor did he; the music halls and cafés soon rang with skits and songs and sketches. The general effort to discredit the movement appears in retrospect as a rehearsal by the philistines and the reactionary intellectuals for their longer-lasting and more virulent attacks on the Impressionists eight years later; the difference being that the one was in part deserved, the other not at all.

Some surprising developments followed the anti-Parnasse attacks, including a duel fought by Mendès which he successfully weathered and, on another occasion, the hitting of Daudet by Verlaine—in the back. This was the result of the publication of the *Parnassiculet Contemporain*, a skit largely written by Daudet making cruel fun of the denizens of the Hôtel de Pérou under the name of the Dragon Bleu. Zola, who had quizzed the Parnassians' struggles to get into print—"these reviews of theirs never last long but as one succeeds another the little army marching after Monsieur Mendès doesn't lose heart at all and falls into step once again with the utmost conviction"—now said briefly but unkindly, "like the fakirs of India absorbed in contemplation of their navel, the Parnassians pass the evenings admiring each other".

Another lance was broken by a would-be Parnassian rejected by Mendès, the young Jean Richepin, who promptly published an anti-Parnassian periodical which he named meaningfully *Les*

Vivants. But the main attack, and the one that really made the movement, was launched by Barbey d'Aurevilly. Annoyed both by Parnassian criticisms and by the omission of a young friend of his, he published in the *Nain Jaune* in the late autumn of 1866 a series of Médaillonets, reviews of every contribution to the *Parnasse Contemporain*. Barbey was a hard-hitting critic and mingled truth with ineptitude. He despatched Verlaine quickly, quoting a line of one of his eight poems

> Elle a
> L'inflèxion des voix chères qui se sont tues

with a "when we listen to M. Paul Verlaine we could wish that his voice had a similar inflection" instead of hearing "a puritan Baudelaire, a droll and unhappy combination, with none of the brilliant talent of M. Baudelaire, and with echoes here and there of M. Hugo and Alfred de Musset".

This last was a palpable hit and the "puritan" rankled for a time, wildly wide of the mark though it was, Baudelaire of course being the puritan, not his admirer. On the other hand this was fame; one was abused, discussed, one was an acknowledged poet. Verlaine, essentially a happy soul, soon regarded the affair entirely on its sunny side and, strong in the belief that he must after all be a man of consequence, a belief nourished by the acceptance of three poems by *La Revue du XIX* Siècle*, began busily to prepare a volume for publication side by side with Coppée. He and Coppée had become good friends and in spare moments were putting together a poetic skit in eleven scenes and an epilogue—*Revue de l'année 1867*—which occupied three of the four pages of a little review *Le Hanneton*, a skit containing two lines:

> Nous mendierons la soupe aux portes des casernes,
> Monsieur, et nous irons coucher dans les platras!

which Verlaine twenty years later was to find "almost prophetic".

But at the time it was a game; he liked nothing better than collaboration in the not too serious exercise of a gift, and nothing better than collaborating with a young man on whose common sense one could rest gratefully whilst relishing the loving atmosphere of his home. And if Coppée had an adoring mother and sister convinced of his genius, why, so had he, the sole difference being that his mother and Elisa substituted for faith in him as poet an all-embracing wish to give him what he thought he wanted. He now wanted to publish a book of verse, and Elisa, following his every move with affectionate interest from her home at Lécluse, offered to pay for it. The printing of the *Parnasse Contemporain* had cost the contributors two thousand francs and the money had to come from the pockets of those who could scrape it together. This included Verlaine, who, though well paid at the Hôtel de Ville, was sufficiently un-French to be more generous than careful. He was therefore chronically hard up and gratefully accepted Elisa's offer. On October 20, then, appeared simultaneously under Lemerre's imprint Coppée's *Le Reliquaire* and Verlaine's *Poèmes Saturniens*.

Coppée's book had a *succès d'estime* after the manner of Glatigny's and Mendès' first volumes; Verlaine's fell flat, only two journals reviewing it, one scathingly. The critics of those days have since been blamed for blindness, but the truth is that Coppée's poems deserved notice, Verlaine's with one exception did not; Coppée did adequately what he set out to do, Verlaine did not. No critic, given such a collection, could be expected to extract one poem from it, still less to deduce from a few hints here and there in versification and melody that a genius had arrived and with him new horizons in French poetry.

In any case genius had not arrived. *Poèmes Saturniens* began with a preface in the form of a poem announcing solemnly that the author's future was predestined and dark like that of all born under the "influence maligne" of that "fauve planète" Saturn, and the poems which follow almost all keep to the declared pattern, the first section, *Mélancholia*, having in it *Résignation*, *Nevermore*, *Lassitude* and *L'Angoisse*, and the rest of the volume being only a little more cheerful. The mood of the book and the Saturnian explanation suggest an unhappy young man of twenty-two foretelling an unhappy life. Actually, though he wrote often enough of the future, his feelings and behaviour were persistently dominated by the present. He was to remain a happy man through most of his miseries and in 1866 the miseries existed in print only: the marriage of Elisa (whom he could see whenever he cared to make the journey and from whom he heard regularly) and the death of his father (the effect of which was not, understandably, life-long) were the sum of his sorrows to date. He had a doting mother, many friends and no enemies, security, ample means and hopes without end, varied and changeable though they might be.

The motto was merely an expression of the melancholy then modish among the young poets who wrote, with Baudelaire well in mind and with hearts bounding with hope and happiness, of doom, death, wretchedness without end. The mood of the volume as a whole was a blend of this youthful morbidity and of Verlaine's wish to be a Parnassian.

He tried hard. The Prologue ranges dutifully through the glories of the mystic East, the classical Aegean, the southern troubadours, to the unhappy lot of the modern poet; in the volume proper one finds the expected nature pieces, historical poems, barbaric names, and the inevitable slighting reference to De Musset; and the Epilogue winds up the whole with an explanation, very well done for a task completely against the grain, of the Parnassian conception of poetry. If one overlooks the occasional un-Parnassian intrusion of "mon pauvre cœur" and the like, and if one does not scan it too searchingly, the volume passes muster as in the main a competent echo of Baudelaire; but, as a man cannot be kept down indefinitely even if he does his utmost to stay under, Verlaine emerges occasionally. The very first poem sets off in good Parnassian style, the personal note excepted:

> Tout enfant, j'allais rêvant Ko-Hinnor,
> Somptuosité persane et papale
> Héliogabale et Sardanapale!
>
> Mon désir créait sous des toits en or,
> Parmi les parfums, au son des musiques,
> Des harems sans fin, paradis physiques!
>
> Aujourd'hui, plus calme et non moins ardent,
> Mais sachant la vie et qu'il faut qu'on plie,
> J'ai du refréner ma belle folie,
> Sans me résigner par trop cependant.
>
> Soit! le grandiose échappe à ma dent,
> Mais, fi de l'aimable et fi de la lie!
> Et je hais toujours la femme jolie,
> La rime assonante et l'ami prudent.

But even in this best-forgotten sonnet the essential man will intrude, and there he is plain enough in the last line of the first quatrain.

The poet is discovered inexplicably in the middle of the little volume, in the section dedicated to Mendès.

> Les sanglots longs
> Des violons
> De l'automne
> Blessent mon cœur
> D'une langueur
> Monotone.

> Tout suffocant
> Et blême, quand
> Sonne l'heure,
> Je me souviens
> Des jours anciens
> Et je pleure;

> Et je m'en vais,
> Au vent mauvais
> Qui m'emporte
> Deçà, delà,
> Pareil à la
> Feuille morte.

Nothing like *Chanson d'Automne* had been written since Ronsard, and it was not Ronsard, it was Verlaine. Only the irony and the unselfconsciousness are missing; for the rest the intimate, un-studied, personal note, the quiet expression of a mood that comes to all from time to time, the economy and the musicality, a sure feeling for words and above all for the placing of words so that the mood is re-created not only in the mind but by actual physical sensation—all this anticipates the mature poet.

Of his friends, the praise of Mallarmé alone was more than mere friendliness. The critics did not detect the originality buried in the book, and one does not blame them. The great men to whom Verlaine, as was the custom, had sent copies did not detect it either. Four replied. Neither Hugo nor Banville had bothered to do more than skim, the latter declaring with his usual exag-geration that he had read it through ten times at a sitting, the former saluting the author as the dawn to his sunset. Verlaine and his friends laughed at this typical Hugoism, but it is possible that Verlaine faintly hoped, as who would not, that the master for once in his life meant what he said. The third man, Jules Goncourt, praised the wrong poem, a juvenile effusion, and the fourth, Sainte-Beuve, said, "We should not take poor good Baudelaire as our starting-point and try to outdo him", which was well said if one can stomach the "poor good", but for the rest praised the historical pieces—the weakest in the book—and the nature poems, and urged Verlaine to concentrate his attention objectively on the descriptive type of verse, which of all things was least suited to his genius.

Verlaine was to take his advice, yet, such is the protection given to the instinctive artist, he was to make, beginning from a false premiss, a thing nearly perfect. But first was to come a different kind of publication.

2

LES AMIES

1867-1868

It is typical of the career and character of Verlaine that his first book should be eminently respectable, the most decorous of revolts conforming to every conventional requirement, and that his second could not be mentioned in polite circles and had to be passed surreptitiously round a selected group of friends. One result of the *Parnasse Contemporain* was to open the columns of some ephemeral periodicals to the contributors, and in 1867 Verlaine published a number of poems (including the joint effort with Coppée) in *Le Hanneton*, a satirical journal edited by Eugène Vermersch, a young and unbalanced man who was well on the way to fancying himself a second Marat but whose chief claim to notice just then was the challenge he sent to the editor of the journal which had belaboured the *Poèmes Saturniens*. To those who know their Toulouse-Lautrec the title will strike a chord, for some twenty years later the painter was to make one of his second homes in this Lesbian café of Montmartre. But Verlaine did not need the example of Lautrec; he had in his room at home a much prized drawing in red chalk of two women embracing rather in the manner of Lautrec's *Le Baiser*. One of the poems published by him that summer was a sonnet to Sappho, and a month or two later he was sending a group of six such sonnets to Poulet-Malassis in Brussels, introducing himself as a friend of Coppée. Poulet-Malassis, the publisher of Baudelaire and the man who introduced Glatigny to Banville, was much admired by the younger Parnassians as Lemerre's daring forerunner, and it is true enough that French poetry would have suffered without his courageous help. He was then printing the last of the poems of the lately dead Baudelaire, printing them in Brussels for the good reason that Louis Napoleon's censors would have clapped him in gaol. He replied gaily that as Coppée wished it he would become the godfather of *Les Amies* (the title Verlaine had given the group) and would treat them like his godmothers and goddaughters: "I'm just the man to fit out these foolish creatures."

The foolish creatures did not get far. In May of the next year the little book was intercepted by the French customs on its way to Paris and in company with Baudelaire's *Les Epaves* was condemned as indecent literature by the *tribunal correctionnel* at Lille and the whole consignment destroyed. Verlaine, who had prudently signed himself Don Pablo Maria de Herlanes (his nom-de-plume for the Prudhomme sonnet) received by roundabout means only eight copies, which he distributed among his friends. These sonnets, very youthful works all but the last, are derivative to a degree; in them Verlaine is first a revolutionary doing his bit to *épater le bourgeois* and defy the government even if only by cocking a snook at the censor; secondly a Parnassian writing of times far away; and lastly the young worshipper leaning heavily on Baudelaire, using throughout a Baudelairean vocabulary, once even borrowing from De Musset and in the example below owing more than a little to the *Erinna* which Banville had just published in a new book of verse. Nevertheless, Verlaine can never quite be someone else; the borrowing is well done, the objectivity is given life by a genuine interest in the subject and the coming poet is observable.

But the reader will wish to know whether or not the censor was justified; was *Les Amies* indecent literature or simply literature? *Sappho* is the last and best of the six:

Furieuse, les yeux caves et les seins roides,
Sappho, que la langueur de son désir irrite,
Comme une louve court le long des grèves froides,

Elle songe à Phaon, oublieuse du Rite,
Et, voyant à ce point ses larmes dédaignées,
Arrache ses cheveux immenses par poignées;

Puis elle évoque, en des remords sans accalmies,
Ces temps où rayonnait, pure, la jeune gloire
De ses amours chantés en vers que la mémoire
De l'âme va redire aux vierges endormies:

Et voilà qu'elle abat ses paupières blêmies
Et saute dans la mer où l'appelle la Moire,—
Tandis qu'au ciel éclate, incendiant l'eau noire,
La pâle Séléné qui venge les Amies.

3

FÊTES GALANTES

1867-1869

Here was objectivity of a kind, referring the ever-present to the past. But at the same time Verlaine, obeying Sainte-Beuve literally as he thought, was writing another kind of objective poem, and between 1867 and the early part of 1869 two of these were printed in *La Gazette rimée* and eight in *L'Artiste*, which with twelve others were published by Lemerre in February 1869 as *Fêtes Galantes*.

The genesis of these poems, Sainte-Beuve's injunction excepted, is uncertain. In fashionable circles there had been for some time a rage for the eighteenth-century painters, a rage begun by the De Goncourts' *L'Art du XVIIIe Siècle*, which began to appear in 1859, and culminating in the opening in 1867 of the Salle Lacaze at the Louvre with its great collection of Watteau, Fragonard, Chardin, Boucher and Lancret. Verlaine read the De Goncourt publication and went often to look at the pictures in the new gallery. He also admired to the point of memorising Hugo's *La Fête chez Thérèse*, a poem which set out to re-create the spirit of the lost age, and he discussed it with the master in Brussels. For there had been a meeting, Verlaine taking his mother for a holiday to his paternal aunt at Paliseul and travelling beyond to Brussels. Hugo was in great form, still fresh from the overwhelming success of his new novel *Les Travailleurs de la Mer* in the year of the *Parnasse Contemporain* and, the year following, the year of the Exposition Universelle, the triumphant restaging of *Hernani*, the first Hugo play to appear in the Paris theatre since the *coup d'état*. He was therefore more than ordinarily the plain old countryman bending the knee to the young hopeful. He took seriously the cultivation of disciples, to the point of learning one or two stanzas from *Poèmes Saturniens* which he repeated to the author with every sign of profound admiration; and although in after years Verlaine was to remember only the "crafty look" in the "beady" eyes of the "sublime and smooth old fox" there is reason to believe that he was flattered by such attention and that when Hugo went on to "tell his fortune" as one of the foremost young poets he quite forgot in delight that this fortune had been told many times before.

Whether the two men discussed *Fêtes Galantes*, about half of which was written, does not appear from their correspondence, and is of no more importance than any other part of the supposed genesis of the volume, for there comes a moment in the creation of every work of art when the creator throws off all his beholdenment and strikes a path for himself. This the young Verlaine (a month under twenty-five when the book was published) achieved with a charm, an originality and a skill that still arouse wonder.

It was a Parnassian shibboleth that one art should be expressible in terms of another ("Poetry only lives through its images", declared Leconte de Lisle, and "All that the poet says in verse must be translatable into a design by the painter", said Banville) and Verlaine was no doubt trying conscientiously to write with these commands in mind: *Fêtes Galantes* are superficially an evocation in words of the age painted by Watteau and his fellow-painters. Had Verlaine succeeded he would have produced a little masterpiece but without much *raison d'être*, an exercise in skill merely. Remarkable enough in all conscience; but what he actually did, because he was incapable of absolute objectivity and could not suppress a sense of the ludicrous, was much more so: he re-created the eighteenth-century scene by one delicate touch after another—the mood, the air, the manner, are all there to perfection—and he then with a delightfully

humorous and kindly irony exposed in a word or two the
essential worthlessness of the age he had brought back to life and
which so many Parisians were sighing over sentimentally in their
boudoirs. The whole thing is done in the lightest imaginable
fashion with a mastery of words and phrasing and an economy
(the twenty-two poems occupying less than twenty pages) that is
past praise.

> Dans le vieux parc solitaire et glacé,
> Deux formes ont tout à l'heure passé.
>
> Leurs yeux sont morts et leurs lèvres sont molles,
> Et l'on entend à peine leurs paroles.
>
> Dans le vieux parc solitaire et glacé,
> Deux spectres ont évoqué le passé.
>
> —Te souvient-il de notre extase ancienne?
> —Pourquoi voulez-vous donc qu'il m'en souvienne?
>
> —Ton cœur bat-il toujours à mon seul nom?
> Toujours vois-tu mon âme en rêve?—Non.
>
> —Ah! les beaux jours de bonheur indicible
> Où nous joignions nos bouches!—C'est possible.
>
> —Qu'il était bleu, le ciel, et grand, l'espoir!
> —L'espoir a fui, vaincu, vers le ciel noir.
>
> Tels ils marchaient dans les avoines folles,
> Et la nuit seule entendit leurs paroles.

The book, which Verlaine had paid for, fell even flatter than
Poèmes Saturniens; only a handful were sold and he received only
two notices of moment, from Hugo and Mallarmé. The latter
learned *Fêtes Galantes* by heart and twenty years later was
recommending the young leaders of the Symbolists to do likewise
with this and *Lèvres Closes* of Dierx published in 1867. Hugo, back
in Marine Terrace, reminded Verlaine of his fortune-telling at
Brussels and proclaimed roundly: "You are one of the first, one
of the strongest, one of the most charming of the new and sacred
legion of poets which I, the old thinker of the solitudes, salute and
love." This was gratifying if not novel, but there was a postscript
which makes one love the man and which must surely have given

the author a moment of real pleasure, for there is no mistaking
the enthusiasm: "What delicate and ingenious things you have
put into this fine little book! . . . *Les Coquillages!* What a jewel
of a last line!"

So Hugo had read the book; and how well he had chosen even
though one knows why he loved that last so-Verlainean line.

> Chaque coquillage incrusté
> Dans la grotte où nous nous aimâmes
> A sa particularité.
>
> L'un a la pourpre de nos âmes
> Dérobée au sang de nos cœurs
> Quand je brûle et quand tu t'enflammes;
>
> Cet autre affecte tes langueurs
> Et tes pâleurs alors que, lasse,
> Tu m'en veux de mes yeux moqueurs;
>
> Celui-ci contrefait la grâce
> De ton oreille, et celui-là
> Ta nuque rose, courte et grasse;
>
> Mais un, entre autres, me troubla.

A modern French scholar has said that *Fêtes Galantes* is
Verlaine's most original, purest and justly his most famous work.
It is certainly his most famous work; beyond the millions who
prize the poems in print, millions more know and love them
because they attracted the genius of Debussy. *Fêtes Galantes*, like
some of the music of Debussy, is near to perfection, the nearest
that Verlaine, or any other poet for that matter, was to reach.
But the originality and the "justly" most famous are true only
if each volume of Verlaine's verse is to be considered as a whole;
and in a poet whose strength lay normally in the occasional poem
this is not the best method of comparison. It is difficult to resist
the charm of the book, and there seems no point in trying, but
all the same if the irony, which is part of the charm, the light
touch and the technical virtuosity are excepted, one is left with
something that any clever young man might have done. It is not
the true Verlaine; he was to become pre-eminently a personal
poet, his work expressing his life; and it is with his life that we
must now concern ourselves.

Chapter Six

"VILE SORCERESS"

1867-1869

VERLAINE the young man was last seen working without enthusiasm at the Hôtel de Ville, taking protracted "elevenses" at the Café du Gaz, where the talk was nine-tenths poetry, sitting the night out at De Ricard's, Mendès' or Nina's, where he sang, acted, recited, flirted and talked, and having in general what he would describe as a very good time. Although he was not one of the leaders in the poets' night life, his curious but likeable face with its sharply angled eyebrows, deep slits of eyes between wide cheekbones and fine hair already thinning above his high brow, had long since become a looked-for feature in the landscape; his laugh was heard often, deep and hoarse, he was an excellent listener, a natural comic, obliging to the point of folly, and absolutely without envy or vanity. His one trouble, if trouble it could be called in one so easy-going, had been that his schoolboy passion for poetry showed signs of going to seed and dissipating itself in footling directions. Then more by luck than judgment he found himself a Parnassian and his natural genius thrust itself through Parnassian rules and a sluggish temperament with an ease that would have puffed up a more self-centred man.

It might reasonably be thought that with two volumes of poetry behind him, a growing reputation among the young literati as one of the coming writers of the day, with a safe if boring job, an adoring mother, a comfortable home and friends by the dozen, his lot was a happy one and his future rosy. But in 1867, in the midst of this undeniably pleasant existence and at the moment when his true vocation was being revealed to him, three events—the death of Elisa, the reappearance of a successful Glatigny in Paris, and the legal separation (divorce then not being permitted) of Nina from her husband—threatened to wreck his life.

He had acquired a taste for drink during his holidays in the north five years earlier, that is to say he had discovered the pleasure of drinking in company, which is not quite the same thing, but for several reasons the taste was kept within bounds during the next few years: the presence of his father until the end of 1865 and a carry-over of filial respect after Captain Verlaine's death; the necessity for putting in regular and respectable appearances at the office; the fact that his first poet friends were comparatively abstemious and in any case were too short of money to overdrink; the strong bourgeois element in Verlaine himself—the "puritan" of Barbey; and finally the lack of motive.

Then, in February 1867, when the reins of his dead father had slackened, the motive appeared. Elisa fell ill suddenly, Verlaine was sent for, and arriving at her home in driving rain and an icy wind, was told brusquely that he was just in time to attend the burial. Drenched to the skin, he followed the cortège and, the ceremony over, stumbled, crazed with grief and shock, to the nearest inn. He stayed there for three days stupefying himself with beer. He had a large capacity for love, he had been shielded from birth from the unpleasant and, meeting it abruptly, could find no consolation; he had no religion, and his mother was too busy with her own sorrow to comfort him. His one thought was oblivion; it was, he knew, at the bottom of every glass, as easy as that. So, in Paris again, he continued the treatment and at once fell foul of his chief in the Hôtel de Ville; he had exceeded his leave and he began to be unpunctual to an extent which could not be covered.

At this moment, in March 1867, Glatigny returned to Paris with a novelty which he sold to the owner of the Alcazar café-concert in Montmartre, that he should do a "turn" every evening as an improviser of sonnets and ballads. The idea caught on and in no time he had become one of the minor rages of Paris —which then included the crowds up for the Exposition. The Alcazar was crammed night after night waiting for the moment when, between Theresa's song and a trapeze act, the long thin form of Glatigny dressed in black from head to foot came on with a piece of paper in one hand, a pencil in the other, bowed, and asked the audience to suggest a theme and to give him twenty words to rhyme in a forty-line poem on that theme. Suggestions were shouted from every corner of the room; he wrote them down and, the moment he had written the last of the twenty rhyming words, began to recite the poem he had improvised. "There were no stops, no hesitations, never a moment's silence", said a fascinated onlooker. "It was prodigious." It soon became a matter of pride for the erudite to trip him by insisting that he rhyme the most intractable words and use the most intangible theme, but he strode over all obstacles, glibly reciting execrable poems which fulfilled all the conditions.

To his friends he was apologetic: "It isn't pleasant, but nothing having gone right for me I've had to become an *equilibriste*, a nightly spectacle. Don't blame me too much, for I must eat a little. I assure you my heart beats with shame under my black suit when the people applaud. The muse must pardon me these exercises if I can see ahead for the first time because of them." He walked the streets in a suit of his own, long legs covered to the smart boots, long arms clad to the fashionable grey gloves.

Gill made an excellent caricature of him at the Alcazar, and the Parnassians, despite the frowns of Leconte de Lisle, the emphatic shoulder-liftings of Heredia and the pained appeals of Sully Prudhomme, the "philosophical" poet of the group, came in a body to hear their comrade display a technical virtuosity that many of them coveted. And after the show Glatigny collected them in his splendour and splashed his money on them with a childish delight; he paid cash down for the publication of his next book of poems, but that done and clothes on his back he had no more need of money, being so unused to it as to feel happier when it was flung away. Verlaine was there, of course, and Verlaine was at the café chosen for celebration (usually the Café de Suède where he had first met Glatigny) long after most of the band had gone home.

Years later, when Glatigny had long been dead, Verlaine looked back to these nights at the Café de Suède with an absence of bitterness extraordinary even for him: "My poor friend! What a droll spirit and in what a droll body, long and lithe as an eel, wide-eared like a faun with sharp, impudent nose, peasant's laugh . . . and noble heart, the best that ever beat." Extraordinary because it was Glatigny, backed by De Sivry, who persuaded Verlaine to change from beer to absinthe.

From that moment Verlaine was in trouble. Beer merely dulled the senses, the "vile sorceress" raised the devil after killing

every resistance to it. What it could do has been shown comprehensively by Degas and Toulouse-Lautrec. "The source of folly
and crime, of idiocy and shame, which governments should tax
heavily if they don't abolish it altogether"; that is Verlaine's
description written with a glass of absinthe in front of him. It has
long been recognised as a deadly drug and suppressed. In his
day, the day of a prudish literary censorship and a cult of
respectability, it was free to all.

Until he began to drink absinthe, none suspected that the mild,
good-natured Verlaine had a devil; it was not easy to imagine.
His mother protested feebly, his better friends forcibly; he
listened, promised, performed, then fell again. He would quarrel,
become violent, was actually thrown out of one café; but though
repenting a thousand times he drank on, for the sorceress
promised forgetfulness of grief, of incessant trouble with his chief,
of lack of notice for his poems, of every trouble great or petty.

In June Glatigny vanished from Paris as abruptly as he had
re-entered it, the brief vogue having expired: "I didn't leave the
Alcazar, it left me", he explained laughing; and once again went
on tour. But De Sivry remained, an able lieutenant if ever there
was one; Verlaine had recovered from the shock of Elisa's death,
but the absinthe habit had been formed and excuses were easy
to find. Not that he ever became the absinthe addict that the
reader of his confessions or of the teetotal Lepelletier might
reasonably imagine. To him absinthe, like every other drink, was
a social act, a stimulation in company; its advantage was that
by the time the company had dispersed and he was alone the
stimulation had given way to a merciful state of no-thinking. One
cannot even say that he could not do without absinthe; precisely,
he felt the need for it but could abstain on occasion. There are
signs that he began to put up some sort of fight after Glatigny
went away; he certainly forced himself back to his poetry from
time to time.

But if he could have controlled himself unaided—and this is
unlikely—Nina made sure that he did not. She gave up hope of
her husband, separated legally from him and, her father dying
soon afterwards, moved to rue de Londres with her mother.
There the soirées continued, but with a difference; some attempt
was made to preserve the decencies, the tea-time concerts
continuing for instance, but by 1868 Nina was plunging into

plots against the government, her house became a notorious rendezvous for Communards, and the soirées, the *Parnasse Contemporain* having been launched and the second number settled, lost most of their artistic purpose and were given over to the wilder spirits. They reminded him, said an onlooker, of students' reunions. He was thinking perhaps of the night *à la* Mürger when, a dozen fiacres bringing back a theatre party, Nina organised a quadrille with Cros at the organ, De Sivry at the piano and a third wielding a cornet. Then, peals at the bell unheard in the din, an agitated figure appeared in nightgown and nightcap demanding, "Are you ever going to end this mad life?" only to be set on by four dancers and paraded round the room in triumph until Nina, helpless with laughter, managed to gasp "The owner of the house!" whereupon he was dropped on the carpet, the cornet player blew a blast, De Sivry cried "To the fields!" and the roomful emptied into the dawn. Or perhaps the onlooker thought of the evening when Heredia came in with his wife to find everyone perched on sideboards, sitting on the tops of chairs and bookcases, sprawled on the carpet and making such a racket that his entrance was overlooked; at which, disgusted, he walked out and, with Leconte de Lisle, Banville, France, Valade, Mérat and Mallarmé, struck the place off his visiting-list.

The staid element banished, the parties degenerated, absinthe appeared and

> Dieux, quel hiver
> Nous passâmes! Ce fut amer
> Et doux. Un sabbat! Une fête!

A witches' sabbath with Nina stirring the pot was an invitation to Verlaine which he did not decline. Even so, he did not lose his sense of humour; after an excursion with Lepelletier to the less savoury quarters of Montmartre he produced a novelty at Nina's in the shape of an argot song after the apache manner. This was a notable moment, and one or two of the applauding crowd might have had a dim idea that the modern Villon was not Glatigny after all—might, had they not been more concerned with egging on the poet, who was good fun when he hadn't drunk too much. In any event this was the only good to come out of Nina's—Nina de Villard once more. Verlaine had already been

informed that his presence was no longer welcome at the Leconte
de Lisle Saturdays, he having in the heat of liquor contradicted
the great man to his face. In Lemerre's bookshop he was earning
a reputation for bad temper and described his rôle there not
unjustly as

> Moi, ma gloire n'est qu'une humble absinthe ephémère
> Prise en castimini, crainte des trahisons
> Et si je n'en bois pas plus, c'est pour des raisons.

Nevertheless, five of his new poems were chosen for the 1869
Parnasse Contemporain, which is interesting in several ways, that
he could still be classed as Parnassian and that opinion of his
poetry was sufficiently high to outweigh the master's personal
disapproval. In rue de Londres Nina's gift for putting people at
their ease had become a menace; the last thing Verlaine should
have had was encouragement to misbehave himself, and more
than once he was escorted out after making free with the sword-
stick he habitually carried.

He rarely left alone; his companions were the ringleaders at
Nina's: De Sivry, Charles Cros and Mendès, the last nursing a
severely wounded vanity, a selection committee of three, Banville,
Coppée and Anatole France, having taken over the work of
himself and De Ricard on the *Parnasse Contemporain*. After some
hours at Mendès' favoured brothel they would end up at the Café
de Suède or some such; and Verlaine, roused from the table at
which he slept by a bottle of water poured over his head, would
shamble off to the Hôtel de Ville. Gone were his fine clothes,
smart monocle and impeccable top-hat; he was dirty, unshaven,
bedraggled, his speech surly. When he was not refreshing himself
at the Café du Gaz he sat at his desk feeling ill and looking hang-
dog, for he was not one who could fall from grace attractively.

After such nights his days were dizzy with good resolutions; he
continued in spurts to collaborate with Lepelletier in a verse
drama of no merit and with Viotti in comic opera, and he wrote
Fêtes Galantes, which seems a near miracle but is actually just
what one would expect, for, disgusted with himself, he grasped
at that past century of decorous dissipation as at a heaven. But
in general he felt hopeless because no one was at the helm. His
mother's reproaches hurt him but did no more than overload
a bad conscience; one can love second fiddles without respecting

them; the years of adoration and compliance were having their reward. He had in any case been brought up in the romantic tradition which called for a rescuer of another kind. But what hope had he, unable to carry off the life he led with a devil-may-care air, of the fair hand outstretched to save?

However, even the novelettish can come true; if a man looks hard enough for a good angel he will assuredly find one. A year earlier, arriving at rue de Londres, he had passed some people leaving one of Nina's afternoon amateur recitals. Keeping his head bent as usual he elbowed rudely past the little crowd in the doorway, but a girl on her mother's arm noticed him, gave one glance at the tall repulsive figure in its dirty raincoat and battered soft hat jammed over the eyes and drew away in an instinctive movement of disgust.

Nina de Callias by Manet

Barricades at the Hôtel de Ville

Chapter Seven

LA BONNE CHANSON

1869-1870

IN the first *Parnasse Contemporain* Verlaine published a poem, *Mon Rêve Familier*, which he reprinted in *Poèmes Saturniens*. It has become well known not so much for its poetical merits—it is excessively Baudelairean—as for the light it throws on Verlaine himself. He was to show that there is tragedy as well as comedy in the life of every man and beauty in the superficially ordinary thought or sensation, and it is his distinction that he gave what is contemptuously dismissed as small beer its true value as legitimate material for great poetry. He proved that poetry could be grand without the grand manner. He wrote down every mood, every thought that entered a mind of peculiar sensibility; he withheld nothing; and the form of his poems perfectly suits the subject.

This last, which seems so obvious, is the reason why he appeals to the reader in English accustomed to the intimacy of lyrical verse; it is equally the reason why his work even today is acknowledged with a certain reservation by so many of his own countrymen. To the occasional visitor the French often appear embarrassingly unreticent; they are for ever talking, for ever gesturing, and they will talk to anyone of what seem to be their inmost thoughts. Yet it is not so. The error arises from the Frenchman's complete unselfconsciousness and his passion for ideas; shyness is virtually unknown to him, awkwardness in society of any kind is a thing undreamt of, as undreamt of as entertaining an idea which he does not at once try to define. The misconception is placed exactly in the saying "the café is the Frenchman's home"—this because he seems to be almost always there and always talking. In truth, the café is the protector of the sanctity of his home; if one listens to the spate of talk there it is found to be nothing more personal than an exchange of ideas. Sit at that café for five years and you will know their ideas to the point of boredom, but you will not know the men. And if after five years you secure an invitation to their houses the polite formality there will baffle all attempt at intimacy.

That is the Frenchman, the most enlivening and exhausting companion in the world and the most reserved of men. And the French poet of the young Verlaine's period, to take the matter a stage further, was yet more limited; in his poetry, with its formal setting and meticulous design, he never dared to allow himself unselfconscious expression of his ideas let alone his personal feelings; he was mesmerised by the national insistence on correctness of utterance within the most rigid bounds, which had driven the Parnassians to mere word play.

But Verlaine was like the Englishman who after travelling from London to Edinburgh in silence will tell a complete stranger his life story between Edinburgh and Aberdeen. Except that Verlaine would begin at Welwyn. He would sit at a café and tell anybody, everybody who would listen, about his latest infatuation, his inability to control his passion for absinthe, anything and everything dearest to his heart or burdening his mind at that particular moment, and specially the ever-growing longing for a stable influence to rescue him from debauch; and how if that influence could take the shape of a beautiful bed companion the world would be perfect indeed.

Nor did he simply talk, he told everybody then in the world and everybody to come in the future who wished to read; luckily for posterity reticence humanly or poetically was not in him. So he confides *Mon Rêve Familier* to the reader.

> Je fais souvent ce rêve étrange et pénétrant
> D'une femme inconnue, et que j'aime, et qui m'aime,
> Et qui n'est, chaque fois, ni tout à fait la même
> Ni tout à fait une autre, et m'aime et me comprend.
>
> Car elle me comprend, et mon cœur, transparent
> Pour elle seule, hélas! cesse d'être un problème
> Pour elle seule, et les moiteurs de mon front blême,
> Elle seule les sait rafraîchir, en pleurant.
>
> Est-elle brune, blonde ou rousse?—Je l'ignore.
> Son nom? Je me souviens qu'il est doux et sonore
> Comme ceux des aimés que la Vie exila.
>
> Son regard est pareil au regard des statues,
> Et, pour sa voix, lointaine, et calme, et grave, elle a
> L'inflexion des voix chères qui se sont tues.

Familiar indeed; but unlike most who write or think so, Verlaine had actually bumped rudely against the ministering angel without recognising her. Nor was his instinct any brighter a few weeks after the first encounter when he deputised with considerable comic success for an absent tenor in an amateur performance of a De Sivry and Chabrier operetta. The girl was in the small audience, but he never so much as noticed her.

She, however, noticed him and this time favourably; she said as much to De Sivry as they walked away together and he praised his friend enthusiastically, his good nature, affection for his mother, intelligence and poetic gift. He lent her Verlaine's two published volumes when they reached home: "He's sure to be famous one day", he told her, a remark which she did not forget.

There was then a gap of nearly a year until, on a certain afternoon of June 1869, Verlaine walked up the hill to see De Sivry. Number 14 rue Nicolet, in the respectable part of Montmartre, was the house of M. Mauté, a retired solicitor with the mutton-chop whiskers, gold-rimmed eyeglasses and well-filled watch-chained waistcoat of the old school. It is not easy to reconcile M. Mauté and De Sivry as room-mates, yet De Sivry had a flat in the same house; the explanation was not the marriage of his widowed mother to M. Mauté but M. Mauté's snobbishness.

Verlaine and his friend were sitting together, De Sivry having as usual just risen from bed, talking over one of their projects for an operetta when the door opened and a girl came in. She hesitated when she saw a visitor and was going to retreat when De Sivry called her back and introduced her to Verlaine.

The half-sister of De Sivry, Mathilde Mauté de Fleurville as she signed herself (the de Fleurville being a picturesque addition without warrant), was an attractive girl of sixteen. She had only two faults, being stupid and vain, and it was hard that weaknesses which are often found in physically attractive women should have led her to so much suffering. She worshipped poets and wrote poetry. Her poems were not good, but the contents are instructive. Here is one:

> How powerful is a woman's tear!
> A signal to the feeling heart
> That takes the lovely, weak one's part
> Of danger drawing near.

A dreadful weapon 'twixt the lids
Of an indomitable She,
That makes deep wounds, as you will see;
Unless you do everything she bids.

Just to begin with, angry looks,
Tho' this is nothing but a skirmish;
'Neath frowning brows her clear eyes burnish
With anger and gleam bright as hooks.

Then bitter tears rain from her eyes,
True tears of mystery are these,
Soon swelling into floods and seas
Broken by sobs and storms of sighs.

But to dry up these brackish springs
Ask pardon as she understands
By pouring in her dimpled hands
Jewels, ribbons, flowers and pretty things.

This, then, was the girl who came timidly back into the room at De Sivry's call. Verlaine, who had been searching with a hungry hopelessness for his good angel for the past three years, did not see her exactly as she was. In fact he saw nothing at all essential, the superficial being far too much for him; he saw perfection in a grey and green dress.

En robe grise et verte avec des ruches,
Un jour de juin que j'étais soucieux,
Elle apparut souriante à mes yeux
Qui l'admiraient sans redouter d'embûches.

Elle alla, vint, revint, s'assit, parla,
Légère et grave, ironique, attendrie:
Et je sentais en mon âme assombrie
Comme un joyeux reflet de tout cela;

Sa voix, étant de la musique fine,
Accompagnait délicieusement
L'esprit sans fiel de son babil charmant
Où la gâité d'un cœur bon se devine.

Aussi soudain fus-je, après le semblant
D'une révolte aussitôt étouffée,
Au plein pouvoir de la petite Fée
Que depuis lors je supplie en tremblant.

He saw too "Ses yeux, qui sont les yeux d'un ange" and, leaving angels to one side for a moment, the fine shoulders, the breasts promising a delicious fullness, "the almost imperceptible pulsing of the blueish veins below her eyes and of the faint violet veins at the side of her forehead, the chaste tip of her tongue appearing and disappearing quickly from time to time as it moistened her lips".

For at once the thought had come to him, could this celestial young creature with her "ethereal body a little disposed to plumpness", could she possibly be the answer to his prayers? And she had no sooner replied to De Sivry's introduction with an 'Oh! I like poetry very much, Monsieur" than certainty came on him and he was struck dumb with rapture, proving if proof is needed that deathless words can be of any quality as long as they are spoken at the right time and by the right speaker.

The conversation languished, Verlaine remaining tongue-tied, until Mathilde murmured that she had heard of him and had read his poems: "They are perhaps a little too . . . strong for me, but I like them very much all the same."

The repetition did not daunt Verlaine, nothing would have daunted him then. He bowed, with a muttered "You are really too kind, Mademoiselle"; and added, "But I hope that I shall soon write poems more deserving of the honour."

And that was all; a few platitudes on the weather and Verlaine got himself somehow out of the room. As for the Mathilde of that afternoon and the later weeks, she was at first confused by the admiration of this man with the bad reputation and brilliant future, confused but not displeased, flattered rather. And if, as quickly became obvious, he wished to place his whole life at her disposal, who was she to tell him that she was not all that he so fervently believed her to be, the pure, strong, intelligent guiding star—if, that is, she could by then see herself as anything but the saint in his mirror? Verlaine behaved as men have always behaved when physically attracted, and conscious, though never conscious enough, of their shortcomings. He too was to suffer in his way and for long after Mathilde was contentedly remarried; and this accurately points the difference between the two.

At the time he retired in a daze from rue Nicolet, his mind a blur familiar to many, at one moment seeing heaven ahead, at the next trying to face the hell of a Mathildeless future; and when that evening De Sivry sought him at one of their regular haunts he found Verlaine meditating "that almost impalpable something which blossoms in the Young Girl in the roseate glory and mystery of innocence" (a meditation which he had just enough sense to keep to himself), sitting over an untasted glass of absinthe which no pleasantries would induce him to drink. The next morning, after a night which can be left to the imagination, Verlaine absented himself from the office and rushed with his mother to Fampoux, where, having decided to think no more of a being so far above him, he drank himself stupid in the bars of Arras and, the morning afterwards, offered his hand to Mathilde by way of De Sivry.

The negotiations dragged on until the late autumn and the engagement for almost another year. M. Mauté regarded his daughter's suitor with disfavour; he did not care for his face, his manner, his absence of aristocratic connections; he disliked most of all his poetical pretensions; the Hôtel de Ville was too plainly a cover for scribbling nonsense. The thought of a Verlaine united to a De Fleurville offended him and he in general liked nothing about the Verlaines, not even their home, which, as he told his wife, was shabby and barely respectable, lacking the potted aspidistra in the drawing-room window. Mme Verlaine was also opposed to the match; she gave as her reasons the girl's age and lack of money; possibly she merely wished to keep her son to herself. On the other hand Mme Mauté, who had had first-hand knowledge of good blood and was an excellent pianist with a genuine artistic connection, took to Verlaine, and De Sivry was strongly partisan. Mathilde, without any hesitation that we know of, allowing for conventional tremors, ranged herself on the side of her mother and half-brother; she had three other suitors, she afterwards declared, including a Vicomte, but she preferred to throw in her lot with the arts; probably she could not resist the temptation of bringing the black sheep back to the Batignolles fold; certainly she was physically attracted. She knew that her suitor drank too much, but it is not known whether De Sivry or Mme Verlaine opened her eyes to the picture of a Verlaine under the influence of absinthe; De Sivry may well have made laughing references which youth and vanity and affection would dismiss easily enough—for Mathilde had come to be flattered into liking a man she had had no opportunity of knowing—and

Mme Verlaine, trying to prevent the match, would not be without obscure hints. All useless in any case: Verlaine had drunk absinthe, had behaved badly under its influence, very well, but who could dream that he would ever touch the stuff again when he had received his heart's desire, as he called Mathilde amongst other things? Mathilde could imagine nothing of the kind.

And to see Verlaine then was to see a man transformed; clothed again in spotless black, top-hatted, his breath innocent of intoxicants, he would visit rue Nicolet each evening at the appointed hour and sit stiffly exchanging polite nothings with a reluctant father and all but speechless girl (when she was allowed to sit in the same room), and when necessary play the appropriate game of cards. His mother also profited for the moment, for her reformed son now accompanied her to her favourite tea-parties, playing cards and munching *petits fours* with a good grace. He had abandoned absinthe, brothels and all harmful companionships; he was, it seemed, the faithful suburbanite restored to his true path; and though he continued to write poetry it was for the most part of a kind acceptable to rue Nicolet.

Verlaine's account of this time and his letters make poor reading; he was earning his Aurora the difficult way and the dishonest way too, although he could scarcely be expected to recognise this in the heat of first love, and his sentimental references to Mathilde's perfections and still more his sly references to future enjoyment of her charms grate unpleasantly. It is interesting to notice how very much less admirable he is when painstakingly on the side of the respectable virtues than when just being himself.

For two months or more he and Mathilde were separated, her father keeping her out of Paris as long as he was able in the hope that the madness would pass. But Verlaine had allies in the camp and love letters reached the bewildered but excited girl—what a triumph to have a real poet at one's feet and a poet who would become famous!—through the hand of the half-brother, who was himself courting a young actress he had met at Nina's. Verlaine's letters consisted of the poems which were to form *La Bonne Chanson*; Mathilde's of confessions that she too wrote poetry and of exhortations to her admirer to act like the knight of old who waited chastely and patiently for his lady, singing love ditties the while.

The love ditties continued—slipped into the hand of a

Mathilde he was not allowed to see alone—throughout the winter and spring of 1870; for M. Mauté, soothed by the substantial settlement that Mme Verlaine promised to pay, had agreed with an indifferent grace to a long engagement and was eventually brought to the idea of a wedding in June when Mathilde would be seventeen. Not all of these poems were to be printed in *La Bonne Chanson*; some were, as Verlaine puts it, "possibly a trifle passionate for a fiancé's engagement gift, but I think they are to the point". They are indeed and make one blush, not because they are indecent or indelicate but because of the unbearably coy approach. One has to remember firmly that Verlaine, who was not accustomed to abstinence of any kind, chose this method of relieving himself.

Anatole France tells the story, in a biographical novel, of a moment shortly before Verlaine met Mathilde when, maddened by despair after one of his bouts of absinthe, he rushed into a church, hammered on the confessional box and shouted, "I must confess! I must receive absolution!" One need not doubt this story, maliciously though it was told; Charlotte Brontë had been driven to the confessional a few years earlier; how much greater the attraction for the indulged Verlaine. He did not confess, being too much beside himself to join the queue he had overlooked.

Verlaine is not the only man and not the only great man who has loved and worshipped on sight, he was merely unluckier than some. Sexual attraction apart, he looked upon Mathilde as the drowning man regards the spar his hands touch at the last moment, and all the rest followed naturally—her purity, beauty, goodness, wisdom being elevated to fantastic heights just as to the drowning man the spar appears the most glorious object he has ever seen. Verlaine did not then believe in God, although his god—love—was not dissimilar, but he was a born worshipper and Mathilde naturally became his idol.

With this in mind the poems of *La Bonne Chanson* are explicable. They have since become popular, but in truth they show Verlaine at his weakest as poet because not himself. These sentimental songs are as unreal as his idea of the girl who had inspired them. One only stands out as worthy of mention. *La Lune Blanche* is heavy with sentimentality too, but the workmanship is superb.

LA BONNE CHANSON

La lune blanche
Luit dans les bois;
De chaque branche
Part une voix
Sous la ramée . . .

O bien-aimée.

L'étang reflète,
Profond miroir,
La silhouette
Du saule noir
Où le vent pleure . . .

Rêvons, c'est l'heure.

Un vaste et tendre
Apaisement
Semble descendre
Du firmament
Que l'astre irise . . .

C'est l'heure exquise.

Not surprisingly the formal visits, month after month, and the
formal words in public with Mathilde soon weighed on Verlaine's
spirits, but he displayed an admirable resolution for a near-
alcoholic, a sexually frustrated man and a creature of impulse;
he drank little, absinthe not at all, and in general succeeded in
putting the years back. He was helped in this by Lepelletier, who,
despite a month in prison with Rigault for slandering the famous
Haussmann, then at the head of the Hôtel de Ville, and despite a
stream of violent revolutionary speech, remained in his private
life extremely proper; by Valade and Mérat, quiet souls at heart
both of them; and by Coppée. His tendency naturally was to
revert to those of whom he had memories more or less unclouded
by a bad conscience; Viotti had shot off to Le Havre, but
whether jealous of Verlaine (as Mathilde claimed) or of Mathilde
herself cannot be said, Verlaine's verses on this subject following
his best fashion of mystification, but for the rest he kept to the
old friends, eschewing Nina's and all temptations and being
drawn particularly to Coppée, a kind of Verlaine with the genius

left out—simple, sentimental, humorous. Coppée had sown his mild oats at speed and was already beginning the climb, one could almost say the leap, to popularity and rectitude. He had so far, like almost all the other Parnassians, contained his true gift, but early in 1869, defying Leconte de Lisle's injunctions to despise the public, he succeeded in getting his one-act play *Le Passant* put on at the Odéon with the famous tragedienne Agar for whom it had been written and with Sarah Bernhardt in travesty. The play had such a success that Coppée became practically a made man overnight. This led to two developments: to bad feeling amongst the Parnassians, Leconte de Lisle, Heredia, France and a few others, disapproving and envious in equal degree, sneering at "the popular poet of the Parnasse"; and to a new and delightful gathering of Coppée's supporters, who turned up at the Odéon to salute the piece with such obstreperous applause that one of the critics, eyeing them with distaste, wrote, "Well, that was certainly a jolly meeting of the *vilains bonshommes!*"

No better excuse was needed; a regular dinner of the "*vilains bonshommes*" was at once arranged with Valade as secretary and the young artist Felix Régamey as the designer of the invitation cards. After moving about from café to café it settled down at the café attached to the Bobino Theatre in rue de Fleurus, a place well known to Verlaine from his early days at the Hôtel de Ville, and there Régamey first met the young poet. He had heard much about him, of course, for *Fêtes Galantes* had already given Verlaine the name amongst the anti-Leconte de Lisle Parnassians and their friends of "a master of the *belles funérailles*"; and by the time they met in the winter of 1869 some of the poems that were to form *La Bonne Chanson* had also leaked out.

Régamey, charmed, sketched him at table, long-haired to counteract the thinning on top, nose with its comical upward turn, small moustache and beard ornamenting the long upper lip and long chin, pipe belching smoke, whilst Verlaine, no mean caricaturist Régamey thought, made a sketch of "*Les Trois*". The dinners were high-spirited affairs with much free speech, and Verlaine was one of the liveliest there—it is not difficult to imagine how he would rebound from the frigid civilities of M. Mauté's salon—and Régamey never forgot the sight or sound of him as he stood, dessert over, "looking like a nice young monkey taking a pleasure in mystifying his audience". For instance, having improvised a poem during dinner, he began reciting it in a tone of voice so completely at variance with the meaning that when the climax, a trick ending, came, everyone was staggered. But his *chef d'œuvre* was the recitation of *Les Coquillages*—an exquisite treat, says Régamey—which Verlaine ended with an irresistible smiling grimace as he sighed

> Mais un, entre autres, me troubla.

At this the company, who knew their Verlaine and his position *vis-à-vis* Mathilde, howled with laughter—an unmalicious reception which he received with more comical twists of his mobile face.

A visit to Sainte-Beuve with Coppée was less happy. This "whimsical pope" with a malign grin on his ugly face correctly warned Verlaine against long words beginning with K, G and C —the legacy of his Leconte de Lisle enthusiasm—but when Verlaine announced his engagement and began to expatiate on the great happiness awaiting him, all the cynic in Sainte-Beuve appeared, and he said comprehensibly "without enthusiasm" as Verlaine mildly reported, "We shall see. Wait and see."

Verlaine was waiting indeed and much against the grain; and he needed all the diversions which the "*vilains bonshommes*" and his quieter friends' inventions could provide. The contract of marriage had been drawn up after the usual haggling, in which Verlaine, supremely uninterested, took no part, and the wedding was fixed for the third week in June. "Wait and see", Sainte-Beuve had said; but as the day at last crawled near it seemed that Verlaine was likely to wait endlessly and see nothing. The evening before he had to put up the banns, three weeks before the wedding date, he arrived at rue Nicolet in great good humour to find the house in turmoil, Mathilde in bed, smallpox (which had been raging in Paris for some time) suspected. His optimism collapsed with a bang and something of a whimper when, the next day, having uneasily put up the banns, he found Antoine Cros, the doctor brother of Charles, at the bedside with another doctor, smallpox confirmed and the marriage postponed, if all went well, to the middle of June. He insisted on seeing Mathilde, which for him was tantamount to a bayonet charge against a forest of machine-guns, and left the house in considerable mental confusion, anxiety struggling with what he engagingly confesses as "a disappointment that one might almost describe as carnal".

His "wicked" disappointment was to last some time, for no sooner had Mathilde recovered than her mother went down, and the despairing Verlaine was told that the wedding could not take place before the middle of August. He continued his "abstinence and fast" with an effort, but his nerves cried out for absinthe and his body for the brothels. Towards the end of July he reached such a pitiful state of nervous excitement and fear that the newly married De Sivry carried him off with Mathilde's younger sister to the Normandy house of the Marquis de Manoury, a friend of Nina, for an enforced rest cure in the country. Verlaine took with him the proofs of *La Bonne Chanson* which Lemerre had just printed, but could scarcely bear to look at them; he had planned to give the volume to Mathilde as a surprise wedding present, but what opportunity, he moodily asked himself, was he likely to have? His mother still reluctant; M. Mauté barely troubling to conceal his relief at the successive postponements; smallpox; and, as if smallpox were not enough, another little obstacle, war. For on July 19 France declared war on Prussia.

Chapter Eight

THE COMMUNE

1870-1871

VERLAINE described his new enemies comprehensively as "The Corps Législatif, the Garde Mobile, the King of Prussia, the Emperor, the Prince of Hohenzollern". The war, he complained, "gave every sign of threatening my happiness in a horridly legal way". It was certainly hard, having suffered the double menace of smallpox, to be faced with a war in which he was not at all interested and in which he might even be obliged to take part. He, perhaps the least militaristic, least chauvinist man in France at that moment, felt injured and apprehensive for his person as well as his marriage. What, he wondered dismally, were all these people about, interfering with peaceable poets who wished simply to be allowed to marry, enjoy themselves in bed, avoid the sorceress and write love poems *ad infinitum*?

He was not alone nor, though he was supposed to be an active revolutionary, was his shocked surprise entirely without reason. Ever since the Prussian victory over Austria in 1866 it had been an understood thing in France that one day the Prussians would have to be put in their place. Paris had been stuffed with men in highly coloured uniforms for as long as Verlaine could remember; almost every day he had seen the sky-blue steel helmets and cuirasses of the Cent Gardes, the bearskinned grenadiers of the Imperial Guard, the veterans of the first Napoleon in their white breeches and black gaiters, and the Zouaves swaggering romantically in baggy black-and-green trousers, broad white sash, tasselled caps and cutaway jackets trimmed with yellow lace. He saw, at first with a boy's excitement, then with the distaste of the republican, because no one could live in Paris and fail to see. Scarcely a day went by without an imperial review, a spectacular parade on the Champ de Mars or the sound of a military band on the march.

But the inevitable war proclaimed by the army and the jingoistic press for the best part of four years lost its inevitability when nothing untoward happened. The bands and uniforms and parades roused in him eventually nothing but a revolutionary growl as meaningless as the pageantry of dictatorship seemed likely to become. By the late 'sixties he, like a good half of the population, thought no more of it than of the circuses intended to preserve Parisians from pondering on the price of bread, the rising taxes, the unemployment which had jumped to alarming heights after the end of the Exposition, and other shortcomings of everyday life: the *foires* with their gilt gingerbread, dancing and performing apes, the Carnival masques in Place de la Concorde, the congresses of Orphéonistes bearing standards showing the great lyre, the marches of the Pompiers with their enormous brass helmets glittering in the sun and the innumerable religious processions headed by choirs, followed by large bands of girls wearing blue sashes and the effigies of saints borne high by the priests and acolytes.

Yet war was coming nearer day by day, year by year. Like every dictator, the wretched Louis Napoleon found himself, poor soldier though he was, obliged to take to the sword again and again in order to keep himself on the Imperial throne. He had given much to France—prosperity, good communications, a beautiful modern Paris, tourists by the million and glory besides, but in the end nothing mattered but the glory. Let the trains run to time, no matter, the people had a short memory for benefits of this kind, they wanted more glory or . . .

The "or" was political and social reform which Louis dared not grant since it would make an end of him. Glory, then, it had to be, or so his wife Eugénie, the power behind the throne, decided. Opportunity came on July 3 when news reached Paris that Prince Leopold of Hohenzollern had accepted the vacant throne of Spain. Four days later the *Corps Législatif* heard from the Prime Minister what amounted to an ultimatum to Prussia and responded with cries of *"Vive la France! Vive l'armée! Vive l'Empereur! A Berlin!"*—cries which the Paris newspapers reported the next day.

For a moment war appeared to recede when Leopold withdrew his name, but Eugénie and the army, their heads turned by the shouts of "A Berlin!" that greeted them everywhere, made certain of it by a new demand, that the King of Prussia should denounce a possible repetition of Leopold's candidature. The demand was refused and the refusal announced in such a way by the adroit Bismarck's "Ems telegram" that both in Paris and Berlin war was felt to be inevitable. And on the 19th it came, with France in warlike mood if public demonstrations were to be trusted, crowds parading every city singing the Marseillaise and chanting "*A bas la Prussie! A Berlin!*", booksellers advertising French-German dictionaries "for use at Berlin".

Verlaine did not buy a dictionary and was not amongst the demonstrators; his mind was not on Berlin but the church of Notre-Dame de Clignancourt, where, if he was spared (what an idea for a peaceful man to have to entertain!), he would at last be joined to his Mathilde.

Yet at first he was not unduly perturbed and, had his nerves been steadier, would probably never have given a second thought to the matter. War, though deplorable, could scarcely be said to touch such a one as he; every Frenchman was agreed that a Prussian army would collapse like a house of cards as soon as it clapped eyes on a French soldier; this had been a foregone conclusion ever since Verlaine could remember. On August 2, just before he left Normandy, came news of the first French success—Saarbrucken captured. And on August 6, when he was back in Paris, a great victory by MacMahon was announced, every window was beflagged and the boulevards were black with people singing the Marseillaise. So the army was after all, as his father had said a thousand times, the greatest in the world and would, incidentally, save him.

The rejoicing was brief. By midnight a telegram from the front gave the facts; the French army in Lorraine had been beaten in three battles and was in a general retreat. Eugénie, who did not lack courage, drove to the Tuileries that night and ordered placards to be posted throughout Paris the next day announcing the news. Verlaine, hearing of it in the Place Vendôme, bought a newspaper and retired shattered to the Café de Madrid to calm himself over a drink, his scruples automatically relaxed in the hour of need. He perhaps had several drinks, having run into several friends, mostly of the literary-political sort, because when a regiment marched by, the band playing the Marseillaise, and a cry of "*Vive la République!*"

was set up, Verlaine was amongst the most vociferous. He even left his seat to shout *"Vive la République!"* at the kerbside; and, conspicuous because of his height, was seized by the police. His friends snatched him free and made a cordon whilst he slipped away and down Passage Jouffroy to safety.

To safety? Mockery was now in that word. That evening Verlaine had his first and last taste of the discomforts of being a true political prophet and, like every young revolutionary whose theories begin to come true, he felt shocked and unbelieving. What was Louis Napoleon thinking of, to prove himself in practice—and such practice—the hopeless bungler he, Verlaine, following Lepelletier, Rigault, Vermersch and the rest, had always declared he was? Verlaine's indignation, fighting alarm, rose to a pitch: to endanger the innocent, no, that was too much, was not to be borne, was not at all what he had meant when he cried out on the dictator and demanded liberty. Naturally he had expected that Louis Napoleon would abdicate in due course and be succeeded by the millennium whatever that might be; but here was the insane man still on the throne, fighting and busily losing a war that everyone had assumed he must win. The distressing possibility soon emerged that Verlaine, as pure as the driven snow of all violence except when under the influence of absinthe, might be entrapped into at least a show of it because of the criminal incompetence of this fellow, might again have to endure a postponed marriage, might perhaps go so far as to lose, or injure, an arm or leg, might even . . .

He tried to comfort himself by recalling that the position, though distasteful, was not utterly desperate; his age group had not yet been called up and there were only four days to go before the marriage. He was uneasy, however, and could not thrust from his mind's eye the dismal series of pictures that had greeted him at every station on the way back from Normandy, of reservists crowding into the train, of wives, mothers, children weeping.

As he was sitting in his office the next day moodily filling in "orders for quarterly payment", a young friend burst into the room, pale, dishevelled. He pulled a revolver from his pocket and told the startled Verlaine that he was going to shoot himself; his mistress had just died in childbirth and he no longer wished to live. With this he threw a bulky envelope on the desk and hurried out. Verlaine pursued him, but was given the slip in the crowded corridors. Returning, he opened the envelope, hoping that it would give an address; it contained only a will.

This at least disengaged his attention from himself, and the next morning, two days before his wedding, came a telegram summoning him to Passy. There he found his friend dead on his bed, a shot through his head. Horrified and sick—for he shrank from every form of physical suffering—Verlaine forced himself to attend to the unpleasant details, breaking the news to his friend's mother, interviewing the doctor, the police, begging the priest to give his friend a Church burial. Anyone who has been unfortunate enough to interview French officials on any matter not as plain as daylight will understand a little of what Verlaine undertook in the wake of a suicide; for a supposedly lazy, cowardly and inefficient man his activity and perseverance were surprising.

He returned to his reward at rue Nicolet, passing through drunken crowds despondently singing the Marseillaise and little knowing what was brewing for him at the Tuileries where Eugénie had given orders for the garrisoning and provisioning of Paris for a siege.

The next day, August 10, he saw his friend buried and, in a state of near collapse, returned to the centre of Paris. He could not face Mathilde so shaken; he sat at a café, the Café de Mulhouse (he never forgot the name although in his memoirs he relates it to the wrong occasion), on the site of which the Musée Grevin now stands, and, it being no time for half measures, ordered an absinthe.

He had greater need of that drink than he knew. He picked up a newspaper as usual and his horrified eyes fastened at once on an official notice: "All unmarried men of the 1844, 1845 classes are called to the colours."

2

The marriage took place as arranged—presumably the date of the contract, June 24, exempted him from this call-up—and the scene at rue Nicolet on the previous night, with the last farewells of a distraught Verlaine on his knees before Mathilde, was thrown away. Valade was a witness at the wedding, as was

Louise Michel, soon to be notorious as the fanatical Red Virgin, who had taught the bride in her school at Batignolles. Thereafter Verlaine disappeared from public life for two days, after which he had to return to work, to his indignation but not to the surprise of anyone else, since he had done little but take days off since meeting Mathilde.

He is next found a week or two later nicely installed in an apartment hung with portraits of himself by Bazille and Cros, a Courbet landscape, a Monticelli and etchings of Dürer and Rembrandt, at the corner of Quai de la Tournelle and rue Cardinal Lemoine with the Hôtel de Ville almost facing him across the river; and at the Hôtel de Ville on September 3 he heard with the rest of Paris of the surrender of Louis Napoleon and his army at Sedan, and on the following day, the famous Quatre Septembre, he saw the Republic once more proclaimed. He, like all his friends, greeted the fall of Louis Napoleon with immense enthusiasm, believing that the millennium had come and that all men would now become brothers, an enthusiasm soon known as siege fever. For the Prussians were closing in on Paris, which they invested a few days later.

Before then Verlaine's enthusiasm had carried him to the drastic length of joining the volunteer Garde Nationale; this despite the exemption which could be claimed by any married civil servant. He did not go so far as to volunteer for a dangerous section of the fortifications, his 160th battalion guarding the Issy, Vanves, Montrouge sector.

So there, in September, the unmilitary Verlaine was to be seen every other day on his way to the southern suburbs with his percussion gun, as absurd a sight as Coleridge in the dragoons. Yet for a time he enjoyed himself, alarmingly so for a newly married man; the weather was superb, as so often in Paris in autumn, the early rising held no horrors, and even the drill seemed a pleasant novelty to the bored clerk from a stuffy office; there were no alarms to stir a timid heart, the enemy keeping their distance with admirable discretion. For the moment all went well and better than well because, as he explained, his absences from home were more than made up by "double rations" every time he returned. That this development of an already old excitement could be the first stage of a mortal wearying he would be the last man to suspect.

In the first days of December *La Bonne Chanson* was printed, announced but not published, Lemerre holding it back for better times; but Verlaine was able to distribute copies to friends, including Hugo, who had made a triumphant return to Paris. Hugo described the book as a bouquet in a bombshell, and it is true that its sweetness came like a breath of flowers—hothouse ones—into a Paris deep in the rigours of the siege, bombarded daily by the Prussians, with wood and coal unobtainable, rats and horses a staple food.

Lemerre did not show similar caution with the second *Parnasse Contemporain*; having withheld it since 1869, he published early in 1871. Perhaps he feared that the Parnassians would have disintegrated by the end of the war. If so he judged wrongly, and the *Parnasse Contemporain*, in which Verlaine's *Les Vaincus* was not the least good thing, was thrown away, obtaining virtually no notice from the few critics still left in their jobs.

Physically disintegrated the Parnassian circle certainly was; Lepelletier was in the army, De Sivry in garrison service outside Paris, Heredia had retired to Nice, Glatigny was in Corsica, Ménard in London writing furious letters to the press about the widespread calumny of France. Only Gautier had come back to share in the siege and to fall foul of Mendès, who married his daughter against his wishes. Gautier refused to attend the ceremony and publicly attacked the Leconte-de-Lislean poetry of the "Crapulle Membête" as he called him: "This pundit pupil of the school of the brahmin Leconte de Lisle now explains the mysteries of the lotus flower and worships the child Krishna." This sneer, not without justice, caused more trouble amongst the Parnassians, Gautier and Leconte de Lisle not acknowledging each other.

Leconte de Lisle had in any case fallen from his self-elevation. He first astonished every Parnassian by writing strongly patriotic verses in the newspapers before the fall of Louis Napoleon. It then leaked out that Louis had been paying him a pension of three hundred francs a month since 1864. When Heredia, who had himself been lending money to Leconte de Lisle, demanded the reason, his former god replied haughtily, "When I go to the lavatory I don't boast about it." "No," said Heredia, "but one can take a thing or leave it." And Leconte de Lisle retired into an involuntary isolation, an isolation not lessened when, after serving like Verlaine but without Verlaine's camaraderie with the soldiers at the fortifications, he demanded the deportation of all republicans, men, women and children.

The Parnasse had also begun to show signs of mental disintegration although the name was to linger on into a third *Parnasse Contemporain*. Coppée was becoming too successful; Mallarmé gracefully, Mérat cynically, Valade without a word retired from the Leconte de Lisle soirées, De Ricard was freely spoken of as no poet, Sully Prudhomme was writing poems which were nothing but philosophical treatises, and Verlaine—well, had *La Bonne Chanson* been published earlier he would have declared himself as fatally un-Parnassian, but he was to be expelled for other reasons.

Happily unconscious of his fate, he enjoyed his "double rations", his drink and games with the soldiers, his talks with other Parnassians turned volunteer soldier (Régamey sketched him again that autumn at the Café du Gaz on one of his office days, velvet-collared, beard rather longer and wider, sitting with Mérat and Valade), and in spare moments, being a gourmand of no mean order, toured the city in search of beef that was beef, even, such was his appetite, braving M. Mauté, who had moved his family to Boulevard Saint-Germain to try to avoid the Prussian shells and whose larder was not to be despised. Here too —for Mme Mauté was hospitable and musical and her husband felt under an obligation to Charles Cros' doctor brother—came from time to time the Parnassians who sympathised with Coppée.

As always when men share a common danger, the Coppée group felt a special bond, and these evenings revived something of past joys and even, when M. Mauté was absent, the light-heartedness of the pre-war soirées. But with a difference, the light-heartedness being close to desperate gaiety. Paris in the winter of 1870 was not a pleasant place; the Parisians were not simply suffering a siege, they were suffering it in disunity. After the first flare of enthusiasm, many began to complain that September 4, far from being another July 14, had simply substituted one form of reaction for another; ugly crowd scenes took place week after week, the red flag of the Commune showed itself, the Garde Mobile (the militia) was dissatisfied almost to the point of mutiny, and it became a question whether the siege would not be broken by civil war rather than by the

Prussians. By the middle of October the government was building barricades in all the main streets—against the Garde Mobile, not the Prussians—and Verlaine on his days at the Hôtel de Ville had to pass through a maze of obstructions.

For the Hôtel de Ville had become the headquarters of rebellion; during October it was crowded by Gardes Mobiles, many half drunk; large red "Vive la Commune" and "Death to Thiers" were scrawled on the walls; there came the formidable Jules Vallès and Rigault, peering through his glasses and muffled in three or four overcoats against the cold, to plot with the slovenly one-eyed Andrieu; and there were read the articles by Vermersch in his revival of Marat's scurrilous *Le Père Duchesne* reminding the Garde Mobile how the first Commune had dealt with nobles, priests and other reactionaries eighty years earlier. During that month Verlaine eyed apprehensively the little flotilla of gunboats moored off Pont Neuf, and on the 29th and the two following days his feelings pass beyond imagination, for then the Commune was proclaimed in Place de l'Hôtel de Ville, the Hôtel de Ville was invaded and the rising put down only after a bloody struggle.

But in such an atmosphere the wilder spirits flourished and a group within a group began to form based on the members of the *vilains bonshommes* dinners, but having as their bond political sympathies rather than the dubious poetical affinity with Coppée. They met at Nina's occasionally, but Nina's for Verlaine at any rate held awkward memories and had besides become one of the more notorious meeting-places of Communard leaders; he much preferred the evenings in his own cosy apartment or at the Mautés'. The leading lights were Cros and his brothers, De Sivry, Villiers, Chabrier, Blémont, Silvestre, Cabaner, who had not yet noticed that France was at war, and the photographer Carjat. But Carjat was a poet too and a personality besides, a dandy who would not allow a mere siege to disturb the symmetry of his smart velvet-collared frock-coat, frilled waistcoat, top-hat and shining monocle. He was accompanied by a man, boy rather, Louis Forain, friend of Cros, who was learning to paint, who was to become one of the greatest caricaturists of the century, but who then was notable only for a spirit of devilment. Verlaine, the good mixer, the poet of repute, and trying hard to forget the violence he had seen and heard of, the ardent

Communard, was not the least lively member of the gatherings. They by no means abandoned poetry, nor Charles Cros invention; he was busy between guard duties making artificial rubies at enormous cost, helped by a De Sivry convalescing after smallpox, and during one of the evenings he initiated a new type of ditty which was to become the latest craze in the café-concert some years later. Villiers, who had turned soldier in his spare time, arrived with a pickled herring (each guest bringing what food he could muster), exhibited his rare find with the air of a man presenting Mme Mauté with a sweet-smelling bouquet, then sank on to the sofa and immediately slept. Cros suspended the fish by a string from a pair of steps straddling the sofa and chanted:

> Il était un grand mur blanc, nu, nu, nu;
> Contre le mur, une échelle haute, haute, haute;
> Et par terre un hareng saur, sec, sec, sec.
>
> J'ai composé cette histoire simple, simple, simple,
> Pour mettre en fureur les gens graves, graves, graves,
> Et amuser les enfants petits, petits, petits.

3

Verlaine, then, appeared to have good reason for happiness, siege and deprivations notwithstanding. Yet before the winter was done, before even the year was over, he was in the thick of trouble. It began ostensibly (had it not been one thing it would have been another) with the coming of bad weather. The winter was late but severe. The pleasures of amateur soldiering faded abruptly when Verlaine found himself wet through or frozen night after night; he caught cold, rheumatism fastened on him (the effects of which he was never to lose) and he became utterly miserable. And when Verlaine was miserable he knew of one remedy only, to stop doing whatever was causing the misery. This led to two days' detention, which he endured philosophically, then to more guard duty, which he was not prepared to endure at all. And if he must, then again only one remedy occurred to him; his friendly drink with his comrades, who included porters from the wine market, extended itself into prolonged drinking bouts, and from beer and wine he moved at last to absinthe. Paris was short of everything but drink; of this it had too much and the Garde Mobile most of all.

The day came when he arrived home as he had arrived at his mother's house, quarrelsome, violent. He forced a quarrel on Mathilde, struck her. She ran to her parents. He fetched her back. The quarrel extended into the night.

The next morning, when the effect of the absinthe had worn off, he was horrified, prostrated himself before the girl and there was a grand reconciliation. A few days later the scene was repeated. Their life together degenerated into a series of violent quarrels followed by the nauseating spectacle of a penitent Verlaine on his knees and of not less nauseating reconciliations—nauseating because all element of reality, such as there ever was, had gone out of the marriage.

In later years Verlaine reproached himself bitterly, but in the matter of Mathilde he was never to become realistic, or, to be exact, only when absinthe released the truth. The general explanation of this disastrous end to the marriage has been that Verlaine was a dipsomaniac, but within a few years he was to show that, given the necessary incentive, he could fight the absinthe habit successfully for years. Rheumatism proved a convenient excuse for him to return to absinthe; the truth came out when, brimmed with absinthe, he accused her of failing him: she had not the necessary patience, the necessary sweetness of disposition, she did not understand his "tigerish love", his simplicity, did not this, did not that; in short, she was not the inspiring saint who was to carry him on the wings of love to everlasting bliss.

All the poor girl had done to deserve such a charge was to be herself. Verlaine found himself in the position of every intelligent man who has married for reasons which nature disguises as spiritual. Out of bed, Mathilde showed herself the naïve, vain and stupid philistine that she was. Illusion gone, every remark she made on poetry was an insult, every idiotic political enthusiasm jarred, every escape to her father became a bourgeois treachery; she stood revealed as a good-looking nonentity, veritable wife to the Monsieur Prudhomme he had castigated years earlier, and he as a man who had made a fatal error.

Even in bed she failed him, though the fault was neither in her nor in him; they were badly matched, that was all. Verlaine, coddled from birth, demanded coddling still; he wanted to be mothered in love as in life. Yet who would dream of such a thing to look at the tall, virile man? Not Mathilde, and not Verlaine himself, then. Later he understood, and that was the meaning, or one meaning, of his reproachful

"You could not understand my simplicity."

But Mathilde understood nothing; her husband's attitude was bewildering and one which she could never understand to the day of her death. Why did he dislike or grow impatient with that which he had loved to the point of fatuity? She had not changed; and this indeed was the trouble.

Verlaine equally would not face the truth because he dared not. Few men will admit even to themselves that their marriage, a few months after it has begun, is a failure; but Verlaine did not fear loss of face, he feared the collapse of his life, the reversion to the aimless, degrading pre-Mathilde years, if he once confessed that he had married not a saviour but a rather silly little girl. He would have been kinder to Mathilde and to himself if he had simply allowed her to stay with her parents, but this, feeling as he did, was impossible. Instead he soaked himself in absinthe and at the end of the year, when his mother (then living in rue Lécluse) suggested that he come to her to recuperate after an attack of bronchitis, she having a good stock of food, he brought Mathilde with him.

During their stay with Mme Verlaine one can feel only unalloyed pity for Mathilde. Verlaine had escaped the Garde Nationale at last by the move and the bronchitis, and was less inclined to drink to excess, but his mother made sure that their life together was not the happier; in the worst tradition of the mother-in-law she was for ever "getting at" the girl for failing to minister to Verlaine in the manner he was accustomed to. They were not there long, a few weeks only, but Verlaine had been given what he always sought, moral support.

In Batignolles they were out of the worst of the excitements though chronically short of food and fuel, but on his way to the Hôtel de Ville Verlaine saw uncomfortable evidence of trouble ahead; the failure of the great Champigny sortie at the end of November led to widespread accusations of treachery and a few days later red posters appeared all over Paris overnight demanding the impeachment of the government. On January 19 came the Buzenval sortie into which thirty thousand Gardes Mobiles were thrown with the regulars to keep them out of mischief. The sortie failed with heavy loss of life. Two days later the Communard leaders imprisoned after the repulse of the October revolt were rescued by a large and angry crowd. The next day a second attack was made on the Hôtel de Ville and the horrified Verlaine heard the frightening sounds of battle not a hundred feet from his room.

The revolt was again broken after much bloodshed. Six days later the government capitulated to the Prussians and civil war was suspended to await the result of a general election. Hugo was triumphantly returned as a republican member for Paris, but the elections as a whole showed a decided swing to the monarchists, and the situation in Paris looked so ugly with vast unemployment, heavy drinking and continued shortage of food that the Prime Minister, Thiers, decided to base his government on Versailles. Before the Prussians made their ceremonial entry on the first of March there had been calls for a Commune by an enormous crowd overflowing Place de la Bastille, and cannon were seized and dragged from the centre of the city to the Garde Mobile headquarters on the heights of Montmartre. When the invaders marched in they were received in absolute silence by all Parisians and throughout their three-day occupation they were contemptuously ignored by the whole city. The enemy gone, the unspoken truce collapsed; within a week the Communards had placarded Paris with an appeal "Unite to save the Republic". Verlaine saw these posters as he walked to work from his apartment, for Mathilde had without difficulty persuaded him to return home after the signing of the armistice.

The next few weeks were too hectic for personal differences to reappear. On March 18, following the failure of the government attempt to disarm the Garde Mobile and capture their cannon, the Commune was successfully set up at the Hôtel de Ville and the remnant of the French army retired to Versailles. Verlaine greeted the Commune as he had greeted the return of the Republic, with ecstatic joy. Rigault had been made public prosecutor, Andrieu Minister of Works, Vermersch in charge of propaganda, De Ricard, Régamey and Louise Michel were all fire-eating republicans, and Verlaine believed with them that a second and more glorious revolution demanded his services. He felt himself to be in the midst of great events and supported by like-minded friends. Even such a man as Courbet, the friend of Vermesch and Gill, was staunchly on their side. Verlaine was not alone; thousands of men took literally the promises of the Communards that France should become a federation of free and independent communes in which all would live in peace and prosperity. Therefore when the Thiers government called on every loyal civil servant to go to Versailles, Verlaine stayed where he was; not only stayed, but, remarkable reversal of rôles, when his alarmed mother sent Lepelletier to insist that he obey the order, he persuaded Lepelletier to stay also and soon got De Sivry a job in the Hôtel de Ville.

The millennium quickly showed itself to consist solely of free meals; open house was held at the Hôtel de Ville, which was stocked to bursting point with food and wine. In all else the Commune proved a disappointment, his friends at each other's throats, Paris filled with discontent, and his job, grandiloquently named Press officer, little livelier than his old one, for all he had to do was to go through the daily papers and mark references for and against the Commune in red and blue chalk.

The job did not last long. The Versaillais laid siege to Paris at the beginning of April and on May 22 Verlaine was wakened by the maid, Louise, with the rumour that they had broken in and reached the Porte Maillot. The truth was even more unpleasant; MacMahon had captured the Trocadéro on the previous day, his troops were advancing along both sides of the river and the Palais de Bourbon was on the point of falling. A few minutes after Verlaine leapt hurriedly out of bed he heard drums beating to arms, people began to run down the street and the bells of Notre Dame sounded the alarm. Then came the noise of artillery far too close, and Verlaine, going on to his balcony, could see shells bursting over the Arc de Triomphe, aimed, he thought, at the centre of the Champs-Elysées, from the Garde Mobile cannon at Montmartre. Mathilde begged to be allowed to see her parents, who had returned to rue Nicolet, and he saw her off with poor grace, feeling forsaken and worse than forsaken, obliged to do likewise. He therefore left the flat in search of his mother, but not with resolute step. The sight from the quayside understandably daunted him; the palace of the Tuileries, the Louvre, the Palais Royal and the Ministry of Finance had been set on fire with petroleum supplied by Andrieu and the shelling of the Champs-Elysées was increasing; smoke, flames, noise, crash of timbers filled the air. He managed to force himself on despite his terror, but was eventually turned back so brusquely—the sentry's rifle pointed directly at him and to his imagination on the half-cock—that nothing would induce him to show his head again even on the balcony.

Alarm expresses itself in the human body in the oddest, the most disconcerting forms, but Verlaine's fear, rising to a pitch as the clamour increased outside, took a novel shape; he wanted nothing so much as to go to bed with the maid. No thought of disloyalty to Mathilde, still less of punishing her for leaving him, came into his mind. With a desperation known only to the thoroughly frightened he longed for company and for distraction, and where could he find both but under the sheets with Louise? There was one hindrance, however; he could not be induced to use the bedroom, insisting after much argument that they retire to a tiny windowless closet. This, stuffed with mattresses, seemed to him to provide reasonable safety in a hideously unsafe world. At least the noise would be muffled. But when at last, arguments over and the mattresses dragged and pushed into place, he and Louise squeezed themselves into the closet they could move no further; even the ingenuity of a roused Verlaine could not devise the means or the possibility of pleasure. And it seems that frustration still reigned when there came a thunderous knock at the front door.

Believing it to be Mathilde, Verlaine rushed downstairs, to find to his dismay Lepelletier and a friend seeking shelter; they had been caught between Thiers' troops and the retreating Communards in Boulevard St-Germain. They found Verlaine a bundle of nerves which they did not improve by telling him that Paris had become a battlefield, the Versaillais already at Pont d'Alma, the barricaded streets cluttered with dead and wounded. The Hôtel de Ville was blazing, the arsenal in the Luxembourg had blown up with a terrific roar, the sound of street firing was growing ominously closer and the guns at Montmartre thundered hour after hour. Nor was he reassured when Lepelletier predicted that Verlaine's *quartier* would inevitably be occupied by government troops within a few hours and that the Communards were fighting a losing battle; he, as a Communard sympathiser, was suspect, and he was now harbouring two active members of the movement, one of them in uniform. Between them they stripped off and destroyed the stripes on the trousers of Lepelletier's friend and burned his *képi*. After this Verlaine was sufficiently relieved to eat a good meal, though he absolutely refused to regard from the balcony the scene of a blazing, smoking Paris, the Seine glinting red. Lepelletier thought him in a highly emotional state, which would be scarcely surprising even in a bold man; and significantly he expressed greater fear for his mother than for his wife.

They had one shock when the building was invaded by a crowd of people fleeing from the neighbourhood of the Panthéon, which they declared was about to blow up, but the rest of the day passed with nothing worse to endure than the incessant and alarming noises from outside. They slept, but early the next morning Verlaine was wakened by a knock at the door; his mother stood there, having crossed Paris during the night; the stories she told of the fires, massacres and fights through which she had passed shook the nerves of all.

Later in the morning Mathilde arrived, having made the journey from Montmartre after several failures; this too showed courage, for she was without escort for much of the way, and Verlaine, ashamed of himself, welcomed her warmly. He was preoccupied, however, by the presence of Lepelletier and his friend, and the prospect, looming ever closer, of a shooting squad for the three of them; and his relief was not veiled at all when they had the good fortune to see Lepelletier's old army regiment marching past. The embarrassing visitors joined them and got away safely.

Two days later the Panthéon and the Luxembourg had been taken and the Communards expelled from the left bank with a loss of fifteen thousand men; within a week all fighting was over, though the fires still burned and smoke covered Paris. The civil war ended as usual in a widespread witch hunt; of the leading Communards whom Verlaine knew, Rigault was shot, Louise Michel was transported to an overseas prison and the remainder escaped death only because they managed to make their way abroad, Nina to Switzerland, De Ricard to South America, most of them to London; even De Sivry, who had done nothing more than act as registrar of births and deaths, was imprisoned and treated brutally. Everywhere men were being denounced for working under the Commune; within a few months thirty-eight thousand people had been arrested, of whom a third were put into prison on the flimsiest of pretexts; executions were still going on two years later. Verlaine took fright, and not without reason: how could he, who had refused to go to Versailles and was friendly with Communard leaders, expect to be allowed to resume his work as though nothing had happened? He decided that the chance was not worth taking, and especially in a career that he was finding increasingly tedious. He stayed away.

At once he felt the pinch of his father's optimistic gambles on the stock exchange; since his mother had paid over the marriage settlement of twenty thousand francs, the comfortable little Verlaine fortune, what Captain Verlaine had left of it, was much reduced. This meant, since he was without a salary, that he must either get another job or live with one of the families until his poetry began to pay. Mathilde objected with reason to a further trial with her mother-in-law; she was also pregnant, a fact which clinched her arguments in favour of her parents' home. And to rue Nicolet they returned.

Here there was almost immediate trouble. M. Mauté had never liked his son-in-law; he now detested him. Verlaine, trying to control his craving for absinthe because of Mathilde's pregnancy, was in no mood to endure his father-in-law's pompous protests; there were undignified scenes day after day. Had it not been for Mme Mauté, who liked Verlaine and had a sense of humour, the double *ménage* must have collapsed almost as soon as it began.

In the summer Verlaine temporarily avoided further trouble by taking Mathilde on a round of family visits in the Pas de Calais, staying with Dujardin at Lécluse and his mother's relatives at Fampoux. For some months there was peace, the last he and Mathilde were to know together. Relieved from fear of arrest, relieved to be away from M. Mauté, his optimism shot up, a natural optimism fortified by a generous supply of beer, absinthe being self-forbidden and, what was more to the point, difficult to obtain. All would be well, the countryside was the place for him, he would not worry about the future. Soon he was writing light-hearted notes to his friends in Paris, commenting to Blémont, for example, on the destruction of the Vendôme column by the Communards in the following fashion: "Our window looks out on a large courtyard in the centre of which rises a Vendôme column which, less pretentious and more useful than the defunct, is content with the humble name of chimney. Beyond it are roofs pierced with a thousand pipes, each more bizarre than the other, then vats, more vats and yet more vats; and if you like treacle you will find it everywhere." And for himself "my cousin possesses a *very comfortable* garden. . . . To smoke a couple of pipes here after a midday dinner, to have seven or eight drinks at the inn between four and five o'clock and to watch night fall in the woods whilst reading some tranquillising book, this is my new life."

There was another side to this life, of course, and he could not fail to feel it. "Yes, it's charming, this existence here," he told Valade, "but absolutely devoid of the literary. All talk is restricted to war stories in which the words *treason* and *revenge* play a prominent part . . . in short, all this gossip about the siege, MacMahon this, Bazaine that—no, my dear chap, I've had enough! These are the real horrors of war! When I can get into a corner with some good man who is kind enough to talk to me about beetroots . . . I'm happy . . . like a Coppée still drawing his salary."

The reference to Coppée is significant; Coppée had gone back to the War Office, Coppée's growing rectitude had begun to irritate the little *vilains bonshommes* group. Before the civil war broke it up the group had decided to put together an album in which parody would play a large part, and the only stroke of work Verlaine did in the country was to write good but unkind parodies of Banville, Heredia and "the abbé Coppée".

For the rest, such was his power of self-deception, which is a cold way of describing a natural bent for happiness, that after a few weeks of sitting in the open, walking, fishing, reading and talking to his hosts (all of whom made a great fuss of him), he persuaded himself without difficulty that the coming of a child would restore all the lost harmony between himself and Mathilde; a picture rose before him of the fond father dandling the child on his knees, watching the growth of the infant poet and once again worshipping the woman who had brought the marvel into the world. The fact that he had abandoned the writing of serious poetry, the artist being a sounder judge of circumstance than the man, either escaped him or was put out of mind. Instead he sounded the depths of false contentment when he urged the newly engaged Blémont to "try to draw a good number" in the marriage lottery: "I can't complain of mine."

In this spirit he returned to rue Nicolet early in September, for Mathilde's confinement was expected the following month. Before his contentment and good resolutions had time to collapse he found waiting for him in Passage Choiseul two letters which were to make an end of both. Yet Verlaine could not have suspected any threat to his specious security in the letters which had been written from the town of Charleville in the Ardennes a few miles south of the country he knew so well; they were the kind of letter familiar to published writers, praising his work, complaining of the lack of opportunity in the provinces and begging him to read the poems enclosed. It is possible that Verlaine might like many another author have put the letters aside, the poems unread, possible but not probable because he was a kind man. But in this case his kindness was not put to the test for there was a postscript by a man known to him, a Charles Bretagne who had once been customs officer at Fampoux, asking him to do what he could for the writer. This writer signed himself Arthur Rimbaud.

Chapter Nine

RIMBAUD

1854-1871

ARTHUR RIMBAUD was born in October 1854, more than ten years after Verlaine. His parents bore a superficial resemblance to Verlaine's; his father was an army man, had risen from the ranks and cut a fine figure in his regimentals; his mother was from the north and was of peasant stock. But in every important respect two couples could scarcely have differed more: Captain Rimbaud, a southerner, was a restless, wild and charming man; Mme Rimbaud had remained the well-to-do peasant and had the peasant's virtues and failings to the point of caricature; she was dour, deeply pious, inarticulate except in anger, and close.

Vitalie Cuif's surrender to the charm of Captain Rimbaud was the major weakness of her life; she accepted its penalties as a just punishment and a lesson for the future. Their brief life together (he was usually away with the army) was a disaster; his open-handedness, light behaviour and unstable disposition offended all the peasant in his wife; they differed on every important point of conduct; violent scenes were frequent. By the time Arthur was a small boy the marriage had collapsed; Captain Rimbaud retired to Dijon and was never seen again.

If Mme Rimbaud had need of further warning that her children's blood might be spiritually contaminated, she found it in the sordid lives of her brothers, both dissolute and worthless men, but the failure of her marriage was enough to raise all the Spartan in her character; she devoted herself with a grim passion to the upbringing of the children, determined that they should be everything that her husband and brothers were not, worthy and God-fearing citizens above all.

Arthur soon showed himself to be the most promising of her four living children. Indeed, promising is hardly the word, for the boy was beautiful, clever and good; he had the noble forehead, wavy light brown hair and startlingly clear blue eyes of his father, his disposition seemed sweet and it was clear to all

Mathilde after the Divorce

14 Rue Nicolet

Rimbaud, 1871

who had to do with him that he possessed a brain of exceptional brilliance. His mother's hopes inevitably centred themselves on him.

The parallel with Verlaine and his mother is plain, but Mme Rimbaud expressed her pride and love in different fashion; the greater her hopes, the stronger her fears, and she was if anything stricter with this model child than with the others. His physical likeness to his father was enough to keep her on perpetual guard. Moreover, for she was far from stupid, she sensed the depth of Arthur's resentment at the restrictions she put on him, the ban on intercourse with other children, the refusals to give him a sou to spend, the home-made clothes which affronted his pride; and she realised that this child had a formidable strength of will which must be subdued for the good of his soul.

Nor did her iron régime relax after the boy had begun his sensational career at the College of Charleville; on the whole she was severer, afraid no doubt that his head would be turned. His triumphs would unquestionably have made an ordinary child insupportable. He was not popular, the boys at first envious, suspicious of his angelic expression and manner and making cruel but natural fun of his clothes. But eventually they took pride in the prodigy, a pride shared, with misgivings, by the masters. Not without reason; his reading was encyclopaedic for a school-boy, his memory prodigious, his vocabulary enormous, his facility on paper amazing. In his early teens, for instance, he one day wrote Latin verses on a set subject for every boy in his class, each series of verses differing in style so that the trick should not be observed—and this in the short intervals when the master was demonstrating a geometrical theorem on the blackboard. At an examination held when he was just fourteen he wrote fifty-nine Latin hexameters in three hours.

By the age of fifteen the young Rimbaud had become the prize pupil. He had to find satisfaction in this public approbation, for he did not receive it at home. He searched inevitably for a "soul mate" and intellectual leader, and found him unsurprisingly in a master at school. Georges Izambard joined the college at the beginning of 1870 and was as much impressed as his predecessors by this remarkable pupil; but perhaps because he was more of an age with him—twenty-one to Rimbaud's fifteen—he understood something of the frustration beneath the shy and staid demeanour. He opened his library to the boy, talked to him, encouraged him to talk; they became close friends.

The immediate result of this friendship was the appearance of Rimbaud as poet. Before Izambard's arrival he had read some Romantics and one or two Parnassians, the moderns of the late 'sixties; he had even managed to publish a poem in a review taken by his mother, a poem plainly yet individually based on Coppée's *Reliquaire*. Made free of Izambard's books, he swept at great speed through French literature, the poets foremost, and wrote poems showing first this influence then that, yet almost always with a fresh and original approach. But the books of Izambard's that most fascinated him were the complete *Parnasse Contemporain* of 1866 and several volumes of poetry by Parnassians, Banville and Leconte de Lisle particularly. He heard that a second *Parnasse Contemporain* was being prepared and in May he wrote to Banville, his god of the moment, sending him three poems and begging him to insert at least one in the anthology.

The letter, an uneasy mixture of arrogance and humility, reminds one of Branwell Brontë's "CONDEMN NOT UNHEARD" letter to Blackwood, and though Banville replied with his usual courtesy, he is unlikely to have reached the end of it or, if he did, would have been discouraged from reading the poems. This was a pity; the letter could have been written by a thousand boys infatuated with poetry—Banville must have received many such —but the poems could have been written only by one person in the world, they were as mature and original in everything but subject as the accompanying letter was juvenile. The poem mentioned particularly by Rimbaud, *Credo in unam*, beat the Parnassians at their own game; it was an astonishingly successful evocation of ancient Greece, the spirit and the appearance.

Foiled for the moment, the boy of fifteen continued to read enormously, to win first prize after first prize at school and to write poems, one of which, the charming *Première Soirée*, was printed in the satirical weekly *La Charge*. And it was apparently through this journal that he was first led to the work of Verlaine; at the end of July a note by the editor strongly recommended *La Bonne Chanson* by the "well-known author" of *Poèmes Saturniens* and *Fêtes Galantes*. Three weeks later Rimbaud is exclaiming to

Izambard that these last are "most unusual, very strange and truly adorable!" and urging him to buy *La Bonne Chanson*. Rimbaud had not then read it, but explains that "many journals have praised it".

He was not talking but writing to Izambard; term had ended, war had begun and Izambard was not going to return. The war completed the boy's unsettlement; it had been just possible for a would-be Parnassian to live in a cultureless Charleville with Izambard to encourage him. But Izambard gone and all the excitements of a war raging not many miles away abruptly snapped his patience. He would run away, he told his friend, a threat which he carried out late in August after his seventeen-year-old brother had led the way by secretly going off with a regiment on its way to the front. The escapade was a dismal failure; he managed to slip into a train bound for Paris, but the moment he reached the terminus was arrested for travelling without a ticket, and put into prison. He at once became the frightened small boy and appealed to Izambard, who obtained his release and put him up for a week or two in his aunts' home at Douai. Then, reluctantly, he was persuaded to go back to a bewildered and furious mother. His one satisfaction was his temporary membership of the Douai Garde Nationale.

He listened sullenly to his mother's reproaches. A few days later he ran away again, this time walking to Brussels by way of the homes of school friends and ending again at Douai. He was still writing poetry.

Once again he was returned to his mother, a mother convinced that she had to deal with the spit of her happy-go-lucky husband. His school had not reopened; Sédan, not far away, had fallen, Charleville was besieged and at the end of the year the Prussians entered the town. Rimbaud spent most of his time walking, talking and reading with one of his best school friends, Ernest Delahaye; they talked poetry, of course, and Rimbaud read and praised the Parnassians, and Verlaine in particular; he was much struck by the hints (broad to him) in Verlaine's work of a new poetry, his inversions, repetitions, his mastery of cadence, his humour, his musicality and modernity in choice and placing of words, and above all by the signs of versification freed from classical forms. His own poems showed something of Verlaine's gift for lyricism and he now took the other hints, becoming as

Verlainean as he had formerly been Banvillean, but here too with a certain note of his own.

The two boys also discussed politics; faced with the Prussians investing and then occupying Charleville, with the shock of the collapse of the much-vaunted French army, with Paris under siege for months and rumours of discord and treachery everywhere freely repeated, no boy of spirit and intelligence could fail to react vehemently. Both were, as might be expected, violently republican, and both echoed dark suspicions of the government. But there they parted company; Delahaye, at heart a prudent young man, would criticise but saw nothing that he could usefully do other than walk past the Prussian soldiers with a contemptuous expression and fit himself to teach young Frenchmen to make their country truly great once more.

To Rimbaud this was weak-kneed, unthinkable. He panted for action. "I've something in me, I don't know what, that wants to soar", he had told Banville, and neither the non-appearance of his poems in the *Parnasse Contemporain* nor the failure of his two breaks for freedom daunted him; they merely determined him to be off again as soon as possible. In vain his mother kept him without money, in vain she insisted that he return to school when the Prussians marched out and the college reopened; he had read in the newspapers how the reported peace terms agreed to by the newly elected government were stirring the Garde Mobile to revolt; was he to stay in Charleville, to go to school, to shelter under his mother's skirts when history was being made in Paris? In February of the new year, 1871, without a word he pawned his watch, bought a ticket to Paris and walked late in the evening to the rue Lepic studio of Gill, whose work he had admired in *La Charge*. There was no reply to his knock but, Gill's door being unlocked as usual, Rimbaud pushed it open, and feeling tired and seeing a bed lay on it and slept.

Gill returned from the cafés in the small hours, saw in astonishment a boy on his bed, shook the sleeper and asked what he was doing there. Rimbaud, rubbing his eyes, complained that he had been enjoying delightful dreams and would have preferred not to be wakened—a typical remark which Gill received with a laugh, being a good-tempered man, and a "I have delightful dreams also, but in my own bed". Being kind, too, he questioned the "lugubrious monster"; and when the boy explained that he

was a poet and had come to Paris to make his name, Gill advised
him to go home and gave him all the money he had in his
pocket, some ten francs.

Rimbaud took the money but not the advice. He was still in
the city, living no one knows how, when an army of Garde
Mobile and their women marched up the Champs-Elysées in
protest against the peace treaty then being signed with the
Prussians, was there three days later when the Prussians marched
in and when they left two days afterwards. If he tried to join the
Garde Mobile he did not remain, nor did he manage to find
Vermersch, whom he knew to be a power amongst the
Communards. He spent most of his time reading at the bookstalls
on the quays as Verlaine had done before him, reading almost
under Verlaine's windows had he known it. Soon after the
Prussians had left Paris he followed suit, impatient perhaps
because the long-promised Commune had not come to pass, no
doubt discouraged because he had not met anyone of note except
Gill, certainly forced to go by shortage of food. Having no money,
he made the return journey of 150 miles by the simple expedient
of passing himself off as a franc-tireur, successfully living off the
country folk (applying to the local mayor for food and lodging
when people turned him away) and getting through the Prussian
lines without detection.

By this time Rimbaud had shown himself as more than an
infant prodigy with exceptional physical appeal; this boy with
the face of a sulky angel and the brain of a double first was also
as cool, daring and determined as the most adult of adventurers.
He remained nevertheless a boy of sixteen returning home again
and again, every hope frustrated. But he bided his time, taking
his mother's punishments and reproaches with outward sang-
froid, and perhaps meditated another escape to Paris, stirred no
doubt by the formation of the Commune and the new siege of
the city.

Whether he did in fact go is not known. What actually
happened to him has never been discovered, but that he under-
went some sort of shock is plain. Some say that he joined the
Garde Mobile and experienced an unhappy sexual awakening in
barracks. Others believe that he reached Paris only to find that
the Versaillais had broken in, that the millennium had collapsed
and that reaction was triumphing. The suggestions are many but

the truth eludes us. It may simply be that the collapse of the Commune filled the boy with bitterness—he had become an ardent Communard—and that he vented this bitterness on the comfortable Charleville bourgeois. Certainly he changed, and for the worse. He had suddenly become a problem child in every sense of the term. He wore the air of a cynical and depraved youth. He refused to return to school, refused to work, refused to wash, refused to cut his hair, and in general refused to conform to civilised life as Charleville understood it. The boy of the many prizes, quiet, well-behaved, neat to the point of excess, disappeared and in his place walked the streets of a shocked town a dirty, long-haired, foul-mouthed lad who hung about the school with a sneer on his face, wrote obscene poetry and sat for hours at the cafés reviling Church, Christianity, women, government, the bourgeoisie and any other institution he could think of, and with such a choice vocabulary that his questionable audience would pay him in drink and tobacco for the pleasure of hearing a boy demean himself so artistically.

One of the more regular of this audience was Bretagne, a man of parts who not only had a nose for tax evasion but was poet, musician, draughtsman and demonologist besides. He let Rimbaud loose in his library, curious no doubt to see what the brilliant boy would make of it. He must have been pleasantly surprised, for within a few weeks Rimbaud was evolving rapidly a theory of poetry that had been hovering in his mind ever since he had first read Baudelaire. The poet, he told a friend of Izambard, must become a seer. Gautier, Leconte de Lisle and Banville were great seers, but Baudelaire was greater, "King of poets, *a very God*!" Yet even Baudelaire had failed to reach his goal, the infinity lying beyond reality; he lived in too artistic a milieu and the form of his work was paltry. New forms were needed, a new language and a new struggle to elevate oneself. This demanded "a long, immense and deliberate *derangement of all the senses*, the poet seeking every possible experience of love, pain and madness, tasting every poison, so that he can keep their quintessence". It also demanded superhuman fortitude and faith, for he would have to undergo "inexpressible torture" and would appear in the eyes of all men as "the great diseased, the great criminal, the great accursed". Only then would he become "the supreme seer! For he arrives at the *unknown*!" The "unimaginable, unnamable things" he finds there might drive him frantic so that he no longer understands his visions, but no matter, "he has seen them!" and others will take over from him at the point where he collapsed.

The theory is not original and could have been stated so only by a very young man and one who after the manner of Vincent van Gogh, though for other reasons, considered himself despised and rejected. Psychoanalysts have a name for this state of mind and for the compensatory dreams which accompany it. In this case its difference and danger lay in the fact that it was set out as a plan of life by one who, having no humility, failed to understand that the aim of the great *voyants* was self-abnegation not self-assertion. Nor did he realise that his hero Baudelaire's overriding sense of sin made quite another thing of the theory of self-assertion that he had taken over.

The remarkable aspect of this declaration by a sixteen-year-old provincial was not the ambitiousness of his plan but his recognition of Baudelaire's greatness at a time when the work of Baudelaire was known only to the few and his genius barely suspected. And no less remarkable are the poems which Rimbaud began to write. Charleville understandably presented pitifully few opportunities for deranging the senses, and the eager iconoclast could do nothing worse than drink too much if his patrons would sponsor him as far, scrawl chalk slogans of "M . . . . to God" on church doors and seats in public gardens, draw savage caricatures of respectable Charleville citizens and talk filth in the lesser cafés. But there was nothing to prevent him from experimenting in the necessary poetic "new forms", and this he did. The first of these poems, *Ce qu'on dit au poète à propos de fleurs*, he sent to Banville in the middle of July with a letter different in tone from the one of the year before but still youthful: "Have I improved?" he asked.

Banville did not answer, and one cannot be surprised; there was a limit to his tolerance. If he read the poem, he must have appreciated the verbal dexterity, but his pleasure would have been of the wry kind, for the boy had made cruel fun of his "cher Maître"; using a wide and original vocabulary, he destroyed with diabolical ingenuity the lilies, roses, violets, forget-me-nots spread so lavishly through the poems of Banville and of the Parnassians who followed him; the only flowers that he will put into his poetry, he said, are flowers never yet seen by man and existing only in the imagination. The "new form" consisted in the use of words and images then considered unpoetical; vulgarisms, colloquialisms, words from the sciences and from the gutter.

Rimbaud had begun to write his second "new form" poem and was worried by Banville's silence. But he had another hope up his sleeve; Baudelaire being dead, he had already distinguished two contemporary poets as the hope of the future: "the new school, called Parnassian, of the two seers, Albert Mérat and Paul Verlaine, a true poet". And when towards the end of August his confidant Bretagne suggested an approach to Verlaine and offered to write a covering note Rimbaud accepted eagerly and wrote straightway enclosing several poems; he was an admirer, he said, and a fellow-poet incarcerated in a provincial town where his talent, his hopes, his ideals were all stifled.

Again he had no reply (Verlaine was then in the Pas de Calais), and in the first days of September he wrote once more. "I have a great poem under way and I don't want to work at Charleville. I can't come to Paris without resources. My mother is a widow and extremely devout. She only gives me ten centimes every Sunday to pay for a seat in the church." He sent more poems.

Verlaine, back in rue Nicolet, read the poems. He was astounded: "You have a prodigious talent", he replied at once enthusiastically. But he was also disgusted with many of Rimbaud's vulgarisms: "Your lycanthropy makes me feel as if I'd caught a whiff from a sewer." And he was cautious, anxious not to encourage a young man to plunge into Paris without adequate backing: he must, he said, show the poems to other poets before helping him to leave Charleville.

He showed them to Cros and Valade. They too were impressed by the originality of the poems, and Verlaine hesitated no longer; he wrote at once: "Come, dear great soul, we summon you, we await you!" He invited Rimbaud to stay with him (M. Mauté providentially still shooting in the country) and sent him the fare to Paris.

A day or two later, on September 10, Rimbaud arrived, bringing with him as luggage the manuscript of *Le Bateau Ivre*.

Chapter Ten

RIMBE

1871-1872

I

VERLAINE and Cros went to the station to meet him, waited at the wrong platform, and returned to rue Nicolet to find Rimbaud with Mme Mauté and Mathilde in the salon. Mathilde hovered between amusement and disgust. Mme Mauté, like every Parisienne with pretensions to culture, had never lost hope of astonishing her world with a real live genius, but she had not reckoned on a genius at once dirty, surly and insolent, and by the time Verlaine arrived she had virtually written off Rimbaud as nothing but a nasty boy and her son-in-law's praise of his poems as yet another case of that too amiable, too trusting young man being led astray.

Verlaine was flabbergasted by his first sight of the author of the poems he had praised so highly. He had expected to find a man in his twenties or thirties; he saw a disreputable youth sitting awkwardly and sullenly on the edge of his chair, a youth wearing a home-made suit of slate-blue serge out of which protruded in the manner of Glatigny a length of leg in coarse home-knitted blue cotton socks ending in heavy labourer's boots, bony wrists and large black-nailed red hands. His face was red and rough, a dirty string tie was tied loosely at the back of a dirty shirt, his hair had obviously not seen comb, brush or soap for weeks. His expression was ugly with the obstinate angry embarrassment of one who finds himself out of place.

But Verlaine was not only astonished, he was attracted. The others saw nothing but a dirty, sullen lower-class boy growing out of his clothes; he divined the charm and intelligence beyond the dirt and surly monosyllables. He remembered the extraordinary poems and with the insight of physical attraction he understood something of what the visitor must be feeling. The others were kind but patronising; he spoke to Rimbaud as to an

F* 153

equal, and he spoke little where the rest rushed in with chatter intended to put the boy at his ease.

Rimbaud's feelings are not difficult to imagine; he felt his uncouthness, his lack of table manners, his inability to speak fluent nothings or move gracefully, he felt the incongruity of sitting in a daintily furnished drawing-room or at a luxuriously appointed table—felt all and resented all. When the women spoke to him, he sensed behind their polite façade of interest the curious, disgusted regard: Mme Mauté's secret fear that her silken cushions were being soiled, Mathilde's playful bedroom comments on his provincial accent, and the perplexity of both at the invitation of Verlaine which had brought such a creature into their home. The fooling of the rattle De Sivry, who joined them for dinner, struck him, already rubbed the wrong way, as insulting and decadent. Even the serious enquiries of Cros could not mollify him; Cros wanted to know something of his political theories, how he had come to write, what his plans were. Rimbaud had plenty to say on this matter, but would not say it in such company; Cros was "talking down" to him, he thought angrily, he was to be made an exhibit, the subject for their latest gossip.

He would not oblige. He was in a fury of hatred. That these people should dare to condescend to him, the genius who was to pierce the heart of the mystery, to be a god among men! His reaction was inevitable and he told himself he had the best of warrants for it; his King of Poets had said a thousand times, "épater le bourgeois". He had followed Baudelaire to the letter, as he thought, in Charleville; was a smooth-speaking, well-clothed, addle-pated group of Paris suburbanites to escape correction?

But he was perplexed and chagrined to find Verlaine in this bourgeois milieu. How reconcile the "seer", the great poet of the future and one of his guiding lights, with such a setting? Evidently he decided to give him the benefit of the doubt; the difference in Verlaine's manner was impossible to ignore; the most touchy could not take offence at it. But to the rest he behaved abominably. He replied in monosyllables to every question; he listened with an insolent sneer whilst the others talked, and when in despair Mme Mauté rose for dinner thinking perhaps that food might soften her difficult guest, he set himself to shock, eating noisily and, the moment he had done, resting both elbows on the table and lighting a pipe which he puffed over the plates of those who had not yet finished. He abandoned all pretence of listening to the conversation, moodily watching his hostess's little dog running from chair to chair begging for scraps. "Les chiens, ce sont des libéraux," he said at last, the only remark Verlaine could remember during that unhappy evening. Then with a muttered "I'm tired" he took himself to bed.

That night Verlaine read the manuscript Rimbaud had brought from Charleville, and if he had had doubts of the boy after the fiasco of the evening he doubted no more. No admirer of Baudelaire could miss *Le Voyage* as the starting-point of *Le Bateau Ivre*, but the sweep of imagination, the verbal originality were Rimbaud's own.

The next day Verlaine took him off for a round of the cafés and introduced him proudly as the poetic prodigy of the age. His pride had to endure many shocks; Rimbaud, he discovered not without uneasiness, said exactly what he thought in the most pungent language to everybody's face, he respected nothing and nobody, would make no concessions, would endure no cant. But, the first shocks over, this was exhilarating and, to a man with a strong sense of humour, irresistible. Verlaine began to love the boy with a passion. With one or two intimates, the young Forain chiefly, Rimbaud displayed an uninhibited zest for life that warmed the heart; the sulky monosyllabic youth of rue Nicolet disappeared, and the clothes, the gangling body, the awkwardness were of no account beside the winged words of a fiery, tow-headed angel. Never had Verlaine heard such enthusiasm; beside it the talks at the Café du Gaz, at Lemerre's and at the pre-war soirées paled to pettiness. And not merely enthusiasm; Rimbaud spoke with a fervour, a knowledge and a certainty of the triumph and glory to come; he would experience all things, dare all to write poetry of a kind undreamed of, the poetry of a man who had plumbed the depths and scaled the heights of sensation. And Verlaine, if he had the courage and the vision, could travel with him, could become a "son of the Sun", an immortal.

Listening by the hour, Verlaine's doubts receded and something of his schoolboy faith returned. Who could doubt, hearing that eager voice with its northern burr, looking at the burning blue eyes? Not Verlaine, and for a time not Verlaine's intimates. After a *vilains bonshommes* dinner at which Verlaine presented Rimbaud, Valade wrote to Blémont: "You missed a great deal by not being there. A most daring poet not yet eighteen was introduced by Paul Verlaine his inventor and in fact his John the Baptist. Big hands, big feet, a wholly babyish face like a child of thirteen, deep blue eyes! Such is this boy whose imagination combines great power with unheard-of corruption and who has fascinated and terrified all our friends." One of them said, "Behold Jesus in the midst of the doctors." Another replied, "More likely Satan!" Valade thought "we are witnessing the birth of a genius".

"His John the Baptist" was a fairly accurate description of Verlaine's rôle. His delight at seeing pretensions demolished right and left rose to an ecstasy. What integrity, what an intellect and what charm! And when the winged words changed to obscenities, blasphemies and strange oaths, that too was a marvel of another kind coming from the sulky mouth of this youthful Lucifer. Everybody must see and hear. Verlaine proudly took his "Rimbe", as he fondly called him, to visit Hugo, who, if Lepelletier is accurate, promptly described him as the child Shakespeare. Another returned celebrity, Nina, back from Switzerland, made a great fuss of the boy, and the writers' cafés generally were intrigued by the contrast of brief but devastating criticism, claims of greatness, and boasts of tasting every form of depravity backed by foul language coming incongruously from this coltish, baby-faced youth with the candid blue eyes and charming smile who moved about like an unwashed and very carelessly dressed young god. Forain shrewdly sketched him with the chubby face of a two- or three-year-old child. Carjat took photographs of him, photographs which explain how fascinating he must have been.

Rimbaud was far from fascinating rue Nicolet. Verlaine, light-heartedly accepting the necessity expounded forcefully by his young friend of "a long and deliberate derangement of all the senses" as a good excuse for reverting to absinthe, began to arrive home the worse for wear. This was naturally put down by the women to the influence of the rapscallion from Charleville, and Rimbaud's welcome wore thin. He accepted the hostility with a will and laid himself out to make sure that his hostess had a good cause for it; his bed, for instance, was found to be crawling with lice and his favourite resting-place on the few occasions when he showed himself seems to have been the gravelled path in front of the house, where Verlaine found him stretched at full length in the sun smoking his pipe.

The return of M. Mauté before the birth of Verlaine's son brought matters to a head. The opinion he and Rimbaud had of each other was automatic, and almost before he could demand the withdrawal of the viper from the love nest Rimbaud had taken himself away no one knew where.

Verlaine searched for him and eventually ran into him in the street a week or two later, thin, pale and wretched, his efforts to support himself having sunk to peddling key-rings. Overjoyed, he gave him a good meal, then put him into the hands of Cros and Gill whilst he looked round for a permanent shelter. Cros and Gill bore no ill will, nor did Banville when Verlaine begged him to look after his friend; he rented and his mother with some trouble furnished the attic of their apartment house in rue de Buci for the destitute young poet, whilst Verlaine and his intimates clubbed together to give him three francs a day to live on.

2

Had Rimbaud been able to settle down on Banville's doorstep, so to speak, and had he allowed Mme Banville to mother him, his future would have been assured. But this, given Rimbaud as he was and the Parnassians as they were, remains a pleasant dream. On the very first evening of Rimbaud's arrival Banville heard a clamour in the courtyard and looking out saw the boy naked at the window throwing his clothes to the ground far below. Nothing can be hidden in Parisian apartment houses, and the other tenants were soon in an uproar—one had already sent for the police, thinking that Rimbaud was either mad or a sexual exhibitionist.

Banville ran upstairs. Rimbaud explained that he was not used to such a clean and tidy room and that he could not wear his clothes, "full of fleas", in it. Banville hurriedly rigged him out with clothes of his own and invited him to dinner. But that too did not please the boy; the conversation bored, the condescension (as he thought it) angered him and he began fingering a knife with an expression on his face that embarrassed and silenced everyone. Mallarmé tells this story; he is a reliable witness and coming events were to confirm him.

For this was the beginning of the end of Rimbaud as a figure of any moment in Parisian literary circles and by corollary of Verlaine also. He departed from Banville's, leaving the room filthy, and Verlaine found him a home with Cabaner in the Hôtel des Etrangers in rue Racine. The dreamy Cabaner, who had gone through both sieges of Paris under the vague impression that they were both by the Prussians, was not easy to offend nor could he easily give offence, his life being disreputable enough to satisfy Rimbaud and his forbearance on the rare occasions when he noticed the outside world being almost without limit. There for a few weeks Rimbaud remained with his "Tronche" as he called the big hairy man with the mild eyes, writing poems, playing Cabaner's lute, drinking and talking with a crowd of literary men—the little set of the wartime soirées—and taking his first new step towards the derangement of the senses, the step consisting of the hashish praised so alarmingly by Baudelaire.

Delahaye, anxious about his friend, had come to Paris to look him up, and, conducted by Verlaine, found him at the Hôtel just coming out of a hashish trance, lying on a couch in a tattered overcoat much too large for him and with a shabby grey felt hat crammed on his head. He had grown rapidly in the few weeks since Delahaye had seen him, was emaciated and appallingly dirty, and was disgruntled by the failure of the hashish: rubbing his eyes, he confessed with a grimace that he had seen nothing in his dreams but black and white moons chasing each other.

He was busy at odd moments compiling with his companions the "Album des Vilains Bonshommes" which Verlaine, Blémont, Valade, Mérat, Cabaner, Richepin, Carjat, Gill and Cros had been planning for their amusement during the siege. It was to consist, as Verlaine explained, of parodies; having done Coppée and Heredia, he was at work on a *Joyeuseté galante* after Glatigny; and Rimbaud contributed, besides a sketch or two, parodies of Dierx, Coppée and De Ricard amongst others and a brilliant "new version" of a *Fêtes Galantes* poem. The contributors also amused themselves, being Frenchmen, by trying to settle on a name for the group; their chief aim seems to have been to differentiate themselves from the too respectable poets of the Parnasse, though they would have been surprised to learn that their true distinction was to harbour two of the most famous poets of the century. To these young men the choice of a name provided a good excuse for fun over drinks; and Valade tells how he and other members, some known, some unknown, tried to find it, Rimbaud contributing his favourite monosyllable.

(*Mérat*) Cinq sous! c'est ruineux! Me demander cinq sous?
Tas d'insolents! . . . (*Pénoutet*) Mon vieux! Je viens du café Riche,
J'ai vu Catulle . . . (*Keck*) Moi, je voudrais être riche.
(*Verlaine*) Cabaner, de l'eau d'aff! . . . (*H. Cros*) Messieurs, vous
    êtes saouls!

(*Valade*) Morbleu, pas tant de bruit! La femme d'en dessous
    accouche . . .
(*Mérat*) Avez-vous lu l'article sur l'Autriche
Dans ma revue? . . . (*Mercier*) Horreur! Messieurs, Cabaner triche
Sur la cantine! (*Cabaner*) Je . . . ne . . . pu . . . is répondre à tous!

(*Gill*) Je ne bois rien, je paye! Allez cherchez à boire.
Voilà dix sous! (*Antoine Cros*) Si! Si! Mérat, veuillez m'en croire,
Zutisme est le vrai nom du cercle! (*Charles Cros*) En vérité,

L'autorité c'est moi! C'est moi l'autorité.
(*Jacquet*) Personne au piano! C'est fâcheux que l'on perde
Son temps, Mercier, jouez *Le Joyeux vio* . . . (*Rimbaud*) Ah! merde!

Rimbaud, it will be seen, was tiring even of the set into which he had temporarily settled. He had already antagonised all the respectable, beginning with Lepelletier, whom he addressed contemptuously as an "excreter of ink" and "saluter of the dead" because he had seen him raise his hat to a funeral. When Lepelletier told him to be quiet, he grasped a knife from the table and threatened him. For this, Lepelletier, more than a little jealous, had his revenge when the Parnassians trooped to the first performance of a one-act play by Glatigny, who, mortally ill, was still making spasmodic appearances in Paris without a sou to his name. Reviewing the play in a periodical, Lepelletier wrote under a pen name that amongst the bevy of writers was "the Saturnine poet Paul Verlaine, who gave his arm to a charming young person named Mlle Rimbaud", thus beginning the gossip which was to end in Verlaine's ostracism.

Lepelletier was an obvious butt; too obvious perhaps to be worth Rimbaud's notice; but the boy was soon extending his field, stretching himself at full length on a seat in the poets' cafés, feigning sleep or grunting scornfully from time to time when he did not care for the poem someone was reciting. Such behaviour from a mere child who would normally be expected to listen wide-eyed had the charm of novelty, especially to those lacking the moral courage to express their true feelings, but as the number of victims increased, the fun wore thin and Rimbaud's contemptuous attitude appeared first tedious then unendurable. He began to be cold-shouldered.

The first open sign of disapproval came when Fantin-Latour proceeded with his projected *Hommage à Baudelaire* as a companion picture to his *Hommage à Delacroix*. The composition suffered one setback after another. Verlaine insisted that Rimbaud should be included as a Baudelaire enthusiast and a poet who was successfully assuming the mantle of the master. Leconte de Lisle thereupon refused to sit. Then Banville withdrew, Rimbaud having upset even his equanimity. Finally Mérat, who found Valade's admiration for Rimbaud tiresome, retired; he took part in the opening sittings reluctantly but delivered an ultimatum after listening impatiently to Verlaine and Rimbaud, who spent most of the time in verbal sparring, Rimbaud criticising one thing after another in laconic tones which were too much like Mérat's own form of interjection to be bearable. Eventually Mérat declared that he would not sit with him; Fantin-Latour must choose between him and the inseparables. The picture then lost its last remnant of original purpose, to include "*Les Trois*", and became according to the sitters *Dîner des Poètes*, according to their critics *Repas des Communards*. Eventually the name *Coin de Table* was agreed, Mérat's head being replaced by a pot of flowers. It is a poor picture, Fantin-Latour's gift not being for portraiture. Rimbaud in particular suffered, his portrait being an absurdly romanticised unlikeness.

By this time Rimbaud's attempts to exhaust the possibilities of alcohol were proving unhappy; he had not the head for it and felt sick and quarrelsome instead of god- or devil-like. In some such spasm of angry disappointment he broke with Cabaner on the grounds that he drank milk; and departed, having as a final gesture of disgust used the current milk bottle as a receptacle for urine.

His choice of homes narrowed as his reputation spread—and it was a small world he lived in—and narrowed still further when, Cros having offered shelter, he tore up and used as toilet paper the pages of an expensive album particularly prized by his host. He also, if Mathilde is to be believed, doctored Cros' drink with sulphuric acid to express his displeasure at the criticism of his use of the album. But as the good-natured Cros merely asked him to leave and met him afterwards from time to time without recriminations, it would seem that Mathilde allowed an understandable malevolence to lead her too far.

Verlaine was hard put to it to know where to place the boy. Before the coming of Rimbaud he had found himself treated coolly in certain quarters of the Parnasse. Leconte de Lisle's demand for the banishment of every Communard included Verlaine; indeed, Verlaine was at the top of the list as being an intemperate drinker and far too good a poet. In the diminished circle at Boulevard des Invalides it would be difficult to say which name, Verlaine or Hugo, blurted out by an unthinking youngster, caused the lines to compress the deeper at the side of the great man's austere but slightly flabby mouth; the irritating apparition of the returned Hugo acclaimed Prince of Poets and receiving the despised plaudits of the crowd could with an effort be dismissed with a shrug of the well-tailored shoulders and an expression which the few disciples would interpret as one of benevolent pity; the mention of Verlaine, possibly the greater danger (for Leconte de Lisle was not without acumen), brought out the judge on his bench, fingers tipped: this loose-living rascal would assuredly end on the scaffold; he had been given his chance but . . . And the master waved away with the graceful if rather pudgy right hand all further consideration of "this animal". Anatole France had gone to Versailles when the Commune took control of the city and on his return proclaimed his detestation of those "*fripouillards*" the Communards; and France was then even more of a power in the Parnasse, having managed to quarrel with Leconte de Lisle without losing his place on the selection committee.

In short, "I have too many enemies—why, God knows!—at Lemerre's to go there any more", complained Verlaine pathetically. He was a little too fond of seeing enemies where they did not exist and he exaggerated here, but it was true enough that he had backed the wrong political horse, had written excessively un-Parnassian poetry (copies of *La Bonne Chanson*, officially published the next year, had found their way into disapproving quarters) and had been, openly, living an un-Parnassian life before his marriage. He now, by his association with Rimbaud, gave the envious and disapproving a handle which they used with relish.

By the end of the year, after going the rounds of the more long-suffering friends, Rimbaud had made sure that he and Verlaine were virtually isolated. The last dinner of the *vilains Bonshommes* (the "*Zutistes*" of Cros not yet having found general favour) that year was held over a wine shop on the corner of rue Bonaparte and rue du Vieux-Colombine facing Place Saint-Sulpice. All went well until the meal was over and a poet, Jean Aicard according to most reports, began to read his latest work. Rimbaud, who had as usual drunk more than he could master, disliked the poem as he disliked most of the poems he had heard read in Paris. He expressed his disapproval by an unmistakable "*merde*" every time Aicard came to the end of a line. At first the company tried not to notice him, listening with what must have been a comical over-attention to the reciting poet. But Rimbaud was not to be discouraged; his "*merdes*" grew louder and louder until the general pretence that he was silent, was not even there, collapsed. Carjat told him to be quiet. Rimbaud said loudly that he would stop for no one; he continued to punctuate the poem with his one-word comment. Carjat took hold of him, shook him and threatened to teach him his manners. At this Rimbaud leapt from the table, rushed to a corner of the room where Verlaine had leaned his sword-stick, drew the sword, advanced menacingly on Carjat and wounded him in the hand. He was then carried bodily by a burly painter to his room and thrown on the bed, where he at once slept.

Verlaine, meanwhile, was warned that the boy must be kept from all future gatherings; he would be welcome as usual, not Rimbaud. His reaction was an angry both or none.

3

From this time their ostracism was almost complete. In the new year of 1872 Verlaine rented a room for Rimbaud in rue Campagne-Première and their society there and in the cafés was restricted virtually to the young Forain (Gavroche to them), Blémont, Richepin and Cros if he happened to be present—that is to say he would not, like most others, go away or move his seat when they came into a café.

The view generally held of the disgraced couple was that, as Mérat had said, Rimbaud was an intolerable young hooligan who had bewitched Verlaine. This view was natural at the time —one would have had to be a most exceptional man to see beyond it—but it will not do now. Rimbaud behaved like a young "spiv" of today but he was not a spiv and his behaviour was due to something other than mere nastiness. He came to Paris to make a name as poet—a great name; he had good reason for his hopes, he believed rightly that his work was remarkable and he had been encouraged by Verlaine to expect a remarkable welcome. What he found was quite different; he was welcomed, but not as the eighth wonder of the world, one who would revolutionise poetry; he was treated with affectionate curiosity as just another of the sensations which stirred parts of Paris from time to time, a Glatigny rhyming at the Alcazar, a rat with two heads, the novelty being all. One or two men excepted, no real interest was shown in his work, and his theory of elevating the poet to a seer through deliberate self-abandonment to every experience was received with tolerant smiles as a passing extravagance of youth.

Simultaneously he discovered, with what emotions may be imagined, that these people who declined politely to take him seriously were not as he had imagined them from the intellectual desert of Charleville, that life in Paris at the very heart of the literary world was little more than a frivolous enlargement of that first dinner at rue Nicolet, that it consisted in the main of men talking cleverly but without conviction, of some giant game that all were wittily engaged in. Banville revealed himself as a clown, a trickster, Leconte de Lisle as a sham, and almost all the men with whom Verlaine was surrounded appeared as pale shadows of one or the other. Their conversation infuriated the boy as a mess of gossip, insincerity and spite, their work as rubbishy. For to value the work by the man was instinctive, and it took a matter of weeks only for Rimbaud to reject the entire Parnassian theory and attitude. The Parnassians, he saw, lived in a world of cosy ideals where all was beauty, order and reason, their poetry a bloodless abstraction.

Any talented boy with the strength of mind to resist the flattery of attention from older men might have gone as far. But at this point Rimbaud parts company with all; for to himself he was Rimbaud, the great Rimbe, he was right, they were wrong, the entire literary world of Paris was wrong except one man, whom he would save to be his companion in greatness. So thinking, with next to no sense of humour, with no head for liquor and an inexhaustible supply of moral courage, he began to show this world what he thought of it; he made himself impossible as Vincent van Gogh was to make himself impossible—for the two men, outwardly so different, had much in common. His reaction to insult, as he saw it, took the form of an unparalleled rudeness. It was a youthful reaction—he was only seventeen in October— the reaction of a boy who became quarrelsome in his cups, who burned to parade his contempt for the world he had mistakenly envied, and whose arrogant belief in his greatness drove him to court this world's dislike as a necessary part of his suffering; the poet, he had said, must seek every possible experience of love, pain and madness, and what greater pain could he discover than ostracism by the gods of yesterday—was not this a form of "inexpressible torture"?

And the man he had picked out, wisely, as the one great contemporary poet, the man he had most unwisely "*pris l'engagement de le rendre à son état primitif de fils du Soleil*", the "infatuated" Verlaine, what is to be said of him? Verlaine thought that Rimbaud was the most wonderful person he had ever met. Angel or devil? Verlaine was to ask himself that question for the rest of his life, answering first this then that; but whichever he decided, Rimbaud remained head and shoulders above other men as poet, in force of intellect, strength of character, beauty of looks and, when he chose, charm of manner. To Verlaine, who was deficient in three of these qualities, and too modest to claim the other two, the boy seemed marvellous in almost all he did. Almost, for Verlaine was neither blind nor a fool. But one does not cease to love when the loved one behaves badly; the convivial Verlaine was embarrassed and unhappy when his friends were insulted by Rimbaud, but he understood something of the reasons for it and his chief feeling was irritation that they had not the perception to see the boy as the wonder he was. He knew; he had read, seen, heard; if they could see only a conceited young puppy, so much the worse for them. For him, he chose to live fully for the first time in his life.

These bold thoughts were not consistent with life in rue Nicolet, but consistency did not interest this impetuous man; sufficient for him was the good of the moment whether it was come by in a café with Rimbaud or in bed with Mathilde. Nobody was willing to play his game; Mathilde, Mme Mauté and M. Mauté continued to protest in their different ways against the association with the young monster; Rimbaud for his part, determined to save a great poet and companion in spiritual adventure from the living death of suburban domesticity, threw spanner after spanner into the works in the shape of caustic remarks whenever Verlaine said he would have to be going home. Verlaine, eternally hopeful of getting the best of both worlds, eternally self-deceptive, parried as best he could these attempts to force him into an unpleasant decision; why, he wondered, should he have to choose between a sensual love for Mathilde with a home to which he could retire at any moment, and a romantic love for Rimbaud with a glorious future as poet?

The birth of his son Georges at the end of October swung the balance heavily in Mathilde's direction; for a few weeks he became the model husband and father. But Rimbaud was not to be denied; and what Rimbaud had to say about a reconciliation by the good offices of baby fingers and a baby smile was too frightfully true to escape the proudest of parents.

He recommended "deranging his senses", which, hashish having so lamentably failed, boiled down to absinthe and plenty of it. Rimbaud had not a sou, but Verlaine, generous to a fault, paid for everything, merely asking his mother whenever he ran short. In this manner the francs sped on their way and Verlaine returned home drunk many a night, and truculent too. Stung by the jibes of Rimbaud, he faced the shortcomings of his life with Mathilde; reproaches followed, and sometimes blows, before insensibility came and he slept to wake without knowledge of what he had done and, when told, to apologise abjectly.

In January, a few days after the scene at the *vilains bonshommes* dinner and following a night of threats by a drunken Verlaine, Mathilde told her parents what had been going on in her portion of the house. They were appalled—a little surprising, this, since mother and daughter spent most of the day together. They acted immediately, sent Mathilde to the south, shut Verlaine out of the house and refused to give him her address.

For Verlaine did not accept the liberty freely offered him; three parts emotion, he was instantly struck to the heart; his conscience reproached him for villainy; he could think of nothing but the happy times he and Mathilde had passed together, of the security of their home, the child lost to him. He besieged the house in a panic, demanding to know where his wife was. His letters would be forwarded, that was the only satisfaction he could get. He wrote, begging Mathilde to come back.

When Rimbaud had been sent away, Mathilde replied, she would return. And when Verlaine showed signs of resisting she threatened him with a legal separation. This so much alarmed him that he gave way; Rimbaud should go. By March Rimbaud was back in Charleville and the Verlaine household had been set up again.

4

Mathilde had made the further stipulation that Verlaine and Rimbaud should not correspond. This promise, made under duress, Verlaine promptly broke; and although he had given way to his wife he privately held it against her and intended to right the matter as soon as possible. Meanwhile he extracted a certain pleasure from his dilemma, the mystery-loving side of him revelling in the situation. Thus he is found instructing Rimbaud to send his "*martyriques*" letters to the rue Lécluse so that the elder Mme Verlaine might the more readily part with money for his keep at Charleville and eventually support the idea of his return, while his letters "*touchant les revoir, prudences etc.*" should go to Forain's new studio on Quai d'Anjou in the house where Baudelaire had lived. No doubt he enjoyed himself crossing Paris in search of secret missives; no doubt he persuaded himself that

Mathilde would open the letters if sent to rue Nicolet; certainly he feared her discovery of their plans to meet again. But as he invariably carried all the letters back to rue Nicolet and left them where they could easily be read, his elaborate precautions disclose themselves for what they were, a game that might have been played by two rather silly schoolboys.

His letters are on a par with his behaviour, peppered with "*merdes*" and talking with absurd gusto of the "*joies, affres, hypocrisies, cynismes*" they would enjoy together and of the "*tigerish* things" they would do to the villain in chief, M. Mauté, whom Verlaine discerned behind Mathilde's firm stand. Filled too with penny-paper mystery heroics: "*Certes, nous nous verrons! Quand? Attendre un peu! Nécéssités dures! Opportunités roides! Soit! Et merde pour les unes comme merde pour les autres! Et comme merde pour moi!— et pour toi!*" He was having the time of his life and at the same moment—very cunning this, he prided himself—living up as he thought to Rimbaud's determination that they should descend to the depths before rising to the heights; doing his best to earn the title of "*fils du soleil*". It scarcely convinces readers today and did not convince the reader then. Yet the only scrap of Rimbaud's replies (mentioned by Mathilde) is on a similar level, distinguished by a row of nine "*merdes*" in a few lines.

Rimbaud, however, was at least practical. Verlaine, finding money hard to come by to send to Charleville, bent to the desperate expedient of taking a job in an insurance office and had the temerity to suggest that his Rimbe might do likewise. Rimbaud was shocked by this surrender to bourgeois influence the moment his back was turned, hurt too by the implication that Verlaine was tiring of supporting him. He dismissed the blasphemy in a few words. "Work is farther from me than my nail is from my eye," he said with a string of "*merdes*": "When you see me reduced to the point of eating *merde* you won't think any longer that I'm too expensive to feed."

To this there was for Verlaine, a Verlaine already finding domesticity decidedly dull without the alternative electric shocks of Rimbaud, one answer only—surrender: "Love me, protect me, trust me. Being very weak, I've much need of kindness." And he made no more bones about getting Rimbaud back to Paris; he and Forain, he assured his friend, had moved all the belongings from "rue Campe" (Campagne-Première, where he had last

rented a room for Rimbaud) and would put them safely in a
room he was taking in the Hôtel de Cluny in rue Victor Cousin.

By May, Rimbaud was back again and he and Verlaine took
up where they had left off, or so it seemed at first. They began
to speak and write with rather too much dotting of i's and
crossing of t's of mysterious goings-on in the Hôtel de Cluny as
in Rimbaud's earlier room. It is obvious, reading between the
lines, that they were hard driven to devise new methods of
deranging the senses. Others have found a similar difficulty;
monotony will creep in. Hence the need for mystification, to
which Verlaine lent himself with a will: "Ah, but it wasn't at
all what you thought it was!" he wrote at the end of a sonnet
brimful of horrid hints, and one can see the finger to the up-
turned nose and the schoolboy gleam in those greenish eyes.

To hear Verlaine in this mood one might think that he and
Rimbaud spent their time in one long orgy, and if his listener
or reader were naïve enough to believe him, he would be
delighted. But alongside this nonsense ran something very
different. There are poets who write, talk and live as dedicated
men—Mallarmé provides a good example—but Verlaine was
not of this kind; he did his work, his talking and thinking at the
table of a noisy café, walking crowded streets or perched on the
bed of Rimbaud's wretched room, and his behaviour in public
was chiefly that of a man dedicated to drink and fooling. A less
serious man would be hard to find, one could reasonably assume;
his life since the coming of Rimbaud seemed to consist mainly
in drinking-parties and quarrels with his wife and father-in-law.
Nevertheless, between them he and Rimbaud were to change the
face of French poetry, and not by accident; they worked for it.
The compulsion came more often than not from Rimbaud, for
he was a serious young man. But Verlaine contributed the
experience and the prestige; he was, after all, the "seer" picked
out by Rimbaud at Charleville to be the leader of a new school.

So they talked over their drinks, talked in Rimbaud's room,
talked in Forain's apartment, talked in the cold, talked on empty
stomachs, talked, talked, talked sober and not so sober but
almost always to the purpose. An occasional listener who did not
know them well would be unable to recognise a purpose, he
would distinguish only an apparently aimless bickering, but the
purpose was there, disguised as Verlaine loved to disguise the

serious, and its first results appeared soon after Rimbaud came
back to Paris.

Their main problem lay in the long-accepted laws of prosody,
laws so restrictive that French poetry had in the course of the
centuries fallen sufficiently behind the true life of the French
language to demand a pronunciation differing widely from that
of everyday speech. As a result poetry came to be regarded in
France as an artificial pleasure, and was relegated, except for the
small "literary" class, to the gorgeously bound uncut volumes
dustily placed behind glass and mahogany. It bore no relation
to life and, the French saving their thoughts and energies for
tangible rewards, its exponents had their eyes on the Academy
rather than on any possible poetical immortality.

The Parnassians' unorthodoxy was confined to verbal dexterity
and emphasis on the rhyme. To Verlaine and Rimbaud this
emphasis, which Banville had hoped would disguise the monotony of the line, in practice added to it, the weight being always
in the same place, and went far to restrict the poet's message to
the actual rhyming words. They set themselves to erase the
barrier between poet and reader by using French as then
spoken, by throwing the emphasis where the sense lay, and in
general by breaking all the laws. Rimbaud, the obviously
adventurous one, began to write *Illuminations*. Verlaine confined
himself to the intimate, personal note. He looks, for instance, at
the sleeping Rimbaud and expresses simply but profoundly the
fear and the wonder known to so many;

> Ce soir je m'étais penché sur ton sommeil,
> Tout ton corps dormait chaste sur l'humble lit,
> Et j'ai vu, comme un qui s'applique et qui lit,
> Ah! j'ai vu que tout est vain sous le soleil!
>
> Qu'on vive, ô quelle délicate merveille,
> Tant notre appareil est une fleur qui plie!
> O pensée aboutissant à la folie!
> Va, pauvre, dors! moi, l'effroi pour toi m'éveille.
>
> Ah! misère de t'aimer, mon frêle amour
> Qui vas respirant comme on expire un jour!
> O regard fermé que la mort fera tel!
>
> O bouche qui ris en songe sur ma bouche,
> En attendant l'autre rire plus farouche!
> Vite, éveille-toi. Dis, l'âme est immortelle?

Again, later, he turns from sonnet to song and sings with a deceptive *naïveté* of a sensation common to all sensitive people:

> Il pleure dans mon cœur
> Comme il pleut sur la ville.
> Quelle est cette langueur
> Qui pénètre mon cœur?
>
> O bruit doux de la pluie
> Par terre et sur les toits!
> Pour un cœur qui s'ennuie,
> O le chant de la pluie!
>
> Il pleure sans raison
> Dans ce cœur qui s'écœure.
> Quoi! nulle trahison?
> Ce deuil est sans raison.
>
> C'est bien la pire peine
> De ne savoir pourquoi,
> Sans amour et sans haine,
> Mon cœur a tant de peine.

5

Their one steadfast companion during these months was Verlaine's "little brown cat" Forain, two years older than Rimbaud. Although unconcerned with the need to plumb every sensation, Forain managed to do so well for himself in this line that of the three he was regarded as the wildest. He and Rimbaud were much together, and thirteen years later, when Forain had become the most renowned caricaturist of modern times, he remembered vividly "the days when we used to wait for you, Rimbaud and I, in that little café in rue Drouot, smoking our clay pipes and wetting our whistles with plenty of bitter-curaçao".

Verlaine, in other words, remained so much the family and business man, having somehow kept his job, Rimbaud acquiescing lugubriously in this lip service to Mammon since one must eat and still more drink, that his friends had often to cross the river to collect him. There were few scenes at rue Nicolet; Mathilde said later that she did not suspect Rimbaud's return to Paris—a confession which tells its tale about Verlaine's behaviour at home. And Verlaine, far from entertaining a wish to break with Mathilde, had a positive terror of it; he was simply enjoying domesticity and Rimbaud in piquant snatches and was pained when he struck obstacles. Moreover, there were omens in the air that made him feel the need of an ally even if the ally happened to be his wife. He was not without prescience, could read in Rimbaud the signs of increasing impatience, and scented the coming of a crisis.

He was right; Rimbaud was becoming impatient, and not only with Paris. Signs of frailty in his companion were disturbingly evident and had been ever since "Love me, protect me, trust me." These were scarcely the words of a superman, and Rimbaud, who did not hoodwink himself, not at least in the obvious way, began from time to time to look darkly at his innocently happy companion: was he at heart just another empty, smooth-speaking Parnassian, lost in the fleshpots; and why did he not leave the woman instead of complaining about her—were some suburban ties still unbroken there? At such times he could scarcely speak civilly to Verlaine, feeling that he had committed sacrilege in revealing his destiny to one of the herd.

A sensualist, too. For Rimbaud was above all the son of his mother, an implacable Puritan, and it was agony to his soul, gulping down noxious liquors which made him sick and quarrelsome but enduring all for the cause of future spiritual glory, to see this impossible Verlaine draining glass after glass with a disgusting relish as if he really liked the revolting stuff, and not one thought of a desperate duty in his feather-brained mind. What kind of soul mate was this! At times he despaired. At other times he was savagely angry, for hell has no fury like the fury of the earnest young man foiled. His irritation boiled over one night. He, Cros and Verlaine were sitting drinking. He said suddenly to Verlaine, holding a knife over the table, "Hold your hands out." To his disgust Verlaine was fool enough, as Rimbaud saw trust, to obey. Furious, he dragged the blade across the open wrists, and when the hurt and startled Verlaine leapt up and ran off, pursued him into the street and hacked his leg.

This was how Mathilde learned of Rimbaud's return; Verlaine laughed off the limp and the bandaged wrists as fencing wounds, but the Cros brothers were visitors at rue Nicolet and Charles had been horrified by Rimbaud's apparently senseless attack. He explained. There was immediate trouble, trouble which ended in Mathilde locking the bedroom door to her husband: he must choose, she intimated.

But before Verlaine and Mathilde could come to a conclusion Rimbaud had acted. Often enough he despised and almost hated Verlaine, but who else was there to keep him company? With Verlaine he could at least have his way; besides, a thrifty soul like his mother, he needed his cash; and he also knew well enough in affectionate moments that in Verlaine he had found an exceptionally generous, loving and obliging man. Above all, Verlaine was a great poet.

So Rimbaud swallowed the disadvantages of this excessively human disciple and put him to the test. One day early in July Verlaine, walking to the chemist to buy medicine for Mathilde, who had developed a sore throat, ran across his friend in the street. Rimbaud was carrying a letter which he had intended to leave at the house for Verlaine. It was to say that he was sick of Paris and intended to leave it at once.

Shocked, Verlaine asked when he was going. That moment, replied Rimbaud. Was Verlaine coming too? Verlaine hesitated: "What about my wife?" he asked. "To hell with your wife," said Rimbaud contemptuously.

That tone had never failed to make Verlaine feel ashamed of himself. He threw his misgivings overboard, turned and went off with Rimbaud.

Chapter Eleven

FOOLISH VIRGIN

1872-1873

I

THIS was the end of Verlaine's marriage, even the shadow of
it, yet none thought so at the time, he least of all. He did
not consider that he had left his wife, told her so a little
belatedly ("Don't grieve or cry. I'm in the middle of a bad
dream. I'll come back one day"), and remained for ever
after aggrieved that such an intention could be attributed to
him.

And curiously enough he meant what he said. He was a man
of impulse, but of what he would call calculation too; he went
off with Rimbaud without a moment's notice yet not positively
without thought; he had a habit of reasoning which possessed as
its main supports an inveterate optimism and a firm bias
towards his wellbeing. His mind had run something like this:
that absence made the heart grow fonder; that any little rift
between himself and Mathilde would close itself automatically
when each learned the other's value; that she could not suffer
hardship since she was in no way financially dependent on him
at the moment; that her time was very much given to the child,
who would in a year or so be of real interest to him and would
constitute a strong and necessary bond between them; that he,
Verlaine, was a man who needed a home as pivot, even if he
did not happen to be living in it for the while, and who would
never dream of abandoning it; that there had been rumours in
Paris of a fresh drive against Communards still at large; and
finally that with Rimbaud he would devote himself to becoming
a great poet—had not Rimbaud promised as much?—and this,
with his consequent fame and fortune, would benefit all and all
would be proud of him.

Mathilde, and still more her father, to Verlaine's everlasting
chagrin, failed absolutely to follow this method of reasoning
("You never understood me", he was to complain again and

again); all they could see was a married man who without a word left his wife and child, to rollick off with a dissolute boy. To her the only other fact of moment was the unavoidable, almost unforgivable truth that his chief pleasure was no longer to be with her. For there was the small matter which even Verlaine could not blink, that he wanted to go with Rimbaud and expected to enjoy himself enormously playing the carefree truant.

Having taken the plunge, there was no feeling in him at first other than delight in a lark. He passed the mood on to Rimbaud, who could be young enough on occasion, and they shot off light-heartedly, Verlaine insisting that Rimbaud meet his aunt at Arras, his uncle at Fampoux, his cousins at Lécluse—a wish which suggests that he could see no harm in the friendship or the journey.

However, they got no further than Arras police station. Arriving at the railway station in the early hours they waited in the buffet until they could call on Verlaine's aunt. But the spirit of the lark was still strongly in them and the sight and sound of the respectable men sitting at the tables set it roaring. Rimbaud began to speak in an audible *sotto voce* of crimes they had recently committed and Verlaine went one better with a loudly whispered reference to their break from jail. They were soon rewarded by the sight of two gendarmes entering the buffet, summoned by an alarmed counter hand, and Verlaine, feigning not to have seen them, expressed great disappointment that they had failed to "pull that job" and assured Rimbaud that they would have another crack at it the next day.

This was enough for the gendarmes, who took them in charge. At the magistrate's court the farce continued gaily, Rimbaud bursting into sobs and claiming protection from Verlaine, who he declared had led him astray. And when Verlaine was asked what he was doing in Arras he took a high line, showing his papers and announcing that, having been born in Metz, then annexed to Germany, he had the right to choose between German and French nationality and: "upon my soul, after this illegal detention I doubt whether I shall continue to be a Frenchman".

By this time the magistrate had begun to scent a hoax and told the gendarmes to escort the two friends to the next train for

Paris. But Verlaine, by then thoroughly in his part, protested that they had been forcibly removed in the midst of their breakfast; he demanded the right to finish it. The gendarmes escorted them back to the restaurant, where they finished their breakfast glee-fully, and by evening they were back in Paris. They crossed at once to the Gare de l'Est and took the first train for Charleville. There they looked up Bretagne, who provided a horse and cart that same evening to take them across the frontier into Belgium. The next day they were in Brussels.

For a time the light-hearted mood held. Tireless walkers both, they explored a large area round the city. They did not care much where they went or what they saw; movement was its own reward, a movement paralleled by the activity of their minds. For they were possessed by exhilaration, free to go where they pleased, free to think and talk as they pleased. Verlaine felt as though he had been born again, watching Rimbaud, who had shot up in the last months, striding along like a young god, listening to the prophecies, surely inspired, of words used as words had never been used before, of a literature originated by the two of them. He was never to forget those days on the roads of Belgium, he and Rimbaud "intoxicated to a frenzy with art, talking and living art". He felt himself in the presence of genius and for the first time felt the possibility of genius in himself. He did not always go the whole way with his daring companion, but this too had its charm, the charm of defying one principle after another with a catch of the breath. "Atrociously delicious", he said long afterwards, and one understands his feeling; caught up by enthusiasm, he would out-devil Rimbaud and out-prophesy him; he was eloquent on their future greatness; all was possible when he felt the sun on his face, drew breath after breath of country air, knew himself to be absolutely unrestricted and had by his side the "devilishly seductive" boy leading him from one glorious fantasy to another.

Practically, these rambles brought from him a small series of poems on the Belgian countryside in which the mood of the writer is reflected by the scene. Yet one of the most delightful and technically one of the most brilliant poems he was ever to write was inspired by Saint-Gilles Fair in Brussels itself, where Verlaine, strongly taken by the roundabouts, came straight back to their hotel to write:

Tournez, tournez, bons chevaux de bois,
Tournez cent tours, tournez mille tours,
Tournez souvent et tournez toujours,
Tournez, tournez au son des hautbois.

.   .   .   .

C'est ravissant comme ça vous soûle,
D'aller ainsi dans ce cirque bête!
Bien dans le ventre et mal dans la tête,
Du mal en masse et du bien en foule.

Tournez, tournez, sans qu'il soit besoin
D'user jamais de nuls éperons,
Pour commander à vos galops ronds,
Tournez, tournez, sans espoir de foin.

But there were less happy moments. Rimbaud, not yet eighteen, could not always avoid being his age when for the first time in his life he wandered where he liked, expressed any thought that came into his head and could forget mothers, punishments and the question of where the next sou would come from. In these moods he was charming, irresistible. But he was a man of action too, a dedicated soul; all he did must further the grand design, all things, pleasures and pains, had their purpose. And when the taskmaster bade him examine his soul and the soul of his companion trouble followed. Verlaine was obviously not a thorough-going *"fils du soleil"* and perhaps would never be one. He talked largely on occasion, but was not the truth less palatable, that he was just enjoying himself like any other philistine and without taking thought for the morrow? Worse still, it became plain that this man whom he had rescued from the spiritual death of domesticity had left Mathilde in body only, and that provisionally; the deluded creature was actually writing what he fondly hoped were secret messages to the woman. It became clear that Verlaine lacked the power to cut adrift from a hampering past; in some inexplicable fashion he continued to cherish it.

Deluded creature perhaps; but in his sterner moments Rimbaud's opinion of his companion was even less charitable; he was dealing with a traitor who would have to be led the hard way. He became angry, an anger fed by subconscious envy of Verlaine's uncomplicated enjoyment of this hateful world. And

FOOLISH VIRGIN

Verlaine suffered, one foot still on rue Nicolet, one on Rimbaud, and the two drawing violently apart. Rimbaud could be unkind, none more so. No need to slash wrists, there were other and sharper ways of wounding; Verlaine's weaknesses were open to him, and in exasperation he began to play on them. The man was a masochist as well as all the rest, he discovered with a new contempt. Certainly he, Rimbaud, intended to be leader, but where was the glory in dominating a man who asked nothing better than to be dominated? The defrauded idealist—and there is none so implacable—set himself to frighten Verlaine out of his wits by practical jokes.

Verlaine spent wretched hours; all he asked were love, companionship, drink and time to write his poems, happy ones for preference. But the poems became mournful, sometimes querulous.

> O triste, triste était mon âme
> A cause, à cause d'une femme.
>
> Je ne me suis pas consolé
> Bien que mon cœur s'en soit allé,
>
> Bien que mon cœur, bien que mon âme
> Eussent fui loin de cette femme.
>
> Je ne me suis pas consolé,
> Bien que mon cœur s'en soit allé.
>
> Et mon cœur, mon cœur trop sensible
> Dit à mon âme: Est-il possible,
>
> Est-il possible,—le fût-il,—
> Ce fier exil, ce triste exil?
>
> Mon âme dit à mon cœur: Sais-je
> Moi-même, que nous veut ce piège
>
> D'être présents bien qu'exilés,
> Encore que loin en allés?

Another matter was causing him misgiving. He sent this and other poems to Blémont, the man who had printed earlier poems in the journal he had founded, *La Renaissance littéraire*, the man who had been the first to assure him after the collapse of the

G

177

Commune that he thought none the worse of him. Now nothing happened; Blémont admired the new poems, would have been proud to print them, but . . . The very marrow began to desert Verlaine's bones; he forgot the trails of mystery laid so industriously by Rimbaud and himself, he forgot Rimbaud's behaviour in Paris, he saw only an innocent man trying to reach infinity and write deathless poetry by the side of a loved friend or, in another mood, a man on a harmless spree, whichever sounded best. But innocent. And in his absence, while his back was turned, this horror! His imagination rushed to the most disagreeable conclusion; he was being cut by his friends, his career as poet was broken, Paris, wife, child, home were all barred to him. And he could not discuss his fears with Rimbaud; Rimbaud had a short way with those who indulged in despondent imaginings. He had to keep an anguished silence.

Then, suddenly, came a note from Mathilde; she had followed him to Brussels with her mother, she was in the hotel from which he had first written to her.

At that moment Verlaine was perhaps feeling one of his revulsions against life with Rimbaud; he was certainly suffering severely from lack of sex; and when, entering the hotel bedroom, he saw Mathilde stretched invitingly on the bed he joined her without thought, without any sensation but joyful relief.

Mathilde had come to take him from Rimbaud, but the method she used made absolutely certain that he would not go. When they at last got up from the bed Verlaine made the motions of surrender but with a sinking heart and a growing sense of shame. And when Mathilde was fully dressed and he saw before him not a beautiful body but a pert and rather silly young Parisienne, his guilt stared him in the face. He agreed to meet the triumphant girl and her mother on the train for Paris in a few hours and he went out to find and tell Rimbaud. Until the train was due he and Rimbaud sat together drinking, then he joined the train and travelled in silence with the two women as far as the frontier. There they had to change coaches. When Mathilde and her mother had found their new seats there was no sign of Verlaine. He did not appear until the train began to move, and then only on the platform. Mme Mauté leaned out of the window and urged him to jump in. He simply shook his head and the train steamed off without him.

It has been said that Rimbaud was in another compartment of the train from Brussels to the frontier. The practical joke that is not really funny certainly bears all the marks of Rimbaud, as does Verlaine's shamefaced silence in the train. But Verlaine's note to Mathilde suggests that he is rejoining Rimbaud in Brussels and one can easily imagine a contemptuous last command from Rimbaud at the café: "Oh, go off with your precious woman—she's all you're fit for!"—which would send Verlaine to the train but would effectually prevent him from reaching Paris.

Before leaving the frontier for Brussels Verlaine sent off what for him was a savage note to his wife: "Misérable fée carotte, princesse souris, punaise qu'attendent les deux doigts et le pot. Vous m'avez fait tout; vous avez peut-être tué le cœur de mon ami. Je rejoins Rimbaud, s'il veut encore de moi après cette trahison que vous m'avez fait faire."

Then, more calmly, he began in *Birds in the Night* to sublimate this dramatic rejection of his wife. The poem, though unrealistic, was one of the most moving he was ever to compose.

2

The effect of Mathilde's foray was to bind Verlaine firmly to Rimbaud. For some time to come, when the boy was difficult or disagreeable, Verlaine could tell himself that he had the right to be all that and more. Naïvely, but nicely too, he attributed his own feelings to Rimbaud. Not that he had abandoned Mathilde; it was not long before he was proposing enthusiastically that she join him and Rimbaud in Brussels in a *ménage à trois*. Rimbaud, he assured her, was doing very well there—a bait scarcely calculated to entice her. Actually she was leaving his letters unopened, a chilly procedure unknown to Verlaine, who wrote on outlining his plans.

Rimbaud might have been doing well in Brussels, though there is no sign of it, but Verlaine unquestionably was not. He could find no work, and his mother, though taking his side in the dispute, was not being very forthcoming with the funds. Early in September, therefore, they moved to London, Verlaine believing that he could find work there, knowing that he would meet Communard friends in exile and, having heard much about

London from Blémont, curious to see it. Moreover, his extensive reading in English literature had made him something of an anglophile; he had not failed to see part of himself in the English lyrical poets.

Rimbaud's reasons for agreeing to the move—and doubtless he had the major say—remain uncertain. But he was anxious to master as many languages as possible so that he could write a universal poetry, and Verlaine, who liked to flourish his knowledge of English by incorrect phrases in his letters, had whetted his appetite. In any case he was restless and yearned for fresh worlds to conquer. Brussels seemed even less conquerable—or worth conquering—than Paris. And as one can despise and feel the lack of a thing at the same moment, the social oblivion in Brussels would contrast unpleasantly with the attention he had first received in Paris. He may have expected better things from London. It may even be that he hoped to find there new methods of deranging the senses; he was young enough and innocent enough for that.

They crossed from Ostend on a Saturday, a rough crossing which did not disturb them, slept at Dover and were up early walking through the town and along the cliffs. About eight o'clock, feeling hungry, they looked for breakfast and found most places closed, the others turning them away with looks of suspicion. Only when they ran across a French interpreter did they get served, and then only by declaring themselves bona fide travellers. That, says Verlaine, "was my first experience of an English Sunday".

In London they found a room in Soho, then called on Régamey, who had a studio in Langham Street. Régamey remembered the *vilains bonshommes* dinners vividly and gave Verlaine a hearty welcome. He thought that the manner of the unexpected visitor was charming "and although most scantily provided for in the linen department he didn't show the slightest sign of embarrassment". Rimbaud also "didn't exactly sparkle with elegance", which was a kind way of saying that both looked like tramps, as a sketch by Régamey was to show, a sketch of them walking the streets, a policeman pointedly ignoring their existence.

Verlaine was in high spirits; he fancied his English, quite without cause, he was delighted to be in the country of the poets he admired; and in his vague optimistic way hoped for good from the change. It was true that his poetry was to appeal more directly to the English than to his own countrymen, that the light ironical note was an English form of humour as was his forte of suggestion and avoidance of heavy emotion; but for the moment England, as represented by the London police, barmaids and dispensers of jobs, cast a chilly eye on the seedy man who proclaimed himself by his exuberant gestures as yet another political refugee.

He worked off some of his good spirits at Régamey's with a couple of satirical sketches to which, with Rimbaud's help, he attached clever but unkind parodies of Coppée, who, having won another success in the Paris theatre, was testing the generosity of his friends to breaking point. Régamey told them that Vermersch was about to get married—"insane", commented Verlaine with greater accuracy than he knew—and that they could probably take over his room in Howland Street. Within a week they were living a few steps from fashionable Fitzroy Square, and Verlaine, heading his letters 34-35 Howland Street, was full of mock complaints that the street numbers "instead of going by odds and evens fluttered about scandalously with every breath of wind".

Free to look about them, they sightsaw with a thoroughness, walking vast distances through and about the city. In the first few weeks they made the usual rounds of the tourist, with the difference that they did all on foot and that Rimbaud strode the streets with a shiny top-hat on his head which contrasted oddly with the shabby clothes below. They made themselves at home in the West End and City, examined the docks at Woolwich, walked through the Tower subway and the Thames tunnel, went over the Tower and Madame Tussaud's, stared at the children with blackened faces and strange rig-outs collecting farthings for Guy Fawkes Day, watched the changing of the Guard and the Lord Mayor's procession, listened to the orators in Hyde Park, visited the National Gallery and Wallace collection and one of the exhibitions at the French Gallery. Here, to their astonishment, they saw themselves on the wall where *Coin de Table* was hanging with the Impressionists. "Fantin for ever!" exclaimed Verlaine, vaunting his enlarged vocabulary—enlarged chiefly, however, by unprintable English words. They became regular theatregoers, listening to Offenbach and Hervé at the Alhambra, Shakespeare at the Queen's and Princess, Sheridan at the Vaudeville and the French players at the Royalty. And they were delighted with the popular minstrel shows, one of which specially pleased Verlaine because the clowns in a skit on the Jesuits "all looked like Leconte de Lisle!"

At first Verlaine was disappointed not to say horrified by the look of London, "as flat as a blackboard", and the Londoners, noisy, quarrelsome and unwashed—"the reek of humanity in the theatres!"; by the atrocious climate, thick grey skies, fog and "rain, rain, rain!"; and by the hypocritical life in this city "black as a crow, noisy as a duck, prudish *in the face of every kind of flaunting vice*, for ever drunken in spite of ridiculous tracts against insobriety". He realised quickly that the Sunday at Dover had been a dream of freedom compared with the shattering austerity of London: "passers-by dressed up in their Sunday best like savages, few cabs, *no carriages, not one! . . . Everything* closed. No trade. The letter boxes closed too. . . . No theatres open, naturally. . . . Oh! Very dull!" With stupefaction he heard a policeman threaten the bootblack who dared to ply his trade on the sabbath, saw policemen "watch in hand timing the opening and closing" of the few pubs and dining-rooms permitted to open from one until three and six until eleven.

And what meals they served in these eating-houses! "So-called oxtail soup" an abomination; "coffee PLAIN per cup" a ghastly mixture of milk and dried chicory; fish "horrible . . . all looking like octopus, soft, sticky and *slippery*"; gin "concentrated sewage water"; and, final insult to the man with a palate, "warm beer!" Nor was he less shocked by the places in which men and women were expected to enjoy their food and drink: the public houses with their slatternly, blowzy barmaids and taciturn barmen, the customers tippling furtively, jammed against one another at a bar and breathing foetid air, or, tiresomely loquacious, being thrust outside unceremoniously. And outside he looked with disgust at the dirt lying thickly everywhere, the garbage blowing about, the drunks reeling along the narrow pavements, the incessant brawls, the rags and beggars side by side with elegance and wealth. Even their tobacco was dirty, their cigars unfit to touch, and their matches . . . ! On English matches he became lyrical; they never lit, "*never*, you understand, *never*". He predicted a fortune for the first enterprising man to import French matches. He longed for the sparkle, the cleanliness, the good meals, the beauty of Paris and above all for the cafés where one could sit indefinitely over a drink and hear intelligent talk.

But within a week or two he began to change his mind. He was a perceptive man; the poet in him responded to the charm of London, so much less obvious than the beauty of Paris. He was a domestic man clinging to security the further removed he found himself from it; the cosy, homelike atmosphere of London which he saw as "a collection of small towns", an atmosphere in which dirt played its part, soothed him with its suggestion of safety in permanence. He was a man with a strong sense of humour; he found this echoed in the frequent exchanges between Londoners. He was a friendly man; the English, he thought, though less polite than his own people, were kind beneath an uncouth manner as the French were not. And, to see the matter from another angle, he was a man unaccustomed until he met Rimbaud to plain speech; he admired "the very great candour" of the English.

His first stay in England, Verlaine confessed later, "was of a rather frivolous nature, to use no stronger expression". But he was then writing for a special audience towards whom he adopted the manner of the reformed rake as being what was expected of him. The truth was less exciting: he and Rimbaud drank a fair amount, but not the unobtainable absinthe; their language was deliberately foul; they seem to have sampled opium in Limehouse following their reading of Baudelaire's translation of De Quincey, and if so this was their solitary success in the search for fresh experience of evil. If Verlaine tried it, the effects are unnoticeable in his life or work; he got more, no doubt, from patronising the prostitutes who to his amazement openly solicited in the main streets. In general, the lives of the two young men were harmless enough; if Verlaine failed to get work, it was not only for want of trying but because of his connection with the Communards, the competition among the many refugees, the indifference of his English and his dilapidated appearance which Rimbaud's top-hat merely emphasised.

From Verlaine, writing briskly to Lepelletier and Blémont, came one optimistic announcement after another: he was working hard, he was no lazy blackguard to live on women, he assured them. Positively, he proposed to write for two *"serious"* French newspapers being launched in London and for American newspapers there—"they pay well"; he also hoped to become a business man in spare moments, "employing myself in French correspondence" for a friend "at the head of a big business"; finally he had written some "extremely curious notes" on Belgium and was writing his travel sketches *Croquis Londiniens* which he pressed his Paris friends to print in their journals, both being editors. Little came of all this. Blémont and Lepelletier showed no eagerness to print anything of his, and their apologetic evasions led to anxious enquiries "who is for me and who against me?" which his few friends in Paris avoided as best they could; led also to sarcastic references to "the *nice* little poets who write *nice* little books on their *nice* little companions in exile", this chiefly because Richepin had attacked Jules Vallès, whom Verlaine had met in London. Mérat, whose withdrawal from *Coin de Table* still rankled, did not escape; it was not for another year, when Verlaine heard a rumour that he had hanged himself in the forest of Fontainebleau, that he was forgiven.

No money to be earned in Paris, that was clear; no money from big business either. Verlaine did in fact know a businessman: a relation, a M. Istace, who owned the Baccarat Crystal Glass Company of Hatton Garden, but there the matter rested. The newspapers also proved broken reeds: no dollars found their way into his pockets, one of the French newspapers never appeared and the other, though serious enough in its way, turned out to be Vermersch's *L'Avenir*, which did not survive the winter.

It is unlikely that these failures to earn a living—or, to be precise, a single halfpenny—weighed on Verlaine for more than an hour or two at a time. He could tell himself that he had done his best and, this said, could with a clear conscience spend much of his time enjoying with Rimbaud the novelties of the biggest city in the world at the expense of his ever-obliging mother. They saw a good deal of Régamey, Andrieu and Vermersch, joined their revolutionary and literary club, attended a club meeting on the first floor of a public house in Old Compton Street to honour the memory of Gautier, who had just died, and listened to a fiery speech on the martyrs of 1832, a speech which inspired Verlaine to write *Des Morts* for *L'Avenir*, a poem which did him no good on either side of the Channel; it merely convinced certain quarters in Paris that he was a dyed-in-the-wool Communard and made quite sure that the London police would report him to the police in Paris as one of the plotters against the Republic. His call on the Consul General to opt for French nationality (the first of October being the final date for those born in the lost departments) was, the Paris authorities might well have thought, a dubious compliment.

Verlaine spoke hopefully of a meeting with Swinburne, one of the advanced poets in French eyes, but this seems never to have taken place. He also spoke of meeting another "astonishing" poet, almost certainly the prodigy son of Ford Madox Brown, who was tutored by Andrieu and lived in Fitzroy Square. Whether he met any English writer of moment seems very doubtful; that he enjoyed himself is clear; he liked London more and more, liked the company he was keeping, he even found a café, the Café de la Sablonnerie et de Provence, in which he could write his letters and poems and from which he looked out on the life of Leicester Square, giving occasional horrified exclamations of "What drunkards!"

Leicester Square was his centre, for there were grouped the French cafés and "tolerable" eating-houses; a dreary centre with its border of "dirty trees in the middle of which is a zinc horse painted red, its rider—George IV I think—fallen to the ground". For the rest he and Rimbaud drank with their friends, talked with them, heard the barrel organs trundle out the serenade from Coppée's *Passant*, patronised the theatres and music halls, listened to concerts and walked, walked indefatigably.

Verlaine said at the time, "My life is entirely intellectual. I devote myself to poetry, to intellectual pursuits and to serious artistic conversations in a small group of artists and literary men"; and although this sounds unlikely in the light of the activities dealt with so far it was, though no more exact than the later apology for his "rather frivolous" existence in London, a good deal nearer the truth. In the midst of their apparently aimless life in Paris he and Rimbaud had talked poetry and written poetry. In London they did likewise, Rimbaud pressing insistently towards a poetry that should be absolutely modern. This he produced in his London sections of *Illuminations*. Verlaine too described his own work as being "more and more *modernistic*", and so in its way it was. In these months before the end of the year he wrote much of what was later to be published as *Romances sans Paroles*, an echo of the vogue for Mendelssohn in the London of those years; he wrote most of the poem about Mathilde which he first intended to call *La Mauvaise Chanson*, a better title than the eventual *Birds in the Night* which he took from Sullivan; he one day sat in a bar at the corner of Greek Street and Old Compton Street after watching the fair in Soho Square and wrote the now well-known *Dansons la gigue!*; and he composed *Green*, which was to be made popular by the settings of Debussy and Fauré.

3

Verlaine's contentment with life in London was marred by two things. First and least by Rimbaud's behaviour from time to time. Verlaine's letters are spattered with "geindres", a sure sign that Rimbaud had been whining, about him, about his friends, about shortage of money, about anything. The boy's usual way of speaking except in moments of enthusiasm was a cross between drawl and whine, lips barely opened, an exaggerated version of the manner of the Ardennais. In his good-humoured moments this formed part of his charm—one has only to remember the vogue of the "sulky" film star to understand how fascinating the quick and sharp-speaking Parisians found his slow, reluctant, blurred speech. But when Rimbaud was displeased—and he found much wrong with the world—the sulk lost its charm and degenerated into the whinings of an indulged prig. This pained Verlaine, who alternated between fears that he could never live up to his spiritually strait-laced companion and annoyance that he, his friends, and especially the amount of money provided by his mother, should be criticised.

But far more disturbing was the bad news from rue Nicolet. When he heard from Lepelletier in November that Mathilde was taking steps to obtain a legal separation Verlaine was shattered, or made a convincing show of it. He ought not to have been surprised, though he did not know that his letters were remaining unopened, but was undoubtedly shocked and his indignation was genuine enough, being merely the customary reaction to shock. So he is found protesting with all the conviction of injured virtue; and when Lepelletier told him that one of the grounds for the separation was to be the relations of the two friends he exploded in fury and alarm. He was writing a full statement of the case "in which I reduce the foul accusation to pulp" he declared; a statement which he believed would constitute a landmark in medical, psychological and legal studies. He would defend the case and call witnesses. He challenged any doctor to examine Rimbaud and himself and find them guilty of unnatural practices. As for his feeling for Rimbaud, his statement would show clearly and soberly "my very real, very profound and *very persevering* friendship for Rimbaud—I don't need to add *very pure*".

Agitated letters flew to Lepelletier, who had read in law. He was not too optimistic, but dropped hints that a *rapprochement* with Mathilde might not prove impossible if Verlaine would return to Paris. This Verlaine refused to do, though whether he most feared the police, snubs by former friends, or a rebuff at rue Nicolet perhaps even he did not know. Instead he begged his mother to intervene, and incidentally to bring away from rue Nicolet his papers and clothes and the manuscript of what he described as Rimbaud's greatest poem. Mme Verlaine obeyed, but the interview was not pleasant, M. Mauté, who had taken on with some relish the job of putting an end to the connection with Verlaine, refusing all requests. Verlaine then appealed to La Mère des Gracchi as he had nicknamed Mme Rimbaud, a strange appeal on the face of it; but his instinct was right. Yet she too failed to move M. Mauté.

The one tangible effect of these interventions proved distasteful to Verlaine; M. Mauté's attitude convinced both mothers that Verlaine and Rimbaud must separate if there was to be any hope of a reconciliation between husband and wife; and Verlaine, after protesting that this would merely provide M. Mauté with precisely the tacit admission of guilt he sought, gave way—gave way, it appears, in the belief that his mother would replace Rimbaud and set up a home in London where they could live "respectably".

By the beginning of December Rimbaud was back in Charleville. Mme Verlaine, however, was not to be persuaded to abandon France and by Christmas her son had begun to languish in solitude. Christmas in London was "like Sunday only worse and practically as hypocritical", he complained on Boxing Day, "which is almost as bad". He was not too unhappy to comment in passing that "the goose is delicious" and, though missing Rimbaud, enjoyed himself well enough until he caught influenza. This was an illness unknown to him and he at once decided that he was dying. An element of calculation entered into this solemn moment; urgent messages sped to Rimbaud and his friends and telegrams to his mother and, with a deathbed reconciliation in mind, to Mathilde. To Rimbaud he enclosed notes for Blémont, Forain and, it seems, Delahaye: "I am *dying* of grief, of illness, of boredom, of loneliness", he said. "Excuse this brevity from one who is very ill. Goodbye, perhaps for ever."

The result of this barrage of farewells fell some way short of expectations. "*Only* my mother has come!!" he was soon crying; for Mme Verlaine accompanied by a niece had hurried to London. She found the corpse very much alive but wretched, and, unable to deny him anything, sent the fare to Rimbaud, who was horribly bored in Charleville. He diagnosed his friend's condition, with what mixture of weariness, contempt and affection can be imagined: "Verlaine is like a child left in a room without a light, sobbing with fear. If I come back to him the talks and long walks will cure the body quickly because they'll cheer the mind."

It was so; after a week or two Verlaine was recovering and by February his mother left London happy to see her son on his feet again but worried by the intimacy she had re-established. For his part Verlaine showed a natural reluctance to admit to those who had so recently received his dying farewells that he was in fact still alive: "I'm feeling better but I'm afraid that my health is likely to remain precarious. In fact I fear—shall I say fear or hope?—that I shan't live very long. My life has been wrecked by a thousand gross and treacherous injuries." The after-influenza depression persisted long enough for him to tell Blémont, "You will soon be receiving my little book, perhaps a posthumous one."

The little book was *Chansons sans Paroles*, which he had failed to get published by the printers of *L'Avenir* and was now urging upon Blémont and Lepelletier. Then no more complaints are heard; he and Rimbaud resumed their explorations of London, visiting Hampton Court, the Crystal Palace, Kew Gardens. "We know the whole of London", Verlaine claimed. "Drury Lane, Whitechapel, Pimlico, Angel, the City, Hyde Park etc. have no more mystery for us." He believed himself to be quite the Englishman, enjoying his glass of beer, his seat in the gallery, his Sunday perambulations of Hyde Park, accepting dirt, smell, noise and even fog with what he hoped was English phlegm. He and Rimbaud were reading and writing hard at home and in the British Museum; quarrelling too. Verlaine's frailties had grown no fewer; he would follow Rimbaud in attempts at dissipation and follow him as far as he could in poetic theory—"I'm soon hoping to write poems after a system which will be very musical without the puerilities of Poe", he was to announce—but he was intellectually lazy, he was decidedly taken with pretty girls, commenting frequently how much better looking the English women were than the French; and most depressing and infuriating of all, he was still worrying about Mathilde.

This led to scenes. Rimbaud regarded him as a brand plucked from the burning—"Remember what you were before you met me" was one of his favourite maxims when Verlaine showed retrograde motions—but Verlaine continued obstinately to smoulder. Irritated by his financial dependence—for he could not even leave him—Rimbaud worked off his irritation in characteristic fashion.

Then, abruptly, in the midst of work, pleasures, quarrels, they left London at the beginning of April.

4

It is not known why they left so quickly or even why they left at all. But some facts are known which suggest reasonable assumptions. Mme Verlaine, Lepelletier and Blémont had all continued to press Verlaine to return to Paris; and Mme Verlaine directly and Lepelletier by implication had urged him in any case to separate from Rimbaud, at least for a period, if he wished to stand any chance of preventing Mathilde's application for a separation. Verlaine had resisted this flow of advice, but it had not left him unaffected. As in Belgium, whenever Rimbaud showed his unpleasant side his friend thought longingly of his wife. He went so far as to tell Blémont that although "the recent arrests demand prudence" he would come to Paris if *Chansons sans Paroles* were published. The book was not published, neither Blémont nor Lepelletier being able to find a publisher. Robbed of a dignified reason for capitulation, Verlaine decided at the beginning of April to capitulate without giving any reason. Whether Rimbaud was to come with him, to stay in London or to return home does not appear; but as Verlaine was coming round to a short separation as a diplomatic gesture and a means of allowing some of his companion's spleen to subside, it seems probable that he proposed to go alone.

He did not get further than Newhaven, or to be precise the ship in harbour. There, he said, he overheard a conversation which convinced him that he was being watched by police agents. He hurriedly left the ship and returned to London.

This story, which may have had some romantic touches thrown in, was nevertheless substantially true; Verlaine, like all refugees regarded as political, was being watched by police agents; his visits to Victoria Station to ask about trains and buy his ticket were noted and reported to Paris; he was on his way there, a police report said later. But this was an error; Verlaine, badly frightened, had quickly changed his destination; for the moment he was almost as scared of London as of Paris and returned only to leave it again the next day for Dover and Ostend.

Rimbaud went with him and the friends disappeared for more than a week. Verlaine is next heard of ten days later with his aunt at Jehonville, near the Bertrix of his grandfather, a few miles from the French frontier; he explained inadequately that the missing days had been spent mostly at Namur, where he had suffered "a kind of brain fever". This fever remains a mystery, for he settled down with his aunt and no more is heard of it. Rimbaud was already at the family farm at Roche, where he appeared on Good Friday, April 11.

Separated from Rimbaud for a time, Verlaine at once approached Mathilde and renewed his requests to all and sundry, Hugo included, to bring her to reason. This done, he amused himself by the making of more literary plans, including a prose drama, the completion of the lyrics for the operetta begun with De Sivry years earlier, a novel to be written "very crisply", a series of sonnets and a book of poems from which mankind was to be "banished completely". He had the titles, all that remained was for the poems to be written, but this, like all that went before, seemed unlikely: "perhaps it's a foolish idea after all", he admitted. He was enjoying a prolonged discussion with Lepelletier, who approved the *Romances sans Paroles* with reservations about the "heresies of versification" and the proposed dedication to Rimbaud—a protest against vile rumours, said Verlaine, and in gratitude because Rimbaud had urged him to write the poems. Verlaine gave way on the dedication but held firm to the heresies; he was aiming, he explained, at Glatigny's facility without his banality, a remark which shows that he had travelled far from the Parnasse.

For the rest the holiday (for that is what it was) slipped by pleasantly with self-taught lessons in English, with hour after hour of trout fishing and in the evenings a round of friends and relations anxious to honour this Parisian poet. For a few weeks the peace, the friendliness and the favours soothed one who had come to look on Paris as a nest of enemies. Eventually, however, boredom set in; better than most Verlaine could make himself at home with all kinds of men, but he was too intelligent not to wish for intellectual companionship and the sense of progress, too intelligent and by that time too much dependent on Rimbaud as mental stimulator to endure life without him. Then he had a letter from Mathilde, a short note asking him not to pester her further, and the last reason, if it could be called a reason, for him to stay on disappeared. He decided that it was time to return to London and, forgetting all the recent quarrels, summoned Rimbaud and Delahaye (then teaching at Charleville) to meet him on the frontier at Bouillon. Rimbaud was a little difficult to prise from his retreat, not surprisingly when the nature of his work at Roche is known, but he was penniless, drinkless and bored—"what a horror this French countryside is", he wrote from Roche. He gave way to Verlaine's importunities and by the end of May they were back in London, this time in a room at Great College Street in Camden Town.

5

This new settlement in England lasted barely six weeks and ended in disaster. It was a hopeless enterprise from the beginning, yet from the emotional Verlaine's short-sighted point of view there was reason to hope for good things in London; he had come to like England and the English, he believed the same of Rimbaud; he had visions, optimistic but not impossible, of earning a living there in a manner not entirely distasteful to him; he felt that responsibility for the break with his wife had been put firmly on to her shoulders and he had temporarily persuaded himself that, this being so, he could rest easy. In any case he wanted to be with Rimbaud, and when Verlaine wanted something, difficulties melted; no man was more adept at persuading himself that the desired course was the wisest, and no man was less able to maintain the fiction.

And to judge by what his few friends in Paris heard of it, this second attempt to get a foothold in London was altogether more successful than the first. He was, Verlaine told them, delighted with his new home in a "gay" and picturesque district, near Vermersch and within striking distance of the hills and woods of Hampstead and Highgate. He and Rimbaud walked there often, they were often at the theatre, they saw all the sights, including the Shah of Persia during his state visit, they sailed again on the Thames, they read enormously in the British Museum, they wrote poems and even began to earn some money.

This last was perhaps a doubtful satisfaction, but was forced on them. Mme Verlaine indefatigably travelled once more to London, to see her darling well settled in, no doubt, but also to warn him that the drain on the family capital must stop; he had spent 30,000 francs since meeting Rimbaud, she complained. Verlaine was intermittently aware that he and Rimbaud could not live on his mother indefinitely, hence the plans and vast prospects bulking largely in his letters to Paris. He now used some of the money his mother gave him before she returned home to advertise for pupils. Before long he and presumably Rimbaud too were actually giving an occasional French lesson; sometimes accepting English lessons in return. Verlaine even reached the point of an interview for a post as assistant master in a school, a post he thought he might take if the headmaster "wasn't too much of a Dickensian type"—for Dickens was included in his bouts of reading. Possibly he was not given the chance to decide; nothing came of it; but the idea stuck.

The lessons seem to have been no more than moderately successful. "Perfection, finesse", he claimed in his advertisement. It may have been so, but in hard cash "it isn't a gold mine but it pays for the room and my tobacco". And it is clear from the tone of his letters that he felt a certain pride in acting the practical man, boring though the lessons often were.

Rimbaud felt no pride, only disgust. But then Rimbaud was disgusted with virtually everything, himself not least, Verlaine most of all; he could not forgive himself for the weakness of the return to London, he could not forgive Verlaine for tempting him to return. For a king of men to accept a bribe is an ugly thought, but in effect that is what he had done; he had no money at Roche, he would have money in London, and for that he rejoined a man he despised, a man he was about to satirise savagely in his latest work. He was fond of Verlaine too, even a would-be god felt the attraction, but this he saw as yet another betrayal of his principles; to be moved by Verlaine's affection or kindness or generosity or trust was to compromise with the world and the flesh, it was a weakness that must be stamped out.

Brave thoughts; meanwhile he remained a dependent boy; he literally could not move without begging the fare home. He did not blink the facts, that was not his way; he faced them, accepted them and began to try to write them out of his system. Verlaine watched him writing and sketched him as he wrote, bowler-hatted, long pipe smoking, in a public house. "How he wrote *Saison en Enfer*" he scribbled under the sketch. Did he read what Rimbaud was writing? The answer is not of much moment for he was soon to live it. Rimbaud could not write the bitterness out of himself, what he wrote merely sharpened it. Rimbaud, plunged in *Faust*, the book and the opera, felt the need of behaving devilishly; to write devilishly was child's play. At his side, never leaving him, was the man who had made him sin against his convictions. It was not a temptation, it was a duty to give this creature a taste of hell.

This was what Rimbaud was writing, from the life: "Pitiful brother! What a lot of atrocious night watches I owe to him! 'I wasn't taking this enterprise seriously. I made fun of his weakness. We should go back into exile, slavery, and it would be my fault.' . . . And almost every night the moment he had gone to sleep the poor brother would get up, mouth putrid, eyes starting from his head—as he had dreamed!—and drag me into the room howling his dream of idiotic grief."

Again, regarding "The Infernal Bridegroom" through the eyes of "The Foolish Virgin", he wrote:

"Hear the confession of a companion in Hell:

'O heavenly Bridegroom, my Lord, do not deny the confession of the most unhappy of Thy servants. I am lost. I am drunken. I am unclean. What a life!

'Forgive me, heavenly Lord, forgive me! Ah! forgive me! What a lot of tears! And even more tears later on I hope!

'Later on I shall know the heavenly Bridegroom! I was born subject to Him.—The other can beat me now!

'At present I am at the bottom of the world. . . . I am the slave of the infernal Bridegroom, the one who ruined the foolish virgins . . . I am a widow . . . I used to be a widow . . . why, yes, I was perfectly respectable at one time. . . . He was almost a child. . . . His mysterious delicacy seduced me. I forgot all human duties to follow him. What a life! Real life is absent. We are no longer in the world. I go where he goes, I must. And often he grows furious with me, *me, poor soul*. The Demon!—He is a demon, you know, *he is not a man*.

'I listen to him making a glory of infamy, a charm of cruelty. . . . On several nights, his demon seizing me, we used to fight, I wrestled with him! Often at night, drunk, he stations himself in streets or houses to frighten me to death.—"I shall have my throat cut; it will be disgusting." Oh! those days when he wants to walk about with a criminal air! . . .

'Oh! the life of adventure which exists in children's books, to reward me, I've suffered so much, will you give it to me? He cannot. . . . Perhaps I ought to appeal to God. I am at the very bottom of the abyss and no longer know how to pray.

'If he were to explain his sorrows to me, should I understand them better than his mockeries? He attacks me, spends hours in making me ashamed of all that has touched me in the world and becomes indignant if I weep.'"

Under the satisfactions of Verlaine's letters to Paris, then, letters in which Rimbaud is rarely mentioned and always happily, ran this other nightmarish life of dependence on a boy who played the devil; not the kind of devilry Verlaine understood but a satanic impulse ranging from schoolboy tricks to a merciless malevolence. Rimbaud would wait for him in hiding, pounce on him and laugh at the shock he had caused. He revealed a genius for mockery; he mocked Verlaine for his cowardice, for his looks, his position as a *mélange* of hanger-on and lickspittle, his beliefs; every good feeling was dragged into the open and made to appear despicable and weak. He even reproached him for unsociability

and meanness. So preposterous was this last that the mild
Verlaine, too easily convinced of guilt, reacted angrily.

Naturally there were breaks in the torture; Rimbaud was not
the fiend he tried to ape but a self-disgusted and exceedingly
critical young man. But for every sign of affection that he permitted himself there were several attacks and matters between
them soon reached a crisis. No matter what Verlaine persuaded
himself in daring or drunken moments, his thoughts returned to
Mathilde whenever Rimbaud scathingly pictured his degraded
and hopeless state. It was true, he told himself, he had become
an outcast not only from rue Nicolet but from the entire world of
Paris in which he had moved so light-heartedly. Even more
dreadful, he had been led not only to deny his God but taught to
blaspheme Him and to spit on Him. He did not believe in God?
Small comfort at such moments; for Verlaine unbelief was
practically impossible at heart; he could talk, bluster, blaspheme,
outshout his mentor, no matter, the childhood teaching would
come back, the need for protection rise up. And was he damned,
then, eternally, irrevocably damned? And when he and Rimbaud
quarrelled, he saw himself lost and cheated, having, for nothing,
thrown up all that he cared for in this world and the next.

Not even thrown up; and this was perhaps the bitterest
reflection. He had never intended to leave Mathilde finally,
witness the letters he had written to her, but somehow what he
saw as a harmless spree had been turned into a possibly unbridg-
able separation. And by whom? By his own weakness, certainly,
but who had taken advantage of it? He became frantic with fear
and self-loathing and he looked at the mocking, japing boy with
a horror sometimes not far from hatred. And it was he, not the
disgusted Rimbaud, who finally made the break.

It came, as these things do, after the mildest of spurs, the jeers
of Rimbaud at Verlaine's appearance as he came home with the
shopping one day early in July, a herring in one hand, a bottle
of olive oil in the other: "What a c.... [an English word that
had replaced 'merde' in favour] you look with that fish!" That
was all, but it was enough; Verlaine took the next ship leaving
for Antwerp.

Evidently he left a note, or Rimbaud guessed that he had really
done what he had so often threatened to do. He followed him,
but by the time he reached the docks the gangway had been

raised and Verlaine, standing on the deck, shook his head against all the frantic signs to him to come back.

The ship sailed and Rimbaud returned to Great College Street feeling respect for Verlaine for the first time since their meeting. Before this solitary act of firmness the boy collapsed, sitting down the next day to write a letter ludicrously out of character:

"Come back, come back, dear friend, only friend come back. I swear to you that I'll be good. If I was unpleasant to you it was only a joke I obstinately persisted in; I'm more sorry than I can say. Come back and all will be forgotten. What a pity you took the joke to heart. I haven't stopped crying for two days. Come back. Be brave, dear friend. Nothing is lost. You have only to make the journey again. We will live here again bravely, patiently. Ah, I beg you. It's for your own good too. Come back, you'll find all your things here. I hope you've realised by this time that our argument was meaningless. Frightful moment! But when I signalled you to leave the ship, why didn't you come? Fancy living together for two years only to end up like this! What are you going to do? If you don't want to come back here, do you want me to join you? Yes, I was in the wrong.

Oh say you won't forget me.

No, you can't forget me.

As for me, I think of you always.

Speak, reply to your friend, aren't we to live together any more? Be brave. Reply to me quickly.

I can't stay here much longer.

Listen only to your heart.

Quick, tell me if I'm to join you.

Yours for life."

He added a postscript in the same uncharacteristic manner, showing as he was to show more seriously a few days later that a shock to his confidence could reduce him to his true age, without courage, pride, dignity, and with no more trace in him than Verlaine of a "*fils du soleil*".

"Quick, reply; I can't stay here later than Monday evening. I haven't a penny; I can't even post this. I've given Vermersch your books and papers.

If I am not to see you again I shall enlist in the marines or the army. O come back, I cry for you all the time. Tell me where I can find you and I'll come. Tell me, wire me. I must leave Monday evening. Where are you going? What are you going to do?"

Verlaine, however, threw away his one chance of asserting himself; before Rimbaud could post the letter, before he had been on the ship more than an hour or two, the enormity of his conduct struck him. He remembered, not the last sordid quarrelsome weeks, but the days of wandering in Belgium, godlike, carefree, happy. All that and the poet who had sprung from it he owed to Rimbaud. Was he mad, to leave the boy and leave him without a penny? Conscience-stricken, he tried to justify himself with heroics:

> "I want to tell you that you must *at heart* understand *at last* that it was absolutely necessary for me to leave, that this life of violence and *scenes* with no better excuse than your whim couldn't go on any longer. As I have loved you tremendously (*honi soit qui mal y pense!*) I also want you to know that if I'm not reconciled in full amity with my wife in three days I shall blow out my brains! My last thought, my friend, will be for you, for you who were calling to me from the pier recently and whom I didn't want to rejoin *because it was necessary for me to make an end of myself*—AT LAST! Will you accept my dying embrace?"

At this and more Rimbaud came to his senses; he metaphorically tore up his letter and wrote another. "As for dying," he commented, "I know you! And whilst you're waiting for your wife and your death you'll be going all over the place in a great state and boring everyone you meet."

Having dismissed the suicide, he tried to bring Verlaine back to realities as he saw them. But he had his own weaknesses to grapple with; by this time he could neither bear to have Verlaine with him nor away from him; the first sign that Verlaine hankered after his wife was enough for him, all past experience going for nothing, to try to recall the backslider to his duty and the glorious future:

> "Do you really believe you would be happier with others than with me? *Think!* Of course you wouldn't! You can only be free with me, and as I've sworn to be very kind in future, as I'm sorry for all the wrong I've done, as I've at last got my mind clear and as I love you very much, if you don't want to come back or for me to rejoin you you are committing a crime *for which you'll suffer MANY LONG YEARS by the loss of all freedom and by miseries more atrocious* perhaps than those you've already endured. After all, remember what you were before you knew me!"

This letter discovered Verlaine at an embarrassing moment. As soon as he had reached Brussels three days earlier he had despatched letters and telegrams in all directions; three to his wife, one to his mother, one to Mme Rimbaud and to sundry others, including Hugo, announcing his imminent decease at his own hands if Mathilde did not join him within three days. He outlined his manifold miseries, said a fairly elaborate farewell and gave directions for the disposal of his literary remains. As usual his mother was the only one to respond immediately; she hurried to Brussels, where she spent her time trying to dissuade him from putting an end to himself. He found it desirable to retire publicly from this resolution by degrees, solemnly telling Lepelletier that "my mother is trying to weaken my resolve, but I don't think she'll succeed". Knowing privately how well she would succeed, his rancour fastened itself once more on Mathilde, who had again failed to respond to an appeal, and such an appeal. Nor had his dying words to his friends done the trick; no one hastened to Mathilde, as he had hoped, and begged her to save his life. He was left to save it himself.

Bogged in this dilemma, he had a reply from Mme Rimbaud which pointed to an honourable way out. This letter took him more seriously than he deserved, Mme Rimbaud not being the kind of woman who could imagine a man threatening to take his life without the slightest intention of doing so. But she did understand that he was wretched and her letter dealt nobly with that situation.

"I hope that by this time your mind has become calm and thoughtful. To commit suicide just because one is stricken by misfortune is *despicable*; to kill oneself when one possesses a godly and loving mother who would give her life for you and whom your death would kill, and when one is the father of a little being who is stretching his arms towards you now, who will smile at you tomorrow and who one day will need your guidance and support— to kill oneself in such circumstances is *infamous*: the world condemns those who die by their own hand and God Himself can't pardon so great a crime and casts the sinner from His bosom.

Monsieur, I know nothing about your quarrels with Arthur, but I have always foreseen that your relationship would end unhappily. You will ask me why. Because whatever has not been authorised and approved by good and upright parents cannot bring happiness to the children. . . .

You complain of your unhappy life, poor child! How do you know what the morrow has in store? Hope then! What do you understand of happiness on earth? You are too sensible to think that happiness consists in the success of a plan or the satisfaction of a whim, a fancy: No, anyone who had all his wishes granted, all his desires satisfied, certainly would not be happy; for the moment that the heart ceases to feel aspirations no more emotion is possible and so no more happiness. Therefore as the heart must beat let it beat at the thought of good—good that one has done or wants to do.

I too have been most unhappy. I have suffered much, wept much, and I have been able to turn all my afflictions to my advantage. God has given me a stout heart full of energy and courage. I have fought against every kind of adversity; then I have reflected, I have looked about me and I am sure, absolutely sure that each one of us has a wound more or less deep in our hearts. To me my wound seems much deeper than those of others; that is natural enough; I could feel my own injury but not those of others. Then I said to myself—and I see every day that I am right—that true happiness consists in doing one's duties however painful they may be.

Do as I do, dear Sir; be strong and courageous in the face of every affliction; drive all bad thoughts from your heart. Fight, fight without ceasing against what is called the injustice of fate and you will find that misfortune will stop pursuing you and you will become happy once more. It is necessary to work hard and give one's life an aim to follow; no doubt you will still have plenty of unhappy days, but however wicked men may be never despair of God's help. Believe me, He alone can console and heal."

Verlaine never commented on this letter; it is unlikely to have touched him deeply then although he was soon to understand its truth; for the moment it seemed to offer him sanction to remain alive without loss of face. He forthwith renounced even the pretence of suicide.

But he could not follow Mme Rimbaud into stoicism, could not even abandon romantic attitudes. Should he return to London as Rimbaud urged (though with a sadistic "what will Andrieu and company think?" to punish him) or should he take his courage in both hands and seek out Mathilde? Better still, could he cut free from them both? This thought had no sooner come into his mind than he met an acquaintance, unburdened himself, and was advised to volunteer for the Carlist army.

Anything less congenial than this mad project would be hard

to imagine, yet by then the almost hysterical Verlaine saw it as
the only escape from an emotional situation which had become
too much for him. If he died fighting he would at least die in a
good cause. Besides, would not his friends, would not even the
flint-hearted Mathilde relent when they heard of his gesture—
relent, forgive and love again?

But to die! Second thoughts followed quickly. He must have
been insane. Feverishly he looked round for someone to deliver
him from his stupidity. His mother? No help there: Mme
Verlaine was an all-acquiescent shadow of himself. Mathilde?
But she had not even replied to his suicide threat. In sudden
terror he telegraphed to Rimbaud.

Rimbaud was still at Great College Street. Verlaine had long
since written to Matuszewicz, one of their London circle, to look
after him; and as Rimbaud had promptly sold most of his friend's
clothes for ready cash he was in no great hurry to move. He
believed that Verlaine could not do without him and would
return to London.

Then he received the telegram "Volunteering Spain. Come
here, Hôtel Liégeois. Laundry, manuscripts if possible." He left
at once and was in Brussels that evening, July 8.

6

Rimbaud found Verlaine a civilian still, the Carlists refusing
to accept foreign volunteers. He was not pleased; to inveigle him
to Brussels for nothing! He became angry as the next day dragged
on without decision. They sat at the cafés drinking and arguing.
Verlaine wanted to return to London, but Rimbaud would not
hear of it; they would look ridiculous in the eyes of their friends,
he said. This from Rimbaud was unconvincing, preposterous. He
had begged him more than once to come back, Verlaine objected,
and had written "It would be a mark of courage" to do so.

Verlaine could not move him; he wanted to go to Paris, he
said, and demanded the fare.

As the evening wore on Verlaine became terrified; Rimbaud
was tired of him, wanted to leave him—was it not obvious? But
if he showed fear, Rimbaud would certainly go; that was a sure
way to lose him. To gain courage he drank more, and the more
he drank the more confused he grew. Should he go to Paris with

the boy, risk trouble with the authorities? But where would they live, and how? And how could he face the cut direct?—for Blémont had not left him in much doubt about the Parnassian view of the flight from Mathilde. And Mathilde? If he went to Paris . . .

The thoughts jostled one another, there was no end to them. What to do for the best? Rimbaud, watching him and contemptuously parrying one suggestion after another, seemed to the wretched Verlaine to be icy with scorn, immovable.

The next morning the one-sided argument was still going on; they had moved to the hotel, nothing else had changed. To every entreaty Rimbaud, leaning against the communicating door between the bedrooms of Verlaine and his mother, replied with a monotonous chant of "Money, money" and holding out a hand.

At last Verlaine ran out of the hotel, drank himself silly at the nearest café, returned and showed Rimbaud a revolver. He would shoot the lot of them, he swore. He sat on the end of the bed and begged the boy to stay.

He was never to forget the next few minutes; for the rest of his life he saw Rimbaud standing near the door to the corridor "his arms folded, defiance in every line of his body, the cruel light of a damned archangel in his eyes". He felt absolute despair, knowing that nothing he could say would move him.

Mme Verlaine, realising that her son was beside himself, put a hand on his shoulder, fearing that he would leap up and attack Rimbaud. For several minutes there was silence, Verlaine and Rimbaud staring at each other. Neither moved.

Then Rimbaud turned away. "I'm off," he said. He went out. Verlaine could hear the wooden boards creak as he rushed down the stairs.

Verlaine "saw red". He felt that Rimbaud was "carrying away his brain and heart". When the sound of the boy's footsteps could no longer be heard he got up as if in a trance and hurried to the door, determined to bring him back and lock him in the bedroom. His mother tried to bar the way. "You're mad, Paul!" she cried. "Come to your senses. Think of yourself."

Verlaine, carried away by anger, flung her aside with such force that she was thrown against the window-frame on the far side of the room. He ran downstairs and out of the front door.

Ahead of him was Rimbaud walking slowly "and with an indecisive air" on the pavement leading towards Boulevard Botanique. He caught him up. "You'd better come back or there'll be trouble," he said.

"Let me alone," said Rimbaud without looking at him. But he went back.

Once they were in the bedroom again Verlaine locked the door, placed a chair against it, sat down, drew his revolver and aimed it at Rimbaud. "Go, will you?" he shouted.

The boy lolled against the wall mockingly. He said only the same maddening refrain, "Money, money," hand held out.

Verlaine fired. The first shot hit Rimbaud just above the left wrist, the second missed him and burried itself in the wall.

Stupefied by what he had done, Verlaine, suddenly sober, sat staring at Rimbaud. Then he burst into his mother's room and flung himself on the bed sobbing. After a moment Rimbaud followed him, watched by the petrified Mme Verlaine. Seeing him, Verlaine raised himself on the bed, handed him the revolver and begged him to shoot. Rimbaud waved the weapon away and told his friend not to be a fool.

For a time Verlaine was inconsolable. Then his mother, recovering her wits, said that Rimbaud's wound must be properly treated. She bound it and all three walked off to the hospital. No one in the hotel seemed to have heard the shots.

At the hospital the wound was dressed, but the bullet could not be extracted that day. They returned to the hotel, where argument broke out again. Verlaine begged Rimbaud to change his mind. Mme Verlaine advised him to stay and let them look after him or at least to wait until he had been into hospital the next day. Rimbaud refused to change his mind, refused to stay the night, refused to wait until the bullet could be taken out. He declared that he was going to Charleville that afternoon. Once more he held out a hand with his chanted "Money, money".

Mme Verlaine opposed him no further and gave him twenty francs to buy his ticket. In the early evening the three walked out together again, towards the station. They had not gone far, they were crossing Place Rouppe, when Verlaine, who had not ceased to beg Rimbaud vehemently to stay in Brussels for the moment, ran ahead a few paces, turned and faced him.

At this point the accounts of Verlaine and Rimbaud differ.

Rimbaud declared, though with decreasing emphasis in successive statements, that Verlaine threatened to shoot him if he did
not abandon his intention of leaving. Verlaine declared that he
threatened to blow out his own brains if Rimbaud persisted in
taking the train.

The truth is not difficult to come by. The time was seven in
the evening; Verlaine had drunk nothing since early morning
and Verlaine sober was incapable of hurting a fly. But he had
eaten nothing, he had been in continuous emotional excitement
for days, he was light-headed and desperate. The idea that
having shot Rimbaud when drunk he could repeat the shooting
when sober is fantastic; few men could do such a thing twice on
the same day whatever their state, and certainly not Verlaine.
But he had bought the revolver with the purpose of shooting
himself and he could threaten once more to do it—that, he would
reckon, would cost nothing and might gain his point.

He did not draw the revolver; even Rimbaud in his first fright
never suggested it. But he put his hand in his pocket and Rimbaud was taking no chances. And having appealed to a policeman Rimbaud was obliged to make some sort of charge; hence
his account. If he thought at all in those few seconds, he thought
only of putting Verlaine out of the way until he could reach
Charleville; the whole question could be discussed by letter
when heads had cooled. He did not think that Verlaine would
be detained for more than a day or two; not even a man versed
in the law could have foreseen what was to happen. So Verlaine
put a hand in his pocket, Rimbaud cried for help, ran to a
policeman and demanded protection. The policeman arrested
Verlaine. Depositions were taken from all three at the police
station, Verlaine was put in the lock-up for the night charged
with attempted murder and the other two were told not to leave
the city.

Verlaine was searched and the next morning taken to the
Petits-Carmes prison, where he was interrogated by an inspector.
It was then that the affair changed its character. The offence, an
unpremeditated attack, was not serious; but when Verlaine
declared that the cause of the shooting, which he did when he
was not himself, was the intention of Rimbaud to go back to
France, "which threw me into despair", the inspector at once
suspected that he was dealing with a homosexual who must be

rigorously punished—not for the shooting but the homosexuality.

Why, he asked, was Verlaine thrown into despair by the departure of a male friend? Were the relations between them other than friendship?

"No," replied Verlaine. "That is a calumny invented by my wife and her family to injure me." It was, he believed, one of the means being used to obtain a separation.

The denial was useless. From that moment Verlaine's fate was decided; all further questioning, and there was much of it, was directed to the one end; the original offence was pushed into the background.

The next day Rimbaud, in hospital waiting for the bullet to be taken out, was interviewed by the same man. He repeated the story told at the police station and extended the details of their life together. Two of his statements were curious: that one cause of their quarrel in London was his complaints of Verlaine's "idleness"; and that when he came to Brussels he wanted to take up their life together again "because there was no reason why we should separate". The first comes strangely from him; the second made nonsense of his wish to go to France. But the inspector was interested only in their relationship: had Verlaine's wife ever complained about his intimacy with her husband? "Yes," said Rimbaud, "she has accused us of having immoral relations, but I shan't give myself the trouble of denying such calumnies."

Neither this frankness nor the contemptuous denial—a most significant reply from one with the moral courage of Rimbaud—had the slightest effect on the inspector. He had established that Rimbaud was kept by Verlaine, that Verlaine shot him when he threatened to leave, and that Verlaine's wife believed them to be homosexuals: to him this meant one thing only.

The police doctors then got to work; instructed to try to discover traces of homosexual practices, they examined Verlaine and stated that the traces "ne sont pas tellement marqués qu'il y ait lieu de suspecter des *habitudes invétérées et anciennes*, mais des pratiques plus ou moins récentes"—a statement which they had no medical warrant for making and which is in fact meaningless. To the police inspector, however, the report was excellent. To it he could add various letters and poems found on Verlaine which could without difficulty be interpreted as indecent and—

another useful titbit—some evidence that the company he had kept in London was not only immoral but politically undesirable.

It was a strong case even though it had no bearing on the charge, and one made stronger by the arrival in Brussels of Mathilde's solicitor, who worked hand in glove with the police to secure Verlaine's condemnation; a Verlaine shut away for a substantial prison term could not defend the separation case in Paris and his sentence would without doubt make the judgment certain in the wife's favour.

After this all else—collection of evidence, further examinations of Verlaine, Rimbaud and Mme Verlaine—were formalities. To Verlaine, herded under disgusting conditions with common criminals in the prison and trying to save sanity by composing poetry, the whole thing was a nightmare out of which he tried to believe that he must soon be delivered. To Rimbaud, the more obviously realistic of the two, the portents were ominous; lying in his hospital bed after the third examination and considering the direction of the questions put by the police inspector, he regretted the moment of panic and the appeal to the policeman in the Place Rouppe. He began to see that Verlaine was likely to be used as a scapegoat. The next morning, July 19, released from hospital, he went straight to the law courts and insisted on making a final statement. Verlaine, he declared, was so drunk in the hotel bedroom that he did not know what he was doing; he had no premeditated or hostile thought in his mind; and the cause of his drunkenness was his troubles with his wife. He withdrew all claim to compensation and said that he did not wish to bring any charge against Verlaine.

Having done what he could to repair the damage he had unintentionally caused, Rimbaud went off to Charleville. His final gesture was useless; he was regarded as a fellow-sinner with Verlaine and nothing that he could say had any weight.

Verlaine's sufferings in prison soon afterwards came to a welcome end. His mother, horrified by his forced company and labour, had petitioned the prosecutor for him to be treated more leniently, and her appeal was unexpectedly strengthened by a letter which arrived for Verlaine and was opened by the police. The letter was from Hugo, a belated reply to Verlaine's "suicide" letter, promising to intercede with his wife. Hugo was held in honour in Brussels and Verlaine was promptly transferred to a detention ward where he could have some privacy and buy food.

The respite was short-lived, was in fact an added misfortune since the ebullient Verlaine, treated with a certain respect for the first time, at once jumped to the conclusion that he would be fined and allowed to go free. And on August 8, when he was brought to trial, he entered the court room comparatively light-hearted.

His complacence collapsed in the first few minutes and was succeeded by incredulous horror. The prosecutor at once attacked him and Rimbaud as sexual perverts of whom the prisoner, as the elder, was the chief culprit. Verlaine's counsel protested in vain that this was irrelevant and inadmissible evidence; the judge permitted the prosecutor to continue and from that moment Verlaine was a lost man, used by the police as an example to deter the homosexuals of Brussels. Rimbaud's final statement was passed over on the grounds that he was a biassed witness despite the fact that the whole case against Verlaine depended on him. The jury found Verlaine guilty and he was sentenced to two years' hard labour and a fine of two hundred francs. An analysis of this sentence abundantly proves bias: Verlaine was given the maximum term of six months for criminal assault; the maximum term of one year for premeditated assault; and a further six months for incapacitating Rimbaud from work. Of these only the first could be described as justifiable and in view of the evidence would be considered severe in any court of law. The second—premeditation—was plainly untrue. And the third was not only ridiculous but directly conflicted with the whole purpose of the prosecution—to prove that Rimbaud had been deliberately kept by Verlaine for immoral purposes.

Shattered by the sentence, Verlaine broke down after he had been taken out of court, but he pulled himself together when the warders explained sympathetically that he could appeal. He did so. The prosecution retaliated by demanding a longer sentence.

Verlaine's misfortunes continued. The Brussels police applied to Paris for his dossier. A few days earlier, on July 24, Matusze-wicz had decided to return to France to try to trace his mistress, who had been missing since the defeat of the Commune. He had no sooner reached Paris than he was caught, arrested and condemned to death. On him was found Verlaine's letter asking him to help Rimbaud. This led the Paris police to trace Verlaine's record, which, when finally sent to Brussels on August 21, was damning though, like the accusation of homosexuality, absolutely irrelevant: Verlaine was described as an intimate friend of Vermersch and Andrieu, influential Communards, his action in working under the Commune was condemned and his private life was described, after he had conceived his "passion honteuse" for Rimbaud, as one long gratification of the "goûts dépravés" he had formed with that youth.

Six days later, on August 27, the appeal was dismissed with costs.

Chapter Twelve

PRISON

1873-1874

I

THE savage sentence of the Brussels court, intended to crush Verlaine, proved the making of him. Before the shooting he remained at twenty-seven years of age a rudderless adolescent drifting from mood to mood, taking pleasure where he found it, his one constant background the sea of his affections. During his two years with Rimbaud, Verlaine was regarded by his friends as completely bewitched. They forgot his sense of humour. To a point he was alarmingly dependent on Rimbaud and could be swayed by him and hurt by him with ease, at his mercy as the warm-hearted are always at the mercy of the cold. But there was another side to their relationship; Verlaine understood the boy well in some respects, loving him through his faults; he laughed at him, mocked his peculiarities, recognised his weaknesses. And as always he expressed this knowledge in poetry. Here, for instance, is one of his brilliant take-offs of the countrified Rimbaud with his coarse provincial burr that mangled the French language, his peasant meannesses, his complaints of this, that and the other.

> C'est pas injuss' de s'voir dans un' pareill' situate! . . .
> Et pas la queu' d'un pauv' keretzer sous la patte! . . .
> J'arrive à Vienne avec les meyeurs intentions,
> —Sans compter que j'compt' sur des brevets d'inventions—
> En arrêvant je m'coll' quéq' Fanta comm' de jusse,
> Bon! V'là qu'un cocher d'fiac' m'vol' tout! . . . C'est pas injusse? . . .
> Voui, m'fait tout jusqu'à ma limace et mon grimpant
> Et m'plant'là dans la strass par un froid. Pas foutant?
> Non! vrai, pour le début en v'là-t-y un triomphe:
> Ah! la sale bête! Encor plus pir' que la daromphe.
>
> .   .   .   .
>
> Je renonce à Satan, à ses pomp', à ses œuffs!
> Je vous gobe, ô profonds mugissements des bœufs.
> J'fonde eun' nouvelle école, et sans coll', j'agricole.
> Coll'-toi ça dans l'fusil, mond' frivole, et racole-

208

PRISON

Z-en d'autres. Désormais j'dis merd' a les Gatti,
A les Russ', à les Vienne et aux Scaferlati
D'contrebande, et j'vas faire un très chouett' mariache.
Je m'cramponne à toi, Roche, et j'défends qu'on m'arrache
Eud'toi . . . Viv' le lard dans la soupe—et soillions
Sérillieux,—et qu'nout'sueur alle abreuff' nos sillions!

Each had influenced the other for good as well as bad. Rimbaud had saved Verlaine from living as so many of his Parnassian friends lived, playing at poetry from the shelter of a safe job or an adoring parent; he had forced him to balance artistic integrity against all that he loved so well—comfortable home, friends, respectability and licence neatly mixed, good feeling everywhere —and to come down on the side of the first; and he more than any other man had made Verlaine the poet. But that lesson had been taught and, with backslidings, learned. Rimbaud had had more than enough of everything to do with Verlaine except his money.

Verlaine would not recognise that their friendship was at an end. He characteristically bore no ill will for his deliverance into the hands of the police—he made no complaint against Rimbaud, but blamed himself steadily—and if he ever suspected the truth he closed his eyes to it at once in sheer terror of loneliness and lovelessness. He had, it seemed, lost his wife, lost his friends in Paris, lost his freedom; the thought of losing the person for whom he had thrown these overboard was unbearable.

Perhaps a prison sentence was the least painful way of cutting the knot, and although Verlaine could not know it the successor to Rimbaud was already at work in him. Intellectually Rimbaud had emancipated him as poet; humanly something else was needed. In prison his poetry at once took on a new depth. Consider, for instance, the poem he composed during his first night in prison, when, sleepless and stupefied with horror and fright, he watched mice running over the floor of the cell crossing the stripes of moonlight thrown through the barred window. A line of La Fontaine came into his mind, "Mais attendons la fin", and he wrote *Impression Fausse*.

Dame souris trotte,
Noire dans le gris du soir,
Dame souris trotte,
Grise dans le noir.

On sonne la cloche:
Dormez, les bons prisonniers,
On sonne la cloche:
Faut que vous dormiez.

Pas de mauvais rêve,
Ne pensez qu'à vos amours,
Pas de mauvais rêve:
Les belles toujours!

Le grand clair de lune!
On ronfle ferme à coté.
Le grand clair de lune
En réalité!

Un nuage passe,
Il fait noir comme en un four,
Un nuage passe.
Tiens, le petit jour!

Dame souris trotte,
Rose dans les rayons bleus,
Dame souris trotte:
Debout, paresseux!

Impression Fausse, with its overtone of Verlainean humour, its undertone of sorrow, was the work of a poet who had gained in artistry but to whom artistry was no longer the chief consideration, a man who like the Russians wrote under the eye of death, in a manner distinctly English but with a delicacy of touch wholly French. And no sooner had the court passed sentence than he wrote a second and stronger poem. *La Chanson de Gaspard Hauser*, as he first called it, dealt ostensibly with the boy whose mysterious career had long attracted the Parnassians, Villiers in particular. Verlaine now, like Villiers, identified himself with the unhappy Gaspard Hauser who claimed noble birth, but, unlike Villiers, he was concerned with the unhappiness and not the nobility and, again unlike Villiers, with marvellous tenderness he crystallises the feelings of the world's misfits.

Je suis venu, calme orphelin,
Riche de mes seuls yeux tranquilles,
Vers les hommes des grandes villes:
Ils ne m'ont pas trouvé malin.

PRISON

A vingt ans un trouble nouveau,
Sous le nom d'amoureuses flammes,
M'a fait trouver belles les femmes:
Elles ne m'ont pas trouvé beau.

Bien que sans patrie et sans roi
Et très brave ne l'étant guère,
J'ai voulu mourir à la guerre:
La mort n'a pas voulu de moi.

Suis-je né trop tôt ou trop tard?
Qu'est-ce que je fais en ce monde?
O vous tous, ma peine est profonde:
Priez pour le pauvre Gaspard!

2

Verlaine, naturally enough, did not view his imprisonment as providential. He was not normally a reflective man, but a man responsible to every emotion and impression; that these latest verses showed a new depth was not his concern; he was preoccupied by his rôle as man of sorrows, for once with apparent good reason. Many men, perhaps most, would have given way to despair when so harshly sentenced; how much more the gregarious Verlaine, hating and fearing loneliness? He imagined himself bitter and broken, but optimism and an inborn sweetness of temperament would bubble up. Moreover, he was poet before man, or perhaps one should say above man; anything and everything served him as poetic material and a prison provided him with novelty. The reader has seen what he could do with the apparently slender motive of mice scampering across the floor of a cell. And when there was absolutely no incident—and for a man sentenced to solitary confinement incident does not abound—he had his thoughts and feelings.

Le ciel est, par-dessus le toit,
   Si bleu, si calme!
Un arbre, par-dessus le toit,
   Berce sa palme.

La cloche, dans le ciel qu'on voit,
   Doucement tinte.
Un oiseau sur l'arbre qu'on voit
   Chante sa plainte.

Mon Dieu, mon Dieu, la vie est là,
  Simple et tranquille.
Cette paisible rumeur-là
  Vient de la ville.

—Qu'as-tu fait, ô toi que voilà
  Pleurant sans cesse,
Dis, qu'as-tu fait, toi que voilà,
  De ta jeunesse?

So this would-be man of sorrows passed his days and weeks at
the Petits-Carmes in a prevailing mood of peaceful detachment
which would appear incredible were it not that prison routine,
like the routine of an army, conveys in the midst of its unpleasantness a certain sense of security. Yet even granted this
aid to sanity, the sang-froid of the so-called weakling amazes.
Unquestionably he was a coward in the popular sense of the
word: he would quiver at the sound of a pop-gun, he hated the
sight of blood, he was far from easy when left alone in the dark.
He has also been voted a moral coward, but perhaps moral
sluggard is the *mot juste*; if he could find someone to deal with
his problems he never hesitated to hand them over with relief.
In prison he had no one to lean on and, worse, was separated
abruptly from the all-obliterating absinthe. Doctors have told
us in no uncertain terms what that means. We wait, therefore,
for the sobs, the collapses, the piteous screeds, the appeals to
warders, governors, anyone within reach by this man who,
deprived at one blow of companions, drink, comfort, hope for
two years, could not possibly sustain existence. But we wait in
vain. And even when, caged in the open prison van of those
days, he was transferred to the prison at Mons in October and
was locked away by himself day and night except for one hour
each day, and during that hour forbidden to look at his fellow-
prisoners, his main reaction was a pleased comment on how
much nicer a building the pink stone prison was than the Petits-
Carmes, and how much cleaner. All of which suggests that he
was not the absinthe addict his critics claimed and that some-
where in that apparently will-less human being was an unexpected source of strength.

He did of course suffer, no feeling man could do otherwise,

PRISON

and one of his most powerful poems tersely communicates this
suffering:

> Un grand sommeil noir
> Tombe sur ma vie:
> Dormez, tout espoir,
> Dormez, toute envie!
>
> Je ne vois plus rien,
> Je perds la mémoire
> Du mal et du bien . . .
> O la triste histoire!
>
> Je suis un berceau
> Qu'une main balance
> Au creux d'un caveau:
> Silence, silence!

But in general, during the next six months until April 1874, his
only serious complaint was of boredom: he could do nothing, not
even write, he said. He exaggerated; he could and did write
masterly poems in this vacuum. One of them he wrote, typically,
in a moment of disgust with "poetical" poetry; wrote it and
thought no more of it than that it was another step towards
another volume that would surely make his fame and fortune.
This *jeu d'esprit* was to become a gospel of the new generation of
poets.

> De la musique avant toute chose,
> Et pour cela préfère l'Impair
> Plus vague et plus soluble dans l'air,
> Sans rien en lui qui pèse ou qui pose.
>
> Il faut aussi que tu n'ailles point
> Choisir tes mots sans quelque méprise:
> Rien de plus cher que la chanson grise
> Où l'Indécis au Précis se joint.
>
> .   .   .   .
>
> Prends l'éloquence et tords-lui son cou!
> Tu feras bien, en train d'énergie,
> De rendre un peu la Rime assagie.
> Si l'on n'y veille, elle ira jusqu'où?
>
> .   .   .   .

213

De la musique encore et toujours!
Que ton vers soit la chose envolée
Qu'on sent qui fuit d'une âme en allée
Vers d'autres cieux à d'autres amours.

Que ton vers soit la bonne aventure
Eparse au vent crispé du matin
Qui va fleurant la menthe et le thym . . .
Et tout le reste est littérature.

3

Here then was Verlaine, in his "château" as he described it, clothed in a coarse green serge uniform, heavy clogs on his feet and on his shaven head a leather cap with linen face flap which he was forced to lower whenever he met another prisoner. His cell measured ten feet by six, its only furniture an upright chair and a board which served as bed by night and table by day. He was forbidden to speak to anyone but the warder, and, as the warder took an instant dislike to him, this meant that he spent every day in silence except when he tried to answer the man's daily reprimands for untidiness. His food was barley soup, bread and water every weekday, pea soup on Sundays. He had no books, no newspapers, nothing to distract his mind from the day-long task of grinding coffee. His one amenity was the pipe of tobacco permitted to every prisoner during the silent midday break. He composed poetry because he could not help it, writing on odd scraps of paper, and that kept him sane. He saw his mother twice, and each time she had to tell him that there was no hope of a reprieve, the French ambassador in Brussels refusing to intercede for a former Communard. No one else attempted to visit him; Rimbaud had returned temporarily to Brussels to arrange for the printing of *Une Saison en Enfer* but did not come near him. He seemed a dead man.

The strain of such an existence on such a man does not need emphasising. His poetry saved him but can scarcely account for the exemplary behaviour which in a few weeks and despite the dislike of the warder led to a certain relaxation of the austerity of his life; for this one must look to Verlaine. He was plainly of a different type from most of the prisoners and was fortunate to have a perceptive Chaplain and Governor. Late in November he was moved to the detention ward. He was given a bed, slightly more palatable food and, saving grace, was allowed books to read and the free use of paper for composition and letter writing. At once he sprang into activity, reading hard, mostly in Shakespeare, trying to improve his English, and elaborating a host of Verlainean plans: to write plays for the French Players in London, to make translations from the English, to fit himself for a lucrative post in England, to turn publisher and, choicest delusion, to resume his job at the Hôtel de Ville—all this in addition to the preparation of his next book, *Romances sans Paroles*, for the press.

This last appeared a lost labour, but Verlaine, to whom the book meant Rimbaud, persevered against every set-back. The little collection had met one obstacle after another ever since Vermersch had failed to publish it. In Paris one publisher after another refused it. Lemerre, the first to see it, spoke for every Parnassian when he gave as reason not the shortcomings of the poems but of their author. Literary judgment was not to be found there nor, it seemed, anywhere in Paris. Lepelletier, entrusted by Verlaine with the task of placing the manuscript, did not speak as plainly as he might—a tactful gesture which did him credit—and Verlaine either did not or would not realise how thoroughly he had damned himself in the eyes of the contemporaries with whom he had mixed in apparent good fellowship so short a time before. Friendship in the arts is a transitory thing at the best of times, but Verlaine, having little of the cynic in him, did not understand just how transitory. There was the matter of Rimbaud, certainly, but Rimbaud had gone and his companion was in prison. He felt something of the apprehensions of the small boy locked in his bedroom for committing a petty crime, but he had like the small boy a belief, without which he could scarcely have continued to live, that the punishment was too bad to be true and must surely absolve him.

He deceived himself; the prison sentence, bad though it was, was limited, the other sentence was for life. As far as most of the men were concerned with whom he had disported himself in the Paris cafés, at Nina's, at Mendès' and the rest of the gatherings, he was beyond the pale; the mere suspicion of unnatural practices frightened the most licentious. And when to this suspicion was added another, that this reprobate was also a dangerously good poet, no hope existed that he would obtain a hearing or, if he somehow obtained it, that his work would be judged on its merits. A few, Valade and Blémont chief among them, were more charitable than most, but had not the courage to defend him. De Sivry missed a lively companion and was always ready with a "Oh, come now, he's a good sort", but De Sivry had no say in Parnassian or any other poetic circles; nor had Cabaner, Forain, Carjat or the erratic Richepin, the minor Bohemians of their time. Neither Banville nor Coppée wished to impair their comfortable positions, Banville's assured, Coppée's more and more flourishing. For the rest, Mendès' comments were lewd, Leconte de Lisle's libellous, and their followers acted as followers do; Glatigny was dead, Nina's mind beginning to give way, Villiers grown too remote from reality to take a stand, Cros siding ingloriously against the grain with the Mauté family.

Yet from his prison cell, lovably or laughably ignoring reality, Verlaine was exhorting Lepelletier to get the poems printed and, anticipating his friend's success, was making lists of the men he had talked and drunk and fooled with, each of whom was to receive a complimentary copy. He varied his inscriptions with an absurdly naïve calculation—Hugo and Banville remaining his "dear Master", Leconte de Lisle receiving only his "duty", others being given his "respects", others again his "cordial friendship" and so on—but he might have saved himself the trouble. The book did indeed see the light of day thanks to Lepelletier's admirable efforts; puzzling efforts too until one remembers what Lepelletier goes out of his way to belittle, the irresistible charm of his friend. There is no more convincing evidence of it than the lifelong loyalty of Edmond Lepelletier.

Lepelletier, denied by every Paris publisher, eventually placed the manuscript outside the city. His own political journal, *Le Peuple Souverain*, the title explaining its outlook, was banned by the authorities and he moved it to Sens, south of Paris and outside the city boundaries. And he persuaded the printer at Sens to print *Romances sans Paroles*.

The optimist in his detention ward at Mons began happily to correct proofs between spells of coffee-grinding and the weaving of dreams. Lepelletier, he said, must be sure to send him every review. He began to calculate how many copies he would sell and what he could do with the money when his sentence had ended.

All in vain. The dedication to Rimbaud had been removed, but Lepelletier's caution and Verlaine's regrets were both wasted. One review—by Blémont—appeared. Not one copy was sold.

Too much indignation has been wasted on this silence. The recognition of genius has almost always been left to the next generation. Great poems are to be found in most of the volumes written by Verlaine; there were great poems in *Romances sans Paroles*, some of which have already been quoted; but its chief distinction as a book is that it shows Verlaine emancipated by the proselytising Rimbaud. Occasionally Rimbaud's influence is excessive, as when Verlaine's preoccupation with form leads him to an overdone simplicity, but in general there is found here a rhythm and a directness of speech long lost to French poetry. Yet Verlaine was far from the usual self-conscious rebel: "L'Art, mes enfants," he was to say, "c'est d'être absolument soi-même"; that was to be his sole rule. *Romances sans Paroles* is mainly composed of experiments, but such was Verlaine's taste and sincerity that very few of them read like experiments and the book marks a notable advance towards "being absolutely oneself".

But there it was: one review, not one sale. And before Verlaine could recover from this underlining of his isolation a blow fell that drove from his mind every thought of failure as poet. The book was published early in March 1874. Two weeks later the Governor came to his cell and explained as gently as he could that Mathilde had just been awarded a separation by the court in Paris, Verlaine to pay the costs and alimony of one hundred francs a month; this on the grounds of habitual drunkenness and physical ill-treatment of his wife.

4

During his months of imprisonment Verlaine had thought and written much about Mathilde, veering between abuse of a wife who had betrayed him and a longing for reconciliation. The latter attitude predominated. "I don't feel any bitterness towards her," he told Lepelletier. "God is my witness that *even today* I would forgive her everything." And again: "It's astonishing the way I grieve for her with all my heart when I think of what is going on, knowing her to be in a milieu unworthy of her and separated from the only person who really understands her—I mean *myself*." He regarded the lawsuit at one moment as a chimera, at another as a vile plot fostered by M. Mauté and which must be defended to the last; though how he was to fight it from prison did not appear.

It is easy, too easy, to dismiss Verlaine as a hypocrite; he was a blend of the naïve, the cunning and the self-deceiver, and in his way loved Mathilde, not the Mathilde of fact but the shy poet-adorer of their first meeting and the willing bed companion of the early months of marriage, the beautiful body and the receptive mind. He deceived himself but, being what he was, the deception was essential. Rimbaud silent, his whereabouts, thoughts and plans all unknown, Verlaine was thrown back on his second string. So he loved the Mathilde of fiction, dreamed of a reconciliation and a firm base on which to rest his life and affections. He had never once abandoned her in mind. If at times he suspected that he could not be content with Mathilde and would seek distraction elsewhere, he dared not face these moments of clear-sightedness; he had an unhappily strong sense of what the world expected from him, a relic of his bourgeois upbringing, and a desperate desire for security. Hence the whipped-up tirades against M. Mauté, the pose of the injured man, the pretence that Mathilde, left to him, would be ideally happy, the dismissal of their differences with a light-hearted reference to an occasional drunken spree.

And hence the overwhelming shock when he heard the Governor's news; every prop struck at one blow from under his feet. It is useless for the onlooker to protest that the props did not exist; he believed them to exist and that is the only thing that matters.

When the Governor pityingly handed over the copy of the court's judgment Verlaine collapsed. A short time afterwards he sent for the Chaplain and said that he wished to be received back into the Church. He was given devotional books. Some days later he told the Chaplain that he had recovered his faith. The Chaplain, impressed but cautious, imposed a further delay before confession and a yet longer one before absolution, but Verlaine remained steadfast and ardent. He amazed all who had to do with him, the Governor, Chaplain, warders in the prison, his mother and even the sceptical Lepelletier who visited him; he was a changed man, mild, contented and at times even radiantly happy and eager to do good to others. There was little scope for this last in prison, but he managed to give French lessons to one of the Flemish warders. Like all converts he rushed to extremes, declaring that he would abandon the writing of verse and the reading of secular books; fortunately for him the Chaplain, a sensible man, advised him to put his gifts to good use rather than to bury them. Verlaine happily began to write religious poems; the kind of poems one would expect from him, dialogues between himself and God, descriptions of his state of mind simply and ardently set down. He had a new love, and this was his theme.

Looked at in a certain light, Verlaine's conversion is both comic and insincere. But there are other lights. A sceptic would say that he sank into the comforts of religion only when denied earthly comfort. The fallacy lies in the assumption that an act loses validity because it appears forced. Verlaine could neither live without love nor exist without moral support; the Church offered both; he flew to it. His conversion was as simple as that. How sincere he was in the moment of decision, who shall say? The proof of belief, then or later, is shown in deeds. Verlaine was not made into a new man; all the old Adam remained, but he managed to live cheerfully for years without love and to live soberly—this from a highly sexual man who had been the near-slave of absinthe for the past ten years.

As for the poetical expression of this new element in his life, *Sagesse* was to be the eventual title of the collection of poems and Verlaine tells how the book was born, tells it in a letter showing that he had lost neither sense of proportion nor sense of humour. "One night in June of 1874 at Mons," he said, "after having thought for week after week, yes and fought and struggled too!, I prostrated myself before a distinctly vulgar image—but what did that matter!—of the Sacré-Cœur and remained there in tears until the bell sounded for the morning rising and the cleaning out of the cells. From that moment *Sagesse* was conceived." Like most poets, when Verlaine tries too hard he fails, and like most converts he often protests too much; some of his religious poetry is self-conscious argument which reads insincerely and therefore embarrassingly. But at times he wrote

from the heart; then he is convincing, as in this sonnet from the
sequence *Mon Dieu m'a dit.*

  —Seigneur, c'est trop! Vraiment je n'ose. Aimer qui? VOUS?
  O! non! Je tremble et n'ose. O vous aimer, je n'ose,
  Je ne veux pas! Je suis indigne. Vous, la Rose
  Immense des purs vents de l'Amour, ô Vous, tous

  Les cœurs des Saints, ô Vous qui fûtes le Jaloux
  D'Israël, Vous, la chaste abeille qui se pose
  Sur la seule fleur d'une innocence mi-close,
  Quoi, *moi, moi,* pouvoir *Vous* aimer. Êtes-vous fous,

  Père, Fils, Esprit? Moi, ce pécheur-ci, ce lâche,
  Ce superbe, qui fait le mal comme sa tâche
  Et n'a dans tous les sens, odorat, toucher, goût,

  Vue, ouïe, et dans tout son être—hélas! dans tout
  Son espoir et dans tout son remords, que l'extase
  D'une caresse où le seul vieil Adam s'embrase?

Chapter Thirteen

NOUVEAU

1875

I

O N the morning of January 16, 1875, he was released from
prison, having earned the full remission for good conduct.
He went off with his mother to Fampoux in a state of
apprehensive exaltation. Not for him the wild unthinking breath
of freedom; he was leaving not only a prison but a protection.
How would his vows survive in the midst of worldly temptation?
He had changed physically, was thinner, and as his hair reappeared his head took on the outline by which he is best known,
bald from forehead to crown, the hair growing bushily at the
sides and back. The thick eyebrows remained, shielding the long
slits of eyes, and a moustache drooped over the wide mouth and
covered much of the deep upper lip. He gave the impression at
one and the same time of benevolence and of a kind of faunish
humour. He looked much older than his age, yet when he smiled,
as he often did, the venerability dissolved into a childlike promise
of mischief.

In manner he had changed too; always affable, he was then
sweetness itself. Regular at meals, drinking only an occasional
beer, walking daily over the flat fields, anxious to help his mother
and her family, he was a model companion round the table and
fireside, punctilious in his churchgoing, a man whose weekly
confessions were so whole-hearted, so thorough as to become not
far removed from orgies.

However, man does not change but only promotes one aspect
of himself above another; Verlaine was after all not yet thirty-
one, strong, healthy, eating and sleeping well in the brisk air
of the north. In such a mood as he then was there could be no
working off his sexual energy with the girls of the village. But
some form of release was imperative. The poet came to the
rescue. Had not the Chaplain expressly counselled him not to
avoid the profane? Possibly their interpretations of the word

221

differed although even this is uncertain, the Catholic Church's view of venial sins being profoundly sensible, but before he left prison Verlaine had returned to his Shakespeare and all that Shakespeare implied and had dropped into the habit of paralleling (this being the word he was later to use) his religious poems with poems frankly and at times startlingly profane; his argument being, the first untenable ecstasy over, that man is a spiritual and physical being and that ideally for moral health both sides should be fully expressed. In fact he could do no other than express the other side, but justification is man's privilege and he freely availed himself of it.

Another thought was agitating him in those first weeks at Fampoux. As a man who had seen the light he was filled with love for all, he burned to wipe away all stains from his past, and yearned to forgive and to be forgiven. He and Mathilde were legally separated, but what of it? in the eyes of God they remained man and wife, sinners both. The thought, together with the blessed prospect of relief from alimony, was no sooner in his head than he wrote straight away to Mathilde and commanded Lepelletier to make a *démarche* at rue Nicolet.

Rue Nicolet maintained a contemptuous silence and repulsed Lepelletier's attempt to intercede. The collapse of Verlaine's dreams, by then solidified into the essence of reason, cut cruelly into the calm he had imposed on himself. In a twinkling he was back in the first days of his conversion; he had held out a hand to the world and the world had rejected him. Very well: he would withdraw himself from the world. He had heard of a Trappist monastery at Chimay a few miles inside Belgium, and although forbidden to re-enter that country he crossed the frontier secretly (the many paths had been known to him since youth), presented himself at the monastery and announced that a new monk stood before them. The father, accustomed to statements of this kind, imposed a week's trial of fasting and silence. Within a few days Verlaine was reminded unpleasantly of his first months in prison; the flesh nagged at him violently, given the strength of ten men by hour after hour of meditation on an empty stomach. Nothing would put it down. Poems not always of the godliest or chastest sort thrust themselves unbidden into his brain and on to his lips. By the end of the week he was wondering whether zeal had not carried him too far. The father mercifully thought likewise and the novice retired from the lists and sought the world again at Fampoux.

By no means satisfied, however. He lusted after converts. And as Mathilde was obdurate, what greater prize than the one whom he had helped to lead astray? Far from bearing ill will towards Rimbaud he had come to feel responsibility as the elder; and being Verlaine he could no more discard love than stop breathing. He wrote to Delahaye, then master in a college at Rethel, enclosing a letter for Rimbaud. The letter was in pious vein, begging Rimbaud to follow the writer's example: "Let us love one another in Jesus", it ended, and, as argument, pointed out that the conversion was no hurried matter lightly undertaken: "I have meditated on the subject for these last six months."

The tone of the letter came as no surprise to Rimbaud; some religious poems smuggled out of prison had been used by him as lavatory paper at Roche. He replied to Delahaye with a string of blasphemies and a contemptuous permission for "Loyola" to visit him. "A pretty thin piece of meditation", he said acidly, foreshadowing the reception Verlaine was to get.

During Verlaine's prison sentence Rimbaud had continued *Illuminations* and printed *Une Saison en Enfer*, copies of which he took to Paris, where he and his work were pointedly ignored. He had not yet reached the point at which he would see these writings as extraordinarily clever examples of precocity leading, if anywhere, straight to the madhouse. But his aims were already changing; the vast literary aspirations had given way to a wish to make money and with this money to conquer fresh fields. When Verlaine's proselytising letter reached him he was living as tutor with a family in Stuttgart so that he could learn German—this being the first stage in a campaign to master as many foreign languages as possible.

The idea of his old disciple in evil panting to convert him was a joke after his mind, an excellent opportunity of power-demonstration and unveiling of hypocrisy; he would show Verlaine exactly how much his new-found consolation was worth.

A few days later, at the beginning of March, in a letter partly occupied by drawings of a fantastic creature spitting all the way down the left-hand margin, he was writing delightedly to Delahaye: "Verlaine arrived here the other day with a rosary between his claws. . . . Three hours later he had denied his God and had made the ninety-eight wounds of our Saviour bleed afresh."

The meeting had up to a point followed its expected course, Verlaine arguing, Rimbaud leading him from bar to bar until he was tipsy, ashamed and angry. The day ended in a walk by the Neckar, the discussion still incoherently raging, and a fight on the bank of the river. The older man, not yet recovered from his prison austerities, was no match for Rimbaud; he was finally knocked insensible. Rimbaud left him lying there and walked back to the city. Some peasants discovered Verlaine, carried him to their hut for the night, washed his wounds and sent him off the next day shaken and bruised.

It would be fitting and even romantic to record that this was the last meeting of the two men, but it seems clear that they not only met again but met in amity, a fact which will surprise no one who imagines Verlaine's guilt feelings and remembers his inextinguishable fondness for Rimbaud. On Rimbaud's side there may have been some compunction; certainly he would bear in mind his ever-present need of money. He handed *Illuminations* to Verlaine in the hope that it might be published after the fashion of *Romances sans Paroles*; he also advised him or agreed with his plan (whichever was the case) to seek a teaching job in England after the visit to Paris on which Verlaine was then determined.

Yet though Rimbaud remained in essence the young man who had exercised his peculiar fascination on Verlaine, and though Verlaine had succumbed to it yet again only a few hours earlier, he had changed more than his young friend, changed to the extent that Rimbaud had influenced him for the last time. Verlaine is unlikely to have imagined any such thing, but he had the sense to leave Stuttgart. If he tried to persuade Rimbaud to join him in London, which is doubtful, he was not successful. So he went off to Paris and to a succession of failures: failure to meet Mathilde, failure to obtain a reduction of the alimony, failure to convert Lepelletier (learning no lesson, he embarked enthusiastically on this formidable task), failure to publish Rimbaud's prose poems, failure to ingratiate himself with his former companions. Not that he tried this last very hard, he was too timid, too fearful of public snubs; but in Paris one could tell without difficulty how the wind was blowing, and clearly it was not blowing his way; he met a preoccupied, harassed Villiers, shabby and prematurely worn about the face; he was received by a Blémont genuinely impressed by his latest poetry; and that was all, this was the full extent of his attempt to take up his old life.

For other reasons he feared Paris, though longing for the life there. The final executions of Communards were only two years gone and many men and women remained in prison. Feelings still ran bitter. He could not feel absolutely safe; he remembered the police agents with a shudder. Another fear, and a more serious one, was that the bars and cafés would tempt him beyond his strength. Once again he limited himself to an occasional glass of wine or beer, but Rimbaud had exposed his weaknesses and he longed to be gone. To long was to do; two days later, towards the end of March, he was in London.

2

England with or without Rimbaud's recommendation was an obvious choice for a man who had so recently endured the disgrace of a prison sentence and the shock of realising that his conversion did not necessarily protect him from a relapse into alcoholism. In England his prison record would be unknown, he would not be encouraged to drink by ever-open cafés or convivial friends, and even if watched by police agents he could not be arrested or imprisoned for his part in the Commune. Besides, the agents, if they troubled to follow his movements, would discover nothing to his disadvantage; he had done with revolutionary politics as he had done with drink and prisons. From now on he would tread the straight and narrow path; not quite so straight and narrow as the Trappist régime, there was such a thing as overdoing virtue, but far from the primrose. His natural impulses must be fettered but the fetters must not chafe, and the English were past masters at this kind of thing.

For once his calculations were correct and he was fortunate too; having registered with a scholastic agency and waited in London for a few days seeing friends and reading in the British Museum, he was told that a William Andrews of Stickney in Lincolnshire would engage him as French and drawing master in exchange for board, lodging and laundry; and he found himself by chance whisked as far from temptation as he could wish and living amidst as pleasant a set of people as he could have imagined. At Sibsey, the station nearest to Stickney, he was met by a pony-cart driven by a groom and accompanied by a chubby-faced boy of twelve. The pony, Taffy, the Andrews' main link with civilisation, took to Verlaine at once. As they bowled sedately through the twilit lanes Verlaine looked with contentment on this first rural scene he had known in England, a scene which had something in common with his mother's Pas de Calais, and the experience was embodied as usual in verse.

Opposite Stickney church in the village street they turned into the yard of a large thatched Tudor cottage with lattice windows. Whether Andrews was there to greet him seems uncertain, but he soon appeared, a man of about Verlaine's age, with a large moustache and enormous whiskers. A short dialogue followed, each man doing his best with the other's language:

"Welcome, moussou."

"Excuse me, I have got plenty of dust."

"Veux-tu laver?"

"Yes."

They went into the kitchen, where Verlaine washed his hands, and then into the parlour. To the astonishment of the visitor, unused to the vagaries of English cottage architecture, every room appeared to have been built on a different level; there were "steps everywhere" and, another English peculiarity, every chair flaunted its lace antimacassar. In the parlour Mrs Andrews bent anxiously over a cradle in which lay a little girl apparently dying. Formality, which could never live long with Verlaine, at once collapsed. Moved by the mother's distress, he burst into sympathetic tears. He tried to express his sympathy, but as Mrs Andrews had no French, her husband only a word or two, and as his English broke down under the strain he was driven to gestures. But his tears were sympathy enough; Mrs Andrews wept too, and from that moment all three became good friends.

This story, like so many of Verlaine's, should not be and need not be taken as exact truth; he was not a stickler for accuracy when his imagination ran away with him, and he wrote his reminiscences of Stickney twenty years later. In her old age Mrs Andrews could not remember the incident. The "dying" is pure

Verlaine; enough for him to see a child in a cradle and a mother in tears. But the essential point is Verlaine's immediate sympathy; it was practically impossible, living with him, to remain on anything but intimate terms, and the Andrews took to him at once; he was strange, certainly, with his black clothes, premature baldness, restless deep-set eyes, eloquent hands perpetually waving and his absurd attempts at English, but he quickly showed himself kind, considerate and wonderfully good fun; as far as his sense of humour was concerned, he might have been born an Englishman.

Next morning he was up as usual soon after dawn and went for an exploratory ramble. The macadam playground rather shocked him ("too much like French courtyards"), but he revelled in a bowling green enclosed by hedges and poplars of a greenness rarely to be seen in France. Strolling here and writing, in the notebook he always carried, a sketch of the poem inspired by the drive from the station, he was greeted by a white-bearded man who introduced himself as Canon Cottman, rector of Stickney for the past forty years. The Canon delighted Verlaine by speaking a tolerable French and still more by revealing that he had been a neighbour and admirer of Tennyson, who was born in the same county. The Canon modestly confessed himself an author, though of a different kind, having published five years earlier his *Flowers from Fatherland transplanted into English Soil*—for he was a travelled man. They got on famously, discussing under a slowly rising sun literature, art and theology. Verlaine was nothing if not accommodating and could and did attend service at the village church just as he could talk about comparative religion without trace of acrimony. In church he sat in bliss through Handel voluntaries ("what soul-stirring music!") and was pleasantly surprised by the poetry of the hymns, and out of church he fell into a friendship with the old rector, dining with him frequently, and saying of him, "I am sure if there be a God, and this God is Catholic, he must be saved; he was so charitable in addition to all his other virtues."

On this first morning, after visiting Taffy in his stall, a pig and chickens, in proper English fashion, he breakfasted with the Andrews at eight o'clock. He was then introduced to the mixed class of boys and girls as "M. Verlaine, who is a B.A. of the University of Paris. . . . He knows English as well as an English-

man, but of course he cannot pronounce it quite well"—a statement which Verlaine accepted complacently. "I am convinced",
continued Mr Andrews, "that you will like and respect this
gentleman. But should any of you take advantage of his foreign
accent to show him the least want of respect I shall lose no time
in correcting the error."

The correction seems to have been unnecessary. Verlaine as
teacher depended on his gift for drawing and his sense of humour
rather than on the knowledge he could communicate: "I teach
in English—and what English!" he told Lepelletier with a grin.
But he found his pupils "well bred and industrious", which was
another way of saying that the boys and girls, intrigued from the
beginning by his comic feats on the blackboard, accepted him
and even came to be fond of him. And as he was quickly on
excellent terms with the family and pets, a great favourite of
George the boy and Lily the little girl, of Nero the fat poodle, of
Taffy and even the "funny black kitten", his post at the
Grammar School was assured. And this meant that he was
received—and soon gladly welcomed—by the gentry as a gentleman and excellent company. He began to give private lessons to
bring in a little pocket-money: to a pupil of the vicar of Sibsey;
to the four daughters of a Sibsey doctor; to the three daughters
and son of the local Colonel; dining from time to time at these
houses and with another cleric, a former curate of Stickney, who
had a living in the next village. He also arranged for Mr Andrews
to teach him the elements of the classics in return for lessons in
French.

In no time he had become a recognised village character,
punctiliously attending church Sunday by Sunday, walking
daily with the children, even taking part in their games. Every
Saturday he walked when he could not get a lift the eight miles
into Boston to attend Mass at the Catholic church, and this too
pleased everybody but the most rabid Protestants; Frenchmen
were Frenchmen after all, knowing no better, and regularity was
regularity even though it led to Papistry. Vastly encouraged, he
began to plan a future for himself in England, a hazy but
enthusiastic one, when he had perfected his English; he liked the
people, loved their poetry and could see himself and his mother
settled in some picturesque cottage, happy, honoured and
respectable. Happy days and industrious too. He read largely

in English, notably Tennyson, spurred by the Canon's enthusiasm which he quickly reciprocated to the point of a wish to translate, Milton, Browning, Goldsmith and Bunyan, and he made some progress in Dante and *Don Quixote* in the original. And he wrote poetry, walking the garden daily, notebook open, pencil busy—Mrs Andrews used to watch him with puzzled affection—his plans heavy with greatness: an epic poem on Joan of Arc, a set of up-to-date Verlainean psalms, a "huge" sacred poem that would "turn on the Virgin . . . span from Adam and Eve to the present day, include all civilisations, all legends", a poem of which he had, he assured Delahaye, the "framework nearly ready". Fortunately what he actually wrote, or finished, in that notebook were some religious poems later to appear in *Sagesse* and in which *Hymns Ancient and Modern* played their part, and some profane poems which he began to speak of publishing as *Cellulairement*.

Mrs Andrews would no doubt have been surprised, possibly scandalised, had she read some of the poems that the strange but eminently respectable foreign gentleman was writing in his little book; but she would have been wrong, for what Verlaine was doing was not indulging his lust but working it off harmlessly or at least keeping it at bay. To live those happy days was not always the simple matter it appeared. Verlaine the potential drunkard, the potential wencher, remained very much alive under the black clothes and amiable talk, and Verlaine the Parisian lived under the surface of that admirer of the Lincolnshire countryside. The country was well enough, gave one pleasant thoughts and built up self-respect, but from time to time he felt nostalgic for the brightly lit bars, the brisk exchange of ideas in the cafés, the piles of newspapers, the scent of caporal. No, it was not easy. "I'm fighting to put down that old Me of Brussels and of London 1872-3, fighting with a kind of ferocity", he told Delahaye. He claimed no credit. Unaided, he confessed, he would have fallen and the English idyll would have collapsed, but he was not unaided and he did not fall. He remained chaste, sober and, in the main, contented.

One homely item played its part; Mrs Andrews was an excellent cook. Verlaine had never before known English home cooking and he was ravished, his letters ecstatic with descriptions of puddings and other dishes strange to him. He ate, as he did everything, with gusto; longings, regrets, ambitions were all smothered by the soporific weight of those huge meals.

Happy days; and one can imagine the shock of receiving through Delahaye a letter from Rimbaud demanding money for pianoforte lessons and to support him whilst he worked for the *baccalauréat*, and hinting that if no money were forthcoming the prison-past of the "B.A. from the University of Paris" would be revealed in the right quarters. The letter was a shock but scarcely a surprise; Verlaine was accustomed to Rimbaud's demands and to threats of one kind or another, the one serious the other usually playacting, and he was accustomed to think of the demands as justified by Rimbaud's precocious brilliance. The habit was difficult to discard, particularly when a fondness remained: what would Rimbaud do with that talent and assurance, where would he go? Greatness surely awaited him. However, Verlaine had no money, Rimbaud might just possibly do what he threatened, and he was reduced to the delightfully conspiratorial device of concealing his address and to swopping military anecdotes with the Colonel, anecdotes so heavily embroidered that the Gardes Nationales of the Ivry sector would not have recognised in him one of the modest heroes of the siege. A hero still light-heartedly facing danger; even at that late hour, he explained, he was harassed, perhaps in peril, not daring to return to Paris and followed to the very haven of Stickney by horrid threats. And he replied at length to Rimbaud: "I explained in detail my arithmetical reasons for not sending him money." He also took the opportunity, demonstrating as never before his unconquerable optimism, of once again attempting Rimbaud's conversion by argument and by further religious poems. "Loyola's latest vulgarities" shared the fate of the first batch: "I've no more time or energy to waste on him", commented Rimbaud incorrectly, for he was soon feeling the pinch again and, irritated by this unexpected firmness in Verlaine, was writing further pseudo-blackmail demands, this time to Arras, where he had heard that Mme Verlaine had taken a small house.

3

Verlaine came back to this house for his summer holidays after a first meeting with Germain Nouveau at King's Cross which produced one of the *Dédicaces*, in which poems are addressed to everybody Verlaine had known as well as to some he had never met, poems including at least one of the finest of this genre ever written. This, however, was not the poem to Nouveau, which, sobered in tone no doubt by their meeting-place, tells how they repaired to one of the "attractive bars" where they were served with bitter ale by "tall misses whiter than ermine"—a picture which demonstrates Verlaine's anglophilism at its height. Or perhaps the after-friendship with Nouveau coloured his recollection, for the men took to each other at once.

Nouveau was seven years younger than Verlaine. He had been born in the rock town of Pourrières under the shadow of Cézanne's Mont Saint-Victoire, and had been persuaded by Richepin to try his luck in Paris, a luck so inconspicuous that unlike Verlaine he had gone off with Rimbaud without the slightest harm to his reputation. He first saw Rimbaud sitting at a café, alone, ignored. He went up to him, praised his poems. Rimbaud said that he was going to London there and then; would Nouveau care to come? The magic worked; Nouveau, fascinated, accompanied him at once with only the clothes he stood up in, the key to his lodgings still in his pocket. They worked together and separately in London, parted after a typical Rimbaldian stroke, and Nouveau, bearing no malice, ranged through Belgium, Holland and northern France writing poems and making pictures: to the point—since he had to live—of selling love lyrics to a wealthy but inarticulate Russian courting a Belgian actress; a lucrative business until Nouveau, allowing his imagination too much play, wrote a poem which earned the Russian a box on the ears.

All this and more Verlaine had heard from Delahaye and Blémont; naturally it intrigued him. He sent Nouveau the poems Rimbaud had given him at Stuttgart, for, having won the liking of Charles Cros, the young man from the Midi seemed to have a better chance of placing them in Paris. An exchange of letters so much impressed Verlaine that he urged Nouveau, who talked of a return to England, to meet him in London.

They compared notes, talked of Rimbaud, with what emotion on the part of the susceptible Verlaine can be imagined. The words "fils du soleil" were repeated by Nouveau; so Rimbaud had tried again! They also compared impressions of those extraordinary English amidst whose silence, broken only by the shouted order, the occasional dirty joke whispered in a corner, the drunken laugh rising above a littered table, they drank and talked. "Undocile, incurious, calm, never amused"— so Nouveau saw them. "In France", he said, "one goes out to live; in England one goes in . . . a disgusting life for the unmarried."

But if Verlaine had been moved primarily by curiosity to see his successor with "The Being", one of his names for Rimbaud, he had other reasons for the journey from Stickney, planned originally to meet his mother and bring her back to Lincolnshire. He also thirsted for news of Paris as well as of Rimbaud, for talk of poetry, of the Parnassians, in a word for intellectual discussion. He quickly rated Nouveau as a "lover of learning" and honoured him in a scribble at the bottom of a letter by admission as junior member to the group of "seekers" Rimbaud—Delahaye—Verlaine. Nor was this the end or even the major part of Nouveau's attraction; he was, Verlaine discovered, violently impressionable and wonderful material for a man hankering after converts; Rimbaud, Delahaye, Lepelletier had all rejected Verlaine's good offices, but Nouveau, though calling himself atheist, was made of different stuff, with a strong religious background and a nature which, like Verlaine's, demanded a strong hand. Verlaine got to work in the short time allowed him. Not without success; he did not convert Nouveau, but his warnings against the temptations of London and the stultifying effect of a small school had immediate effect; Nouveau withdrew hurriedly from London, where he had intended to spend many months, and from the country school where he acted as assistant master for two days; returning to Paris and then to Pourrières with a thankful "I should have been properly caught if God hadn't been waiting for me there." For God in this instance one reads Verlaine, who returned to Stickney with the glow of well-doing, leaving Nouveau after agreeing that they should meet at Arras as soon as possible.

At Arras that summer Verlaine was sweetness and light; Delahaye, influenced by the cynical jokes of Rimbaud, came over from Rethel with a friend expecting to unmask a hypocrite, but he could find no trace of insincerity, no excess of religious emotionalism; Verlaine went his long walks because he liked them, avoided the cafés because he had made up his mind to keep sober, talked and joked freely with the air of a man with a good conscience, worked hard at his English and in spurts at his poetry. Only one incident marred the harmony. Verlaine at his mother's request showed Delahaye the inevitable book of photographs. As he turned to the page on which a photograph of Mathilde was fixed, another photograph slipped to the ground. Mme Verlaine picked it up with an exclamation. "Yes, it's my bane, Mossieu Rimbaud," said Verlaine, mimicking Rimbaud's uncouth accent. He held out a hand, and despite his mother's protest fitted the photo of Rimbaud on the page opposite the photo of Mathilde and slammed the book shut "with a mischievous grin". "There!" he said, "I've united the two creatures who have caused me the most suffering."

If proof were needed of Verlaine's humility, the chance was offered this same holiday. The rump of the Parnassians was preparing for a third and, as everyone else realised, a last *Parnasse Contemporain*. The Parnassian movement was dead, though not unexpectedly none of the survivors would confess to it. Leconte de Lisle indeed had never been more master of all he surveyed, which was not now very much. Banville continued charmingly witty about less and less, and the rotundity of the middle fifties made his boyish fun seem a little, ever so little, absurd; he had to face increasing danger that he would be laughed at for himself instead of for what he said. Mendès had become the laughing-stock of Paris; the ageing Hugo had made a cuckold of him, had ravished his young and beautiful wife under his very eyes, so to speak. Already displaced from all influence in the Parnasse, Mendès blustered his way out of this new reverse by a display of riotous living which offended many. The *Comité des Grâces* of Banville, Coppée and France not only privately criticised each other (Coppée was marked for early extinction as altogether too popular) but together, led by France, resolved to throw overboard all who were unsympathetic to them. The jettisoning was considerable; Mérat and Valade went, Sully Prudhomme ("He is not of this house," Leconte de Lisle ruled), De Ricard ("His poems need cleaning," France said), Charles Cros, who had become *persona non grata* at Leconte de Lisle's apartment ("I resign if he goes in," threatened France) and even Mallarmé, both Coppée and France rejecting him.

"He is making a mock of us," the latter declared. The rejected poem was *L'Après-midi d'un Faune*.

Then in blundered the ever-hopeful Verlaine. Surely, he reasoned, he would be taken back into the fold now that he had paid for his transgressions, had seen the light and could offer work demonstrating his advance as poet. He submitted a number of recent and near-recent poems including *Beauté des femmes*, which was in another world of inspiration and artistry from the accepted Parnassian contributions. His entry caused an embarrassed sensation. Banville and Coppée refused to vote one way or the other. The decision was left to France, who settled his place in literary criticism by writing: "No. The author is unworthy and his lines are some of the worst I've ever read."

Verlaine's overtures to this *passé* remnant will seem comical to the most cursory reader of French literary history, yet from his point of view he had good reason. As a young man he had tried to be a good Parnassian because he hated the thought of being a poet (or anything else for that matter) in isolation; his friends were or wanted to be Parnassians—that was argument enough. And the argument held good for him in 1875 as in 1861; to be received into the third *Parnasse Contemporain* would have meant reconciliation with his old companions of the 'sixties, the lifting of the moral ban, the prospect of walking the familiar streets or sitting at the familiar cafés without being obliged to avert his eyes every five minutes. That was the purpose of his application, the purpose of his whole life one might almost say. "L'amour, voyez-vous, croyez-m'en plutôt que de m'en blâmer d'avance, c'est sinon le tout, ah! du moins le presque tout, le mobile quasiment unique de toutes les actions dignes de ce nom, et ne me parlez pas d'autre chose, ambition, lucre, gloire! tout au plus peut-être de l'Art. Et encore, et encore, l'Art, tout seul . . . ?"

He reacted well to Anatole France's display of bigotry, to the cowardice of Coppée and Banville; his first remark was a "this is laughable, this proscription of Lemerre's; it began with the Commune don't you think? Ever since then Leconte de Lisle has regarded me as an ogre." He did well to point to Leconte de Lisle, "who has been a pig to me after most friendly relations", for Leconte de Lisle had dismissed Verlaine with a "people with more merit than this animal have been shot on sight". But after the first shock Verlaine followed the true Christian tradition, turned the other cheek and offered, when the anthology appeared, to try to sell it in England. This too was refused, and he returned to Stickney to make the best of schoolmastering.

He had not long been back when Rimbaud began to pester him again. Verlaine protested to Delahaye, who remained their intermediary. Delahaye, one of Rimbaud's admirers, was shocked by the decline of his god. Rimbaud, he reported, was declaring that he would write no more, that he despised literature. "What insolence!" Rimbaud was impious and sneered at religion. "Unhappy wretch!" Rimbaud would stoop to the meanest deceit to screw a little money out of his few friends in Charleville. Was he going mad? Delahaye thought that this was the most charitable conclusion; he would surely end in Charenton.

Verlaine knew Rimbaud better; no madness there; but he was hurt: "First he replied with impertinences garnished with vague threats of blackmail, then with ridiculous calculations by which he demonstrates that it would be good business for me to lend him the money. Not to mention a letter written in a kind of drunken gibberish amidst which I made out the statement that future letters would include the demand that I 'fork out' or else —*zut!*

"In a word he is still banking on my old foolishness, on my wicked stupidity not so long past of wanting to live only through him and by him. Add the intolerable rudeness of a child whom I spoilt and who repays me—the logic, the justice of it!—with criminal ingratitude. Hasn't he in fact killed the goose who laid the golden eggs?"

He could not see Rimbaud in Charenton, he told Delahaye, but he believed that a young man who thought that to be insolent was to be strong and that to swindle one's friends was a sign of cleverness was no better than a cad who at thirty might prove a very nasty customer. In a real sense this exceedingly brilliant youth was behaving unintelligently. Verlaine's admiration, he admitted, was perhaps built on sand, nevertheless if Rimbaud would only show a sign of change of heart his affection and friendship were "Christianly available, that goes without saying".

This letter, passed on by Delahaye, silenced Rimbaud. But Verlaine, who was nothing if not contrary, or, to put the matter more charitably, who longed to share his blessings, was not easy in his mind. He feared for the blasphemer and grieved over the lost poet who had written such masterly verses at Charleville. His conscience worried him. How much was he responsible?

Such thoughts clouded some of the autumn and early winter days at Stickney, days otherwise of a calm and delightful monotony, days which began with the morning ramble, Verlaine light-heartedly leaping stiles, continued with the little morning service before school ("but what a sad cult, this, and absolutely without reason", he told Delahaye) and was enlivened by huge helpings of Mrs Andrews' masterpieces, gooseberry fool and seedcake. At length, before leaving for Arras for the Christmas holidays, Verlaine's anxiety broke out in a final appeal:

"Despite my promise (if I remember rightly), I haven't written to you earlier because I was waiting for a satisfactory letter from you. Nothing received, nothing answered. Today, however, I break my long silence to confirm all that I wrote you some two months ago.

I remain the same always. Strictly religious because this is the only good and intelligent thing to be. Everything else is trickery, wickedness, stupidity. The Church has made modern civilisation, science, literature: she has made France particularly, and France is dying because she has broken with her. That's clear enough. And the Church makes men too, *creates* them. I'm astonished you don't see this, it's so strikingly obvious. I had plenty of time during those eighteen months to think again and again on these things and I assure you that I cling to it as my only plank. And seven months spent amongst Protestants has confirmed me in my Catholicism, my legitimism, my resigned courage.

Resigned for the good reason that I see and feel myself as justly punished, justly humiliated, and know that the severer the lesson the greater the pardon and the obligation to respond to it.

How can you think that this is a pose or a pretext? Why do you write to me of (I can't remember the exact words) *'modifications of the same sensitive individual'*, *'rubbish'*, *'tommy-rot'*—all bunkum and a medley of nonsense . . .

So I'm always the same. The same affection (modified) for you. I greatly wish I could see you enlightened, reflective. It's a great grief to me to see you following such idiotic paths, you so intelligent, so *ready* (however much this may surprise you!). As proof of it I point to your own disgust with everything and everybody, your perpetual anger against all things—reasonable enough at bottom, this anger, though you don't know *why*.

As for this matter of money, you can't really fail to recognise that I am *generosity itself*: this is one of my very rare virtues—or one of my very many faults, as you please. But, this granted, and the need to repair, by little economies, the enormous breaches made in my tiny capital by *our* absurd and shameful life three years ago— and bearing my son in mind also, and also my new and firm principles, you must understand perfectly well that I can't support you. In any case, where would my money go? On drinks and pub owners! Piano lessons? What *humbug*! Hang it all, wouldn't your mother agree to pay for them?

In April you wrote me letters so revelatory of your base and wicked plans that I can't risk giving you my address—although any attempts to harm me would be ridiculous and powerless from the outset, and besides I warn you that they would be answered *legally*, with evidence. But I pass over this odious hypothesis. It's some fugitive *caprice* of yours I'm sure, some unhappy brainstorm which a little reflection will drive away. However, prudence is the mother of safety, so I won't give you my address until I'm certain of you. . . .

Come, confound it all, show a good impulse, a little heart, some consideration and feeling for one who remains always, as you know, your very cordial P. V.

PS. I'll explain my plans—very simple!—and the counsels I should like to see you follow, religion apart, though this would be my great, great, great counsel, when you have replied *properly via* Delahaye."

Rimbaud did not reply.

Chapter Fourteen

NOUVE

1876-1879

I

VERLAINE had intended the Christmas term at Stickney to be his last. He believed, a shade optimistically, that his English was good enough for him to strike out on his own and earn some money, and he planned to establish himself at Boston, where he had made friends. But the Andrews were reluctant to let him go, a fact which says much for him as master or more probably as enlivening companion, and he was offered a small salary and some lessons in German if he would stay on. He agreed to remain for the spring term.

"L'*arrrgent* avant tout, vous savez", he told Blémont, mocking the pronunciation and abiding weakness of Rimbaud, but his plan to move was not made solely for money. Stickney and its people were as near perfection as Verlaine was likely to reach, they had given him almost everything he had dreamed of in prison—safety, respectability, affection, good living. But he discovered that there were other things; for an intelligent Parisian in his early thirties an English village showed itself after a few months as not far distant from death, a pleasant death but death all the same; and he realised that he would prefer less perfection and more life. Boston was a town, it had life of a kind, and if Verlaine had his way it would have more. It was not his intention to set up in Boston on his own; he hoped to persuade Nouveau to join him, either as French master in his place at Stickney or at Boston helping in the decoration of the Catholic church.

He had been thinking a great deal about Nouveau; in him he had found, it seemed, a substitute for Rimbaud and a more amenable if less exciting one, master and pupil changing places. Nouveau was flatteringly conscious of Verlaine's status as poet and responded eagerly to his encouragement, writing and sending him poems for criticism. A correspondence was soon in full swing, Verlaine presenting his "Nouve", as he quickly became, with a photograph of himself taken in Boston. For his part Nouveau tried to persuade his new leader back to Paris: Why bother about the Parnasse? he asked; it was "a detestable milieu and generally sickening. I shall arrange in the future to have nothing more to do with *them*." Nina, whose advice he asked, said: "If I were Verlaine I should definitely come back to Paris and get along very nicely without going to the Voltaire or seeing my former comrades—not very amusing anyway. As soon as I was successful in the press or theatre they'd come round all right—if I still wanted them."

Verlaine, however, was not Nina, and after he had spent a few days of his Christmas holidays in Paris Nouveau recognised his objections as just and eventually agreed with a "Knowing you so much changed, I ask myself whether you don't do well to go to Boston." Yes, he had changed, but this did not mean that he was resigned to a lifetime of exile, not merely physical exile but mental and emotional too; he still had a heart and a tongue, and was less than half a man with both virtually out of action. If Paris was undesirable on several counts, perhaps a snatch of Paris could be brought to him. Rimbaud's obduracy had left a gap, not in his affections, which were inexhaustible, but in his opportunities for tangible expression of them. But if God took with one hand He gave with the other. "Nouve" had a look of "Rimbe" if one was not hair-splitting; his eye blazed, fascinated; he was as wilful, he dressed as weirdly, he was just as dirty. He had not Rimbaud's ambitions, which was perhaps as well, he was often timid and hesitant where Rimbaud was bold and assured, he showed no sign of Rimbaud's extraordinary intelligence. This too was doubtless a mercy. But his potentialities had won over the critical Rimbaud and he possessed a sense of humour and a temperament which Rimbaud was without. One could call it madness, this temperament—it was to be called that—but to Verlaine the flashes of excessive emotion, the queer flights of imagination, the posturing, the inexplicable japes, appeared chiefly as an intimation that in Nouveau he had found pupil, convert, companion and stimulator all in one. There was besides a kind of poetic justice in the event; Rimbaud gone, his chosen lieutenant takes his place.

And not Nouveau only; Nouveau had a sister who admired Verlaine's poetry, who wrote poetry herself ("not bad", said her brother), who even had a look of Verlaine in the oriental setting of her eyes, who was "very loving" and whom Nouveau "would much like to see married". Marriage was not on Verlaine's cards but all else was possible. So let them both come! And let them found in the Lincolnshire wilds a little Paris in which love, art and religion would go hand in hand.

But the new year of 1876 had not ended its first month before these hopes were dashed in a manner well known to Verlaine: "her poverty as well as mine", reported Nouveau, prevented them from raising even the fare. And the move to Boston at once took on a new and less promising aspect.

He summoned his mother; having gone so far, having spoken to Andrews more than once about his wish to leave, he would try to establish that respectable little English home which had been hovering in his mind for years. If his hopes were realised, he might after all be able to pay for Nouveau and his sister to join them.

Mme Verlaine arrived late in February or the beginning of March. She knew only one word of English, but at once made a good impression; what struck everybody was the deep affection between mother and son, an affection shown a little too openly for English tastes (their morning embrace, for instance, was almost loverlike) but which nevertheless went to the heart. Verlaine, who had already added to his popularity by a display of virtuosity on the ice—the winter was a hard one—won golden opinions by his touching attentions to his ageing mother, then in her sixty-eighth year.

Mme Verlaine amused the village by her talkativeness and vivacity and quickly made herself at home. She lodged with the tailor, the man who made such queer noises in the choir every Sunday, but took her meals with the Andrews. She had the gift which her son displayed in even greater degree, of getting on terms with the most varied of people; the children took to her and she went the round of the pets with Verlaine, fed Taffy and the rest and in short displayed the kind heart and streak of sentimentality beloved of the English. She was asked out to dinner with her son and finally crowned her popularity by responding to a village disaster, a small fire, by unmistakable gestures of sympathy and by the royal gift to the unfortunates of a sovereign.

When she and Verlaine left for Boston at the end of the month,

Verlaine at Boston, 1876

Verlaine at Bournemouth, 1877

Germain Nouveau: Self-portrait, 1880

they were seen off by a little crowd truly sorry to see them go. For perhaps the first time in his life Verlaine left no mixed feelings behind him; he had shown in that year at Stickney all the best side of his nature and not one serious weakness. Yet the move was inevitable; he did good work at Stickney because he was inspired by the novel life; the moment the novelty wore thin, the poet was doomed; and whether he knew it or not the man was motivated by the poet.

Stickney had been a lucky chance; Boston was a mistake. Verlaine perhaps counted on a paid post at the Grammar School there; this seems to explain his reference to finding "a more lucrative position at Boston" and his daily hopes of a letter about it. But the good news never arrived and he set off with his mother into the blue with nothing more encouraging ahead of him than his friendships with an Italian photographer (the one who had taken the portrait sent to Nouveau and others), an Irish customs officer and the Catholic priest, the German Père Sabela; there were no more free meals, lodging and laundry; everything had to be paid for.

He and his mother put up at an inn and Verlaine advertised two or three times for pupils in French, Latin and elementary drawing. The result was disappointing; at the end of two months he could muster only three pupils, one of them Père Sabela's brother, who was decorating the little church—the work in which Verlaine had hoped Nouveau might join.

He called regularly at the Sabela house for tea and taught French as best he could in English, their one common tongue. The best was not very good, but for a few weeks he and his mother lived happily enough, visiting the Sabelas and attending mass at the chapel. Canon Cottman, an open-minded man, had contributed to the decoration of the little building, the Haydn and Mozart played there pleased Verlaine, the congregation, made up of foreigners, Irish and one or two of the old English Catholic families, interested him. For the rest he spent much of his time in a museum in the form of a grotto which belonged to the inn. The museum exhibits were except in one particular un-remarkable—queer shells, pebbles, old weapons and armour—but the complete skeleton of a whale fascinated him; he loved to sit inside it with his friend the Italian, smoking his pipe and drinking a glass of beer like a modern Jonah.

By the beginning of June he abandoned hope of earning a living on his own and, as his mother feared for the remnant of her capital, he went back with her to Arras, leaving his name once more with the agency in London. He was soon engaged as French and Latin master in a school at Bournemouth (Bournemouse to him) and took up the post in September.

Although he was paid sixty pounds a year all found except laundry, this new post proved to be far from another Stickney. Frederick Remington, a Protestant clergyman converted to Catholicism, had founded St Aloysius College for boys whose parents considered their health too "delicate" for a public school, which was a delicate way of attracting the snob, the stupid and the misfit. Despite the impressive name, Verlaine found no more than a dozen or so pupils to be taught, but the dozen included some "absolute devils" of Irish boys, one of whom was to throw a snowball weighted by a stone which knocked him unconscious. Unlike Stickney, the classes were all male and the average age of the boys at Bournemouth was higher; there were no more comic blackboard sketches, and Verlaine's disciplinary weaknesses must have been rudely exposed.

He managed nevertheless to earn Remington's approval, though this may have been more by charming the principal than disciplining the boys; and it was not so much the classes which worried him as his obligation to "superintend the pupils generally". Ominous words, which in practice meant daily walks and monitorial duties out of classroom hours. As long as the warmth lasted, the walks were tolerable since they ended in sea bathing for all, but in winter, with conversation practically at a standstill, they became an unmitigated bore.

As consolation he enjoyed his Sunday services at the church attached to a picturesque Jesuitière, services fortified by good music; and when he was free to walk alone the miles of sea with its foreground of gorse-covered cliffs pleased the poet. As at Stickney, grandiose plans abounded, but the poems actually written remained genuine impressions and not a moral hotchpotch conceived in duty. But though he could write poetry, worship Shakespeare and adulate Tennyson, promising himself to translate *In Memoriam*, though he could enjoy the quiet voices, the soft country and seascapes, hard facts would intrude.

He was bored, he had no outlet for his affections. His mind turned as always to Paris. News from there was politically reassuring; the *Comité des Grâces* had at last finished its work, most of the people arrested for complicity with the Commune had been freed from prison, there was even talk of a general amnesty. Surely he would be safe. And he would again be within reach of Mathilde and his son Georges.

For he had not given up hope of Mathilde. What was a separation, as legal as man could make it? When he thought of her he loved no part of Catholicism quite so much as the decree that man and wife once joined are inseparable in the eyes of God. He had consulted Delahaye amongst others, had even, it appears, meditated proposing, had his Boston venture succeeded, that Mathilde should join him there. The best thing, Delahaye had advised, "would be perhaps to get the young person *alone*— carefully avoiding contact with the papa—and speak some frank and simple words in which you would categorically propose to her that she come to join you in England. Who knows if this little *coup d'état* wouldn't tear aside the spiders' webs?"

Verlaine did not forget his friend's advice. Boston had failed, he had not made a home for himself in England, but the advice still applied. Moreover, he had thought up a new tactic, one which had the merit of unambiguous feeling: he would recover Mathilde by way of the fatherless child. Georges was then almost six years old. Verlaine had not seen him out of swaddling clothes. Georges would love his father; why should he not enjoy a father's love? Verlaine lashed himself into a passion, and the thing, in imagination, was done: childish arms round his neck and the rest would follow.

He was enormously encouraged by a chance remark of Hugo. He sent some poems to the old man with the customary assurance that such merit as they might possess had come from the master's example. "Your poems", replied Hugo, "are simply superb. I am proud to have inspired them; you should be not less so to have written them." And he ended: "Give my compliments to your charming wife." So Hugo believed that husband and wife were happily reunited! If he believed it, a reunion must be possible, reasonable, not just an optimistic delusion of the husband. Verlaine's reply has unfortunately been lost, but the encouragement was plain.

But to be with Mathilde and his son he would have to regain Paris and earn a living there, if only to appease M. Mauté. Lessons in English in a French school: that was the obvious answer. Hugo's letter reached him at Christmas when he and his mother were on a visit to Paris. He at once consulted Lepelletier. "Testimonials from your English schools," answered Lepelletier; anything less than a year's residence might sound a little thin.

Verlaine soared back to Bournemouth, dreams gloriously weaving; he would earn the second of his testimonials and then! "for the Capital of the world, 'where one has a good laugh' as the poet says!" But for himself, he assured Lepelletier, "I shall lead a more monastic life than ever, my only pleasure an occasional sight of my little boy."

The year dragged itself out. The snowball fight was a grand incident in a life of futile agitations, of tedious hours with the boys, of pipes smoked slowly over Remington's fire in the winter evenings, of long spring walks across the heath to Poole, the pocket-book busy. At last *Sagesse* was ready, blend of the boring and the inexpressibly beautiful, with its inimitable Verlainean line

Vous voilà, vous voilà, pauvres bonnes pensées!

Again he called on the help of Lepelletier: a religious publisher this time, he urged; but even that kind seemed wary; nothing happened. Evidently he ought to place the book himself; a final argument in favour of a return to Paris.

Another and very different matter worried the militant Catholic he had become. It seemed to him at times that England was almost entirely composed of Protestants turned Catholic; there was Remington, in the Jesuitière were two more converted parsons, one of them a nephew of Manning, at Boston there had been English strong in the Faith, even the Canon had contributed towards the decorations of the church on the canal bank. Manning's nephew, Anderton, had given a series of talks at Bournemouth on the Catholic Church and its doctrines; heard, read or repeated, these too helped to influence the impressionable Verlaine; everywhere the tide was turning, yet he, a brand snatched from the burning if ever there were one, a magnificent example of what the Church could do for the least of wretches, remained without a scalp to his name, he was taking no part in the great movement that was sweeping England and that must regenerate France.

The fact was that Verlaine's face would not satisfactorily absorb a pious expression. In religious mood he looked the hypocrite; the piety dissolved into a Tartuffian smugness. This he did not know; he felt that if the world would not hear the poet it might listen to the preacher, and he yearned in proselytising moments to bring others into the fold. He yearned vainly until the summer of 1877, when, having completed his year at Bournemouth by "superintending" through the holidays, he went back to Arras with a testimonial from Remington in his pocket. He was joined there by Nouveau, and lo, the miracle!

Hitherto Nouveau had repulsed all attempts at conversion. Not that he was fundamentally unsympathetic in so far as he could be said to have any guiding light in him at all; two of his family were in a convent in Pourrières; but he remained in essence a disciple of Rimbaud, wrote weak and incomprehensible poetry, painted lascivious pictures, disported himself when in Paris at rue des Moines where Nina was rapidly going down the hill, and in brief followed every whim and said whatever came into his head, being governed only by the need to earn a living. This in 1877 had brought him to Charleville as *surveillant* in an institution. Perhaps this experience led him to Arras in thoughtful mood; he may well have noticed a certain resemblance between the patients and their keeper; whatever the occasion or the cause, he lent an ear to the voluble Verlaine and to his mentor's joy announced himself a reclaimed Catholic.

There followed a few days of spiritual revelry as the lost lamb was welcomed home. Then perplexity reared its head as Nouveau made clear that the revelry was to remain strictly spiritual. Nouveau was a young man who did not comprehend the meaning of half measures; his religious ardour became frightening, almost indecent in its ferocity, and the piety of his converter was exposed as having the consistency of water. There were long and, to one of the party, slightly wearisome discussions on the nature of faith, the precise duties of the true Catholic; dogma seemed to dog all their conversations. "Nouveau is charming, isn't he; but what a Jansenist!" wrote Verlaine uneasily. "Verlaine", wrote Nouveau firmly, "is a child who needs to be led. Sometimes I am very fierce with him; but without it one would achieve nothing." "Here I'm living more and more like a hermit", wrote the child with a decidedly mutinous pout. "I've given up the 'Sanpeur' café or at the most go there on Saturday afternoons to look at the illustrated papers." For there had been trouble over the Christianly glass of beer at the Arras cafés. One, perhaps; two at a pinch; but when Verlaine made motions to order a third Nouveau's thick eyebrows would contract and his eyes flash remonstrance. At home Mme Verlaine, bewildered, watched the struggle between the two sons of the Church. Opposition merely whetted Verlaine's appetite. The day came when he and Nouveau faced each other across a café table close to hatred. Verlaine, unexpectedly obstinate, had managed to persuade eight glasses of beer to slip down the throat of the sultry convert; he was about to order the ninth, a light not recently seen illuminating his eye, when Nouveau rose and took an angry leave.

Verlaine, back to his senses, sought his friend in vain: Nouveau had left for Paris. Verlaine wrote to him apologetically, prostrating himself. Useless; Nouveau would not answer. Verlaine played his last card: meet me, he begged, "at High Mass at Saint-Sulpice" on such and such a day. An agitated backslider attended the mass; no Nouveau.

It was about this time that Delahaye gave him news of Rimbaud. Verlaine and Rimbaud were not to meet again or to correspond, but one at least did not forget the other. Verlaine heard then of Rimbaud's wanderings through Italy, his enlistment at Marseilles as would-be Carlist volunteer, enlistment in Holland in the Dutch colonial army, voyage to Batavia, desertion and escape to France, journey to Vienna, to Hamburg as interpreter in a circus, to Sweden, to Denmark—a flight from himself that aroused loving bitterness in the heart of the one man who truly cared for him. How well he knew the boy and how futile he knew this odyssey to be! He put all this into the inimitable *Dargnières Nouvelles*. This poem, written in the lazy, sulky Ardennais of Rimbaud and employing the argot, the crudities and the "secret" language of abbreviations and associations used by them together, exposed the boy with a devastatingly humorous and penetrating irony. Here is Rimbaud as he spoke, lived and thought; not only the Rimbaud of past and present but the Rimbaud of the future.

Rimbaud lost, Nouveau gone, he turned to his own flesh and

blood; if all the world rejected him, there remained his son. In Paris again, he sent a peremptory note demanding that Georges be allowed to spend some days with him. Georges did not appear.

Lepelletier could not cheer him: no one would publish *Sagesse*; no one wished to engage him as English master. That the baffled Verlaine, a step from the Paris cafés and their absinthe, somehow shunned the sorceress said much for the faith that Nouveau had found so weak. He had made up his mind to apply for another post at an English school, when he ran into Delahaye. They adjourned to a café. Delahaye explained that he was on his way to Orléans, where he had found a new and better post. Verlaine raised his eyebrows at this and Delahaye explained why he had left the college at Rethel. Verlaine was a good and sympathetic listener—Delahaye, like many others, comments on his ability, so rare, to hear the other man out and really to listen, not merely to wait for his own turn to speak. And as usual he had the reward of a good listener; Delahaye went on too long, his complaints amounting to nothing more serious than that the atmosphere at Rethel was a little too religious for his liking.

At this Verlaine leaned back with a dreamy laugh: "What you give up so cheerfully would be paradise to me. To live in the midst of good priests . . . myself as a Christian profiting from all . . . if I had had this happiness, this half-monastic life without the rigidity—too much for me—of vows and total renunciation . . . !"

Delahaye, however, did not see the college at Rethel in this light; the conversation moved to other things, including Verlaine's imminent departure for London and the scholastic agency. They dined together, drank a beer or two at the cafés, Verlaine laughed and joked as always in company he liked; apparently he had not a care in the world and nothing more to say about Rethel.

One week later Delahaye received a letter which opened "Dear Predecessor". The morning after their evening together Verlaine, precipitately abandoning England, had taken the train to Rethel, sought out the man in charge of lay teachers, introduced himself as a friend of Delahaye and offered his services as English master. The man was impressed by Verlaine's testimonials from Stickney and Bournemouth and by his appearance and behaviour—grave, reverend, judicious, the very soul of propriety. He was engaged.

2

Verlaine's instinct had served him rightly and was to give him two of the happiest years of his life. The college of Notre-Dame at Rethel was an institution after his heart at that particular time, offering peace, security, company, occupation, all within the framework of organised religion. It even provided a familiar and well-liked background, for Rethel was only a few miles below Charleville and the countryside was reminiscent of Paliseul where he had spent so many months of boyhood and of which he had only happy memories.

The college, though founded some twenty years earlier by the Archbishop of Rheims to prepare boys for the priesthood, was open to all and offered a general education to those wishing to lead a secular life. And though staffed mainly by priests, the atmosphere differed little from any ordinary secondary school; the religious background was not obtrusive. If Verlaine at first felt out of his depth it was because his exaggerated assumption of all the Christian virtues set him apart from the human and quite jolly staff; he declined their modest daily glass of wine with a scarcely concealed gesture of horror, he regarded the smoking briar with apparent disgust, stood aloof when after-dinner tales circulated, and was in every respect too good to be true.

But to his fellow-teachers Verlaine's piety appeared suspiciously close to hypocrisy. Far from being thought, as he had fondly imagined, a model master, he was shunned as—of all things—a *pudeur* employed secretly by the Archbishop. Happily this object lesson in misguided hypocrisy ended abruptly one day when Verlaine's sense of humour, tickled beyond control, came out in a great burst of jovial laughter. This unexpected sound from the college Malvolio staggered and relieved everyone; he was immediately offered and readily accepted a glass of wine, he lit up the hungry pipe, he told a fairly decorous story or two and was suddenly found to be a very good fellow.

From then onwards his path was smooth. He may not have been a good teacher, but he was certainly a most unusual one. His method of teaching English was to persuade his pupils to pronounce French with an English accent; the lesson began each day as Verlaine entered the room with the class on its feet chorusing "Baoun-jaur, maossiun Voeulaine!" Nor does the following dialogue suggest that he was the ideal teacher of history, although it does show how far he had moved from the politics of Parnassian days.

"Who were the Girondins?"

"The Girondins, sir . . . the Girondins . . . were . . . the deputies from the Gironde."

"Well?"

"Sir?"

"Their views, the rôle they played?"

"Sir?"

"You don't know. Right! Then who does know?"

"I do, sir."

"Well?"

"They were . . . the moderates."

"They were not the moderates. Someone else . . . yes, you."

"Sir, they wanted to end the revolution."

"Not on your life!"

"Sir, it says so in our history book."

"Never mind what your book says. The Girondins were the maddest, the most dangerous fools in the whole frightful revolutionary crew, do you understand?"

He was popular with the boys, masters and servants (especially with the servants), and every evening made coffee in his room for a little crowd of callers. He accepted gratefully the small bottle of wine supplied with lunch and the liqueur after dinner and showed not the slightest disposition to augment them. He had ample leisure to write his poems but not too much to tempt him elsewhere. He had privacy when he wanted it after classes were over, and if he preferred company, that too was open to him. The daily prayers, the public readings from the scriptures, the prolonged Sunday devotions all wove a comfortable web of good thinking about him. The very position of the college, backing on to the church high above the town, soothed him and promised a lifetime of safety. "This is a kind of paradise to me," he told Lepelletier, "where I have peace and calm and freedom." He wrote in similar sense to Mallarmé, who was still teaching English, and to Delahaye. All that he had to teach, including

I* 249

history, literature and geography, were "amusing and dis-
tracting". Delahaye, witnessing this enthusiasm with a smile,
hoped that he would settle down and not show himself "a
hideous anglophile" incapable of appreciating his own country.
And so it seemed. His behaviour remained exemplary and the
legend (not begun by him) that he was a pious gentleman in
reduced circumstances seemed, if action is the criterion, more
truthful than the facts with which naturally enough he had not
troubled the headmaster.

A year went by. He astonished all in Paris and in Arras, where
he had spent his holidays, by presenting a front resolutely
Christian and by resisting without apparent effort the many
temptations of the Exhibition then filling the capital. And when
the Archbishop made his annual visit to the college he was more
than a little surprised to discover that one of his teachers was
an ex-convict, Communard, drunkard and husband, Verlaine
seizing this opportunity to release the burden of his conscience
in confession. Absolution followed and with it the job remained
safe, for life the exhilarated man began to hope.

Yet it was not to be for life, and perhaps none but Verlaine
would ever have thought so. The security and the guidance
appealed powerfully to him, but he had a body healthy as never
before because of the English years, strong and with strong needs
which could not be balked indefinitely; he was only thirty-four
despite the misleading bald pate, and by no means ready for a
semi-monastic life. The question was, in the long run, whether
his physical needs were to be satisfied in respectability or not.
Would Mathilde accept him again? And there was another
question. At Rethel he endured—the word is not too strong—
chastity, respectability and mental decorum—endured them
mainly in the hope of winning Mathilde back. The last of the
three was not the least agonising to a man with a remarkable
if erratic intellect. How long could he bear the musty common-
room conversation, the very graveyard of intellectual liberty?

In Paris that Exhibition summer he had got in touch with
De Sivry. That happy-go-lucky individual was free from moral
attitudes and welcomed him enthusiastically. In no time they
had arranged to go into partnership again, De Sivry agreeing
readily to write an opera on the Temptations of St Antony,
Verlaine's libretto to follow Flaubert. This was slightly off the

beaten track for the musical director of the Chat Noir, but
De Sivry would agree to anything for the sake of a good huddle
over a drink. Not that Verlaine drank much, but De Sivry could
always drink enough for two.

Verlaine, having salved his conscience with St Antony, used
De Sivry as ambassador at rue Nicolet; he was to present a
beautifully written copy of *Sagesse* to Mathilde with the author's
compliments and with special verses written in honour of her
and of little Georges; he was also to comment in passing on the
astonishing moral reformation of the author and of his fitness
for a second bout of married life.

This the "most brotherly" De Sivry did without visible effect.
Then Verlaine unexpectedly obtained an entrée; his son fell ill,
he begged to be allowed to see him and was permitted. Twice
he came, the second time finding himself alone with Mme
Mauté. He seized the opportunity to speak of his changed
character and his unchanged hopes. Mme Mauté, always well
disposed towards him, did not rule out a reconciliation in time,
perhaps a long time. Back at Rethel, Verlaine began to correspond
with her, sending gifts for Georges, reports on his own progress
and stressing his unalterable devotion to Mathilde and her child.

Months passed and the new year of 1879 came and went with
no more than cordial messages from the mother-in-law to keep
the fire burning. Verlaine was not the most patient of men and
his plans were expected to mature with tropical rapidity. Mme
Mauté's "years" might as well be centuries for all the use they
were to him. But he could not believe her, or thought that he
was cleverer than she. Would she ever have thought, for instance,
of sending Delahaye as formal emissary, Delahaye the correct,
the most obviously respectable of his friends short of a priest?
For that is what the by then feverishly impatient Verlaine did.

Delahaye, who was received courteously by M. Mauté,
explained his errand as tactfully as he could, painting the new
Verlaine in bright colours and offering as tempting background
the view of the rebuilt Hôtel de Ville in which a sober hard-
working official not unknown to rue Nicolet sat at his desk from
nine to five, reinstatement as civil servant remaining high on the
list of Verlaine's designs. But when Delahaye at last spoke of a
possible reunion between husband and wife M. Mauté turned
the conversation.

Delahaye reported failure. Verlaine would not accept it; there had been no direct refusal. Go again, he begged. Delahaye went again and listened to muted praise for Verlaine's regeneration and a polite inability to see in what way it could concern M. Mauté and his family. Again, demanded Verlaine. This third time the somewhat weary Delahaye came straight to the point and was answered to the point: Mathilde would never live with Verlaine again, never.

Mathilde's rebuff drove Verlaine to drink. He accepted the refusal temporarily, but not the reasons for it, and for the rest of his life was to name her as the chief architect of his misfortunes. But his slide from grace was not, as one might expect, rapid and calamitous; the powers of religion and habit were still strong in him and before either could collapse absolutely he had found another reason, and a more compelling one, for sobriety and hope; yet not until his colleagues at the college had witnessed with astonishment and pain a change in the habits of the "pious gentleman". He had long since made friends in the town; visiting them in the evenings, he was invited to take a nightcap before leaving and, when he assented, to take a second. This he had invariably refused. Now he no longer refused. He began to sit on, arriving back at the college slightly fuddled. He also found the customary half pint of wine insufficient for the day, and augmented it, carrying from the town almost every day a bottle or two unskilfully concealed about his person. And these failing to quench the mounting thirst, he began to slip out after lunch to a nearby café for a beer, then for two or three. Sometimes his afternoon class had to be dismissed, the master feeling "indisposed". Apart from the evening liqueur, he still drank nothing stronger than wine or beer, but the deterioration could not be hidden from so self-contained a community. Following the change in habits came change in manner, geniality often giving way to depression and even moroseness. The evening visits for coffee and a talk dropped away, he was avoided and before the summer term ended he was informed that the English course would be suppressed from the opening of the autumn term. This gentle method of dismissal meant that from August he was an unemployed man. At the end of that month he left Rethel for England. Not alone, however; there travelled with him one of the pupils, Lucien Létinois.

Chapter Fifteen

LUCIEN

1879-1883

I

LUCIEN was then eighteen. He was the son of a peasant from Coulommes, near Rethel, who had sent him to the college in the hope that he would raise himself to the priesthood or the teaching profession. Up to a point Lucien had fulfilled these hopes; he showed a fair intelligence, he had become moderately ambitious, and in person seemed far removed from the peasant, wearing a collar as though he had been born to it.

He first caught Verlaine's attention not by his virtues but because of a certain impudence in his tone that at once revived the memory of another boy. And colour apart—for Lucien's eyes and hair were dark brown—there was a resemblance to Rimbaud in this tall, slender youth who spoke with the slow Ardennais burr, who looked his master straight in the eyes and answered him with a directness bordering on insolence. Lucien had not Rimbaud's dazzling good looks, but he had a pleasant face, rounded and childlike, which like Rimbaud's contrasted violently with his manner and speech.

Later Verlaine spoke and wrote of Lucien as the son he had adopted in place of the son he was forbidden to see. This was misleading. If Delahaye has dated his letters correctly, he met M. Mauté late in 1879 and the old man asked why Verlaine had not been to visit Georges—a question which Verlaine, then in England, would find distinctly awkward to answer. It was true, however, that all hope of living with his real son had long since gone; true too that he came to regard Lucien as a son; but the first attraction was not chiefly to a man cut off from his kin but to a man who must love someone and love them at hand; that Verlaine should stress the point merely shows how bad a name the dog had been given.

The likeness to Rimbaud was decisive. Rimbaud was lost, Nouveau though not lost had soared into regions too rare for

253

sinful men to follow; but here, Verlaine had no difficulty in persuading himself, was yet another Rimbaud to be trained, and a Rimbaud with principle, a Rimbaud who would neither wreck his own life nor the life of his patron-father but ennoble both. For Lucien in his sulky and argumentative fashion was a good boy to the point of priggishness. No Rimbaud here, for those frank brown eyes were alight with the faith of the Church. Of Rimbaud's extraordinary intelligence he had no trace, and he had none of the gifts of Nouveau, but this did not worry Verlaine, who on the whole must have felt relieved that for once he could more than hold his own. In fact, when Lucien first forced himself on the notice of a master benevolently expecting good behaviour from all, he was not only impudent but on the lazy side and Verlaine was soon giving much of his spare time to coaching the boy for the *baccalauréat*.

What Lucien thought of Verlaine is difficult to determine. That he responded in some degree to the warm affection is certain; that he was flattered by Verlaine's attentions is clear; for the rest one has to judge by his actions and his later complaint that Verlaine, though extremely good to him, fussed too much and did harm to himself and his family. He also criticised the weaknesses which by that time had become obvious. But granted the weaknesses and the tiresomeness of the adulation heaped on a young man who preferred young company and preferably of the other sex, the remarks leave an unpleasant taste in the mouth and suggest that at heart Lucien was another Rimbaud and that opposites had attracted each other once again. He had not cast off the peasant mentality, for when in spite of Verlaine's efforts he failed in his *baccalauréat* he and his parents agreed without marked enthusiasm or gratitude to all suggestions for his betterment, and took the open-handed man's money without a qualm.

Lucien's failure coincided with Verlaine's failure at rue Nicolet and subsequent dismissal from the college. Verlaine's regrets for this last were therefore less poignant than they might have been. As it happened, he had already received news which made him regard the disasters with positive light-heartedness. The "hideous anglophile" was tenacious of his friendships and since leaving England had corresponded with the Andrews at Stickney, the friends at Boston, and Remington at Bournemouth.

He had just heard that his successor at Stickney was to leave at the end of the term and at once pictured Lucien in his place, perfecting his English, gaining valuable teaching experience and enjoying the pleasantnesses of life with an English family in the English countryside. He put the matter to Lucien and his parents, glowingly no doubt, and carried off the boy in triumph to Boston.

For himself he had no fears, registering again in the London agency; and sure enough by the beginning of the autumn term Lucien was installed as French master and tutor at Stickney and Verlaine had obtained a post in a school at Lymington.

This post was a little more profitable than his others, the Solent Collegiate School having some thirty pupils, and for a short time Verlaine was a truly happy man. He liked the little port with its view of the Isle of Wight where his god Tennyson lived; he liked his walks in that part of the New Forest which runs down to the outskirts of the town, seeing in it the equivalent of the Arden which had inspired his beloved Shakespeare; he liked his evenings, smoking long black cigars over the fire and discussing everything under the sun "until unheard of hours" with his Scottish headmaster William Murdoch and a football- and cricket-playing Irish priest. Everything was delightfully old and delightfully English and he revelled in the belief that he was making himself a part of it. Even Murdoch's sister, "a strict Presbyterian", accepted the foreign Catholic in her good-natured moments.

But above all he loved Lucien's weekly letters. One can imagine his optimistic thoughts as he strolled through the forest or sat up in bed reading these letters; eternal child that he was, he had forgotten the ennui at Stickney, the boredom of Bourne-mouth; he could see only Lucien well placed and protected, himself well liked and mildly prospering, and, the temptress Paris relegated safely to strictly limited holiday visits, a lifetime of steadily improving scholastic posts ahead of them in this calm, quiet country with its glorious literary tradition stirring his own muse.

2

The dream collapsed with cruel rapidity, and, for a change, through no fault of Verlaine but through the weaknesses of the upright Lucien. The boy's letters late that year began to hint that all was not well at Stickney and he did not exaggerate: he was not happy in England, his English was poor, he was an indifferent teacher, he could not keep order and, not being liked (one suspects a lack of humour), was made wretched in class. Worse still, like so many prim young men, he had an eye for women and had committed the unforgivable sin of becoming involved, with whom and to what extent has never been discovered, with a local girl.

Just before Christmas the blow fell. Lucien had not been re-engaged for the spring term, he was leaving for London on Christmas Day. Verlaine announced sadly to a puzzled Murdoch that he would have to give up his post because of his mother's poor health; his one wish then and always was to protect Lucien's reputation. On Christmas morning he left what had probably been his happiest berth in England and left, one gathers, to the regret of all.

As if to emphasise the cloud on Verlaine's spirits, this particular day arrived at the height of a foggy spell. He reached London after a long-drawn-out journey of interminable stops on the line. London was in the grip of a pea-souper, rank in the nostrils, clutching at the throat, fouling all it touched, a blanket of murk through which street flares glimmered inadequately at the crossings. Beset by anxiety, Verlaine crawled in a cab to King's Cross. There he had to wait, every moment increasing his uneasiness, for the long-delayed train to arrive. By the time Lucien stepped off it he was in a panic. He had known another Christmas Day in London seven years earlier and the forsaken feeling it implants in the foreigner. But then at least he could see sky above him, had been in a home of sorts, had been invited to the Christmas meal, had been given an illusion of belonging. Now he and Lucien might have been in another planet for all the likeness London showed to its normal self. They had nowhere to go, Verlaine having broken with his Communard acquaintances. About them everywhere, in every house, families and friends were cheerfully eating and drinking; they had only the station bar.

And there they had it out, an unhappy series of exchanges in keeping with the day, for they could not even take pleasure in each other. Lucien did not like England, never wished to see it again; that was the first blow. His tactlessness in the affair with the girl was likely to affect Verlaine's much-prized friendships at Stickney. His confidence in his ability to teach, never very strong, had disappeared; some other future had to be foreseen for him. And Verlaine, unused to face let alone make decisions, had now to do both and to do it with a heart filled with foreboding. In addition to his grief and embarrassment at the failure of Lucien he was distraught by personal fears. Lucien's fate was his fate, every plan for the future had collapsed and a new life had to be made. He had to say good-bye to the safety of England, where absinthe was unknown, where drinking of all kinds was made so difficult, where the very atmosphere of the country threw a protective mantle of respectability over one's every act, where the "not done" was a godsend to a Verlaine anxious to hold to his prison vows. He would be forced back on France, a France he loved but with reservations. Dreadful premonitions of ruin, of the collapse of his life haunted him.

He was not to forget that day; he was to remember everything, details which for the ordinary man would have been obliterated by emotion. But the poet was unconsciously noting the scene, his and Lucien's feelings, and even the most trifling incidents, all of which he was to embody in the often misinterpreted *O l'odieuse obscurité*.

What did Lucien wish to do? In a few months he would be called up for military service and, unless steps were taken to prevent it, would be due to serve for five years. The answer seemed to lie first in farming, the one job that could be carried on by others in his absence; and after some weeks of discussion in the little house at Coulommes, to which both returned, Lucien decided that he would be a farmer. Verlaine, recalling idyllically his holidays in the Pas de Calais and the Ardennes and ready to try anything to soothe the boy's wounded vanity, promptly declared that he too would like nothing better.

The parents' smallholding at Coulommes was in the eyes of Lucien and Verlaine unworthy of the scholar of Rethel College. Verlaine had just received a legacy from his aunt at Paliseul and with this and the help of his mother he bought a large farm at Juniville ten miles away, bought it in the name of Lucien's father and installed the parents in it. Mme Verlaine completed the family when she chose to leave her friends at Arras.

There remained the shadow of the five years' military service. A payment of fifteen hundred francs and the passing of a not too difficult examination would reduce the term to one year. Verlaine borrowed the money from his mother and gave Lucien the necessary tuition in the evenings.

The farm was not a success. Verlaine's efforts to play the farmer, wearing his battered top-hat and raincoat of English days, led to the neighbours' contemptuous comments that he was an English gentleman amusing himself with a serious job. He liked the animals and, with sentimental memories of Taffy and his sugar lumps, spoiled them hopelessly. He took enormous pride in watching the tall straight figure of Lucien behind a plough, wielding a scythe, threshing, cutting and binding faggots, work in which he lent a hand occasionally but without any real conviction. He bought a dogcart in which he and Lucien inspected the farm, paid visits or merely went for a spin. For the rest he enjoyed the few obvious pleasures, the harvesting *par excellence*, and the mug of beer that ended the day. When rain fell or the fields were damp his rheumatism, legacy of the siege, reappeared; then he sat at home reading and writing or hobbled to the Lion d'Or a hundred yards away, where the hostess gave him the run of her parlour and watched with fond amazement the composition of poems on the oak table. He drank little, she noticed.

That summer Nouveau visited the farm. In Paris a few weeks earlier Verlaine, still trying to find a publisher for *Sagesse*, had paused by a kiosk for a little cheap reading—a weakness of his, this—when his shoulder was slapped and the familiar husky voice cried, "So here's the man who can never resist the news-papers! You light creature, led astray by useless, worldly things!" The quarrel vanished as though it had never been and Nouveau was pressed to inspect the new venture, make his home there if he wished. Come! At once! The Ministry of Public Education, where he then worked side by side with Izambard, Rimbaud's old master, and the young De Maupassant, put un-reasonable obstacles before this ideal grouping of good friends and Catholics; and when, freed by holidays, Nouveau arrived, he was immediately tormented by toothache. This kept him from the fields but not from his crayons; he made a comical self-portrait in the midst of the pangs, and to everybody's delight announced his intention of making a pastel of Lucien. The pastel done, father and mother gazed blankly at auburn hair, beaked nose, rosy complexion: "But his hair and face are brown, his nose straight!" Nouveau reproached them brusquely: these peasants and their craze for outward signs! "You are wrong to want him brown," he said severely: the soul of Lucien, that was what he conveyed. And he had, strangely enough, caught the expression of the eyes, the straight frank look. Verlaine was to revere this pastel; for the moment it remained, Nouveau apart, something of a joke. So did the farm that lively summer, reduced in Verlaine's eyes to a pleasant background for visitors.

Old Létinois, the one man who might have made something of the farm, remained bewildered by its size and reluctant to employ labour. Lucien, too much preoccupied by the threat of the army or succumbing too often to the lure of trips in the dog-cart, seemed never to get a grip of the work. Then he took and passed his examination and late in the summer of 1880 was posted to the Artillery at Rheims.

His departure was the virtual end of the farm, though his father struggled on. Verlaine soon lost the last remnants of what had never been more than amiable acquiescence in a pastime, and followed Lucien to Rheims. There he got himself some sort of work in a school in order to see what he could of Lucien, to see and admire, and eventually to write, somewhat fatuously, proud-fatherly panegyrics on the handsome erect soldier sitting his steed and wearing his uniform with such aplomb.

Lucien accepted the compliments but could not return them whole-heartedly. He had the usual self-righteous intolerance of youth for the frailties of his elders; he chided the venerable-looking Verlaine with his great ivory dome supported by the clusters of side hair: why sit about so much before a mug of beer? It was neither wise nor dignified. Waiting at the café for him to come off duty was a Verlaine sometimes slightly thick in speech. He had had to wait so long? that was no excuse; Lucien was grateful for all he had done for him and was doing, but . . . "But my boy!" A stiff forgiveness would come, Verlaine promising amendment over and over again, at Rheims and, later, at Châlons-sur-Marne whither Lucien was moved and which Verlaine visited whenever he was able.

3

When Lucien was in the army, in the autumn of 1881, *Sagesse* was at last published. It was Verlaine's first book of verse to get into print for six years. The text had been completed in the summer of the previous year by the fine *Vous reviendrez bientôt*, which Verlaine dashed off indignantly after the expulsion of the Jesuits from France at the end of June, and by the pathetic *Et j'ai revu*, written after a further visit to Georges which he had made as soon as he could get down to Paris. The tone of this poem suggests a prevision that this glimpse of his son might be the last, as it proved; the visit, and even more the two poems in *Sagesse* pleading strongly for Mathilde's forgiveness—*"Faites le geste qui pardonne!"* one ended—showed that he continued to hope for reconciliation with his wife. Showed too that he did not place too much store on the permanence of the relationship with Lucien, though he would face such a thought only in poetry.

When in Paris, acting probably on the hint of Lepelletier, who was becoming an editor of some importance, he showed the poems to Victor Palmé, the publisher of Catholic books. Palmé accepted them, but only on payment of six hundred francs, so that in this matter Verlaine at thirty-seven with a body of imperishable poetry behind him was back where he had begun at twenty-two. He paid, of course, and when he had received the proofs announced the forthcoming publication to his old friend Valade, who responded warmly.

Verlaine wrote a preface to the book, breathing the over-confidence of a man who has seen the light; an unfortunate tone which failed absolutely to propitiate those who had ignored his earlier work because of his association with Rimbaud. His moral critics now dubbed him hypocrite. Some of his few friends regretted his change of tone: Mallarmé, a staunch admirer, said that he was disappointed not to read another *Fêtes Galantes*—a compliment to this work but not truly perceptive since Verlaine, most subjective of poets, could not be expected to repeat an objective *tour de force*. Others, Lepelletier and Blémont for example, did their best, but it was not enough. His enemies either turned a blind eye to the new book or made rude remarks about its author. "What, isn't the fellow dead yet!" exclaimed Leconte de Lisle. Most reviewers passed it over. A despairing effort by Verlaine to print a review, written by himself, of what he called "this remarkable book" was disqualified at the starting-post. Sales were negligible.

The failure, as it then seemed, was undeserved. *Sagesse* is an uneven book, but it contains one or two of the finest poems he was to write. But reviewing then was concerned more than now with the standing of the author, and Verlaine had no standing. Nina, one of the few staunch friends, was no longer a power in the literary world, only a mental wreck who, believing herself dead, played extraordinary music on the pianoforte.

Disappointed but not dismayed, Verlaine turned to another form of literature. Although the bulk of the poems in *Sagesse* had been written years earlier, he had still not composed enough poems to make another volume. He had already chosen the title of his next book—*Amour*—but that was almost all. The period at Rethel had been, as far as poetry was concerned, two years taken out of his life; he wrote nothing of value there. He therefore wrote his first prose work, *Voyage en France par un Français*.

This could not find a publisher, and one cannot wonder at it. The *Voyage* was in tone rather like the unfortunate preface to *Sagesse*, and in manner the most prosy of documents. Nothing less edifying has ever existed than Verlaine deliberately being edifying, and in this book he excelled himself; it reads like the work of an excessively hypocritical Colonel Blimp lecturing the youth of France on the way it should think and behave. One asks how a great poet came to labour over it. Its *raison d'être* is found in Lucien's pained reproaches; it was to be proof at once to Lucien and to himself that he knew, no man better, the rules of the good life even if very occasionally he chanced to break one of them. It was also a further and futile effort to impress the world with the picture of a reformed spirit who asked no more than that an appreciative public buy his wares; but this, as the book did not appear, they could not do.

4

By the time Lucien returned to Juniville from the army the farm was as good as gone. For some months into 1882 the hopeless struggle was carried on; then the Létinois, father, mother and son, moved out hurriedly into nearby Belgium, apparently but unnecessarily alarmed by mounting debts. Verlaine put the farm up for sale (quickly receiving about half the purchase price, which he returned to his mother—the one example on record of Mme Verlaine receiving back money paid out) and took rooms in Paris in rue de la Roquette. From there, his first regular Parisian address for eleven years, he made efforts to help Lucien and himself; he applied through Lepelletier to be readmitted to the Hôtel de Ville, and through Delahaye for a school post for Lucien.

This was in October 1882. The first application, though promising well for a week or two, was hopeless; the Communards and their sympathisers might by then be regarded indulgently by a government feeling itself secure, but this did not mean that renegades were to regain official positions; this final effort to return to the old life was denied him; his application was refused.

He had better luck with Delahaye, and a somewhat reluctant Lucien was placed as master in the semi-military Institution Esnault at Boulogne-sur-Seine, and his parents established in the suburb of Ivry close by. Verlaine, retaining his rooms in Paris for the use of himself and his mother (who had gone back to her little house in Arras), took a room near the school in a hotel in rue du Parchamp. Almost every evening he met Lucien, gave him dinner, and when the weather was obliging walked with him in the Bois de Boulogne, listening to the recital of daily events in the school, sympathising with the young man's ambitions, discussing the marriage he foresaw as inevitable though he was quite unable to visualise a girl good enough, and even venturing into philosophical discussions which he and Lucien must have found difficult to sustain. Their one strong link was religious belief; but even in this it seems improbable that the critical and modern Lucien could listen without inward reservations to the childlike faith of Verlaine, who believed that his still infant soul was being guarded by the Holy Mother, Father and Son—a belief that he was to express with touching beauty in his poem *Prière du Matin*.

Lucien no doubt wondered, as a severe and rather stupid young man would wonder, how Verlaine reconciled such a faith with the failings of his everyday life. For inevitably the talk sometimes dwelt on the use to which Verlaine was putting his spare time; what did he do with himself whilst he waited for Lucien? Was there not something feeble in the thought of a man hanging about day after day for the sake of a few hours' conversation at night? Lucien's feelings towards Verlaine had become cooler since the failure of the farm and the uprooting of his parents: "Better if we had never met him," he said privately to Delahaye. But he was a conscientious boy aware of Verlaine's goodness; grateful too, no doubt; greedy, it may be; he continued to see his patron regularly, to talk freely, to be affectionate—it was difficult to dislike Verlaine whatever resentment one felt. But critical he certainly was.

And it was true that Verlaine seemed to be slipping; he took no care of himself, looked seedy in his old raincoat and battered hat, and he was drinking. He continued to keep clear of absinthe, but the beers followed each other down his throat with alarming ease.

He was not helped in this by his one regular outing every week; on Friday evening he took the horse tram from Auteuil to Saint-Sulpice and walked along to the Voltaire, where he found one or two old companions who would drink and talk with him. There was Valade, and, thanks to Valade, there was Verlaine's "Great Albert" shaking his hand again, all ill-feeling gone. There too were Blémont, Dierx and Mendès, a tarnished Apollo nearing forty but tossing golden hair in the manner of the 'sixties, talking as glibly and with a finger in every pie except that of the *Parnasse*, which he was now busily denying to have been a movement. He did not object to Verlaine, he could scarcely afford to in the face of his own life, but he failed to appreciate the poet then as in Parnassian days.

Looking about the Voltaire, one almost received the impression of time standing still: Mérat held his head in the air as ever, cigar puffing, stick tapping, flinging provocative remarks into every silence as if he had just climbed the corkscrew stairs at Lemerre's; Valade, black beard a little fuller, but his old benign self, as shy as if he were hesitating on the threshold of a De Ricard soirée; Mendès, flashily and aggressively youthful as if he were presiding at one of his teas in the rue Douai; Dierx, gentle, pensive and quiet as he had been in Nina's garden night after night; the fair, plumpish Blémont as smooth and comfortable as on that first meeting at Banville's. Only when the eye fell on Verlaine did time rush on; crazily, for Verlaine looked as far beyond his years as the others looked less than theirs, with his shining bald head as venerable as the slits of eyes were youthful. Gone the monocle, the smart stick, the frock-coat and dainty cravat; in their place moved a shabby old ruin not yet forty years of age.

He contrasted so oddly with the company that a stranger would have been puzzled to explain his presence. It was not entirely, not mainly because old friends had relented; they remained conscious of the years between and what had happened in those years; their attitude to the reformed reprobate was not far from condescension. But there were others present at the Voltaire on these Friday evenings; there was a young Greek with dead-white face and great black moustache, Jean Moréas his adopted name; there was a provincial youth, Charles Morice, dark and handsome too but in more conventional style, dressed always in worn but correct and even dandified frock-coat and striped trousers; and there was a sprinkling of young men who broadly followed the lead of these two. These youthful poets were unconcerned with the morals or the past behaviour of this seedy character; they questioned him, read their poems to him, they were not far from deferential; but not the deference of youth for age—this was given, amusingly enough, to the ever-young ex-Parnassian friends of Verlaine. As Mendès had looked back twenty years earlier to Banville, Leconte de Lisle, Hugo and Baudelaire, so Moréas and Morice were fumblingly experimenting with a new theory based on the work of their elders. The theory had not arrived but it was in the air, and their attitude and words made clear that it would be based not on the Parnassians, not on the work of Mérat, Valade or Dierx, not even on the perseveringly youthful and friendly Mendès, but on the two men who in their very different ways had been found wanting by their contemporaries—Mallarmé and Verlaine.

For *Sagesse*, flat though it had fallen, had been noticed by one or two youthful eyes, and Verlaine in the closing stages at Juniville, in the rue de la Roquette and in the hotel bedroom at Boulogne-sur-Seine had done more than swill beer and look fondly on Lucien: he had been writing poetry and this poetry was beginning to appear in print. In June, to celebrate the resumption of relations with Mérat, he wrote one of his most

sparkling sonnets, sparkling with the wit and profundity of a
movement from Mozart.

Et nous voilà très doux à la bêtise humaine,
Lui pardonnant vraiment et même un peu touchés
De sa candeur extrême et des torts très légers,
Dans le fond, qu'elle assume et du train qu'elle mène.

Pauvres gens que les gens! Mourir pour Célimène,
Epouser Angélique ou venir de nuit chez
Agnès et la briser, et tous les sots péchés,
Tel est l'Amour encor plus faible que la Haine!

L'Ambition, l'Orgueil, des tours dont vous tombez,
Le Vin, qui vous imbibe et vous tord imbibés,
L'Argent, le Jeu, le Crime, un tas de pauvres crimes!

C'est pourquoi, mon très cher Mérat, Mérat et moi,
Nous étant dépouillés de tout banal émoi,
Vivons dans un dandysme épris des seules Rimes!

The following month was a landmark; for the first time for ten
years Verlaine's work was printed in a Paris periodical. That bare
statement does not convey the full magnitude of the landmark,
and it is unlikely that Verlaine, used to the vagaries and bank-
ruptcies of publishers and the fleeting appearance of literary
journals, could have guessed what was in store for him. Yet this
unpropitious moment was to be the turning point of his literary
fortunes. For the owner of this new periodical was not in the
ordinary run of publishers; Léon Vanier, an unprepossessing
little man of thirty-six, was a tradesman trying his hand at
publishing, a realist but a man of literary discernment too. He
had read one of the few circulating copies of *Sagesse*, he had then
read everything of Verlaine's he could find, and he at once opened
his periodical *Paris Moderne* to him. He did more, he offered to
publish Verlaine's poetry in book form and to pay for it.

Good fortune when it came, came in good measure. In
November *Paris Moderne* printed more of Verlaine's poems, this
time including the *Art Poétique* he had written in prison at Mons.
Morice protested, in a letter written under a pen name to *La
Nouvelle Rive gauche*, that *Art Poétique* preached a rigidity of poetic
form and a contempt for rhyme that was deplorable coming
from an established poet. Verlaine, replying, explained, "We're

really of the same mind in essentials, that's why I continue the discussion: we both want impeccable rhymes, correct French and above all good poetry no matter what the trimmings are." The discussion continued further; the critical Morice gave way and more than gave way, he became one of Verlaine's first disciples. Verlaine was invited to contribute to the journal in which the battle had been fought, and *Art Poétique* was accepted as a battle-cry by the young men dissatisfied with past and present poetry. The news of it circulated slowly but with effect, and the bewildered Verlaine, who had merely thrown off the poem as the expression of a particular mood, found that he began once more to have the entrée to the *avant-garde* journals—his poems appeared the next year in *La Nouvelle Rive Gauche*, *Le Chat Noir* and *Lutèce*—and he was received at the Voltaire with a certain flattering interest as if a mouldering scarecrow had suddenly put forth a flower. There was, of course, little money in all this, but there was gratification as well as amusement for one who regarded "movements" with a quizzical distrust.

However, there he was, a man with a publisher, at the Voltaire and in company and very glad of it, yet a man who put all his hopes not in this swing of the pendulum but in the young man whom he met, walked with and talked with almost every evening, whose brilliant future was always in his mind.

But if Verlaine's heart sent his sense of proportion toppling, his good angel had other plans; straddled over incongruities, he was to be lifted painfully to safety. After two months Lucien, who had been looking out for something better, found a job with good prospects in a factory at La Chapelle. He began work at once and Verlaine took his place at the school until the end of term.

The evening meetings continued whenever Verlaine could leave the school; he would wait at the foot of the stairs at Auteuil Station for Lucien to arrive in the train from La Chapelle: "Mon pauvre enfant," he was soon to write, "ta voix dans le Bois de Boulogne!"

"Mon pauvre enfant"; for this pleasure too, the breath of life one could say, was to be short-lived. The school term ended and Verlaine went back to his hotel, his beers, his poetry, his Fridays at the Voltaire. Then towards the end of March of the new year, 1883, Lucien fell ill and was taken to the Hôpital de la Pitié at Ivry. He had caught typhoid fever. Verlaine, refusing to believe the inevitable, never left his bedside. On April 7 Lucien died.

Chapter Sixteen

COLLAPSE

1883-1885

I

THE death of Lucien led directly, though not immediately, both to the collapse of Verlaine's remaining hopes of leading a respectable life and to the production of one of his greatest series of poems. The elegy *Lucien Létinois* was written over the years that followed, ending in 1888. It consisted of twenty-four poems. A late addition was written to the memory of Elisa; the rest covered the time, less than four years, that Verlaine had known Lucien.

The elegy was based in theory on *In Memoriam*; in fact there is only the slightest resemblance, and that technical, between the two. Verlaine claimed in 1888 that "this series, sorrowful and I dare to believe moving, is in any case unique in our literature". The claim was correct; some of the poems deal specifically with Lucien, his skill as skater, equestrian, farmer, letter-writer for example, but the great poems transcend their subject and show Verlaine in a new light, as a man and poet ennobled by suffering.

> J'ai la fureur d'aimer. Mon cœur si faible est fou.
> N'importe quand, n'importe quel et n'importe où,
> Qu'un éclair de beauté, de vertu, de vaillance
> Luise, il s'y précipite, il y vole, il s'y lance,
> Et, le temps d'une étreinte, il embrasse cent fois
> L'être ou l'objet qu'il a poursuivi de son choix;
> Puis, quand l'illusion a replié son aile,
> Il revient triste et seul bien souvent, mais fidèle,
> Et laissant aux ingrats quelque chose de lui,
> Sang ou chair. Mais, sans plus mourir dans son ennui,
> Il embarque aussitôt pour l'île des Chimères
> Et n'en apporte rien que des larmes amères
> Qu'il savoure, et d'affreux désespoirs d'un instant,
> Puis rembarque. . . .

To understand the remainder of Verlaine's life it is necessary to be clear about what it was in Lucien that really attracted him,

267

and which resulted in this movingly controlled outpouring of grief. The superficial resemblance to Rimbaud was incidental; the lasting attraction of Lucien was his monumental ordinariness. Handsome, yes; high-minded, yes; but the heart of his appeal was the respectability that every look, every word of that ordinary young man proclaimed. Verlaine could scarcely sustain the loss of anybody he loved, as his collapse after the death of Elisa demonstrated. But he had been young and hopeful when Elisa died, with friends, money, ambitions; the death of Lucien left him with the feeling that he had been robbed of the ideal he had yearned after so intensely. Mathilde, hearing that he had begun to drink again and was without regular employment, and in any case disapproving of the intimacy with Lucien, had on the insistence of M. Mauté refused to let him see Georges again. After his fight of eight years, resisting every natural inclination, he was left entirely on his own—no job at the Hôtel de Ville, no wife, no child, no Lucien, no one whom he could at once love and lean on—and was firmly and finally expelled from his beloved bourgeoisie.

Collapse after that could not long be delayed. One is only surprised that it did not follow at once. He had not lost his faith, however; he was never to lose it, and in poignant verses he cried again and again for strength.

> Et puis, bon pasteur, paissez mon cœur:
> Il est seul désormais sur la terre,
> Et l'horreur de rester solitaire
> Le distrait en l'étrange langueur
> D'un espoir qui ne veut pas se taire,
> Et l'appelle aux prés qu'il ne faut pas.
> Donnez-lui de n'aller qu'en vos pas.

He had not lost his faith but he had lost what was more necessary to a sense of proportion, his sense of humour, and the company he kept did not help him to regain it. After Lucien's funeral at Ivry he went back to his rooms in rue de la Roquette, where he was joined by his mother. She had never been good for him, and she was not so then. She was over seventy, and although she remained active her mind, which had never been normal, was obviously failing. She was embarrassingly skittish with the men who called to see Verlaine, insisting playfully, for instance, in the midst of one of Moréas' dramatic declamations of Baudelaire, that he "shut his eyes and open his mouth", into which she immediately plunged a stick of barley sugar "for his sore throat". The barley sugar had become a symbol of her approval, as had also, to the earnest young visitors' distress, her invitations to join in a game of ball.

Verlaine's main prop in these unhappy days—a self-constituted prop—was Nouveau. But Nouveau was no longer the gay and charming companion. Nouveau had gone from vision to vision and was by that time a rabid Catholic. A few years later he was to dash from a drawing-class, jump into a fiacre, get out in the centre of the city, stop the traffic, sink on to his knees in the middle of the street and kiss the paving-blocks. The police then took him off to a mental home. But in 1883 he roamed freely about Paris when not in his office, or not in the mood for an office; not mad in the certifiable sense but distinctly unbalanced. One delusion was that his mission in life was to rescue Verlaine from alcohol, a worthy aim no doubt if carried out with tact, but defeating its object when pressed home with the kind of ferocious wild-eyed insistence that he called sincerity. He was scarcely a good advertisement for sobriety. Verlaine, obliging to the last and indeed grateful for Nouveau's particular brand of affection, countered by limiting himself to one glass in the evangelist's company. Nouveau gone, Verlaine would be off and round the corner in a twinkling to make up for lost time. He still confined himself to beer; after enough of it he found that his shattering sense of loss subsided in a kind of warm mist, his bowel-weakening fear of lovelessness blurred into a general affection for all who stood at the bar or sat before their glass at the round tables.

But always the effect wore off, and there was his mother, there was Nouveau, there were frightening thoughts beating at his brain. One couldn't drink all the time; not only Nouveau's stern and watchful eye but the shade of a sad, reproving Lucien forbade it. The few visitors reminded him that he was not altogether forgotten, the magazines were slowly opening their pages to him, the poems would be written, nothing could stop that self-explanatory flow; but his main view of these hints of a more promising future was to see them as mockery rather than comfort.

Paris suddenly became unbearable. Then came the thought,

how obvious! that he could be with Lucien, as nowhere else, in the house in which the boy had been born and reared. Moreover, to buy the house, which old Létinois still owned, would be to recompense the parents for the dislocation of their life: Lucien would approve. The thought was scarcely in his head than it became a devouring necessity. His mother—was ever mother of a famous man so unfailingly unfortunate in her advice and encouragement?—enthusiastically seconded the plan; her son, no longer the pariah, was becoming free of the cafés again; to sit and talk was to drink; at Coulommes, companionless and untempted, he would work soberly the day long. So she reasoned, if reasoned is the word.

By July the house was theirs and they left Paris. For some months—until the end of the year—the unpromising gamble seemed to have succeeded; Verlaine drank his luncheon and dinner beer with conscious rectitude, with measured face he walked top-hatted about the countryside, he wrote and revised poems for *Jadis et Naguère*, as he had decided to name his next book, he dreamed nostalgically about the dead Lucien and his life under that roof: here he had been born, here learned his lessons, here eaten his frugal meals, here—in that top room next to the granary—slept and prayed.

Holy ground indeed; and Verlaine, incurable idealist in emotional moments, may well have thought that God had answered his prayer, that the miracle had happened and that, breathed over by Lucien's pure spirit, he would end his days in peace and useful labour. But Verlaine could never be satisfied by a spirit; fleshly he was and fleshly would remain. The explanation of these quiet and fruitful months is found, the charm of novelty apart, in a fresh hope which had entered that unpractical heart. For, incredible though it may seem, he still could not take his mind from the possibility of a reunion with Mathilde. Lucien dead and the isolation of Coulommes beginning to prey on a companionable spirit, his mind turned once more to rue Nicolet. Mathilde had objected to further meetings between Georges and his father, a cruel ban, yet perhaps not utterly without a gleam of reason. But what mother could object to her son associating with a father who led an honourable and diligent country life in his own house in his native Ardennes? And what wife could or ought to resist a *rapprochement* with a husband so solidly placed, a man moreover who now had his own publisher, a following and a future?

The correspondence with Mme Mauté was resumed; she remained kind and guardedly hopeful, she alone of the family having some notion of the man her daughter had married and some pride in the poet. He began to imagine wife and child established contentedly in the house at Coulommes. And had he set eyes on her as she then was, he would never have spent an easy night, for Mathilde had not become less desirable physically; the "hint of plumpness" marked by Verlaine's expert eye at that first interview had come to pass. She is described at this time as a formidable young woman patronising the "poets, musicians, writers, artists" gathered under the wing of "le premier des monologuistes" as Charles Cros styled himself; she is seen one Thursday evening walking with assurance into the headquarters of Cros' Zutistes, the "Maison de bois" in rue de Rennes, to sing the songs of De Sivry: "a piquant brunette, well covered, with superb shoulders, large eyes missing nothing and her nose in the air".

It is impossible to say how Mathilde's mind would have worked if she had been left to make her own decisions. Had she been able to see into the not so distant future, a matter of five or six years only, her view of taking up life with Verlaine again might have been much changed. As it was she obeyed her father, how willingly will never be known. And as M. Mauté was the power in the home, only the presence of her mother preserved a slight element of uncertainty. Early in the new year of 1884 the last element of doubt disappeared. Mme Mauté had a stroke. Paralysed, she lay in rue Nicolet slowly dying.

The news shattered the unnatural calm in which Verlaine had been living for months. He began to write the elegy he did not complete until the tenth anniversary of Mme Mauté's death:

> Vous fûtes bonne et douce en nos tristes tempêtes.
> —L'Esprit et la Raison parmi nos fureurs bêtes,—
> Et si l'on vous eût crue au temps qu'il le fallait
> On se fût épargné que de chagrin plus laid,
> Encor que douloureux! Puis, lorsque sonna l'heure
> Définitive où d'espérer n'était qu'un leurre
> Dorénavant, du moins vous fîtes pour le mieux
> Quant à tel modus vivendi moins odieux

VERLAINE

Que cette guerre sourde ou cette paix armée
Qui succéda l'affreux conflit.
                                        Soyez aimée
Et vénérée, ô morte inopportunément!

A beautiful poem; but the "morte inopportunément" in so far
as Verlaine applied it to himself was unreal. He did not dare to
think so, however, and, temporarily freed from despair and the
bout of drinking in which he had drowned it, busied himself with
the enlistment of new allies. He first begged Cros' wife, a good-
humoured Scandinavian who liked him, to plead his cause. She
fared no better than Delahaye four years earlier. Then he asked
his disciple Moréas to intervene, a strange and unlikely choice
which would have occurred to none other than Verlaine. The
reception given to this excessively proud young man rebounded
on to his hero, admiration thereafter being mingled with
contempt.

The immediate result of these rebuffs, which seemed final
enough, was absolute collapse of the flimsy structure of the
country life. Verlaine had never been accepted at Coulommes,
appearing to his neighbours as at Juniville as a man living "out
of his class"; what had he to do with farms and fields, with
solitude, when terror gripped him, when he saw himself loveless
and unwanted? Yet there he was, master of a house he did not
want, looked at askance by the people, his every movement
known, his prayers unheard. God had forsaken him: he rushed
to that conclusion; he was unworthy of Lucien.

Desperate for company, he consorted with the only people who
would grant him more than a frigid word, the riff-raff of the
district; desperate for forgetfulness, he drank with them, spreading
his money freely abroad until he reached home penniless but
beyond reach of self-criticism. There followed black looks from
neighbours, protestations from Mme Verlaine, more drink, more
forgetfulness. The round was broken by fits of repentance, by a
visit to Paris and by composition, his muse as usual flourishing
in wretchedness.

It is faintly possible that, helped by his writing and his
conscience, he might have pulled himself together, but two events
in the summer demoralised him still further. In June, Valade
died suddenly. He was only forty-three, one of Verlaine's oldest
friends and one of the few who had stuck to him in trouble.

A Verlaine Soirée, 1889

Standing from left : Henry d'Argis, Verlaine, Gabriel Vicaire, Villiers, Cazals, Ary Renan.   *Seated from left :* A. Desvaux, Moréas,
Sophie Harlay, Jules Tellier, Ernest Lefevre, Rachilde (with fan), Paterne Berrichon, Fernand Clerget, Laurent Tailhade

Verlaine at the François Premier, 1892

Verlaine, shattered, sought his usual consolation, and the next month, before he could get back to an approximation of normality, Nina died insane in a mental home. He had not seen much of her recently—her mind had been unhinged for some time—but he remembered her soirées nostalgically. And she, like Valade, had defended him through the years of isolation.

He went to her funeral. There he met Hector de Callias faultlessly dressed and sober for the first time in many years. The effort exhausted De Callias and, the ceremony over, he trailed through the bars of Paris accompanied by Verlaine, discussing wives, discovering belatedly the perfection of Nina and, by contrast, the vileness of Mathilde. Verlaine, meeting sympathy, lashed himself into a factitious hatred. It was then that he first broke the vow made in the prison at Mons ten years earlier and drank absinthe.

Up to this point his differences with the neighbours at Coulommes had been not so much about drink—he had kept to beer—as about dress and demeanour; their complaints of the top-hat had merely changed to criticisms that he did not always trouble to shave or put on a collar. Now he gave them real grounds for disapproval; he moved from one bout of absinthe to another until he became a byword. His violence alarmed Mme Verlaine so much that in the new year of 1885 she took shelter with a grocer and his wife who kept a café on the main road; they counselled her to discipline Verlaine by withholding money and, that failing, urged her to leave him.

The drinking bouts were neither simply nor mainly the result of a relapse into absinthe; they were caused by a crowning blow. At the end of 1884 the disestablishment of the Church in France, so long and so bitterly canvassed, became a fact; and on the first day of the new year divorce was legalised. Mathilde was one of the earliest applicants and was one of the first to receive the decree. On February 9 the divorce was pronounced and Verlaine was ordered to continued the "pension alimentaire" of twelve hundred francs.

As a Catholic Verlaine did not recognise divorce; but morally and spiritually sound though he might feel this attitude to be (and he was to make great play with it in future years), in practice even he could sense an absolute end to hope. The affair was finished. When the news reached him he hurried to Paris and put up for the night at an English hotel. He had never before stayed there and the hotel and district were both outside his customary haunts. Possibly a hope stirred in his muddled brain that an English atmosphere would restore sanity as England had done before. If so his hope failed, as did the notion which had caused the plunge into Paris, of a wild appeal to justice, a dramatic facing of Mathilde, a snatching away of the child, anything but inaction; he sought calm and strength of purpose at the English bar and lost the most rudimentary command of himself. The next morning he rushed back to Coulommes dangerously drunk. There he found that the grocer had forced a way into the house and removed Mme Verlaine's clothes and personal belongings.

This discovery snapped what little restraint he still possessed. He stormed into the grocer's house and made a scene the details of which remain uncertain to this day, since he, his mother and the grocer all told different stories. The upshot was that Verlaine found himself in court once more, charged with violence and threats to kill his mother. He protested that on the contrary he had threatened to kill himself if she did not come back to him. This, which was almost certainly true, was not discounted as a similar statement had been discounted in Brussels twelve years earlier. The magistrate, in view of the conflicting evidence and Verlaine's whole-hearted repentance, imposed the reasonable sentence of one month's imprisonment and a fine of five hundred francs. Verlaine made no appeal; he sold his house, paid the fine and in the second week of April entered the prison at Vouziers.

If the sentence was reasonable the conditions in prison were lax to the point of farce. As the only educated prisoner he read evening prayers with an air that captivated all, and as a born convivial he charmed his warders so thoroughly that the daily tasks were either excused or, when hurriedly and ineffectually done, overlooked. He wrote his poems undisturbed and made friends wholesale, his chief companion being the prostitute Lily— the Vouzinoise as he called her—whom he was to see much of in Paris later. He may well have paid for her to live there, for he continued to splash his money about; almost as soon as he had come out of prison, for example, he gave fifteen hundred francs to a passing drinking companion to buy a merry-go-round.

His movements after leaving prison in May remain obscure.

COLLAPSE

He went to Paris for a few days, where he seems to have rented the room in the Hôtel du Midi, 6 Cour Saint-François off rue Moreau, which he was later to inhabit. But he did not stay there then; he felt restless and he had money to collect, from the sale of the house at Coulommes and from Juniville, where the last part of the purchase price of the farm had only just reached the solicitor.

For Verlaine to possess money in his mood of that time was to invite confusion; he had not yet found anything or anybody to replace Lucien or the ghosts of Georges and Mathilde. To forget was everything. Money therefore melted, and before he reached Juniville he was begging his way, a not unhappy tramp.

He was rescued from drift by the Church. From Juniville he wandered northwards into his beloved Ardennes, and he had no sooner crossed the Semois into Belgium than he ran into an old playmate from his childhood holidays at Paliseul. The playmate had become the Abbé Dewez of Corbion, that romantic frontier village overhanging the river. To meet an old friend and a priest was to confess all. The sinner was forgiven and provided with a home. There he stayed until September, outstaying his welcome one suspects; he was for ever escaping, to collect money here or there, to sprinkle it in Paris on Bastille Day and, in short, to fit himself for renewed repentance at Corbion.

There are limits to clerical patience; in September came a rather strained farewell, an erratic progress back to Paris, and there, the next month, a belated settling in Cour Saint-François. His wanderings were over.

2

No reader could be blamed for imagining that these years between the death of Lucien and the final settlement in Paris were years of excess, disgrace and waste. Nevertheless, the cold facts tell us that, whilst morally and physically Verlaine seemed to be going from bad to worse, he was working hard and was winning in absence a reputation in Paris that present and sober he had never been able to achieve.

As we have seen, the publication of *Art Poétique* at the end of 1882 was to lead gradually to its adoption as a kind of testament by the young Symbolists, led by Moréas and Morice. In June of the next year *Le Chat Noir* published, amongst other poems of Verlaine, his *Langueur*.

> Je suis l'Empire à la fin de la décadence,
> Qui regarde passer les grands Barbares blancs
> En composant des acrostiches indolents
> D'un style d'or où la langueur du soleil danse.
>
> L'âme seulette a mal au cœur d'un ennui dense.
> Là-bas on dit qu'il est de longs combats sanglants.
> O n'y pouvoir, étant si faible aux vœux si lents,
> O n'y vouloir fleurir un peu cette existence!
>
> O n'y vouloir, ô n'y pouvoir mourir un peu!
> Ah! tout est bu! Bathylle, as-tu fini de rire?
> Ah! tout est bu, tout est mangé! Plus rien à dire!
>
> Seul, un poème un peu niais qu'on jette au feu,
> Seul, un esclave un peu coureur qui vous néglige,
> Seul, un ennui d'on ne sait quoi qui vous afflige!

This masterly *jeu d'esprit* became to its author's amusement, the "clarion call" to another group of young poets, the Decadents as they were to name themselves or as Verlaine inadvertently named them. Soon after the publication of *Langueur* he was asked by Anatole Baju, their leader, to contribute to a projected group periodical *La Décade*. He replied bluntly, "The whole bunch of you will be told to go to the devil, you'll be called the Decadents"—a warning which the "ineffable" Baju converted into a challenge by christening the periodical *Le Décadent*.

The rights and wrongs of the matter can be left to the literary critics; the essential point in Verlaine's life at that moment was not whether he was or was not the founder or inspirer of these groups, but the fact that he was increasingly regarded as such by a few young men who were to form the literary judgment of the near future. Nor was this all. Illuminating those years of gloom and restlessness with gleams of cheerful promise was a star which, had Verlaine been more practical or more himself, would have appeared as his saving grace. A curious star indeed, the unromantic Léon Vanier with the fat cheeks and gross leer; but there it was, Verlaine had not only found a publisher but a man who actually welcomed whatever he was given. The relationship was some way from the ideal, but Vanier saw the joke and the genius. The joke was to prove too much for him from time to time, but his faith in the genius persisted. And if one asks how it was that a fat little purveyor of fishing tackle with a hankering for publishing could discern genius—and profitable genius—when the poets and critics had been blind to it for a decade or more, the answer must remain a mystery. On Verlaine's side he saw Vanier as a milch cow miraculously lowered from the skies, a delightful fellow slightly crazed or with more money than he knew what to do with, who was prepared to pay cash for, apparently, anything that Verlaine would write. Better still, who would pay for anything he could extract from the precious bundles of manuscript stuffed into every pocket. Never had he destroyed a line he had written, and how right he had been!

So Verlaine obliged. In these years he wrote much of the Lucien elegy and some of the other poems which were to make up the volume later known as *Amour*, he wrote many occasional poems for the three journals then printing him, he completed his *Jadis et Naguère* and, prose seeming to be as acceptable to Vanier as verse, he relieved his mind of some of its spleen towards Mathilde by writing, after the divorce, an account of life with the Mautés for what was to become his *Mémoires d'un Veuf*. Of the occasional verses, mostly excellent, one was outstanding; *La Dernière Fête Galante*, published in *Lutèce* in December 1884, is a brilliantly amusing attack on his own book.

> Pour une bonne fois, séparons-nous,
> Très chers messieurs et si belles mesdames,
> Assez comme cela d'épithalames,
> Et puis là, nos plaisirs furent trop doux.
>
> Nul remords, nul regret vrai, nul désastre!
> C'est effrayant ce que nous nous sentons
> D'affinités avecque les moutons
> Enrubannés du pire poétastre.
>
> Nous fûmes trop ridicules un peu
> Avec nos airs de n'y toucher qu'à peine.
> Le Dieu d'amour veut qu'on ait de l'haleine,
> Il a raison! Et c'est un jeune Dieu.

Séparons-nous, je vous le dis encore.
O que nos cœurs qui furent trop bêlants,
Dès ce jourd'hui réclament, trop hurlants,
L'embarquement pour Sodome et Gomorrhe!

Jadis et Naguère, published a month earlier, has often been called a hotchpotch. It is true that the presence of the one-act comedy *Les Uns et les Autres*, a mildly amusing extension of *Fêtes Galantes* to the stage, and the *Vers Jeunes*, put in simply because Verlaine could not bear to waste a line he had written, have given the whole book a bad name. But a volume containing the sonnet to Mérat, *Art Poétique*, *Luxures* and *Vers pour être calomnié* cannot be underrated. Nor are these fine poems exceptional; the sections *Jadis* and *Naguère*, the bulk of the book, do not contain a single poem less than first-rate; such a one, for instance, as the early sonnet *Circonspection*, in which expression, feeling and atmosphere are blended superbly.

Donne ta main, retiens ton souffle, asseyons-nous
Sous cet arbre géant où vient mourir la brise
En soupirs inégaux sous la ramure grise
Que caresse le clair de lune blême et doux.

Immobiles, baissons nos yeux vers nos genoux.
Ne pensons pas, rêvons. Laissons faire à leur guise
Le bonheur qui s'enfuit et l'amour qui s'épuise,
Et nos cheveux frôlés par l'aile des hiboux.

Oublions d'espérer. Discrète et contenue,
Que l'âme de chacun de nous deux continue
Ce calme et cette mort sereine du soleil.

Restons silencieux parmi la paix nocturne:
Il n'est pas bon d'aller troubler dans son sommeil
La nature, ce dieu féroce et taciturne.

The merits of the book were not this time ignored. His work was at last being watched, and when *Jadis et Naguère* appeared it immediately increased his growing reputation as one of the first poets of his day. A sign of the times—as noteworthy in its way as the cordiality of Mendès at the Voltaire—was the breaking of Banville's long silence; he, regretting the cowardice of his behaviour over the third *Parnasse Contemporain* and unable to restrain his admiration, came into the open with a letter of congratulation. He had his reservations: "At times you skirt the cliffs of poetry so closely that you risk falling into music"; but even here he wisely chose to waive them with a "Well, you may be right."

But it was neither *Jadis et Naguère* nor his occasional poems which had the decisive effect on Verlaine's reputation. This came curiously but with poetic justice through Rimbaud. Amidst his work in 1884 not yet mentioned was what appeared, and what he certainly thought to be, an easy task; to write introductions and make selections of poetry for a series under the title *Les Poètes Maudits*. The series appeared first in *Lutèce*; then, in April, Vanier published it as separate small books. The work was not particularly well done, Verlaine being too kind-hearted for true criticism, but it was perfectly timed. He chose as his poets Rimbaud, Mallarmé and a Breton, Tristan Corbière, who had published a book of poems, *Les Amours Jaunes*, exactly ten years earlier, when Verlaine was in London. The poems were scarcely noticed and Corbière had died the next year, at the age of thirty, an unknown man. He had something in common with Verlaine and even more with the young Symbolists then struggling for a hearing; Verlaine's selection made a hit amongst the young poets and Corbière was read, studied and elevated to a niche in the Symbolist temple.

The effect of the second book surprised Verlaine, Vanier and its subject. Mallarmé had by that time escaped from the provinces and was teaching English with indifferent success in the Collège Rollin, but he was a choosy man as to companions, no lover of the cafés, and the move to Paris had done little for his reputation. Then *Les Poètes Maudits* appeared and Mallarmé became almost overnight one of the gods of the Symbolists; from that moment he and Verlaine stood as twin pillars of the movement. To Verlaine the little book was intended as an agreeable memento of the mutual admiration subsisting between himself and Mallarmé—one can scarcely call it friendship since in their wisdom the men, differing so markedly in their pleasures outside poetry, took care to avoid all but an occasional meeting. In the event he found himself hailed as the man who, not only himself a fine poet, had brought Corbière and Mallarmé to life.

The third book, on Rimbaud, made even more of a sensation.

By then Rimbaud, although still only twenty-nine, had become a legendary figure in Paris. He was remembered, when at all, as a rather nasty youth who had made a meteoric and unpleasant descent on the city, had seduced Verlaine from his friends and family, and had then gone off no one seemed to know where. Delahaye, who heard something of him from time to time, was a provincial schoolmaster rarely seen and as little listened to; Rimbaud's one-time familiar Forain was uncommunicative; Nouveau his last companion was scarcely sane, and Verlaine was little wiser than the café crowds. The young intellectuals knew nothing of his work and no more than rumours of his life.

Then came Verlaine's book. The *avant-garde* poets read with astonishment *Le Bateau Ivre* and the vowel sonnet, read and marvelled. In the cafés of the Latin Quarter one could hear little but talk about this mysterious man who had written highly original poetry, thrown up literature in his teens, and vanished. A Rimbaud cult began which would lead in time to yet another school of poetry. But for the moment attention and esteem fell almost equally on Verlaine; Verlaine who had brought him to life, who knew him as no other man, who had suffered because of him.

Then came *Jadis et Naguère*, Banville's compliment and, following Banville—the disapproving Leconte de Lisle and Heredia excepted—the rest of the old guard, of whom only Dierx, Mallarmé, Valade, Lepelletier and Blémont had remained more or less faithful at a respectable distance. Middle-aged approval; youthful enthusiasm and imitation: here was change indeed, somewhat ironical when one remembers that at this time the respected author was serving his month in prison for assault, and afterwards wandering on drunken sprees about the Ardennes. But the respect of Banville and company was, all understood, intellectual merely; the days of Parnassian or any other kind of soirées were, so far as Verlaine was concerned, gone for good; he was to be praised at a safe distance. It was to the young and to the few unrespectable faithful among his old companions that he had to look. The last and in many ways best period of his life was about to begin.

Chapter Seventeen

PARADISE BROUSSAIS

1885-1888

I

THE Hôtel du Midi was one of the least prepossessing of the
scruffy lodging-houses in which Paris specialises. It sat
dismally in the apology for a street called Cour Saint-
François, a noisome cul-de-sac behind Place de la Bastille. It was
rat- and bug-ridden like every other house in the neighbourhood,
and was practically without the light of day, huddled under the
arches of the railway to Vincennes and shaking from top to
bottom every time a train rumbled overhead. When its inhabitants
were not deafened by the railway their nerves were torn by the
day-long scream of a saw, for next door was a timber warehouse.

Verlaine's room in this palace with the high-sounding name
was even worse than the imagination bargained for; after
stumbling down the foul-smelling street with its open drains,
most of his visitors recoiled in horror from the den that he
described as his home. Occupying most of the ground floor of the
hotel was a wine shop; visitors had to walk through this to reach
Verlaine's room, "small, sordid and sinister like the cut-throat
place at the bottom of which it squatted. There was no floor, not
even flagstones; one trod on the bare earth, which was damp and
muddy. . . . A tiny cupboard served as Verlaine's library; it was
crammed with books and manuscripts. A narrow table and two
wicker chairs completed the furniture."

To Lepelletier, who wrote this, Verlaine, obliging as ever, said
what Lepelletier expected to hear: that it was all the doing of that
unspeakable Mathilde, *"horrible, horrible, horrible femme!"* and the
old —— her father. Lepelletier would nod sympathetically, a
little shocked by the abuse but familiar with the routine. And
now? What an outlook! He wanted to earn his living by the pen,
but . . . If Lepelletier could give him a few more introductions . . .
And so on until Lepelletier, having done his duty and heroically
concealed his distaste, hurried away with a shudder.

VERLAINE

Most people repeated Lepelletier's shudder, but there was another point of view. The budding young Symbolist poet, Gustave Kahn, a sharp youngster with an eye for weaknesses in his elders and betters, came to persuade Verlaine to give some poems to the opening number of a new periodical, came squelching through the same slush, dodging the same balks of timber, pushing through the same shoddy crowd of prostitutes, pickpockets and down-at-heel labourers in the wine shop. He noted that the great man had chosen to live in a "picturesque quartier". He found Verlaine wrapped in an ancient blue overcoat, a bottle and glass before him on the table. The bottle was not full. He broached his mission, but Verlaine, disliking brevity, went off at a tangent. With "an exaggerated friendliness" which reminded the critical visitor of Banville he spoke of Kahn's growing reputation and, just to prove that there was no deception, quoted some verses of his with an admiration that the young man felt to be excessive.

Kahn came from Metz; Verlaine knew that too and went off into a rhapsody about the beauty of the Esplanade and his happy childhood walks there, his first love affair. Kahn repeated his request: some poems, please. Verlaine replied that he felt the honour deeply: "at the beginning of an infirm old age it is a recompense for living to hear the young men say that I have written good things". Changing the subject again, he spoke lyrically of Mallarmé, whom Kahn particularly admired, and recited his poetry "with curiously grandiloquent intonations". This done, he asked after Kahn's latest work.

Kahn reverted again to his purpose: was not Verlaine writing further *Poètes Maudits* and was there any chance of the new periodical printing them? Ah, the *Poètes Maudits*! Now Desbordes-Valmore, what a poetess: so simple, so direct, so sad, a northerner like himself! Taking up a book and assuming a formidable and heavily blurred pair of spectacles, Verlaine raised his head and, apparently glancing beneath the glasses, read several poems, the tears running down his cheeks.

Reduced to melancholy, he put down the book at last, drained his glass and began to tell his visitor of his return to Paris, of his many sorrows, of his false wife, his imminent poverty, his failing health. Fresh tears fell. Another glass was emptied.

But there were compensations? suggested Kahn; growing

fame, respect from the young poets, a good publisher, a body of superb poetry behind him and even greater to come. And to live in the heart of the working quarter of Paris, this too . . .

Verlaine, who had cheered up, agreed enthusiastically; he would not miss the morning walk, clip-clopping to the Place de la Bastille in search of newspapers. Even to take part in that futile manœuvre, to try to insinuate oneself on to the omnibus of faubourg St-Antoine black with workers reeking of garlic, even that was—well, it was Paris and one loved every wasted moment of it, the abuse that meant nothing, the smell, the incredible noise.

He abruptly went back a decade and with great éclat told stories of his days at the fortifications with the Garde Nationale which made even the purposeful Kahn laugh. Ridiculous, wasn't it, he a soldier, a Communard?

The anecdotes flowed, the bottle was done, the boy from the wine shop replaced it, the glasses filled and emptied, the tireless Verlaine talked on. Kahn repeated his request. Poems? Of course. And Verlaine, scrabbling in the little cupboard, handed his guest a sheaf of papers covered with the beautiful writing. After a moment's hesitation he produced another paper. "I suppose you couldn't use this? A powerful piece of work." Kahn looked at it; it was a scurrilous attack on Mathilde. "No, I'm afraid not." "Oh, well"; and the paper went back into the cupboard.

But there was one more point. The periodical, Kahn explained reluctantly from the doorway, clutching the manuscripts, was new, uncertain of its future, and in short the rates of payment were not high, in fact they were low, practically nothing to be exact. Verlaine spread wide arms from the midst of his squalor. "I had never given it a thought," he assured Kahn with the air of a man beyond money; and Kahn escaped gratefully with his precious papers, which would ensure the sale of the first number. To him the slum was picturesque.

But most people shuddered like Lepelletier. And if the reader asks why Verlaine, who was not entirely without money at the time, had chosen to plant himself there, the explanation is simple: the wine merchant was his friend; he liked wine and he liked friends, and would rather be miserably uncomfortable in company than in comfort and alone.

Miserably uncomfortable, but not miserable. Most visitors thought and most readers would naturally assume that he must be both. But it was not so, as his letters clearly show. "I am filled with joy", he told Vanier, now become his chief correspondent. "Found heaps of things, prose and verse, I thought I had lost. Seen Izambard, who has lent me early Rimbaud poems. Plan definitely fixed for *Madame Aubin*, which will be one act only. In labour with two long chapters for *Mémoires d'un Veuf*. Have written verses for serious, paying periodicals (Prudence and Chastity) which do pay. Some very daring biographical verses are just going to be published by *Lutèce*. Confound it, I'm burning my boats. Chatter and publicity."

That is a sample of Verlaine's state of mind for the greater part of the next two and a half years. He was busy, hopeful and had at his back a publisher who could generally be persuaded to fork out an advance of five francs or so when funds were low. He was having enormous fun chasing the periodicals that sprang up like mushrooms, writing this for that, that for this; he was enjoying the conversion of every experience into reading matter for the insatiable Vanier to put into print.

But to have plenty of work, to feel that it is good work and that it is usually to be paid for, to know that one's reputation is rising, does not compensate for detestable physical discomfort. Knowing Verlaine's happy-go-lucky disregard of fame, knowing him to be a sensuous animal loving comfort as much as any Frenchman can, and brought up from his early years in what most of his countrymen would describe as luxury, one has to look elsewhere for the answer. He had at last come to terms with himself. In future, life was to do what it liked with him and he accepted everything, good and bad, with no more than the famous satyrish grimace and commonly with a joke, rude if possible. Nothing—fame, money, poverty, pain, flattery, malice —could disturb his fundamental balance. As a result the last years, the years of city vagabondage, years of discomfort, homelessness, poverty (self-imposed most of it)—everything that he had struggled against—nevertheless form the most admirable period of his life. He was contented if not happy; to him, whose conscience remained lively, the past was recalled as a time of many errors and downright sins, and his present life, as a direct result of them, appeared a second best; but this decline he no

longer bemoaned; with humility and a good-humoured resignation he made the best of what he had left himself. His life from
1885 onwards is not commonly put forward as an example of
the good life, but it may well be that the general judgment
is at fault.

Moreover, he wore the sign at times incongruous but always
unmistakable of the man who is himself from morning to night,
believes in himself and is not for ever finding himself in a false
position. He had tried to live up to Mathilde, Rimbaud,
Nouveau and Lucien; often with the best intentions, but an act
nevertheless; and in consequence he had invited criticism. Now he
had dignity. Dignity is not the characteristic one would expect to
find in a man who had "sunk low", as the expression goes, whose
tastes were dubious and whose life was to be passed in cafés,
miserable bed-sitting-rooms, and hospitals; yet that was the first
and last impression of every perceptive witness. One will suffice,
the young André Suarès, later to become well known, who
happened to be sitting in the corner of a café when Verlaine
came in, sat down and put his game leg on the chair opposite.
He was quickly "surrounded by young people, some disciples,
some merely curious. He sat silent. He was offered a drink.
Finally he accepted it, but with a dignity not less admirable than
he had previously shown in refusing it. He had the air of one
completely at home with himself." And the witness, who was to
see him often, adds, "Not one of the pharisees who criticised him
as a disgrace could rival in dignity the Verlaine of the 'undignified' life."

In one important way he was helped to throw off restlessness
and idealism. It was no mighty effort of will, of which he was
incapable, it was no miracle; it was simply that he became all
at once unable to do more than potter about city streets and
that he accepted with a grace remarkable in a strong man of
forty-two a life conditioned by an incurable disability. He had
been settled into his room for only a few weeks when his left leg
began to swell. The pain became so great that he called in a
doctor, who diagnosed water on the knee. The knee was put into
plaster. His mother came down from Arras, to which she had
retreated after the court case early in the year, and took the room
above him.

By December he was up and out, which explains Kahn's

"clip-clopping", and it was then that he first took on the appearance which has remained famous: the black slouch hat, shabby macfarlane, the heavy stick in the right hand and the pronounced limp. He could not be missed, first because of his height, secondly because of his clothes, which grew fantastically worn with the passing years, lastly because of his manner: affable, hail-fellow-well-met with all, yet not that of another bum, crank or down-at-heel clerk. He would be heard murmuring as he limped along; not talking to himself as the passer-by might imagine—he had no need of that lonely man's compensation, not being lonely—but sounding out the possibilities of words. He was for ever striving after the perfect word; subjects met him wherever his eyes turned, and when they turned inwards there too was the subject, inexhaustible, of the mystery of man.

So Verlaine limped heavily to Place de la Bastille every morning, mouthing words meticulously, pausing to make a note in his pocket-book, limping on, stick tap, tap, tap, keen eyes darting in every direction, missing nothing from the stir of a leaf in the dirty gutter to the flutter of a handkerchief from some high and uninviting window, comical flat nose registering every scent —caporal, garlic, coffee, *croissants* newly baked—faunlike ears distinguishing every small sound apparently lost in the din of crowded streets.

Arrived at the Place he made a tour of the kiosks, lingering until the owner objected to prolonged free reading, moving on until, the round accomplished, he sat down at a café overlooking the great square, a bundle of newspapers under his arm if in funds; if not, summoning the waiter to bring him what papers the café possessed. Followed a quick but thorough perusal, the lighting of a foul-smelling pipe, more drinks, conversation with any likely neighbour or the making of more notes in the pocket-book. Plans innumerable ran through his head: what he would write and where he would send it; should he stand immovable, rocklike outside Mallarmé's school where Georges was then studying and insist on seeing the boy whom Mathilde was keeping from him? Mathilde—this thought called for another drink with furrowed, angry face; Vanier—how much could he screw out of him, five francs, ten, even fifteen? On and on the thoughts chased, one drink took the place of another, the morning was gone, lunch had to be sought if there was money for a lunch, otherwise a friend or admirer must be found to stand him one. That was not difficult on most days, for he was a character whose conversation repaid hospitality, adapting himself readily to the tone of his companion.

Towards the end of a day he was not always affable, the absinthes having their effect. He did not drink as heavily as in youth, and the after-passions had gone, but he could be irritable, quarrelsome. And one evening, differing from the waiter about the reckoning, he went so far as to call a gendarme, a rash step which ended in a night in a prison cell. This, the penultimate "imprisonment", which he noted in the amusing *Mes Prisons* he was to write for Vanier, was a turning-point in his relations with the police. The time was not far distant when they were to take a pride in preserving him, not simply from a prison cell but from the curious and impertinent bystander, he having won the freedom of a city peculiarly responsive to the arts.

For the moment, however, his drinking resulted in more trouble with his leg. And in January 1886, when he was bedbound again, his mother caught a chill and died; died without him, since he was too heavy and too tall to be carried up the narrow steps to her room. So ended, to the sound of Verlaine's passionate regrets, a relationship which for all the exceptional feeling on both sides can only be regarded as a disaster. The last twenty years of Mme Verlaine's life were sadly harassed, that is to state the obvious; less obvious but equally true were the many satisfactions which only another Mme Verlaine would fully understand. One thing can be appreciated by all, however; that Mme Verlaine, abnormal though she was and wickedly though she spoiled her son, was in the rights of it when she gloried in his loving disposition; he caused her endless trouble, but she weighed the good against the ill and considered that the one amply compensated for the other.

Practically, his mother's death meant that Verlaine once again had money to spend. It was not a great deal, and of what there was Mathilde to his fury demanded and was awarded half; but it was enough to bring his health to a crisis; and in July, all money gone and both legs covered with sores, he was admitted to the Tenon Hospital.

From this time until May 1888, that is for the best part of two years, he moved, with short and penurious intervals, from one hospital to another; from the Tenon to the Broussais, from the Broussais to the Cochin, from the Cochin to the Convalescent Asylum of St Maurice at Vincennes, back again to the Tenon and so on, doing the rounds but with a growing and decided preference for the Broussais.

Any attempt to take this hospital period seriously is defeated by the patient himself, who in many of his letters and in his *Mes Hôpitaux* (hurriedly turned out later on to earn an advance from Vanier) makes high comedy of his efforts to stay put or, having been dislodged from one hospital, to seek shelter in another and, successfully installed, of his life there as undisputed master of the ward. In reality it was not always the joke he pretended, but efforts to discover when exactly he went into hospital because his health demanded it and when he tried to go there because he was penniless end in confusion. But it is of no great moment and one accepts the comedy gladly, remembering that he was a sick man for much of this time and that his sufferings must have been considerable.

Even the exact nature of his ailments remains uncertain. He began with water on the knee, then sores on his legs, then complete rigidity of one limb; he also had acute rheumatic pains. The diagnoses differed, as did the treatments, but there seems little doubt that the main trouble was syphilis; Verlaine at any rate freely blamed the prostitutes of Paris and London. Alcohol was the worst possible thing he could take, but he took plenty, with the result that, out of hospital, he at once began to undo the cure. Scarcely less harmful was his indulgence in the women, including his friend Lily, whom he picked up. In this instance homoeopathy did not work; when not reinfected he was exhausted and wide open to any new infection. Back then he went in a week or two, and the treatments began all over again. When, as sometimes happened despite his best endeavours, he remained on his feet with empty pockets, he would besiege one hospital after another, manufacturing a pain or two if nothing "curable" showed itself at that moment.

At first sight this passion for hospitals appears strange.

Granted the boons of regular and free food, clean clothes and skilled attention to a man who could never save a penny, be sure of a roof over his head or the next meal, the disadvantages of perpetual discipline, loss of freedom and friends would seem to outweigh them. But Verlaine had the habit of bending everything to his comfort, even a hospital. There were times when he was really ill and treated like every other patient. There were times, too, when he felt himself to be badly done by and expressed his feelings in delightfully Coleridgean manner: "But all the same it is hard after a life of work set off, I admit, by accidents in which I have had a large share, catastrophes perhaps vaguely premeditated—it is hard, I say, at forty-seven years of age, in full possession of the reputation (of the *success*, to use the frightful current phrase) to which my highest ambitions could aspire—hard, hard, hard indeed, worse than hard, to find myself—good God!—to find myself *on the streets* and to have nowhere to lay my head and support an ageing body save the pillows and the *menus* of a public charity, even now uncertain and which might at any moment be withdrawn—God forbid!—without, apparently, it being the fault of anyone oh! not even, and above all, not mine!" But this excursion into the pathetic was written for a public, with tongue well in cheek, humour not absent (see the *menus*) and of which the operative words are the opening "But all the same".

Out of hospital he did not dwell on these moments, but thought with absolute longing of the days and weeks when treatment had reduced itself to medicines which he could often slip overboard untasted, and to massage which when the masseuse was pretty or plump he by no means disenjoyed. And thinking so he could not wait to get back to "that paradise, the Broussais" where he was uncrowned king. For rules disintegrated before his blarney and cheerful courage, visiting hours elongated themselves almost round the clock, and his ward became workroom, salon and even bar.

So for much of the time he really did enjoy himself, not so much because he felt well as because it was in his nature to find the good in everything rather than to concentrate on the bad. He suffered a lot from his legs, the doctors did devilish things to them occasionally, that was a bore, an unbearable outrage; he would shout it, then forget it. He was being looked after like a child, he had absolutely no responsibility, that was wonderful and he revelled in it. He was confined to his bed, but that was about all he was confined to; sitting up on his pillows, hospital night cap (his "halo") jauntily askew, he wrote his way through reams of hospital paper, pouring out poems, prose, letters innumerable, presided in state over all the affairs of the ward, dispensed advice, cheer (by much mimicry, quite well done, of visitors, doctors, nurses and men of the day) and, when he judged it necessary, medicines unprescribed by the doctors which he drew cautiously from underneath his bed. Every afternoon he received callers: the successful Coppée, an Academician since 1884, a thought-provoking example of what prosperity does to a man of letters, looking no longer a mild Napoleon but a third-rate actor who had come into money, who when leaving slipped fifty francs into a not unwilling hand; the fat Vanier weaving plan after plan for their joint profit; the youthful Morice and his crowd, who, after listening rapturously to recitations of Verlaine's latest work and to his comments on the poems they recited, would withdraw reluctantly, carefully depositing under the inverted chamber-pot a bottle of brandy or a flask of absinthe, some cigars or a packet of the invalid's favourite tobacco.

The doctors and nurses soon came to take pride in this glorious eccentric. He was incorrigible, he would not be permanently cured, that much was clear. But what good company, what a flow of rakish speech, what bonhomie and, even in melancholy moments, what style! And with a shrug and a wink almost all let him do as he pleased. An occasional reproof, a short repentance, this was the beginning and end of discipline.

The hospital years, therefore, blossom into high comedy, then into downright farce. He is for ever scheming to get back before he has even been discharged: "I *must* leave on Friday, the first of July so that I can return in a few days' time. It's compulsory— a bore, but compulsory"; and, to Vanier, "I beg you to send by return a mandat or note for 50 francs. Without it I'm liable to be discharged any day. See what a spot you've put me in! I absolutely dared not go out yesterday." Again, to the same correspondent from the Broussais after a short absence: "Received back here like the prodigal son. Mild reproaches, that's all. And arrived in very good shape in spite of all the absinthes."

His letters to Vanier become a travesty of the popular idea of author to publisher. Every week, every day or two he dashes off a note to the long-suffering man on Quai St Michel. The requests veer from the piteous cry to the peremptory demand, having in common only their inevitability; scarcely a letter was without the money element; most of them had no other purpose. Always there were promises, as much to himself as to Vanier, who was utterly unconcerned with his author's morals or morale, promises of amendment, promises grandiose, promises descending to the farcical. "It is pitiful to live so. I assure you that my heart weeps as I write all this. But I shall do nothing that is not dignified and straightforward. *Potius mori quam foedari*: that is truly my motto. That and to die a Christian death worthy of my parents and an example to my son. . . . Yours very cordially and very sadly but determined to be strong."

But the cry for money was the great thing. He did not waste space: "Great need of cash. It's true, no kidding. Quick. Quick. Great need of cash"; "Be so good as to send me 50 francs at once." And not only for money as such; the theme was varied. Vanier inevitably assumed more and more the shape of a universal provider: "Don't need money but . . . chocolate, stamps, a small carafe of wine from time to time, etc. (the etceteras aren't numerous or alarming!). In short, please send me a mandat for 15 francs"; "If you aren't a bread and butter publisher . . . you'll recognise and recompense my activity, my zeal, my punctuality, my patience, and all my virtues by coming WITH ALL MANUSCRIPTS AND STAMPED PAPER."

Vanier must also buy clothes: "I hope to get back into hospital . . . but I must look a bit respectable. A pair of shoes at any rate and a reasonably decent hat to liven up this old carcass . . . in short, bring or send me (send by mandat) all you can spare as soon as possible. This business of petty debts, of thinking what is due, etc., bores me without counting the frightful fatigue of keeping up appearances"; "Now if it turns out to be impossible to prolong my 'rest cure' here and to get into another hospital right away (what a life I lead, my dear chap!) . . . I must eat and I shall need one of those hats at 3 fr. 60 not to mention a shirt and some shoes . . . and a nice little sum in my pocket. So, send these . . . so that I can leave here for the 'Great World' well armed for the 'Struggle for life' in the depths. And may heaven bless you"; or again, "Will you—and this is very serious—get me a pair of summer trousers, grey, the same kind that I bought for 3 francs last summer?"

Vanier must repay the few loans which, to Verlaine's horror, the lender seemed to expect to be settled, and Vanier must settle the restaurant bills Verlaine had signed during his few days or weeks between one hospital and another. "Now be a good fellow and don't forget M. Allemoz"—this being the owner of his then favourite restaurant in rue Moreau; and again, "Have you paid good mother Allemoz?"

But Vanier did not always pay. Then, Verlaine having sent Delahaye, Morice, Carjat or some other familiar in vain to Quai St Michel to collect what he had come to consider his due, a haughty letter was despatched to "Monsieur Vanier" ending with the formal "Agréez, Monsieur, mes civilités." "I'm on very distant terms with Vanier," he explained to Lepelletier, "and for a very good reason." He failed to give the reason.

But he was too good-tempered—and too often without a sou— to keep up a tone so widely out of character. He had to be friendly with all; all had to be loved except three people: Mathilde, who had committed the final crime by remarrying— this time a building contractor, the M. Delporte who was later to divorce her; her father; and the implacable Leconte de Lisle. These apart, the world was all love to Verlaine when it was not despair. He and Vanier were quickly reconciled and Vanier usually paid up in the end.

Vanier, however, must not be romanticised. That Verlaine did more than amuse him is unlikely; he had no time for senti- ment in business; if he seems absurdly generous to this indigent author it was because he knew that he had discovered a source of profit. All honour to him for that; he was the first man to realise Verlaine's potentialities. But his advances, numerous though they were, were always very small; Verlaine, who could never assimilate the idea of his growing importance, continued to ask and be grateful for the five odd francs that a beginner would have had a right to. In sum they did not amount to more than he could have demanded legitimately had he possessed the slightest head for business.

In one way only did Vanier take a risk; it was necessary that Verlaine should not merely write about the many works he had in train but should actually produce them. And here the publisher was fortunate; for although Verlaine gives every appearance in his letters of being the cadger to outdo all cadgers and a hopeless weaver of impossible plans, he was in action one of the most prolific writers of his time. "I'm writing very much", he tells Vanier, the "very much" in English; "I work *en masse* and I have great hopes for the future"; "I'm worked to death"; "I continue courageously with my literary work so as to provide if possible for my old age"; "I write verse and lots of prose between a couple of sighs and some ghostly groans when I'm treated with sulphate of copper—not very aphrodisiac, this régime of mine!" So the messages went: wan, rude, humorous, dignified as the case might be; but the burden of them all was work. And astonishingly the work was done.

3

It has become an accepted fact that Verlaine never wrote anything really good in his last years, but even accepted facts need looking into from time to time. It is certainly true that Vanier was a menace as well as a godsend. Put a man like Verlaine, put any man with vigorous appetites and inexhaustible impulses towards generosity into the position where he has only to write to be paid or, even more tempting, to be paid before he writes, and he will write too much. Verlaine was never one to labour overmuch; he would find the right word for his poems but he would do it *en passant* as it were, while he walked, before he went off to sleep. For the rest he was an instinctive poet, writing as naturally as he breathed. He was not a born writer of prose; he could write well but he could also write badly, and he did not take enough trouble; indeed it is a question whether he took any trouble at all.

And here is the basis for the popular belief; here and in his habit, now that ready-money Vanier had come on to the scene, of rescuing from his only too well preserved archives every line he had ever written and of palming off on publisher and public youthful follies, failures put aside years earlier, anything and everything that would fetch a franc or two.

Let us examine the work written and published in these years
to the middle of 1888. In prose, Verlaine's principle was the
journalistic one of converting into cash any and every *rencontre*,
memory, experience that could be fashioned into an article or a
book: hence his confessions, his reminiscences of hospitals and
prisons. But these, although begun or already in mind at this
period, were crowded out by other and more pressing tasks; for
his confessions could end only with his life, he could not be sure
that he had experienced his last prison and he was quite certain
that there were more hospitals to come. In 1886 Vanier published
his *Louise Leclerq*, a book of three long-short stories including *Le
Poteau* and the supposedly autobiographical *Pierre Duchâtelet*—a
book of no more than moderate merit. This was followed by
another short play, *Madame Aubin*, and by the *Mémoires d'un Veuf*
to which he had been making additions over the years, including
a good account of the formation of the Parnasse (a counterblast
to Mendès' much criticised account of two years earlier) and a
slightly shocking but salutary "re-estimate" of Hugo, who had
died just after Mathilde's remarriage.

The reception given to the *Poètes Maudits*, and especially to the
volume on Rimbaud, had encouraged Vanier to advise Verlaine
to prepare for a reprint and an enlargement of the series. Three
more were added, one on Desbordes-Valmore, one on Villiers
and, Verlaine seeing no reason why the inventor should not
benefit from his invention, one on a mysterious "Pauvre Lelian"
which turned out, not to the great surprise of anyone, to be an
anagram of Verlaine himself, an exceedingly clever anagram
which went the rounds of Paris so thoroughly as almost to re-
christen Verlaine for the rest of his life. He was working on all
of these during the hospital years and, thinking this to be a pretty
easy way of earning money and a reputation, began to write for
another series, *Hommes d'aujourd'hui*, in which he would if given the
chance have included every man of any moment he had known,
going as far down the scale of fame as De Ricard, then back
in France in his rightful place as editor of a newspaper at
Montpellier.

Of this last series only the little volume on Rimbaud need be
noticed here. Verlaine on Rimbaud reminds one immediately of
Charlotte Brontë's introduction to the work of Emily; the same
strong, simple prose, the same profound admiration, the same

puzzlement and almost awe before wayward, self-willed genius: "Le tout, simple comme une forêt vierge et beau comme un tigre." Verlaine had already begun to search for the manuscripts of Rimbaud, who was still in Abyssinia, so that he might print and introduce them all. In this period he introduced an edition, the first to be printed, of *Illuminations* published by *La Vogue*, the periodical in whose interests the young editor Kahn had called at the noisome chamber behind the wine shop.

Important though his work on Rimbaud was to prove, and considerable though its effect was on contemporary writers, his own poetry remained his *raison d'être*. In the hospital years he wrote poem after poem, many of them appearing in the left-bank periodicals, poems which ranged from the fragment of the Temptation of St Antony libretto to the decidedly free *Lombes*, from the heart-rending Lucien sonnets to the delightfully witty *Ballade en faveur des dénommés Décadents et Symbolistes* dedicated tactfully to Vanier.

> Quelques-uns dans tout ce Paris
> Nous vivons d'orgueil et de dèche.
> D'alcool encore qu'épris,
> Nous buvons surtout de l'eau fraîche
> En cassant la croûte un peu sèche.
> A d'autres fins mets et grands vins,
> Et la beauté jamais revêche!
> Nous sommes les bons écrivains.
>
> Phoebé, quand tous les chats sont gris,
> Effile d'une pointe rêche
> Nos corps par la gloire nourris,
> Dont l'enfer, au guet, se pourlèche,
> Et Phoebus nous lance sa flèche.
> La nuit nous berce en songes vains
> Sur les lits de noyaux de pêche.
> Nous sommes les bons écrivains.
>
> Beaucoup de beaux esprits ont pris
> L'enseigne de l'Homme qui bêche,
> Et Lemerre tient les paris,
> Plus d'un encore se dépêche
> Et tâche d'entrer par la brèche;
> Mais Vanier à la fin des fins
> Seul eut de la chance à la pêche.
> Nous sommes les bons écrivains.

ENVOI

Bien que la bourse chez nous pèche,
Princes, rions, doux et divins.
Quoi que l'on dise ou que l'on prêche,
Nous sommes les bons écrivains.

To move from the slight to the sublime, by the first month of 1888 Verlaine had completed the poems for his next volume, *Amour*, and almost half the poems for the volume to follow it— completed with a typical letter to Vanier: "To the rescue, infamous publisher! You are a rotter for never turning up. I've waited ages for you! To punish you, here 'herewith' is the TRULY LAST piece for *Amour*, which I hope will soon be coming out. It's now or never, I think."

Amour appeared towards the end of March. It is a pity that those who wish to form an opinion of Verlaine's religious verse do not read this book as well as the more famous *Sagesse*. When he wrote *Sagesse* he was still in the state of exaltation which follows conversion; poetic gift apart, the substance and mood of the religious poems might have been those of any other recent convert—the tendency to hysteria, the divorce from the world, the horror at all he had been; they did not express the true faith of the writer. Later, in the years now reached, Verlaine had begun to explain far and wide, "*Moi*, I am a Catholic of the Middle Ages." This was near the mark; he was, naturally, being compared with "pauvre Villon", and took pleasure in the comparison. In the *Amour* poems we see this modern Villon, this Catholic of the Middle Ages, no mystic but a child often bad, often repenting, again bad, again repenting *ad infinitum*, but always with the touching belief that his sins would truly be forgiven him by a merciful and loving Father—no awful, unapproachable figure, this, but *un vrai Père*. This belief he demonstrates best in *Un Conte*, which first appeared in Moréas' and Kahn's short-lived *Le Symboliste*.

Simplement, comme on verse un parfum sur une flamme
Et comme un soldat répand son sang pour la patrie,
Je voudrais pouvoir mettre mon cœur avec mon âme
Dans un beau cantique à la sainte Vierge Marie.

PARADISE BROUSSAIS

Mais je suis, hélas! un pauvre pécheur trop indigne,
Ma voix hurlerait parmi le chœur des voix des justes:
Ivre encor du vin amer de la terrestre vigne,
Elle pourrait offenser des oreilles augustes.

Il faut un cœur pur comme l'eau qui jaillit des roches,
Il faut qu'un enfant vêtu de lin soit notre emblème,
Qu'un agneau bêlant n'éveille en nous aucuns reproches,
Que l'innocence nous ceigne un brûlant diadème,

Il faut tout cela pour oser dire vos louanges,
O vous, Vierge Mère, ô vous, Marie Immaculée,
Vous blanche à travers les battements d'ailes des anges,
Qui posez vos pieds sur notre terre consolée.

Du moins je ferai savoir à qui voudra l'entendre
Comment il advint qu'une âme des plus égarées,
Grâce à ces regards cléments de votre gloire tendre,
Revint au bercail des Innocences ignorées.

Innocence, ô belle après l'Ignorance inouïe,
Eau claire de cœur après le feu vierge de l'âme,
Paupière de grâce sur la prunelle éblouie,
Désaltèrement du cerf rompu d'amour qui brame!

Chapter Eighteen

PRINCE OF POETS

1888-1894

I

IN May 1888 he took rooms at the Hôtel de Lisbonne, 4 rue Vaugirard, and from this date it is possible to say that he enjoyed some semblance of a home of his own. Not that he had done with hospitals, but in the future he was to go back to them chiefly when he was too unwell to stay away; he no longer had to hang on there or to reinsinuate himself at the earliest possible moment in order to ensure a square meal and a change of clothing.

The move and the "rooms" in the plural were the joint result of improved health and a conglomeration of payments which even Verlaine, lashing out with a will, could not manage to dissipate in a few days or even weeks: he had at last received the final payment on the farm at Juniville, nine hundred francs, the repayment from a friend of the family at Arras of an old loan from Mme Verlaine of a thousand francs and, perhaps more surprising, the repayment, under some pressure, of fifteen hundred francs which he had lent in mysterious circumstances (some say as conscience money on the insistence of the fanatical Nouveau) to the Abbé Salard—"a hard nut to crack, a curate of Saint-Gervais", he told Lepelletier gleefully, "but fifteen hundred francs is a juicy morsel"; and to this windfall of three thousand four hundred francs, a small fortune for him to scatter abroad, was added at much the same time a sum not far removed from this in royalties, advances on books and contributions to periodicals. *Amour* was selling well, the first of his books to pass a sale of one hundred copies, and Vanier was busy with new editions of *Poèmes Saturniens*, *La Bonne Chanson* and *Sagesse*—that is to say, he was wherever possible rescuing unsold stock from the cellars of other publishers to reissue under his imprint—and with the next volume of poems, giving advances on all.

This was not Verlaine's first return to the left bank. After his first stay in hospital, in July 1886, he had abandoned the Hôtel du Midi and the right bank. Afterwards, whenever unsympathetic doctors obliged him to find and pay for lodgings, he would cross the river and camp out in one of the rooms near the Sorbonne favoured by impoverished students. The discomfort there does not have to be imagined; it can be experienced today in, for instance, any of the mean streets favoured by Verlaine on each side of Boulevard St-Michel. It need only be said that, fresh from hospital and with memories of English armchairs and generous heating and floor coverings, he lived wretchedly enough not to rest until he had persuaded some hospital that his state demanded immediate treatment.

Needless to say, compensations offered themselves even in the midst of squalor and physical discomfort. Some, the women, the drinks, the cafés, are obvious; others less so. There was, for example, the *rencontre* with Leconte de Lisle. The two men met at the counter of a tobacconist. Leconte de Lisle, portly, dandified, hair long, thin and white, legs a little unsteady, dignity Olympian (he had assumed the mantle of Hugo as Prince of Poets and grand old man of French literature and had followed— a sad grievance, the followed—Coppée to the Academy), stared through his square monocle, then bowed frigidly to the seedy Verlaine. Verlaine returned the bow and motioned Leconte de Lisle to the counter. After some mutual protestation Leconte de Lisle was served first and with due deliberation bought a box of Corona-Coronas. He paused to extract one, cut and light it, pointedly unaware of Verlaine's continued presence. Verlaine, who had gone with the intention of buying a pinch of caporal, took from his pocket all the money he possessed (a few sous) and planked it on the counter with a grand gesture: "Give me the biggest cigar you've got." The cigar handed over, big, cheap and nasty, he copied the motions of Leconte de Lisle and, turning, inhaled deeply, blew a cloud of rank smoke into the face of the great man, bowed and limped from the shop. Such was their last meeting, and such Verlaine's impromptu revenge for the calumnies of the "old ass".

The other notable satisfaction of the hospital period was of a purer nature, a visit to a Mallarmé soirée. By the time Verlaine visited him, "les mardis" of Mallarmé had become the most exclusive literary soirées in Paris. The stalwarts were Villiers and the Catholic writers J. K. Huysmans and Léon Bloy, but the bulk of the visitors were young Symbolist poets headed by Kahn. The atmosphere in rue de Rome every Tuesday evening from nine until midnight was one of ordered and domestic calm. Mme Mallarmé sat next to her husband, her head bent over embroidery, Mlle Mallarmé sat next to her mother, prepared to open the door to the disciples, who, seated solemnly round the room, helped themselves to tobacco from a Chinese jar on the centre table and listened with devout attention to what was practically a monologue from the master. No sound marred the smooth flow; a thick carpet muffled all footsteps, the door was draped with thick velvet, the windows were tightly shut and Japanese curtains closely drawn before them. The fireplace was sacrosanct; there Mallarmé stood by the small, hot stove or propelled himself softly up and down in the rocking-chair close to the stove. Protecting his feet from draught were thick carpet slippers, over his shoulders rested a large plaid shawl. His urbane voice quietly filled the room, the neatly pointed beard moved up and down, through the long moustache filtered the smoke from the eternal cigarette, the calmly shining eyes veiled by long lashes were fixed on the ground or, in more fervent moments, on the tastefully decorated ceiling. He discussed the theory of poetry and, disliking self-assertion and direct assertion, never permitted himself a plain statement; everything was put in the form of questions. A pause for reflection preceded every question.

Into this exquisite Symbolist paradise limped one evening the disreputable Verlaine. Unhappily next to nothing is known about the visit, but Mallarmé's feelings are not difficult to imagine: liking for Verlaine and admiration for his work struggling with horrid fears: would he be intoxicated, as was only too likely; would he make rude jokes, as was equally probable; would he even mock Symbolism itself, a proceeding of which he was fully capable? Even Verlaine's motive for appearing is lost, but it can be confidently surmised: he was either too drunk to know what he was doing or, more probably, having spent his last sou and having nowhere to lay his head for the night, he called to collect an immediate loan, the soirée evening being preferable because there was a good chance of securing a whip round.

It is just possible that Verlaine's visit coincided with the historic irruption of Heredia, a greying Heredia, stouter, louder,

and even more opulent in his evening-dress, who had left the
Opéra after the first act, who crashed into the quiet room with a
huge "Hm. Stuffy here, isn't it? Hot, eh?", marched heavily to
the rocking-chair, sat himself down with a thud and proceeded
to lecture the guests for the remainder of the evening.

The unhappy host, teetering between stove and table like a
lost soul, said nothing because he was too polite and too much
appalled by the solid vision with the massive expanse of shirt-
front studded with out-size pearls; the disciples remained quiet
because Heredia was a man with a reputation, a man freely
named as Prince of Poets after the ageing Leconte de Lisle.

If Verlaine's visit coincided with that of the mighty Heredia,
who gave him a condescending nod in the streets, keeping well
clear of physical contact, he would have sat quietly enough and
would not have failed to collect an extra five or ten francs from
the great one. In any event Verlaine's reception from the
disciples would be an inimitable blend of intense respect and
uncontrollable laughter. For he was a great man too, even
though he resolutely and comically refused to act the part. Of
those present at the Mallarmé soirée, Bloy, Huysmans and
Villiers of the older generation all admired him, the first two
particularly for his Catholic poems, and the young Félix Fénéon
Edouard Dujardin the Wagnerian, Laurent Tailhade and
Maurice Barrès of the disciples were notable for their persistent
imitation of Verlaine's as of Mallarmé's verse; Barrès was soon
to prove his devotion practically by paying the rent at rue
Vaugirard when the master's money ran out.

Nor was he set up as a Symbolist god simply by those who
admired and imitated; more significantly he was marked out by
the opponents of "modern verse" as its begetter in chief. As far
back as 1885 *Il pleure dans mon cœur* was quoted in Paul Bourde's
famous attack—the attack which put the movement on its feet—
on the "horrible decadents" as embodying all the vices of this
"maladive et bizarre" school. In his reply, and in his "Symbolist
manifesto" published a year later, Moréas proudly claimed
Verlaine as one of the main inspirations of the Symbolist theory,
following Poe, "that the beautiful is the only legitimate domain
of poetry", that the poet "should use suggestion and music as the
basis of his work" and should be the implacable enemy of
"didacticism, of the objectively descriptive and of the insincerely

sensitive". This was followed by Baju's claim, in *Le Décadent*, that Verlaine was the greatest poet of the nineteenth century. And just before Verlaine moved to rue Vaugirard, the better known *Revue Bleue* published an article by Jules Lemaître, one of the most influential critics of the day, in which he confirmed Baju's statement. Morice was writing a critical study of Verlaine's poetry, the young Debussy and Fauré were setting his poems to music and there was even talk of a "Selected Verse".

This last indicates Verlaine's stature. He was not Coppée, who had become the poet of the people, easy, optimistic, sentimental. The growing fame of Verlaine was of another kind; he remained little known to the man in the street, his contemporaries respected and envied his work but avoided him and the youth of the left bank proclaimed him a neglected genius.

In so far as he was becoming popular by association with the Symbolists and Decadents, Verlaine acquiesced with a grimace: "Symbolism?" he exclaimed. "Don't understand it. Must be a German word, eh? Anyway I'm simply not interested. When I suffer, when I enjoy, when I weep, I know quite well that it's not a question of symbols." As for the name Decadent: "fundamentally it doesn't mean anything at all."

Plain speaking; understandable from a man who had thrown off in a couple of not too serious moments the poems which Decadents and Symbolists persisted in seeing as their gospel. It was true enough that he was not the innovator that some of his disciples claimed; Moréas looked back, correctly, to Poe, and the general worship of Wagner (with which Verlaine associated himself) by the adherents of both movements showed that they knew their origins. But it was also true that at a crucial moment the young poets discovered in Verlaine's verse the essence of Symbolism. There is always a time lag in the development of literary modes and it is possible to see a similarity between the co-ordinating work of Mendès in the 'sixties and of Moréas, Morice, Kahn, Baju and the rest twenty years later; Mendès had And he summed up with his:

> A bas le symbolisme, mythe
> Et termite, et encore à bas
> Ce décadisme parasite
> Dont tels rimeurs ne voudraient pas!

gone far to form the Parnasse on the work of Leconte de Lisle, who expressed ideas worked out sketchily by others; and Verlaine expressed the mode of the future already distinguishable in the work of earlier men. But Verlaine's expression was the unselfconscious expression of genius, and what he expressed was, unlike the Parnasse, a true forward movement which was to spread through the arts, to Debussy, Gauguin and the great creators.

This kind of fame caused him to chuckle secretly whilst he revelled in the company of admirers. Another is shown by his enquiry to Vanier: "How goes Fame—that is, how go the sales?" This was all that fame meant to him now, this and drinks, more drinks, friendliness on all sides, talk, gross talk, fine talk, and still more drinks until the hero would lurch home, the gendarme explaining proudly to the enquiring stranger when a crowd gathered: "That's the poet M. Verlaine. He has to be in that condition to write his poetry."

Yet another mood led him to the room in rue Vaugirard over-looking the Luxembourg gardens and within a stone's throw of the Voltaire, the François Premier, the Procope, the Soleil d'Or, at all of which he was to have his special seat for the rest of his life. For at last he could show his face freely again. No more fear of snubs. Salutations everywhere. If this was fame, he liked it; crowds of youngsters round him at the François Premier firing questions, manuscripts and drinks at him. No need to put one's hand into that emptying pocket, the young men insisted on paying all. They would help one home too. They were not always respectful—their worship was modern— but who wanted adulation? Not Verlaine, or not for long, a moment or two enthroned in a hospital bed, perhaps; no, give him young men interested, cheeky, talkative, alive.

In the autumn of 1888 and the spring and summer of the next year he first became the great sight of Boulevard St-Michel. There's Verlaine! Here's Verlaine! And the men would collect, the news passing more quickly than the shambling figure in his black hat and thick stick tapping solidly with every step. He was game for everything, to recite a poem, deliver a judgment, empty so many glasses in a given time, tell an unmentionable anecdote, even to unroll a bandaged leg to show a threatened ulcer. He could be silent too, listening with grave attention, one finger tapping the marble table, head lowered. When he lifted his head his eyes fascinated everyone: "Grey or green," wrote Suarès, "I could never be sure, they looked like sloes. Soft and sharp, weary and lively, at times almost spiteful then mistily veiled as though they had been inwardly drowned in tears, giving themselves up to internal sobbing, to the dream of an unfathomable sadness. These eyes begged; arrogant, hurt, angry, they were heavy with supplication."

Another reason for the settlement, if one dare use such a word of this Bohemian who protested in and out of season that he was nothing of the kind, was the arrival in his life of a boon companion, biographer and portraitist in the person of F. A. Cazals. In the mirror of his room when he had one, Verlaine stuck the portraits, grubby through long life in his pockets, of Lucien and of his son Georges, soon to be removed by his mother to Algiers out of harm's way. Rimbaud he was honouring (and profiting from) by printing the poetry as he discovered it. Cazals, the last of the tribe, was quite another kettle of fish. A dandy who reminds one of the photographer Carjat, this humorous, perky, happily married young rake with the flair with the pencil and crayon had constituted himself a kind of unofficial guardian to Verlaine, looking after him when ill but not ill enough to need a hospital, and restraining occasionally some of his more fanciful extravagances. But he was in no sense a moral guardian, originating as well as playing a leading part in many of the "sprees" with which the ancient-looking (he was forty-five) but lively Verlaine indulged himself. It was just that, being more French than Verlaine in this, an economical streak occasionally uncovered itself in him.

As for the "sprees", it is not known what part Cazals played in the arrival of the delegate from the advanced poets of the south, come to pay homage, who found two naked women reclining on the bed. Verlaine, not at all put out, introduced the young man with courtly gestures to the two ladies and improved the occasion by exclaiming: "How fortunate! Now you can tell all your friends that you've actually seen proof that I'm not the homosexual my enemies have tried to make out." And although one feels that one woman on the bed would have been even more convincing, the young man from the Midi rallied quickly and returned home with a glowing report of the master's liberality.

Edmond
Lepelletier,
1880

Villiers de L'Isle Adam

Verlaine and Eugénie
Krantz

Verlaine at The
Hague, 1892

Cazals certainly had a large hand in the soirées that Verlaine was able to hold for the first and last time; his Wednesdays of 1888 and 1889 became famous throughout the Latin Quarter. The company jammed into the room every Wednesday evening was a mixed bag; Forain was there, Carjat too, but of all the men who had gathered with Verlaine at De Ricard's, Mendès', Nina's and Lemerre's only one remained. Glatigny was dead, Valade, Nina and, the year that Verlaine set up at rue Vaugirard, Charles Cros; and another kind of death explained the absence of Coppée, Mendès and the rest of the band: Verlaine was no longer respectable. In the Parnasse circle it had been consistent with respectability to drink too much, to fool to excess, to womanise; but Verlaine had committed the sin of sins: not the sin of his association with Rimbaud—that had been overlooked—but of failing to keep up appearances; he had "let himself go".

The survivor was Villiers, a subdued, embittered Villiers, beard and moustache turning grey, hat reddened with age, frock-coat threadbare, trousers frayed, face prematurely old. He had outlined the plots of his stories too often; so-called friends had purloined them, written them up, and when Villiers at last put them into shape and sent them to the magazines his manuscripts were returned with accusations of plagiarism. That was sobering even to a volatile spirit. He had almost immediately dissipated the reputation and money his *Contes Cruels* brought him, beggaring himself and making himself a laughing-stock by writing to the papers demanding that the Porte St Martin theatre withdraw a play in which a De l'Isle Adam of the fourteenth century was shown as a traitor. The author of the play was long since dead—it was first staged in 1834—but nothing would mollify Villiers. The only effect of the letter was to fill the theatre night after night. Villiers brought an action against the theatre, prosecuting his suit with a fury that would never have been wasted on a true ancestor. He lost the case and his money. The cafés ridiculed his pretensions and the rumour spread that he was the son of a grocer.

Poor Villiers never lived down the fiasco; within a few months of his appearance at the Verlaine soirées he was dead. By that time, in the late summer of 1889, Verlaine, again having trouble with his legs, had been sent to Aix-les-Bains to take the waters. There he heard of his friend's final humiliation, the death-bed marriage with his mistress "to preserve the title" and the discovery when she came to sign the documents that she could only make a cross. Verlaine had little in common with Villiers except an inability to keep money, but Villiers had not shunned him and that was enough to make him rate the friendship higher than it deserved. He wrote on the spot one of his best *Dédicaces*, as the collection was named the following year.

This poem, lively letters to Cazals and the delightful verses on the statue of Ganymede in the public gardens were the only good things to come out of Aix-les-Bains. Verlaine had never been south of Paris since he was a child, and he never went south again. He was first refused admittance to his *pension*, the owner mistaking him for a drunken beggar or thief, and when he did get settled in he didn't care for it: "an Evangelist asylum, English spoken, water-closets, fixed price, all right"; or for the town: "a kind of Bournemouth with less sea and more mountains . . . fewer cafés than in Paris and dearer". The one really favourable item was the massage after his daily hot baths ("very pleasant, almost voluptuous"), but this was more than cancelled by the sunshine and strong light: "As a man from the North I have little liking or admiration for the sun, it makes me feel sick, giddy, it BLINDS me, and like my dear great Mallarmé I much prefer *lucid winter*." So he was soon writing round to raise his fare back to Paris, arranging to enter the Broussais for a short season, and exhorting Cazals to help him to lead a more careful life so that hospitals and begging letters could be put in their proper place. He went regularly to mass in Aix, and to this, to his detestation of loneliness and to the spa atmosphere his new resolutions were due: he would give lessons in English, he declared, write stories with Cazals, make more poems more often; he would not end like Villiers, dying in the charity of a monastic retreat.

The resolutions did not long survive the sight of Paris, and after a short stay at the Broussais to repair the good that Aix had done he launched himself into short-lived cohabitations with Lily from Vouziers, the notorious Princess Roukine of the poem, and with a new friend Caroline Teisen whose birthplace of Metz first won his attention. Then followed café-crawls, brothels and night clubs, including the Chat Noir, where De Sivry still provided the music, and the Mirliton, where he heard the roars of applause that greeted Aristide Bruant's argot songs. Heard them with a smile, remembering the night at Nina's when he had recited his own amusing little poem, forerunner of all such:

J'crach' pas sur Paris, c'est rien chouett'!
Mais comm' j'ai une âm' de poèt',
Tous les dimanch's j'sors de ma boît'
Et j'm'en vais avec ma compagne
  A la campagne.

Nous prenons un train de banlieu'
Qui nous brouette à quèques lieu's
Dans le vrai pays du p'tit bleu,
Car on n'boit pas toujours d'champagne
  A la campagne.

Ell' met sa rob' de la Rein' Blanch'
Moi, j'emport' ma pip' la plus blanch';
J'ai pas d'chemis', mais j'mets des manch's,
Car il faut bien qu'l'éléganc' règne
  A la campègne.

Nous arrivons, vrai, c'est très batt'!
Des écaill's d'huîtr's comm' chez Baratt'
Et des cocott's qui vont à patt's,
Car on est tout comme chez soi
  A la camp—quoi!

Mais j'vois qu'ma machin' vous em . . . terre,
Fait's-moi signe et j'vous obtempère,
D'autant qu'j'demand' pas mieux qu'de m'taire . . .
Faut pas se gêner plus qu'au bagne,
  A la campagne.

2

There succeeded a confused period of hospitals and mean lodging-houses until the middle of 1894, when he at last regained rue Vaugirard. But this period of four and a half years differed from the "hospitals period" of the late 'eighties; he now went to hospital because he had precipitated his "ageing body" too often into beds not his own or had overdone the absinthes too many days and weeks in succession; he ran out of money—and he was always running out—because he spent everything on friends, drink and women. He was never well off in the sense that Coppée was well off, but his earnings increased steadily. He helped himself and others as before by begging loans—Mendès, Coppée, Blémont and a new admirer Robert de Montesquiou, the rich dilettante immortalised by Proust, being four of the most heavily "tapped" sources—and by a new device; he composed sonnets in praise of all and sundry, sent one copy to a periodical for publication and the other to the honoured subject and waited hopefully for a tangible expression of gratitude. When he had written sufficient to form a book he persuaded Léon Deschamps, editor of the latest Symbolist periodical *La Plume*, to publish it.

The Saturday soirées of *La Plume* were reminiscent of the gatherings at Lemerre's twenty years earlier; almost suffocated by heat and tobacco smoke, and stunned by noise, the newcomer fought his way down to the basement of the Café de l'Avenir, where two hundred poets were sandwiched into a room built for forty. Here poetry was read and discussed and here Verlaine, not only an honoured guest but one of the liveliest men there, recited his poems amidst acclamation. Régamey, long back from London, sketched him at the age of fifty at the *La Plume* banquet when he was proclaimed president by Mallarmé; physically he looked far older than his years but the expression of his face was youthful as ever. Saturday after Saturday his neatly ironical wit set the room in a roar, he drank innumerable free drinks and pocketed a few loans before being assisted out in the small hours. And, more to the point in the first part of this period, he collected advance payments for *Dédicaces*, collected them to such a pitch that even the easy-going Deschamps was shocked; from the book, he told a friend, "Verlaine is drawing more than from all his previous books. The author of *Sagesse* has been on a frightful binge. I've given him six hundred francs in one week. He got through it all. I'm going to put the brake on."

He put the brake on; but the six hundred francs in a week demonstrates not only Verlaine's powers of spending but his powers of earning. No longer was he the great obscure; from all sides public protests arose that one of the foremost French poets should be allowed to live in squalor; journalists, discovering wonderful "copy" in this ragged King of the left-bank cafés, returned with snapshots and inimitable dialogue with the "neglected genius", who, leaning back in his "reserved" seat, clouded glass on the table before him, eye lazily twinkling, gave the man what he expected, exposing his legs and telling hair-raising tales of starvation, freezing rooms, and a cold hand hopelessly tracing one poem after another on lavatory paper.

But the field was not left to the journalists; the young poets entered the lists with letters to the daily papers complaining that their master was denied his due. Baju openly accused Verlaine's Parnassian friends of sitting back in luxury whilst their old companion starved. Even Lepelletier joined in with a dignified complaint of the virtual ostracism of Verlaine by old friends and lesser poets who had turned respectable. This troubled the conscience of Lemerre to the extent of offering Verlaine a hundred francs for a preface to a novel he was just about to publish by Vermersch, who had died insane in an English asylum twelve years earlier; and it stung Mendès into a public reply; he would contribute, he said, to a public fund from which Verlaine could draw regular sums.

Verlaine's reaction to this blast of public appeal and reproof varied comically between gratitude and resentment; declarations that he owed his privations "to a series of legal and other 'accidents'", protests that he did not wish to be classed with "consumptive and 'interesting' poets" and a grandiose finale rejecting "what might resemble an insinuation prejudicial to his honour" and claiming "he has little left to him except his poverty but he insists that this at least shall be respected".

The wave of assistance came to a grand climax in May 1891 with a gala performance at the Théâtre Vaudeville for the joint benefit of Verlaine and Gauguin. The two men had much in common, above all the fact that both were great artists at odds with society. Both had known years of near starvation, both had been isolated from their fellow-artists, both possessed large sexual appetites, and both retained for the greater part of their lives a hopelessly impracticable regard for their wives. Both also shared a distaste for marching under the banner of a movement even when their name was inscribed prominently on the flag; they met occasionally at the Voltaire, where every Monday the Symbolists sat down to dinner, Gauguin having been chosen as the painter-representative of Symbolism. Next to nothing, un-happily, is known of their conversation, but Gauguin chuckled appreciatively at Verlaine's "Bah! these cymbalists!" in the midst of some particularly Symbolist speech from the head of the table. They became friendly enough for Verlaine to visit Gauguin's soirées a year or two later.

Gauguin, holding an unexpectedly profitable auction at the Drouot, was lucky enough to get off to Tahiti before the benefit performance. There he waited hopefully for his estimated share of not less than fifteen hundred francs. Verlaine appeared in person. The foyer of the theatre was hung with Gauguin canvases, *Les Uns et les Autres* was played together with a sketch by Mendès, and poems by Verlaine and others were declaimed from the stage. Unfortunately the organisers had been over-lavish with the extras; almost all the receipts were eaten up by expenses. The profits worked out at two hundred francs to be shared by the two men. Verlaine, hearing the news during the performance, retired to the bar to drown his disappointment: "Bénéfice!" he cried when the "magnificent sum" was handed to him, "Maléfice they mean!"

3

A few months later, and a short while after the death and magnificent funeral of Banville, a train left Paris on August 23 carrying Rimbaud to hospital at Marseilles. He had travelled down from Roche. Had he stopped in Paris he would have found himself the greatest sensation the city had known for many years. But he was desperately ill and he despised the poetry about which the cafés were excitedly talking. He passed straight through; no one knew that he was there; all he saw of Paris was the wet streets between the Gare de l'Est and the Gare de Lyon. In the first week of December the news reached Paris that he had died in Marseilles on the 10th of the previous month; he was thirty-seven years old.

Twice at least false reports of his death in Abyssinia had been circulated in Paris, and each time Verlaine had written a poem to his memory. When he heard of his death at Marseilles Verlaine was busy with a new edition of *Illuminations*, to which he had added *Une Saison en Enfer*, having discovered the manuscript; on the 7th he wrote a postcard to Vanier from the Broussais: "Come then! or write. What about the preface for the Rimbaud? (dead, I hear)." And the next day: "Have received confirmation . . . of the death of Rimbaud and burial at Charleville." And that was all, to Vanier, except that in the weeks following he pressed him to hurry on with the new edition of *Illuminations* so that it would "cash in" on the publicity following Rimbaud's death. That was the journalist. Another Verlaine sat down to write:

Toi mort, mort, mort! Mais mort du moins tel que tu veux,
En nègre blanc, en sauvage splendidement
Civilisé, civilisant négligemment . . .
Ah, mort! Vivant plutôt en moi de mille feux

D'admiration sainte et de souvenirs feux
Mieux que tous les aspects vivants même comment
Grandioses! de mille feux brûlant vraiment
De bonne foi dans l'amour chaste aux fiers aveux.

Poète qui mourus comme tu le voulais,
En dehors de ces Paris-Londres moins que laids,
Je t'admire en ces traits naïfs de ce croquis,

Don précieux à l'ultime postérité
Par une main dont l'art naïf nous est acquis,
Rimbaud! *pax tecum sit, Dominus sit cum te!*

His periods in hospital reflected the change in his status; they had always been pleasant; now, although the treatments were severer, they formed one triumph after another. His visiting hours magnified themselves into crowded receptions, his bedside was besieged by callers, from De Montesquiou to the wealthy American woman "seeing the sights of Paris" who thrust orchids at Verlaine, from the young poet who plumped on his knees by the bed with a "Master! Dear Master!", to the head doctor, by this time a firm friend and admirer, who would stop by the bed with a flourish and a "Gentlemen, the greatest Catholic poet of the century!" His bedside table was heaped with flowers, bowls of fruit, a pile of visiting-cards, manuscripts of youthful poets awaiting his verdict and the paraphernalia of the invalid; all contrasted oddly with the great man at his ease after the receptions, pipe belching, "taking off" his visitors and recounting the latest dirty story with a wealth of telling gesture to a ward roaring with laughter.

After the news of Rimbaud's death the flow of visitors no

longer amused him; he became moody, abstracted, melancholy, until one of his young Symbolist visitors, Adolphe Retté, a protégé of Kahn, called with an article he had written on Rimbaud. Since Rimbaud's death there had been a burst of publicity; Delahaye, Isabelle Rimbaud and Paterne Berrichon, who was to marry her, all began to write accounts of the dead man, and many young men like Retté discussed his work. Retté asked Verlaine to read the article before sending it to a periodical. He found him in a small ward with four beds, sitting near the window looking like a Doge of Venice with white wool cap and long blue dressing-gown and brandishing his cane like a sceptre. He read Retté's article, then sat silent, looking unhappy. Retté got up to go, but Verlaine took his arm: "Let's take a turn in the garden, it's stifling here." They strolled and smoked in the garden—although January, the weather was autumnal—until Verlaine stopped: "I'd like to walk off black thoughts but my leg won't stand it." Could he help? Retté asked. Verlaine shook his head with a melancholy smile: "It's not money this time. My dreams worry me. Since the news of Rimbaud's death I've seen him every night, he dies again and again." He fixed Retté with eyes "like black diamonds" and said in a harsh voice: "I can't accept his death. It's many years since we saw each other, but Rimbaud's face still shines before me, his genius still stirs me to the depths of my soul."

Retté, touched by his misery, urged him to unburden himself, and Verlaine related the history of the shooting in Brussels: he had forgotten nothing. Then he sighed: "There was a devilish seductiveness in that boy. Hordes of memories of the days we spent wandering along the roads come back to me charged with atrociously delicious perfumes. I've known true happiness twice in my life. First through my wife, the only person I've ever loved deeply; a happiness which would have made another man of me if I'd been master of my senses. Then I tasted the painful joys of living intensely, to the very top of my being, in the company of Rimbaud. I've never been able to console myself for the loss of either."

He tapped Retté's manuscript: "You write that Rimbaud is a legend. From the literary point of view you are no doubt right. But to me Rimbaud is always a living reality, an inextinguishable sun flaming on me. That's why I dream of him every night."

And lifting his hand in the familiar gesture he recited the last
stanzas of the poem he had written four years earlier, when
Rimbaud's death in Abyssinia was first reported:

> Mort, tout ce triomphe inouï
> Retentissant sans frein ni fin
> Sur l'air jamais évanoui
> Que bat mon cœur qui fut divin!
>
> Quoi, le miraculeux poème
> Et la toute-philosophie,
> Et ma patrie et ma bohème
> Morts? Allons donc! tu vis ma vie!

4

Retté found Verlaine with a hospital temperature chart in one
hand; he had been writing a poem on the back of it. And had
Retté called another day he would have seen much the same; a
temperature chart, a prescription form, the back of an envelope,
anything would do. For Verlaine was almost always writing;
letters and poems poured from hospitals, lodging-houses, cafés;
he would snatch the nearest scrap of paper or rummage in his
pockets, and head bent, lips mouthing words, would cover the
crumpled, torn, dirty sheet with his neat, legible writing. The
mere list of published books since *Amour*, excluding reprints and
the long roll of insertions in periodicals, gives some idea of his
industry. In 1889, the year after *Amour*, came *Parallèlement*; in
1890 *Dédicaces*; in 1891 no fewer than five books, *Bonheur*, *Mes
Hôpitaux*, *Chansons pour Elle*, *Femmes* and *Choix de Poésies*; in 1892
Liturgies Intimes; in 1893 *Odes en son Honneur*, *Elégies* and *Mes
Prisons*; in 1894 *Quinze Jours en Hollande*, *Dans les Limbes* and
Epigrammes; in 1895 *Confessions*; and after his death *Hombres*,
Chair, *Invectives*, *Biblio-Sonnets*, *Œuvres Oubliées* in two volumes and
Œuvres Posthumes in three, not to speak of the many poems
discovered later and printed in periodicals.

Industry: that is the word; and when one deducts earlier
poems which he had preserved against a rainy day, he still wrote
too much, for the time had come, specially after the appearance
of *Choix de Poésies*, which made him really popular, when he could
sell every line he chose to write. He was also a contented man and

the contented man rarely produces great work. He was hard pressed for cash and this too does not encourage good writing. But one book, *Parallèlement*, was on a different plane. He described it many times, perhaps the most Verlainean effort being in his preface to the religious *Liturgies Intimes*, where he called it "a backsliding deliberately confessed". The "backsliding" had a long history; it began in the prison at Mons when the Chaplain advised the impassioned convert not to confine his poems to religious subjects but to express the other, parallel, side of himself. The poems range from the Lesbian sonnets of 1867 through the *Laeti et Errabundi* of 1887 to the savage *Les Morts que l'on fait saigner* written in the year of publication. There is not one bad poem in the book, many superb ones and at least two masterpieces. Of all the books by Verlaine this best expresses his nature and genius in maturity; he is himself all the time in every kind of mood.

Parallèlement was an immediate success; it led to the appearance of the profitable selection of poems two years later which by 1894 had gone into five editions and was still selling briskly. This in turn led Verlaine back to rue Vaugirard and to comparative, very comparative, affluence for a few months. And there, a few weeks after settling in, he received an honour which, to the old guard at least, came as an unpleasant surprise but which to the reader may seem a rare case of the prophet honoured in his lifetime: on the death of Leconte de Lisle he was elected Prince of Poets by a decisive majority. The affronted Heredia polled less than half the votes given to Verlaine; Coppée was at the bottom of the list.

Moved by this unexpected gesture of sanity, Verlaine promptly spent every sou on a grand celebration in his rooms. And, in character, he made light of the honour. "You have made me Prince of Poets," he said in a mock reply to an address of welcome. "I'm without a palace at the moment, but my royal park is free to all"—and he pointed grandly through the window to the Luxembourg gardens.

Chapter Nineteen

THE LECTURER

1892-1893

I

ONE day late in October 1892, Verlaine was to be seen in Boulevard St-Michel gesturing rather more vivaciously than usual and exposing a wealth of shirt-front. He seemed to be inviting passers-by to examine his linen, and if one joined the crowd which gathered whenever he stopped one would hear him say triumphantly, "Feel it; it's not just clean, it's new!" And he would shoot a pair of fairly spotless cuffs with an air.

Remaining a little longer, one would hear the whole story: he had been invited to lecture in Holland; he or someone—it was not clear—had bought a white shirt, a hat, a jacket and trousers, a respectable shiny pair of boots; he would travel first class from Paris and back again; he was going to turn over a new leaf when he returned, save his lecture fees (he gave details, one thousand francs for six lectures, everything found) and lead a hard-working life, limiting his drinks, keeping his francs under the mattress. No more shortages, no more cadging of loans; probity, economy, respectability, order, were to be the watch-words of the new Verlaine. "Je vais me mettre dans mes meubles!" he said again and again in sprightly tone, "clicking his teeth like castanets".

Those who listened remained sceptical; he had said the same thing with similar emphasis before the publication of each book in turn. But no one wished to deny the significance of an invitation to lecture out of France; the lecture tour was a sign of renown and offered a chance of earning much more money than any book of poems could produce. Besides, one tour was apt to lead to another.

Before he managed to get himself on to the train on November 2 Verlaine's shirt had lost its first freshness, but he arrived sober and cheerful at The Hague, a cheerfulness increased by his

315

having watched from the window *en route* the pink walls of the prison at Mons passing by; a sight which he regarded benevolently and "almost triumphantly", as well he might, and which needless to say he made into a poem.

The tour had been arranged by the young Blok, a Dutch bookseller afterwards to become famous; he had visited Paris, listened to Verlaine at the cafés and, admiring and pitying in equal part, had secured sponsors. It was at the home of one of these, the painter Philippe Zilcken, that Verlaine made his headquarters. Verlaine, said Zilcken afterwards, "was neither black nor white but an impassioned, impressionable, versatile poet". He might have added, an unusual guest; he rose early, before anyone was astir; he retired after breakfast to the studio, where he "surrounded himself with dictionaries", which astonished Zilcken as being quite out of reported character, prepared his lecture and, his host happening to comment on the incomprehensibility of Mallarmé's poetry, said, "But it's very easy, only a question of syntax", and proceeded by analysis of a poem to make everything clear. He won the heart of his hostess's small daughter, soon "the divine little Renée" and "my literary daughter"; and of his hostess, whom he immediately approached with a "lots of things have been said about me and I want you to know exactly what kind of man you are entertaining"; this followed by a complete life history, nothing withheld and not too much excused.

After this all was plain sailing in the Zilcken home. The comfort of the house, and for that matter of all the Dutch houses he visited, overwhelmed him, as did the amount of food they ate, and for a couple of weeks he lived like a lord. He loved the "sweet gravity" of the Dutch, he said, and accepted in good part their "unmalicious chaff"—for, taking immediately to schnapps, he was once or twice only just in shape to stand before his audience. He lectured at The Hague, Amsterdam and Leyden, his lectures consisting of a brief foreword on the Parnassians, Symbolists, Decadents and the latest school of poetry, Moréas' Ecole Romane, with readings from the best of them. His delivery was indifferent—"mediocre, negligible, almost voiceless", he said—and his hostess made him swallow a raw egg before he went off to the hall; but he could be effective, as an onlooker remarked: "His voice, though rather heavy and slow, sometimes had a pleasant timbre and played on all the stops from oratory to invective; it had the hoarseness of one who takes a gloomy pleasure in making a sad avowal." His readings of his own poems were much admired by those who sat in the front seats, but the success of the tour was not in the lectures, which were poorly attended, but in the furore which his visit caused amongst the young literati. After the first lecture Zilcken's house was filled with these young men and Verlaine was entertained at one dinner and soirée after another. His absolute absence of pose struck everybody, and as he somehow managed to carry his drinks with discretion, compliments abounded. "He's an artist from head to foot," one young poet enthusiastically told a friend, "a man who has made the most beautiful poems, a great and pure artist whose every look, every gesture conveys the unique personality"; and he enclosed a buttonhole worn by Verlaine at one of the dinners, which he had begged as a souvenir.

Verlaine returned triumphantly to Paris without having once blotted his scutcheon, with his thousand francs intact, plus an advance from Blok on a Dutch edition of his *Quinze Jours en Hollande*, a little book which he retired to the Broussais to write— this because he immediately lost all the money he had made.

Of this more later; he was soon preoccupied by another invitation, from Maeterlinck and the Belgian Catholic writer Jean Casier, to lecture in Belgium. A few years earlier, Maeterlinck had spent several months in Paris, nominally to finish his legal studies, actually to haunt the cafés. His main centre was the Brassière Pousset, where Villiers recited his unwritten short stories and illustrated them in mime so vivid that one of his listeners, Mallarmé, was terrified that he would throw himself into the crowd in an epileptic fit. He would talk and act for six hours at a stretch, and one of the crowd who never moved while he spoke was the young Belgian law student, who forthwith abandoned the law and returned home to write with Villiers' voice still in his mind. "All I have done I owe to his conversation," he said later. He did not meet Verlaine, who had then just embarked on his hospital period, but he read his poems and pronounced him "the evangelist of dream and irony".

This high-flown description notwithstanding, he had heard enough about the evangelist to know roughly what to expect when the train steamed into Ghent one morning in February

1893. The window of a third-class carriage (no fares paid this time) opened with a great noise and the "faunesque" head of the poet protruded with a cry of, "I take it with sugar!" This war-cry Maeterlinck understood—the correct Casier, who stood with him on the platform, happily did not—to mean that Verlaine sugared his absinthe. All three "fraternised violently", Verlaine being already slightly the worse for wear. Maeterlinck mentioning lunch and a drink, the guest suddenly showed signs of restlessness and was quickly installed in a cab with his luggage, a much worn carpet-bag. They drove to the Taverne St Jean, the best restaurant in the city. Verlaine "wore the enraptured air and smile of a hairy angel" and, offered port, wisely chose gin to welcome the "magnificent lunch".

Verlaine's light-heartedness was due as much to relief at the sight and sound of Maeterlinck as to the flask of absinthe he had emptied during the night, for he had with a sinking heart read the work of his host before setting out. "A phenomenon, Maeterlinck, a revelation!" he said afterwards. "From his plays and verse I expected to find a pale, thin, corpselike man swathed in flannel and drenched with herb tea. But not at all, a great big fellow greeted me most jovially, had a fine drink ready for me and said with a Flemish accent, 'Now, dear Master, we'll eat a good beefsteak.' This Maeterlinck had a formidable appetite. Afterwards he spoke of his bees whilst smoking his pipe." Verlaine breathed again: "I love mystics of this sort." His hosts were less enthusiastic: Casier worked up to reverence the greatest Catholic poet of modern times; Maeterlinck worried, knowing Casier and the "straight-laced and easily offended" Belgian audiences.

The lunch began inauspiciously; Verlaine was no sooner seated at the table decorated in his honour than he asked "with the simplicity of a Franciscan brother: 'Where are the latrines?'" A slight cloud passed over the table, "the seraphic Casier gripping his chair with embarrassment". But Verlaine seemed to notice nothing; he went off and returned radiant; and as the gins followed one another he explained with much laughter, bending forward confidentially, that "all that kind of thing was over long ago". As the meal progressed he began to tell anec-dotes, charming some of them, Maeterlinck thought; but the *maître d'hôtel*, anxious to do honour to the great man, was too zealous with the bottles, and before Maeterlinck could give him a discreet signal Verlaine was well launched. By that time he believed himself, Maeterlinck thought, to be in a bistro and almost imperceptibly the anecdotes changed character; into them "glided obscenities" which, fortunately, "our Saint Casier, comprehending nothing, took for subtle pleasantries".

Another matter was agitating Maeterlinck as he watched the gesticulating, talkative, hairy angel across the table. The new white shirt of the Dutch tour had long since been sold to the second-hand clothes dealer; Verlaine was wearing a grey-pink flannel shirt, "more grey than pink", Maeterlinck observed, closed at the neck by a coloured cord with "alarming" tassels. Maeterlinck remarked that a white shirt and stiff collar would be considered *de rigueur* that evening; would Verlaine care to visit his shirtmaker? Verlaine agreed enthusiastically and off they drove when lunch was done. The shirtmaker laid out many elegant and expensive shirts, but Verlaine, who had been nosing about the shop, pointed out a simple triangular shirt-front and collar as worn by the waiters of lesser cafés: "that one's cheaper and easier". Nothing would dissuade him; he took it.

The problem then was to divert him until evening. Maeterlinck tried a round of "curiosities", but Verlaine showed an increasing tendency to stop *en route* at bars for "a quick one"; he had, he explained, never before tasted "Haselt old style gin", the brand they had served as an apéritif in the restaurant; he believed that it held beauties undreamt of in the French gins; he would like to confirm this belief. What was more, he would obviously prefer to confirm it in the cheaper bars and not at the luxurious ones in which Maeterlinck tried to detain him by the lure of armchairs and illustrated papers.

At last evening came. Verlaine was still on his feet, he had put on his shirt-front and carried his lecture notes purposefully, but his bearing was such a blend of the jaunty and the confused that Maeterlinck prepared for a stormy session. He, Grégoire le Roy the poet and Georges Mince the sculptor, all big men and good boxers, arranged to police the lecture hall. The room was practically full when Verlaine was introduced by the president; as he approached the lecture table, inclining his head, a few stifled laughs came from the audience and Maeterlinck and his friends clenched their fists. Verlaine seemed not to have noticed (though he afterwards complained of the "snobbery" of the Belgians), put down his papers and read some dozens of verses with nothing more untoward than an occasional stutter.

Unhappily the arrangement of his papers had been imperfectly made—he had thrust them pell-mell into the carpetbag in Paris and had not looked at them since—and he stopped in the middle of a line, fumbled ineffectually with the papers and began to improvise with no more than moderate success.

At this moment a door leading from the room to a billiards saloon opened, a man appeared shirt-sleeved and queue in hand, listened to the improvising Verlaine for a moment or two, said loudly, "That fellow is drunk!" and went back into the saloon, closing the door with a crash.

Maeterlinck and his friends, horrified, leapt forward to chastise the billiards player and to overawe the tittering section of the audience. But they reckoned without a Verlaine feeling well disposed towards the entire world: thanks to "the imperturbable calm of our old Master, who lost the thread of his discourse without losing his head", the lecture settled down, continued eventlessly and ended without further hitch and to the sound of applause "scattered but distinguished".

The president handed a sealed envelope to Verlaine, who was quickly surrounded by people demanding his autograph and asking "inane questions". He was rescued by Maeterlinck and his big friends and led outside. There he made straight for the nearest street lamp and feverishly tore open the president's envelope.

"Three hundred francs!" he cried, pale with emotion. "Where is the nearest bank?"

It was then an hour short of midnight. All the banks were closed, they assured him. "Then what shall I do?" he demanded. "You understand that I can't possibly spend the night with such a sum on me."

Maeterlinck promised him that if the money were stolen he and Casier would replace it; then, realising that this was not exactly what Verlaine meant, he begged Le Roy, a nightbird himself, to look after the guest. Le Roy and Verlaine set off into the night and at Verlaine's request towards the still-illuminated bars. Le Roy found his strength tested; he struggled for two hours, until the bars closed, to prevent Verlaine from drinking himself insensible and treating everybody he met. He succeeded to the degree that he was able to conduct Verlaine to the station that morning to catch the train for his next lecture town.

The lectures, at Charleroi, Antwerp, Liège and Verviers were unremarkable and saved, as at Ghent, by Verlaine's readings of his own poems, the poems rather than the readings being so much greater than anything else the audience had heard. The Belgians remained snobbish in Verlaine's eyes, but he fell in love with one of their towns, Bruges: "I should like to spend the rest of my life there," he said.

The last lecture, in Brussels, was an unexpected triumph. It was held in, of all places, the Palais de Justice, where Verlaine had been sentenced to two years' imprisonment. He rose to the occasion, threw aside his usual notes, produced the proofs of *Mes Prisons* and read his account of his sufferings in that very room twenty years earlier almost to the month. The reading and his tears as he read moved his audience as his lectures did not; he was loudly applauded and left Belgium in a blaze of glory and with rather more than a thousand francs in his pocket.

The glory perhaps went to his head, for when, on Taine's death, there was a vacancy at the Academy and a journalist said "Why not you?", Verlaine promptly put his name down. Why not, indeed? Lepelletier, who did not approve of Verlaine's young admirers on the left bank or of anything that his old friend now did, explained why not in an article in the *Echo de Paris*: Verlaine was not respectable. Meanwhile the young poets and the journalists revelled in the situation: the greatest poet in France and the most disreputable; what did the Academy stand for, greatness or respectability? The answer when it came was decisive; Verlaine did not get one vote.

This, however, was almost a year ahead. Before then, at the beginning of November 1893, Verlaine was on tour again, having been invited, to his enormous gratification, to give readings at Nancy and Lunéville. He was greeted with tremendous enthusiasm at both places, and at Nancy the sight on the lecturer's platform of a large beflowered board inscribed "Nancy for Metz" (Metz having been incorporated in Germany since 1871) reduced Verlaine and his audience to tears.

Ten days later he left Paris for his last lecture tour, in his beloved England.

In the past few years there had arisen in England a wider knowledge of pleasures awaiting the tourist across the Channel. In the 'eighties and 'nineties, Paris of the Madeleine, Place de l'Opéra, Boulevard Montmartre and Montmartre itself was thronged with English and Americans; all was ready for them, the glaring lights, the nudity, the vulgarity, whilst to reassure the timid were English bars, English hotels, English tea-rooms, English beggars soliciting alms from the kerbside in good honest cockney.

There was also a small section of London intellectuals aware that they had much to learn from France. The appeal of French culture to the intellectual snob has been strong since the eighteenth century, but there were then as now a few men who appreciated what France had to offer without belittling the culture of their own country. Swinburne and his tiny following excepted, genuine appreciation was restricted almost entirely to painters; it was pretty well established that if a young man wanted to paint seriously he must go through the Paris schools. And it was largely with the help of two young men whose interest was primarily in painting that Verlaine was made known, first in print, then in public, to a select English audience.

The first of these, George Moore, though known now as a writer, spent much time in Paris with the painters. It does not seem that he had met Verlaine before he wrote about him in 1881, but he would have heard sufficient from Manet and his friends Mallarmé and Chabrier to provide a description (not always accurate) of this outcast Parnassian to accompany an appreciation of his work. In the same year another young Irishman, O'Shaughnessy, translated and published *Clair de Lune*.

Neither the article of Moore nor the translation of O'Shaughnessy made the slightest impression in England, and it is probably true that Verlaine first became known to a few English people ten years later, in 1891, when Moore reprinted his article in *Impressions and Opinions*; Moore was beginning to make a name as a writer and the article might well have reminded the travelled reader of certain Paris newspaper snippets about the man whom journalists had pigeonholed as the reincarnation of Villon.

The first Englishman to make the acquaintance of Verlaine,

as opposed to gaping at him in Boulevard St-Michel, was Arthur Symons in the early 'nineties. Symons was poet, essayist, critic and most francophile of all English literary men. He had heard of Verlaine, of course, but it seems that his knowledge of his work had been restricted to a chance reading of *Romances sans Paroles* in Coppée's house. He then met Morice, absorbed his enthusiasm and persuaded him to take him along to the François Premier.

This was one April night in 1892. Verlaine was sitting in the midst of a group of young men—Symons noticed the dark-featured Moréas with his blue-black hair and half-savage, half-sullen black eyes, and the tall thin painter Fernand Langlois. But Verlaine astonished him; he had expected something *"en diable* ending in a green tail"*, having heard many descriptions and seen many portraits, "none pleasant"; he saw a shabbily dressed, collarless man, white scarf round his neck and grey soft hat pushed back on his head, a man with a "spiritual forehead, animal jaw, shifting faun's eyes . . . oblique, constantly in movement, with gestures of the lids and brows" and with a genial expression. Verlaine's air was "manly and gentlemanly". He was all gesture, face, hands, arms, body moving suddenly, violently, convincingly: "As he explodes into conversation his whole body seems to translate meaning into movement."

But what most surprised Symons was Verlaine's natural dignity; he conveyed unmistakably an "ineradicable refinement, impressive sincerity and simplicity with an entire absence of pose or deliberate extravagance—the extravagance when it came, as often, being natural and on the spur of the moment".

Verlaine's conversation veered as violently as his movements. He began with natural courtesy to talk of England, how he admired the poetry of Tennyson and Swinburne, how he loved the English Sunday: "So religious!" he exclaimed, pulling imaginary bell ropes with his hands. Abruptly, having done his duty as host and expressing at the same time one of his thousand enthusiasms, he began to tell "rather shocking stories", interrupting himself from time to time, again courteously, to try to find the exact English equivalents for "unspeakable" French words—the quotes being Symons' of course.

Turning directly to the visitor, he then told some "most dubious" experiences of his past life, told them "in a most matter of fact, impersonal manner with the good-humoured tone of one who tells a curious story that may interest the listener". He wound up with an invitation to Symons and his friend Havelock Ellis, neighbour in his Fountain Court chambers, to visit him the following evening.

When the two young Englishmen climbed the stairs of the Hôtel des Mines in Boul' Mich' the next evening there was no Verlaine. Symons went out and came across the missing host dragging himself along the boulevard on the arm of Bibi-la-Purée, the little man who had one day knelt before Verlaine in the street insisting that he be allowed to sew up the master's torn overcoat and who thereafter refused to leave him. Verlaine had forgotten his invitation, apologised several times with "tremendous" emphasis, and continued to excuse himself on the stairs, stopping every few paces to explain why he had to take his time.

The room was small, mean, frugally furnished. A portrait of Verlaine, a few books, a large Bible were the only personal possessions to be seen; two candles provided the only light. Verlaine was in expansive mood: "I have got *money*," he proclaimed in English, "I will have pleasure." He took out his purse, extracted two francs proudly and handed them to Bibi. Langlois came in and curled himself on the bed, Symons and Havelock Ellis occupied the two chairs, Verlaine limped about the room, and Bibi, returning with glasses and a bottle of rum, perched himself on the chest of drawers. Verlaine dispensed the rum, sipping his own slowly, raising the glass halfway to his lips and holding it suspended whilst he talked "furiously", and sometimes putting it down again untasted. He was "argumentative and explosive, his facial pantomime more frantic than ever".

He picked up the Bible, patted it fondly and showed it to his guests, pointing out the name of the Protestant translator. It was an excellent book, he assured Symons, and he was a religious man. "Je suis Catholique!" he exclaimed again and again, fondling the Bible in one hand, in the other grasping the glass of rum. "Catholique du moyen âge!"

Recalling the nationality of his visitors, he changed the subject and, laughing, quoted several examples of cockney obscenities learned in London with Rimbaud. Finally, as the supreme compliment, he declaimed "in a weird accent" one of Hamlet's soliloquies.

Symons was a man of discernment; after these two short visits he cut through the gossip to a truth. He compared Verlaine with Villon—"picturesque vices, fell in with scum of society, whole nature waiting to turn into poetry"—that much was inevitable, but his summing up is solid. Drinks were offered to Verlaine all day long, he said, by people who said they were his friends (he would have added, had he known Verlaine longer, that the offers were not always accepted), but Verlaine sober "was the most delightful of companions—queer, rambling, confidential talk full of wonder, trouble and gaiety, a condensation of the mood of the moment and always on the verge of poetry". Back in London he promptly began to translate the poetry. Within two years he had published some translations and a critical estimate of Verlaine's work—criticism which compares favourably with anything written at that time by the French critics.

The pioneer efforts of Symons had their effect, and by 1892 a little group of men in London understood that a great poet was living and writing in Paris. Wilde could write, "I look forward . . . to a talk about French art, the one art now in Europe which is worth discussing—Verlaine's art particularly", and Verlaine became the focal point of a pilgrimage obligatory to any of the group who chanced to be in Paris. Most of them came with preconceptions, the young Edmund Gosse, for example, an admirer of Leconte de Lisle. Verlaine obligingly confirmed the literary tourist's expectations; so Gosse sees in the entrance to the cellar of the Restaurant d'Harcourt "a ghostly shape . . . a strange bald head" and "something flopped up out of the darkness like an owl—a timid, shambling figure in soft black hat with jerking hands". The apparition, persuaded to sit by a chorus of "Venez donc, Maître", at once explains (realising by Gosse's surprised stare that he did not quite fill the bill) that his good suit is a legacy of the Belgian tour and, shooting his cuffs, "C'est ma chemise de conférence."

Another of the curious, John Grierson, hunting down his quarry in a café in Place de l'Odéon, first saw Moréas playing dominoes, fixing his eye on his opponent from time to time and thumping his chest with a "J'ai du talent! Moi, j'ai du talent!" An adequate summary of Moréas, but the picture of Verlaine is less happy, a Verlaine who, "to judge by the clothes he wore, might have been a carpenter or bricklayer. But his face! Incarnation of Villon. Over two sleepy, waggish grey eyes a pair of mephistophelian brows curved upwards. . . . When he tipped his slouch hat back on his head he looked like a modern toreador." He smoked incessantly, sipped cognac, raised his brows "and with an inimitable gesture of bonhomie passed a trivial remark". Grierson then sees Verlaine and Bibi in Boul' Mich' "looking like mendicants on their way home after having amassed a few sous at some church door". Verlaine then lived near the Panthéon, which needless to say his interviewer noted was "where Villon lived five hundred years earlier".

But even the journalist stumbles on a truth occasionally though he may not recognise it. To Grierson, as to other Englishmen, Verlaine praised his language: "English is made for sentiment and poetry. . . . I love the English language." He gave examples, the first words to come into his head: "What a difference between *mère* and mother! The English is soft, homely and musical. Then there is the word heaven—how much more beautiful than *ciel*." Grierson reports without comment, unaware that Verlaine had revealed his whole life search in these two words.

It remained for a young English painter, William Rothenstein, to harness the genuine admiration in England to some purpose. Rothenstein, then studying at Julian's, had a kind heart and a gift for admiration. He was struck by the beauty of Verlaine's verse and by the injustice of such a man for ever struggling to avoid starvation whilst his former friends flourished (Rothenstein was young, it must be remembered), and he wrote in this sense to the poet. Charmed, Verlaine invited him to the Broussais in the autumn of 1893. Rothenstein, already at home in Montmartre and the Latin Quarter, had heard much about Verlaine from De Sivry on one hand and Moréas on the other: a great poet but an impossible man, he was told. At first he did not find him so; Verlaine was clean and sober, which seems to have surprised his visitor, very pale with small candid eyes (brown to Rothenstein), heavy moustaches and beard turning grey. The Socratic nose, the comparison with Silenus, were automatic. Verlaine talked amusingly, of his leg which hurt, of the kind doctors and nurses, of the stingy Vanier, of his lectures in Holland and Belgium and, scenting money, of his poverty. Not in vain; for Rothenstein, who was making a series of portraits of well-known men, asked permission to add Verlaine to the list, made three excellent drawings and then suggested a possible lecture tour in England.

Verlaine was enchanted. Symons, consulted, was enthusiastic and John Lane, the *avant-garde* publisher of the time, showed practical interest by commissioning two poems for a review, poems which he paid for in advance. "C'est très honnête!" commented the gratified Verlaine pocketing the hundred francs. But he proved difficult to pin down, hard to find when out of hospital, dubious of his health, uncertain about the times of trains, steamers, and generally helpless. Finally, when all had been settled and Verlaine had gone off to his short lecture tour in the north-east, Rothenstein, then in England, received almost at the last minute an urgent demand for a hundred francs without which the poet could not make the journey. Some of this was apparently to "console" a certain person for his absence, the rest to pay his travelling expenses.

Symons, consulted again, advised against the sending of the money direct; it could melt before Verlaine ever reached the station. Instead, he sent it to an American friend in Paris, with instructions to put the poet on the train. And on November 19 Verlaine, "with a mildness, patience and charm reminding one of Jesus and Socrates", allowed himself to be taken to the station, given dinner and installed in his compartment, his portion of the hundred francs resting undisturbed in his purse.

In London the lecture had been arranged for the evening of November 21 in Barnard's Inn. Verlaine was to talk on contemporary French poetry; the tickets were ten shillings each and a notice circulated amongst the intellectual élite promised a fair audience. Gosse tried to assist by writing an advance "puff" in the *St James's Gazette* on the morning of the lecture, assuring readers that the price of the tickets would relieve a genuine poverty.

All, then, was ready, all but the principal actor. He was due in Symons' rooms for lunch on the 20th. Symons waited in vain. Forebodings gripped him; Verlaine alone with some seventy francs was a sobering thought. But Verlaine was better than his reputation; at that moment he was reposing himself at Dieppe as best he could after a shattering night of storm which had stopped all cross-Channel sailings—a noisy night which reminded him unpleasantly of the bombardment of Paris more than twenty years before. He had spent part of the night on a bench in the waiting-room until offered a sofa in the hotel opposite. On the evening of the 20th the sea fell sufficiently to allow a steamer to set off. He slept through most of the rough crossing and wrote a poem on the "immense caress" of the waves—he was always a good sailor—and arrived at the Temple in the early hours of the 21st, arrived full of good cheer and was at once enraptured by Fountain Court, so enraptured that he could not tear himself away; and the anxious Symons, making yet another excursion in search of him, found his overdue guest, carpet-bag in hand, drinking the water under the light of a pale moon.

Symons made him welcome with gin and a box of biscuits. As he ate and drank they talked "about everything under the sun"—Paris, the lectures, poetry, money, "poets think of nothing else—and with reason!"—talked for two hours. Verlaine found it "one of the best and gayest meals in my life". After a sleep he lunched with Symons and Gosse at a "sumptuous restaurant", dined *à la française* with Lane, Rothenstein, William Heinemann, Frank Harris, Herbert Horne, and Henry Harland the American novelist, then was escorted to Barnard's Inn, where, the lecture being in French, a smallish audience had assembled.

The next morning he read favourable press reports in all but the *Pall Mall Gazette*, which complained that his voice lacked eloquence and his subject matter originality. The critic was disappointed to find no trace of "the true Verlaine" in the sober lecturer. For the rest Verlaine was soon telling Vanier: "A fine press, old chap!"

The day was given to sightseeing, a visit to the French hospital to have his leg dressed—it was giving him much trouble—a lunch with the young francophile poets, dinner with Heinemann and an evening at the Alhambra. Symons drove about with him in a hansom and was struck by his good visual memory. Not a great deal had changed since the year with Rimbaud; Leicester Square had been tidied up and Shakespeare had taken the place of George IV, several restaurants wore a French air, the main streets were lit by electricity, and the crude green and red of the women's lavatories had given way to pearl-grey and rose. This delighted Verlaine, but then almost everything pleased him: "The sombre London of twenty years ago . . . is today an

international and specially a French London." His one substantial criticism was of the men's lavatories: why, he asked,
hobbling painfully down and up the steps, were the English such
prudes? Everyone knew the lavatories were there, why pretend
they were not?

He was on his best behaviour all through the day, and in the
evening whispered to Heinemann, who found him absolutely
charming, that he must not, *absolument pas*, get drunk. Nor did
he, thanks to a limited circulation of the wine, and was able
more or less soberly to revel in the Alhambra: the same old
Alhambra that he and Rimbaud had visited (but how differently
as to seats, clothes and company!), the same old comic songs at
which he roared, the same interludes of ballet. A novelty, a
French one according to the English, was the tableaux of nudes.
But the ballet was the thing: "I love Shakespeare, but I love
ballet better," he told Symons in the heat of enthusiasm, and no
doubt at that moment he did.

The next morning he took the train for Oxford, where he
lunched with York Powell, the professor of history, Rothenstein
and the French poet Charles Bonnier, who lived in England.
Some students tried to catch a glimpse of the famous man
through the window, and Bonnier, who knew the Verlaine of the
Latin Quarter, was tickled by the efforts of the poet to assume
a manner in keeping with his surroundings. Verlaine too saw
the farcical side of this pose of "the sage of Paris" and could not
always keep a straight face.

Then came a tour of the city in hansoms, "the streets rather
like the prim and modest little streets of Boston". Ravished by
the beauty of the colleges, Verlaine exclaimed, "our old
Sorbonne . . . is pitiable compared with this exquisite Oxford".
That evening he lectured in the room behind Blackwell's shop.
The audience was almost all students, and Verlaine, perhaps in
view of their youth, added to his description of what the poet
must be and do an emphatic and profound "le poète doit vivre
beaucoup, vivre dans tous les sens", illustrating this from his own
life.

The next morning he showed no sign of leaving, and Powell,
with an eye on Dodgson, the strict Master, and certain that
Verlaine could not pass two sober days in succession, shadowed
him from morning to night. Unnecessarily, as it happened;

Verlaine, bewitched by Oxford and in no hurry to leave it, knew what was due to it, knew a good deal better than most of its inhabitants. Besides, he had given a promise; he arrived back in London the next day reluctant and sober.

Symons having gone to Italy, Verlaine was given a room in a boarding-house in York Terrace, Regent's Park, but did not see much of it. For the next week he lived "the life of a pasha, and for nothing". Horne, Harland, Dowson and the young poets took over the rôle of Symons with gusto; he was invited to the Cheshire Cheese, the francophile poets' rendezvous; he dined at the Constitutional Club (one's mind boggles at the thought of Verlaine in this milieu), recited his poems in luxurious drawing-rooms, was, in short, lionised by a small and not very distinguished section of London society. But to him all was heaven, a rather wearing heaven: "I'm pretty tired of this game," he told Cazals, "although I take cabs too often. But when I say too often I'm wrong, because I can only walk with great difficulty."

The week in London was unexpected. He had intended to return to Paris after the Oxford visit, but Lane produced a friend from the north, a young intellectual Congregational minister, Theodore London, who urged him to lecture in Manchester. After some hesitation—he was doing too much and doing it without the usual source of stimulation—he accepted, hoping to carry back to Paris a more substantial sum of money.

In this he was disappointed; the lecture at Manchester was badly managed, without advance publicity, and was held on December 1 in a dreary gas-lit Congregational school in Salford. Barely fifty people attended. But Verlaine began his day in determinedly optimistic fashion by praising St Pancras Station, which he had last seen half built, remained cheerful through a Manchester fog, took to the interpreter, a Swiss schoolmaster, and was given a pleasant surprise at London's house before the lecture, where he was offered a retiring room with a bottle of absinthe, procured heaven knows how, on the table. He emerged from the room after a prolonged interval playful (punching his hat into clerical shape and regarding the Rev. Paul Verlaine in the mirror from various angles), but delivered his lecture without incident. The one mischance occurred during the reception afterwards, when his braces snapped. The alarming gap which developed was tactfully drawn to his notice, he gave his trousers a genial hitch, and Lancashire susceptibilities were saved.

Returning to London the next day without, as he wished, seeing *Coin de Table*, then at Manchester, or obtaining a photograph of it, he once more limped into a social round varied by treatment at the hospital. A second London lecture did not materialise; instead he gave a press interview. But his chief satisfaction came, it seemed, from the purchase of a splendid pair of braces: "otherwise I should keep my trousers up with a belt, a sure sign of moral disintegration".

He remained indefatigably anglophile, even to the answering of impertinent questions by a journalist. The questions were for the most part of the usual inanity. Was he the poetic descendant of Villon? To which Verlaine answered: "I haven't killed anyone yet, nor am I a captain of industry. Villon was a great poet, but so were Racine, Corneille, La Fontaine, Victor Hugo. Why these odious comparisons?" The one intelligent question: "Is it true that you take little notice of the rules of French poetry?" he side-stepped with: "It's possible to stretch that theory too far. The amateurs of free verse don't respect rhyme or rhythm. In short, one can't write a sonnet of fifty lines, or a line of fifty feet."

He went back on the 6th. He was not to see England again, although filled with hopes of doing so, and the various projects arising from the visit shrank in the end to little; a selection of poems which Lane was to publish hung fire after the Wilde trial, and Verlaine was paid for no more than a couple or so articles, and for a handful of poems.

He went back "over a sea like glass". He was disappointed with the financial result of the tour, or said he was for tactical reasons; but something in the region of fifteen hundred francs was not to be despised and he changed his third-class return ticket via Dieppe for a second-class via Calais. This change he announced in a letter to Paris, announced apologetically and with a hint of bribery and corruption: "Perhaps I shall bring back some pretty little gift." And thereby hangs a tale, the last tale.

Chapter Twenty

CONJUGAL END

1890-1896

I

THE life of Verlaine fittingly petered out in long-drawn comedy. When he came back triumphantly from Holland in November 1892 with his thousand and more francs and promptly lost the lot, the "lost" was a kindly way of saying that it had been taken. Not stolen, for the woman who took it believed it to be her due, and even in the long run a kindness. The affair was commonplace except for the largeness of the sum.

Verlaine was, in brief, a family man, and had been so for some two years. There was no family, and the one room (two in months of exceptional luxury) in which he lived from time to time was an apology for a home, not only miserably uncomfortable but always changing; he had no fixed address. For that matter he had no wife; but two women, at times three, had come into his life. Not on the face of it an ideal existence, yet he had somehow reached a state which exactly suited him.

The change came to public notice, as it were, on September 24, 1890, when a stocky middle-aged woman with short curly black hair worn close over a low forehead called at Vanier's office with a note from Verlaine promising a hundred lines of *Invectives* the next day "against (I hope) a considerable number of thunes" —one of his innumerable slang expressions for money—and introducing the bearer as "Mademoiselle Krantz, who is worthy of every confidence, whom I love very much, who stops me doing foolish things, who looks after me and my affairs admirably, and who has kindly agreed to fetch from you a hundred sous which I simply must have".

Six months later, in March 1891, another stocky middle-aged woman, but more buxom, with a slight squint and reddish hair, called on Vanier and handed him a note from Verlaine in which he read, presumably with surprise: "Very unwell, I have asked Mlle Philomène, in whom I have *justly* placed all my confidence, to be good enough to drop in at your office and collect the most money possible, 100 francs at least."

More than a year later the Box and Cox act was still going merrily on: "I am sending Mademoiselle Krantz to you to collect *everything you can spare* from the sale of *Mes Prisons*."

Three months later: "Here are some poems. Give all you can to Mlle Philomène, who will hand them to you . . . and who definitely has all my confidence and all my friendship—good sense, gracefulness, honesty, this one!—and is my faithful house-keeper."

One month later: "If Mlle Krantz needs money I can thoroughly recommend this good creature to you."

Two months later: "A good thing I only sent Bibi with a letter purely *opportunist* and not pecuniary. I shall be much obliged if you would say nothing about it to Philomène. Though less beastly, she thinks everyone is spying for *the other*. But never mind! I love this good girl very much and don't want to lose her at any price."

Four months later: "Will you pay my *wife* Philomène for the two poems she will give you."

Vanier's relief can be imagined. After three years the man had at last made up his mind; the interminable procession of women would cease and he would be spared the sight of Bibi's dis-reputable head round the door, a Bibi working impartially for the one who tipped best or for a Verlaine trying to collect a few francs on the side; not to mention a Verlaine, unable to trust any one of the three, limping painfully into the office with anxious looks to right and left before closing the door. What did Verlaine think he was? A charitable institution? A women's institute? He paid up because he could profitably print every line Verlaine wrote, good, bad or indifferent. All the same . . .

But if Vanier's hopes rose uncertainly, they soon collapsed again. All that had happened was that Philomène had paid a visit of state, with a flowery hat perched on her head, to Verlaine in hospital. And at sight of this the ravished Verlaine had introduced her to the ward at large as his wife.

Five months later the game is resumed, for the moment in a third version: "I'm sending you most of my booty to look after *for me*. Neither 'authorisation' nor 'messengers'. I'll draw on it myself from time to time, but no one else, *not even Philomène*. Watch out!"

Six weeks later begins a series of "I authorise Mlle Krantz to collect the money for the 49 lines herewith . . . for the enclosed poem . . . for the two productions she'll hand you" with a rider of familiar hue: "As you know, Mlle Krantz is to be trusted."

As you know! But how could anyone know, least of all Verlaine, who six months later is writing: "Please welcome Mme Esther, *still my best friend*, who is very happy to act just for once as my messenger and to collect the proceeds from you."

2

But to begin at the beginning. On some unspecified night in 1890 Verlaine picked up a streetwalker named Philomène Boudin, who worked professionally under the name of Esther. He took a fancy to her, at first perhaps because she was an Ardennaise, later for several other reasons, and was soon living with her. What might at first sight appear as an obstacle to the romance—the presence in an adjoining room and at meals of Philomène's pimp, who also happened to be her husband—turned out in practice a blessing. This man became greatly attached to Verlaine—he had never before met so helpless a creature, in his sense of the word, nor one so generous—and he soon constituted himself as unofficial guardian to the poet just as Bibi had made himself an unpaid messenger. "If anyone so much as lays a finger on M. Verlaine he'll hear from me," he would announce truculently; and, patting himself on the back, "Many's the time I've followed him home from a café without his knowing it, to make sure he got back safely."

Indeed, had his wishes prevailed, the *ménage à trois* might have continued indefinitely. But Philomène, like Verlaine, splashed her money about royally and regarded him with disfavour when all was spent; in her cups she had a temper and did not hesitate to accuse her protector of withholding supplies for the benefit of others, demanding that all friends be left to their own devices. This Verlaine was unable to promise or, if a promise were extracted, to perform. He would slip out to the cafés from time to time and, returning empty, faced a woman of wrath. And when, as happened occasionally, Vanier drew in his horns, the scenes became longer and more painful.

334

Retiring from one of these to the bar on the ground floor, Verlaine met at the counter a woman whose Ardennais accent at once aroused his interest. He outlined his grievances to her over a few mutual drinks, she sympathised, he accompanied her back to her room, and when morning came, decided to make it his home.

Eugénie Krantz was fifty, six or seven years older than Philomène, and had officially ended her occupation, which she claimed had included spells with several moderately famous men. She was keeping herself alive by making shirts for the Belle Jardinière, but was not averse to a resumption of her old rôle and she perceived more clearly than the emotional Philomène that she had stumbled on a small gold mine. Apparently it was only necessary for this queer customer to scribble a few lines on a piece of paper and the paper could be exchanged for cash in Vanier's office. She had a thirst which shirt-making could not quench; she also had vague ideas of providing for her old age. Verlaine, it seemed, could do both. She began to "organise" him; if he did not write so many lines a day he would hear from her; if he did he was rewarded by drink in plenty, a home of sorts, and her favours in bed.

Verlaine settled down with her, escaping now and then to the cafés, but could not quite resign himself to the loss of Philomène. The problem was admittedly difficult: Philomène represented romance, Eugénie common sense; Philomène was a gadabout, Eugénie offered some prospect of a home of sorts; Philomène spent every sou, Eugénie talked of putting something by for a rainy day; Philomène didn't badger him into writing every hour of the day, Eugénie kept his nose to the grindstone; Philomène was jealous, Eugénie was close. One could go on for ever; all these things were necessary or desirable at one time or another. What to do? But the problem was solved for him; after a month or two, sometimes only a week or two, he was either driven out or walked out; he would not write his daily quota and Eugénie— "sometimes a bit of a shrew", he said with English understatement—would scream at him (rumour even spoke of a beating) until he fled in search of Philomène; he would slip off to a café once too often and Philomène, finding his pockets empty, would shout him into the street. And when both would have nothing to do with him he would search out his third string, Caroline Teiser, who, being made of weaker stuff, would share her all, which was not much, when he assured her that she, unlike those harridans with whom he had lately made the mistake of consorting, was his true muse and inspired him to write immortal poems. An astute move, if he made it with intention; which he partly did, for as soon as Eugénie and Philomène discovered that their goose had found another pen in which to lay his eggs they sank their differences, wrenched him bodily from the more or less gentle Caroline, demanded his money or his poems and gave him a bed under their eye. And the round began again.

3

The benefits of this somewhat stormy existence are not immediately obvious. What one sees at first is that Verlaine's life as the last great Bohemian, dispensing wisdom, good cheer and inspiration from his seat at the François Premier, is merely the outward half of the man and that it was only possible because he had at the back of him a Philomène, a Eugénie, and in the dim distance a Caroline. Also clear is the reason for his perpetual poverty. Even though constitutionally unable to keep a sou in his purse, he could not unaided have got through the money he drew from Vanier and others. Add three women to be kept, two of them voracious females with a practically unquenchable thirst, and the position is reversed: how did he manage it? one wonders, and understands the interminable begging letters which disfigure the last years.

Clear too becomes the reason for the falling away of his work. Not even Verlaine could write poems of quality with Eugénie standing over him day after day for years. The last books he wrote to celebrate the charms of Philomène and Eugénie, his *Chair* and *Odes en son Honneur*, make sad reading. He was too experienced a poet to write many lines bad in themselves, but the poems are nevertheless a travesty; the enlivening bite of humorous irony has disappeared, the source of inspiration is not so much degraded as lifeless. The interminable thighs and breasts and buttocks read like a catalogue, and the attempts to marry physical and spiritual in the persons of Eugénie and Philomène are the reverse of convincing. This late poetry, naïve in thought, unpassionate, inconsequent, reads like the poetry of an old man.

Verlaine the Lecturer, 1893

Bibi-la-Purée by Picasso

Twenty years of emotion, hardship, excess were having their effect even on Verlaine's strong body.

Nevertheless the poetry repays study; read carefully it reveals itself not as pornography, not as the maunderings of an old man, but as the sleepy-ecstatic cries of a child snuggling against his mother. And therein lay the secret of the appeal, otherwise difficult to understand, of these two not particularly prepossessing women. More than most men Verlaine resists summing up in a word or phrase; he was this, that and the other at various moments. But there were constants riding smoothly enough beneath that troubled sea and directing the passage of his apparently rudderless ship. He tells Cazals, for instance, when he hears of the death of Villiers: "His life was certainly more *worthy* than mine but not at bottom more proud. I've made greater efforts than he and I was—alas! I *was*—a more logical Christian. My falls are due to what? Shall I accuse my blood, my upbringing? But I was good, chaste . . . Oh! the drink which has developed the bug, the bacillus, the microbe of Lust to such a point in a body really built for the normal, the orderly! It's true that misfortune, a misfortune without equal I believe, did—for a time—temper me, then perhaps distempered me because I didn't practise the tempering wisely. With all my common sense I lack judgment. The moral of this I don't care for much because it smells of so-called physiology: I am a *feminine*—and this explains lots of things!!" This shows some self-perception, but he would have got nearer the truth if he had recognised that he remained above all a child. His future had been decided by the early years of indulgence, the petting, the caresses of two women, the withholding of all responsibility and practically all rebuke. He came out of this hothouse a nice boy because he had an unspoilably nice nature, but with an inclination to be coddled through life. The absence of the maternal in the young Mathilde drove him to the unbending paternalism of Rimbaud, the revolt of Rimbaud drove him into the arms of the Church, to the soothing lullaby of English country life, to the masculine Lucien, Rimbaudish in face, with his strong athletic body like Verlaine's, his rigid moral code. Then, Rimbaud dead, Lucien dead, Nouveau insupportably righteous, the power of the Church reduced by the years, he turned to the hospitals, where he was fed, dressed, undressed, reprimanded, praised like a baby, all

M

responsibility, even the shadow of it, removed, then to the brisk and dominating Cazals, and at the last reverted completely to the child in the embraces and the reproaches of Eugénie and Philomène.

For his instinct, the one failure of Mathilde apart, was unerring. He did not choose Philomène and Eugénie simply for their Ardennais accent but because that accent stood for what he most needed. The Ardennaises are a recognisable type not only by their short, square, full-bosomed bodies and harsh faces, but by their masculinity of mind, their parsimoniousness and greed. The Ardennes has for centuries housed pre-eminently a matriarchal society; almost everywhere the women rule, not with charm as in so much of southern and central France but by force of character. Eugénie was typical of her countrywomen, Philomène scarcely less so. Both were experienced in the arts of love, both knew well, as successful prostitutes must know, how to deal with their most frequent customer—the old or oldish man losing virility. Verlaine presented no problem to them; they spoiled him in bed, ruled him in and out of it and extracted every sou they could get from him, which was not difficult. He responded with childish revolts and subterfuges, but at bottom always with alacrity and gratitude.

Their rooms were bare and cold, but they were his homes; when there was a fire in the tiny grate they had lit it but he warmed himself at it, when the meal was put on the table they had cooked it but he ate it. And the less pleasant side of the relationship was at heart a consolation. When Philomène had thrown him out and he came sheepishly back to Eugénie, she would say grimly, "All right, I'll take you back, but mind, I know you and if you don't make some money pretty soon I'll send you away again." And when he had made some and they had spent it she would shout at him, "Write ten lines so that I can cash them at Vanier's." These are not the words of a woman to her lover, they are the words of a mother to her son, and as such Verlaine accepted them. And, in character, he would sometimes revolt and limp off with the air of one on a boyish escapade to what appeared at a distance as the romantic charms of Philomène, a Philomène who did not press him so hardly, who spent his money with florid gestures, who was less dour, more lively, but who alas was even more ruthless with him when his pockets had been emptied. Yet even this was in line with the "bad woman" the boy had sought; and the first explosion over he would make his way back to Eugénie with no hard feelings for either.

Hard feelings—why should he have them? They gave him what he wanted: to be cared for, to have excitement, safety, company, a home, discipline, sexual gratification, a certain mental activity and, in bed at least and on the spree, what could be interpreted by a fond man as affection. So, his poverty, his bad leg and all his other troubles notwithstanding, the appearance in his life of Philomène and Eugénie made his last years pre-eminently years of contentment; between them and his café life he could enjoy fame and domesticity, he could sit back happily as the Prince of Poets, fondle maternal limbs and cower contentedly under motherly whips. For these, to him, were all signs of that indispensable good feeling he lived for; disciples, women, all loved him; he was needed, made welcome, and his heart was warmed.

4

Not that these last six years were years of unalloyed bliss. Verlaine, it cannot be too often repeated, was a man of moods; he was not far behind Mrs Welsh, whom Carlyle described as indulging fifteen different humours within the hour. He had practical cause for discontent; he disliked poverty and discomfort, but lived in both most of the time; he disliked, in principle, raucous women, but had them most of the time; he disliked pain, but suffered it constantly; he disliked disapproval, but endured it, at a distance, all the time.

But he was not only a man of moods, he was a man with a sense of sin, not the less strong because he successfully suppressed it most of the time. Not all the time, however. Thus, for example, he was found one night by a young disciple and some friends leaning over Pont au Change staring into the Seine. Asked why he was there and alone, he answered with a sob in his voice: "I'm bored. Oh, I'm so bored! I've been thinking of throwing myself into the river." He was persuaded to dine, but remained silent, pecked at his food and would not drink. They tried to cheer him by reciting *Colloque Sentimentale.* He protested, then brightened as the poem proceeded; his eyes filled with tears at the end and he cried "Encore! Encore!" They recited *Langueur* and he became radiant and demanded that they recite the last poem of *Sagesse, C'est la fête du blé*. This done, he rose, spread his hands wide with his familiar triumphant "Voilà!" and walked back to the bridge with his disciple. He fell silent again and the young man, trying to cheer him, asked what he could do. "Recite Rimbaud's *Derrières Académiques*," said Verlaine, giving his own title to *Les Assis*. The young man spoke the lines so brilliantly parodying Coppée's *Petit-Epicier*, then, as Verlaine remained silent, began to walk away uneasily. At the end of the bridge he turned; Verlaine was looking after him with a smile "so sad and so nice" that he came back. Verlaine put a hand on his shoulder. "I owe you my thanks. Before you turned up tonight I thought of killing myself, after an evening of thoughts I don't care to remember—my loneliness, my desultory life. . . ."

The fact that Verlaine would never have found the courage to kill himself is beside the point. In these moods he had indeed "thoughts I don't care to remember": thoughts of the dead Rimbaud, his inspiration and joy and bane; of Mathilde and Georges, dead to him; of Lucien, Valade, Cros, Glatigny, Nina, Villiers, Chabrier, all gone; of the rubbish that he was sending to Vanier day after day in the name of poetry; of what he had been and what he was. Cruel thoughts, hopeless thoughts, since time could not be turned back and the dead were dead, himself included.

So Verlaine, his power gone, the reason for life gone, chose to play the fool through most of these last years. The farce went on with Verlaine for the most part resigned, in the grip of one storm after another which, as he had not lost his sense of humour, was a source of after-amusement. What to be done, for instance, about the ladies' saints days? One fell on the 14th, the other on the 15th of November. Both must be celebrated to the hilt. Each woman, well aware of the name day of her rival, took some pleasure in wrecking it, Philomène by delaying the agitated Verlaine beyond her span of twenty-four hours, Eugénie by tempting him to skip the preceding day. And whether he succumbed or resisted, the victim was in any case the lover. Verlaine moaned, laughed, dreaded the coming of November, blustered unconvincingly, and more than once ended up with Caroline.

But it was not until the first lecture tour, to Holland, that the fun became really fast and furious. When Verlaine broke the news the women's eyes were opened and he blossomed into the great poet of all time. Never before had he been so kindly treated and his life during those preliminary weeks was a dream of delight, or would have been had he not been obliged always to leave one of the two in a flaming temper.

Unhappily, precise details of the negotiations immediately prior to and after the tour are lacking; it seems either that Philomène, always the less careful of the two, was unwise enough to quarrel with the lecturer just before he set off or, which is more likely, that he chose Eugénie as the most suitable guardian of his forthcoming treasure. If so he regretted it immediately, for she relieved him of the entire one thousand francs the instant he returned, after an unseemly fracas on the landing which brought the police in. It was the last time Verlaine was to have unfriendly dealings with them. He let out a large and dignified wail: "A false welcome awaited me in Paris, hypocrisy, lies, and finally the theft—skilful and crafty as well as plausible—of certain bank-notes. . . . A most violent quarrel on my staircase led to the arrival of the concierge and the calling of the police, who, mistaking my vehement and justifiable anger for the result of stopping too long in places where one drinks, carried me off to the police station for an hour or two, not without unnecessary brutality."

His tale of woe left Philomène so unimpressed that she slammed the door in his face; Caroline was either unavailable or out of funds, and he retired in dudgeon to the Broussais. Perhaps this was just as well, since the tour had tried his leg to the utmost.

He soon discovered that he had done Eugénie an injustice; part at least of the thousand francs she had purloined was taken merely to prevent his spending it rashly elsewhere; so at least she said when news arrived of the Belgian tour. A fairly general harmony spread amongst the three in view of Belgian francs by the hundred, but with Philomène very much on the *qui vive*; and Verlaine, though privately instructing Vanier, to whom he sent some of the profits *en route*, that Eugénie could draw on them, also sent some money direct to Philomène and behaved for the rest with the utmost tact. He wrote practically identical letters to both women, the most striking difference being the opening:

"Bon chéri" to Eugénie and no more than just "Ma grosse chérie" to Philomène who was renowned for her bosom. Tact even spread itself to the final promise, "I shall send you a little more tomorrow", Verlaine not wishing to look too far ahead, "until I can faithfully hand you, bon chéri, the entire proceeds". His last greeting, however, gave "thousands and thousands of kisses" to Philomène as against the "thousands" to Eugénie.

Not surprisingly both women were at the station to meet him. But Philomène was in some respects a frail vessel not always able to keep her eye on the main chance; though it may just be that in this instance she was simply unfortunate and, a big railway station not being the happiest choice for an appearance incognito, some admirer of the moment refused to be shaken off. However this may be, when Verlaine reached the barrier at Gare de l'Est he saw Eugénie alone, Philomène accompanied by a man. He did not hesitate, went off with Eugénie and, possibly shaken by what he had seen, handed over all his profits without a murmur.

There was some talk of banking the proceeds and of leading the life that Verlaine had been promising himself during the tour and, for that matter, ever since the publication of *Amour*. "Je vais me mettre dans mes meubles!" had simply become "Nous allons" in the course of the years. But the "nous" were little better able to hold to their gains than the "je"; in two months the money was gone. He was also homeless, romance having come belatedly to Eugénie, who, without so much as a by-your-leave, set up house with a youthful barber's assistant.

Back to the Broussais went Verlaine, where he was visited amongst others by Rothenstein and by Philomène gorgeously hatted. This was the moment when she was metamorphosed into "my wife" and he introduced her to Rothenstein as such. Eugénie had become "that harlot" and "the cholera". And it was the temporarily victorious Philomène who insisted on the hundred francs advance before Verlaine went off to London a few months later, thirty francs of which she pocketed "just in case". In her miserable room in rue Broca, a room no bigger than an ordinary bathroom, a fire had been lit in honour of the American who brought the money.

The opening of the English tour was all Philomène. He kept in touch with Eugénie as a precautionary measure, but it was to his "Chère femme" that he sent money, from her that he begged a telegram, Yes or No, when the Manchester lecture was suggested, because of her that he abstained, with what effort can be imagined, from absinthe. And it was to her that after no more than five days' absence he proposed marriage or, to be exact, took up a chance remark of hers that it would be nice to be married, nice too if he returned from England with a certain begemmed bracelet which they had spoken of in exalted moments. "As for the bracelet, etc., I shall do your sweet will if at all possible. As for marriage, if you are speaking seriously it would give me *the greatest pleasure of my life* and we will go to M. le Maire as soon as you wish. This would also be the best way of settling something on you after I die. O chérie, yes, let us do it, it was always my idea. I love only you, and how greatly! Here I live the life of a pasha, for nothing, free. Dreadful dinners, theatres, music halls. But this scarcely amuses me and I would infinitely rather be near my Philomène even when she is naughty as can happen . . . sometimes! *And I don't drink* and I won't drink if my dear forbids me . . . sweetly." He thought to add later a reassuring "Don't worry about the women here. London did me great harm in that line twenty years ago. And then I love you too much."

It was to Philomène also that he wrote distractedly from London, Oxford and Manchester; distractedly because he had not spent one week in England before disillusionment set in. Eugénie's affair with the barber's assistant had lost its glamour the moment she heard of the new lecture tour; England, to her, was the land of riches; if Verlaine had made a thousand francs in Holland and in Belgium, what fortune might he not bring back from Albion! She brusquely threw off the hairdressing encumbrance and addressed herself to the work of countering the machinations of Philomène. She had met Rothenstein, who caught a glimpse of her life with Verlaine: the fearful shouting matches when Verlaine accused her of robbing him, of keeping him so short that he could neither clothe himself nor buy a friend a drink, followed by the sudden silences, each walking apart "like two cats in a yard" and Verlaine continuing his talk on literature; she now wrote to Rothenstein at Oxford. "Another person" was intriguing, she said mysteriously, he must on no account divulge Verlaine's movements or address.

The futility of this gesture no doubt struck her after she had posted the letter. She followed it with a note of sinister warning to Verlaine; she had a word of advice to give him if he wished to hear it. Genially from his bed of roses he bade her speak. She did so and to some effect: Philomène was throwing away the money he was sending her, and not on herself alone; she was living openly with a young man. To clinch the revelation she gave his name, Alfred, and, final humiliation, his age.

The news reached Verlaine incongruously in the midst of his lionising. He received it with a mixture of panic and indignation. "If this is true," he wrote to Philomène after tearing up his first attempt, "tell me frankly. It would be frank and honest even though frightful. If it isn't true, prove it. That is to say, deny it strongly. Then pardon me, and the word marriage becomes a reality."

His correspondence became positively frantic; in every spare moment—and he was allowed few—he dashed off an appeal or a warning. When the preternaturally serious lecturer retired, at Oxford, at Manchester, in London, "to prepare his notes", the notes took forms that would have surprised his audience. "Say nothing! Not a word to a soul! Silence!" to a gratified Eugénie; "O don't deceive me! The shadow of that *man* torments me" to Philomène; and, the latter's denials lacking the substance he was looking for, a harassed call for aid to Cazals: "I am jealous in this country of Othello, jealous enough to die of it if I should decide to break with that too much loved, strange and delicious *middle-aged* woman! Is it true that she is deceiving and exploiting me up to the hilt? You can find out and must tell me. Or am I cuckolding and robbing myself?"

But Cazals' report was unnecessary: Philomène, badgered by daily letters, admitted that a man had visited rue Broca, but, she explained, he was merely a young truss-maker fitting her out for a visit she intended to make to her home province in the near future.

At this Verlaine burst into a long lamentation to his "Chérie, trop!" as she had become. "I write this with death in my soul. When a fixed idea takes hold of a man, all is over. I have the impression, everything tells me so, the past, the present, 3000 francs spent or put away without any profit to me, the hints of others—all indicates to me that you have a lover, that you are living with him, and that he couldn't care less about me or you. At your age one doesn't have lovers of 29 *for nothing*! I am crushed by sorrow, I can't think of anything else."

Hope lingered on, however, and in the next sentence he explains that he is enclosing twenty-five francs, apologises for not sending more, "for I must buy some clothes and linen", and suggests a compromise: "Let us remain good friends. We can meet each other and I shall never refuse to do you a service." Then he looked at her letter again and burst out afresh: "But live with you! From the very first we have never been able to manage it with your continual changing of address. It's you who mistrust me, is it—and I don't want to sleep outside a room I've paid for. That's really a bit too expensive. Some 600 francs or thereabouts have disappeared and you want me to trust you with *all* my money. Thanks very much! and to Monsieur Alfred and to all the pimps who would lick their chops over it. You threaten to be angry with me. Mon Dieu, try it, but I have no more, in fact I have never had any confidence in you . . . and I know quite well, for instance, that your journey is imaginary, like your truss-maker, etc., etc."

But it was difficult to remain angry at a distance with the light creature: "Nevertheless I love you too much—one can love without trusting—to give you up." He tried the gentle reproach: "You who only love me—you told me so in rue Pascal—for my money, because I am only a mug, only a client, only the man who keeps you whilst others are your lovers—you said it to someone, in front of me, in rue Saint-Jacques—you ought to write nicely to me, 'Well, yes, it's true, I'm living in furnished rooms with Alfred, 20 rue de la Glacière. I have some sous in hand. When I need more I will tell you.' Then we should remain good friends. Otherwise there will always be quarrels. That's dreadful (for me), but that's how it is."

Remembering the notes to Vanier which he had scattered in happier moments, he added a gentle threat: "All those notes you have, 'I authorise' etc., are useless. *I shall draw all money myself, alone.*"

But the thought would obtrude; suppose, just suppose . . . "For the rest, if you really haven't deceived me odiously, foully, ignobly . . . and if we are to live together, let us marry and I will make sure that you have something to live on after my death. . . . In any case write quickly one way or the other. I'm

M*   345

due to leave Thursday, but will come back earlier if you agree. And, given proof, my confidence will return and I'll make you the happiest of women."

He signed himself "Your too old, alas, it seems, P. Verlaine". Then, overcome again by the sadness of the occasion, he added, "I can't bring myself to write either Mme Alfred! or 'Esther'! It's really too bad."

He waited one more day and, obtaining neither confession nor denial, recalled Eugénie, telling her to meet him at the Gare du Nord. "I am parting from Esther with great grief," he said, and, with a frankness that the occasion seemed to demand, added: "I love and shall always love that woman. But she is dangerous for me and my mind is made up. I love you also. You have always been good for me and I only work well when I'm with you. I won't say any more of the other. If she had had a better character all would have been well." This written, frankness seemed perhaps not the happiest way to regain Eugénie's regard; he hurriedly promised her a good dinner near the station before "making dodo" and assured her, and himself: "We can be happy if we are *wise*. Only it may be better to change our district. I *must* get as far away from Esther as possible. This poor girl has thrown a spell over me and things always go badly when I'm with her."

Evidently the spell was still working, for he wrote at once to his "poor dear" to announce his decision with a "Farewell! It is better so. When you need me give me a sign and I'll do all I can. But to live together is impossible. You would always be paying for young men and that would end in pork butchery."

This sounded tolerably definite; too much so for Verlaine, who made his decision appear rather less irrevocable by suggesting that, "If you want to see me", she should meet the train in Paris, when "I would have the greatest pleasure in embracing you, perhaps for the last time." This with the warning: "But don't bring someone else with you as you did on the other occasion."

History does not record whether Philomène went to meet him. It seems unlikely, since in his agitation Verlaine had given her the wrong day. In any event Eugénie carried him off in triumph, and when the elections for the Academy came up a few months later it was Eugénie who, tickled by the thought of playing Aspasia to his Pericles, stopped all supply of drink for a week so that he could array himself in the frock-coat with which to pay the necessary soliciting calls on the thirty-nine Academicians. Eugénie used afterwards to explain that he failed to become an Immortal because he had no top-hat: "He had some, but smashed them one day in a bad temper"—but this appears improbable since Verlaine, feeling unwell, excused himself when the visiting period arrived.

5

The race, needless to say, went to Eugénie, but was hotly contested almost to the finishing-post. Verlaine continued to alternate between the women and was even thrown back on Caroline for a time. When he retired to hospital for the last time at the end of 1894 Philomène and Eugénie visited him on alternate days. Both were urgently requested beforehand to "Wear a hat!" and both were introduced solemnly to the ward as "ma femme".

But when he left hospital early in 1895 Verlaine was a really sick man, scarcely able to walk. He needed a nurse more than a lover, and the still flighty Philomène scarcely filled the bill. He therefore threw in his lot perforce with Eugénie, "whom I love very much and who despite her changeable nature is to some extent indispensable to me as I cannot at the moment attend to my bad leg myself". They set up house first in rue Monsieur le Prince and finally at 39 rue Descartes behind the Panthéon. The apartment matched the dreary street and consisted of two small rooms and a small kitchen; to the left of the main staircase was the bedroom from which Verlaine rarely moved; to the right was the room where Eugénie did her sewing. The rooms were clean but bare, the only ornaments being an oil painting of Captain Verlaine and a cage of canaries. To cheer the gloomy prospect Verlaine gilded all the chairs and the bird cage.

Here came the visitors, Lepelletier and Cazals (on different days and hours), Delahaye, De Sivry, Dierx, Blémont, a host of young poets, Verlaine's English friends and as many of the crowd of curious as could get past the maid. For Eugénie was determined that Verlaine should end his days in respectability; he and she continued to quarrel violently, they drank themselves back to friendship, they lived in an unsalubrious quarter, they

dressed like beggars, they rarely had a sou to bless themselves
with, but—they had a maid. Zélie was not perhaps in the first
flight of domestics, a blowzy, bad-tempered woman on the wrong
side of fifty and as much addicted to the bottle as her master and
mistress. But, as Eugénie had said, someone must open the door
to all these callers; it was not fitting that the wife (in all but name)
of the most famous man of his time, a man who would have been
in the Academy but for a fit of temper, should have to interview
every Tom, Dick and Harry who tried to catch a glimpse of him,
or asked him to read poems, or to autograph books.

As for money, one is baffled. All Verlaine's books were selling,
he could get a franc a line for anything he cared to write, he had
at last been given a grant by the Ministry of Fine Arts, he was
receiving a hundred and fifty francs a month from a committee
including three leaders of Parisian society, Coppée, Prudhomme,
Barrès and Montesquiou, and he had written a first instalment
(also the last) of his *Confessions* for *Fin de Siècle*, a beautifully
written and wildly inaccurate account of his life up to the coming
of Rimbaud, which sold in vast numbers. Where, then, did it all
go? No one knows. Drink was inexpensive, they had no other out-
goings of moment, yet they were always hard up. One suspects
Eugénie's mattress; Verlaine was obviously failing, and she had
fears for the future.

Towards the end of the year Verlaine received a letter from
Georges, then apprenticed to a watchmaker in Belgium. This
first word from his son for fifteen years provides the most convincing proof of Verlaine's widespread fame. Mathilde had
realised at last that it was no mean thing to have been the wife
of such a man and for the rest of her life his name was to take
precedence of all others in her conversation, even of the Vicomte
she had refused. The ban on intercourse between father and son
was relaxed and the twenty-three-year-old Georges promptly
wrote, wrote in character; he would like to visit Verlaine but
could not raise the fare.

Verlaine was overjoyed. The child's photograph was still stuck
in the corner of his mirror, all his books had been sent to Georges
as they were published, one had been dedicated to him. He sent
the fare, but Georges did not appear; he had been taken ill, had
left the watchmaker and gone to his mother in Brussels. Verlaine
wrote in vain to Mathilde; she too had moved; he asked a

Belgian friend to search for them. All in vain; the boy did not come.

That winter was cold, the room scarcely heated, and a few days after he had heard from his son, late in December, he caught bronchitis. Feeling the approach of the end, he wrote his last poem. It showed that the poet lived in him still and with power:

> Les Armes ont tu leurs ordres en attendant
> De vibrer à nouveau dans des mains admirables
> Ou scélérates, et, tristes, le bras pendant,
> Nous allons, mal rêveurs, dans le vague des Fables.
>
> Les Armes ont tu leurs ordres qu'on attendait
> Même chez les rêveurs mensongers que nous sommes,
> Honteux de notre bras qui pendait et tardait,
> Et nous allons, désappointés, parmi les hommes.
>
> Armes, vibrez! mains admirables, prenez-les,
> Mains scélérates à défaut des admirables!
> Prenez-les donc et faites signe aux En-allés
> Dans les fables plus incertaines que les sables.
>
> Tirez du rêve notre exode, voulez-vous?
> Nous mourons d'être ainsi languides, presque infâmes!
> Armes, parlez! Vos ordres vont être pour nous
> La vie enfin fleurie au bout, s'il faut, des lames.
>
> La mort que nous aimons, que nous eûmes toujours
> Pour but de ce chemin où prospèrent la ronce
> Et l'ortie, ô la mort sans plus ces émois lourds,
> Délicieuse et dont la victoire est l'annonce!

He grew worse; when Delahaye called on the sixth day of the new year he whispered "I'm finished." The next day he was dressed and put into a chair so that he could lunch with two friends. He managed to eat and drink a little and talked proudly of Georges: "I shall leave him a name which will be as worthy as any other."

That night he fell from the bed; Eugénie and Zélie could not lift him back; he lay on the floor all night covered with a blanket and eiderdown.

By the time he had been put back into bed the next morning he was dying. Cazals was horrified when he saw him, but one flicker of the old Verlaine showed itself; he overheard Eugénie's whispered "He's dying", opened his eyes and murmured with a smile, "Don't sole the dead man's shoes yet."

At eight o'clock that evening, January 8, 1896, he died muttering the names of Lepelletier and Coppée. None of the old friends sent for by Cazals had arrived before his death.

The next morning the papers were full of the news and rue Descartes was crowded with people trying to pay their respects at the bedside—poets of every age and school, old patients at the hospitals, waiters from the cafés, neighbours from every street he had lived in for the last eight years, even from Cour Saint-François, not to speak of the merely curious.

There was no money in the house to pay for the funeral, or so Eugénie declared, but the Ministry of Fine Arts contributed five hundred francs and Verlaine's friends made up the rest. After a service in the church of Saint-Etienne-du-Mont the procession slowly crossed Paris to the family tomb in the Batignolles cemetery. The coffin was hidden by a mass of flowers—roses, orchids, lilac, carnations—and the following crowd grew to enormous proportions by the time the cortège began to climb the hill to rue de Clichy, the hill that Verlaine had walked so often as child, boy and man.

The chief mourner, Georges Verlaine, was absent. He had been discovered doing his military service at Lille, was notified, but to the general surprise did not arrive. His place was taken by Delahaye, Vanier, De Sivry and Cazals.

The four corners of the pall were held from rue Descartes to the church by Coppée, Lepelletier, Mendès and Montesquiou. After the service Barrès replaced Montesquiou. Then Coppée, complaining of fatigue, asked Mallarmé to take his place, hailed a cab and followed the procession at his ease, polishing up the notes for his funeral oration. Mendès did not complain of tiredness, but, showing obvious signs of boredom, bought a paper *en route* and, still holding his cord with one hand, made himself *au fait* with the day's news until the long walk was done.

6

The funeral oration in France is a serious and lengthy business. So while the old and young friends of Verlaine are showing their paces before the largest assembly ever seen in the cemetery at Batignolles let us look for a moment into the future.

To begin with Verlaine's women. The victorious Eugénie, clothed from head to foot in widow's weeds, rode in state in a carriage behind the four chief mourners. No doubt she gave an occasional thought to the man in the coffin—Eugénie was far from being heartless—but naturally the future preoccupied her. Delightful preoccupation! The death chamber crowded every hour of the day, and the enormous crowd following her carriage, had given her ideas. What a life! What a death too; for Eugénie, doing a roaring tourist trade in "the pen with which Verlaine wrote his last poem" and "the last manuscript handled by the Master"—including the fragments of the fragment of a play which she had torn to pieces and flung at Verlaine in a fury— drank herself into the grave within a year.

Philomène was there too, in the crowd; and when all had gone home, the speeches over, she knelt by the grave in tears and put a bunch of violets on the heaped wreaths. Soon afterwards she went back to her home in the Ardennes and Paris saw her no more. So she really had meant to make that journey.

Caroline was not there. Caroline, stark naked, was hammering at the door of the house in rue Descartes, shrieking that she was Verlaine's muse and must preach his fame throughout the world. She was removed to an asylum where she died mad.

We have already glanced at Mathilde in her *pension* at Nice. Her stories of the mighty were to be known and feared from one end of the Côte to the other. Yet she was far from unhappy, even though both her marriages had failed; after all, what other woman could claim to have been the wife of Paul Verlaine?

And where was Georges? Accusation and denial followed each other briskly, and hard things were said of Mathilde in the literary circles of Paris; unjust things, as it happened. She had not prevented her son from going to the funeral. The explanation was less complicated; he was in a drunken stupor. Yes, Georges too. But Georges was an alcoholic as his father was not; the poor boy was doomed from birth. He tried one thing after another and Lepelletier finally got him a job as station-master on the Metro. Nothing could save him; he died of delirium tremens in 1926.

Bibi also did not hear the speeches; stealing off with the umbrellas laid aside by the orators, he hurriedly sold them and, temporarily in funds, proudly paraded the Latin Quarter, in Verlaine's clothes, presented by a suddenly generous Eugénie, until they fell to pieces.

Lepelletier, whose oration was so dull that we cannot possibly repeat it, became a Député and secured the inevitable ribbon across his chest. When one talked to him of revolutions he would smile indulgently, the kind of smile he gave whenever Verlaine was mentioned. He was indefatigable in trying to arrange for the erection of a statue of "poor Paul", a statue cleansed, of course, of every trace of riotous living. He died full of honours, respected by all; and if many a hand was lifted to stifle a yawn during his lifetime not a voice was raised against him afterwards.

Mendès remained the persistently golden-haired Apollo of a certain set for many years. He never precisely achieved anything though he was always on the verge of it, but his triumphs with women were prodigious. He produced in company many an anecdote of his old friend Paul, whose genius he had spotted at a glance; the grain of truth in these anecdotes tended to become obscured by the years, but he told them exceedingly well.

Coppée was rich in reminiscences too. He did not exaggerate much, but grew sentimental readily. He died rich, popular, hard-working to the last. If one can barely restrain a shudder when contemplating the successful poetaster who was once a charming and imaginative young poet, that is merely kicking against the pricks.

Heredia, who was not at the funeral, was elected Prince of Poets in Verlaine's place and thereafter talked of his predecessor with majestic magnanimity. He was succeeded after two years by Dierx, melancholy to the last but a good poet.

Within a month of the funeral Vanier too was dead. He had earned his immortality.

7

But it is time to return to the grave. The orators, spurred by the size of their audience, had seized their chance. Eloquence of a kind rarely surpassed in the Batignolles cemetery flowed over the resting place of the dead man. Coppée had polished to some purpose. "Let us respectfully salute the tomb of a true poet and bow before the coffin of a child. Paul Verlaine and I had barely passed our twentieth year when we met each other, exchanged our first confidences and read our earliest verses. I see once more our two heads bent fraternally over the same page and once more I feel our admirations, our enthusiasms, our dreams in all their youthful ardour. We were two children marching confidently towards the future. But Verlaine never encountered experience, that cold and inescapable companion who takes us by the hand and leads us along the thorny path— he remained a child always. . . .

"Happy the child who, falling heavily and raising himself tearfully, immediately forgets his pain and trouble and whose eyes still wet with tears gaze eagerly and rapturously on nature and life. And happy the poet who like our poor friend here preserves the heart of a child, the child's freshness of vision and feeling and instinctive need of love, who sins without perversity, repents whole-heartedly, loves openly and believes in God. . . .

"Happy that poet! I dare to repeat it knowing full well how Paul Verlaine suffered in his sick body and sad heart. Child as he was he faced the world defenceless and life wounded him often and cruelly. But suffering is the privilege of genius, a word which we must use when we speak of Verlaine, for his name will always stand for a new form of poetry which will always remain as one of the most important innovations in French literature. Yes, Verlaine created a type of poetry peculiar to himself, with an inspiration at once naïve and subtle, compounded of fine shades of feeling evoking the most delicate vibrations of the nerves, the most fugitive echoes of the heart, yet a most natural poetry fresh from its source and at times not far from the popular; a poetry in which the free and broken metre preserves a delightful harmony, the stanzas swaying and singing like the chant of a child, the exquisite lines filled with music. And in this inimitable poetry he has told us of the ardours, failings, remorse and tender dreams which have troubled his innocent heart.

"Such poems are made to live and I declare that the companions of Paul Verlaine's youth who have worked hard at their art would instantly renounce the pleasures and vanities of a happy life and accept the hungry days and shelterless nights of 'Pauvre Lelian' if they knew that they would leave behind them, like him, pages that will never die and would see the immortal laurel bloom over their tomb."

Mendès had been reading his newspaper too earnestly: "Paul Verlaine, you who are on the borders of night, my voice expresses the sorrow of the brothers of your youth with a last Adieu! and communicates to you their undying admiration.

"You passed away in suffering. Your martyrdom is ended. May God give you what you hoped for! But amongst us your fame remains imperishable for you have erected a monument like unto none other. By shallow marble steps, through the melancholy whisper of roseate bays we mount to a great white chapel wherein fair wax tapers shine! And as the Kingdom of heaven belongs to the meek in spirit so the Kingdom of fame belongs to the simple in genius. We love you and lament you, poor dead; we adore you, pure immortal."

Mallarmé: "From generation to generation when youthful lips open, *Fêtes Galantes*, *La Bonne Chanson*, *Sagesse*, *Amour* and *Parallèlement* will be poured out in a melodious stream quenching their thirst with an immortal flow of exquisite French. Paul Verlaine, his genius soaring into the future, remains a hero. . . . An example rarely furnished by the centuries, our contemporary faced all the terrors of the fate of the singer and dreamer, for solitude, cold, discomfort, poverty is the lot of him who with ingenuous hardihood walks through life at the bidding of his inspiration."

Kahn: "I desire in the name of myself and of other poets younger than I to bid a last farewell to the most profound, most tender, most exquisite of French poets, the one whom we loved most of all."

Barrès: "Paul Verlaine had neither official position, wealth nor influential friends. He did not belong to the Academy. . . . The essential part of him was his ability to feel and the accents which communicated these feelings, accents French to the core and imbued with those tender and thrilling beauties which have no analogy except in another art. . . . Verlaine, linked to François Villon by the freedom and charm of his genius, helps us to understand one of the principal facets of the French contribution to literature. Henceforth his ideas will take their place amongst those which form the national heritage—and this thanks to the younger generation. It is by our constant propaganda, our generous love, our active clear-sightedness that the work of Paul Verlaine, repulsed by his friends and rivals save a few to whom public opinion renders homage, has triumphed over the obstacles which six years ago might have seemed insurmountable."

Moréas: "I speak as one of Paul Verlaine's oldest friends among those who are called the poets of the new school. But let us leave schools alone. Today we think only of poetry; and from Victor Hugo to Leconte de Lisle, from Leconte de Lisle to the youngest amongst us, just as from Villon to Ronsard, from Ronsard to Malherbe and Jean Racine, this poetry of the French bids us lament the loss of one of its greatest exponents. The author of *Sagesse*, *Jadis et Naguère* and *Amour* must be admired as an illustrious poet in the absolute sense of that word. . . . Adieu, Paul Verlaine . . . your name will not perish."

8

What is one to say of all this? Of the seven men who spoke at Verlaine's graveside Lepelletier had been disapprovingly helpful; Mendès had shunned Verlaine for the last nine years; from the depths of his sheltered existence Mallarmé talked boldly of sufferings he had never experienced and had no intention of experiencing, he admired the poet, but was so obviously distressed by the man that Verlaine kept away from him; Kahn admired the poet with reservations but made public and cruel fun of the man; Barrès admired the poet too but had long since drawn clear of the man, and his assumption that the poet was made by the younger generation, himself well included, was wildly far from the mark; Moréas, blown up with a vanity which time has not justified, admired neither man nor poet. He had quarrelled with Verlaine, a quarrel of his own making, and had written of his work: "Verlaine, aged fifty, has published some little books; the earlier ones had some pretty, musical things in them. But all these small poems of a page or two at most, struck out at random, are all so much wind. They don't make a work of art." Coppée alone had an inkling of the man behind the poems and of the true stature of the poet, though his assertion that he would have changed places with Verlaine if he could must be taken as poetic licence. He had refused to vote for his old friend's inclusion in the third *Parnasse Contemporain*; he had not, a visit or two to the hospital excepted, set eyes on him for twenty-three years; he had given him money but wanted nothing to do with him socially.

What, then, is one to say of these speeches? Rimbaud would have had a word for them, but Rimbaud would have missed the point as he often did. The subject of the eulogies would have seen the point, as he usually did. These seven men were following the tradition of their country in standing up and glorifying the memory of their one-time friend. "Today we think only of poetry," said Moréas. What he meant was, speaking for the whole French nation, "Today we think only of the decencies." They had come to bury Verlaine and to praise him. Yet out of the mouths of these men, mouths filled with formalities, came, all unknown to them, truth.

BIBLIOGRAPHY

MANUSCRIPTS OF OR CONCERNING VERLAINE

Archives du Département de la Seine, Paris.
Bibliothèque Nationale, Paris.
Bibliothèque Royale de Bruxells.
Bibliothèque Sainte-Geneviève, Paris.
Bodleian, Oxford.
British Museum.
Musée Rimbaud, Charleville.
Musée Royale, Brussels.
Préfecture de la Seine, Paris.

WORKS BY VERLAINE

Confessions, Paris, 1895.
Correspondance, Paris, 1922-1929.
Mémoires d'un Veuf, Paris 1886.
Mes Hôpitaux, Paris, 1891.
Mes Prisons, Paris, 1893.
Œuvres Complètes, Paris, 1899, 1911, 1926.
Œuvres Oubliées, Paris, 1926, 1929.
Œuvres Poétiques Complètes. Ed. Dantec, Paris, 1938, 1940, 1947, 1954.
Œuvres Posthumes, Paris, 1903, 1929.
Quinze Jours en Hollande, Paris 1893.

BOOKS ON OR CONCERNING VERLAINE

ADAM, A., *Verlaine, l'homme et l'œuvre*, Paris, 1953.
ANON., *Paul Verlaine et ses contemporains*, Paris, 1897.
CARRÉ, J.-M., *Autour de Verlaine et de Rimbaud*, Paris, 1949.
CAZALS, F.-A., *Paul Verlaine. Ses portraits*, Paris, 1896.
CAZALS, F.-A. & LEROUGE, G., *Les derniers jours de Paul Verlaine*, Paris, 1911.
COULON, M., *Au cœur de Verlaine et de Rimbaud*, Paris, 1925.
—— *Verlaine, Poète saturnien*, Paris, 1933.
DELAHAYE, ERNEST, *Documents relatifs à Verlaine*, Paris, 1919. *Verlaine*, Paris, 1919.
—— *Souvenirs familiers à propos de Rimbaud, Verlaine, etc.*, Paris, 1925.

BIBLIOGRAPHY

DONOS, C., *Verlaine intime*, Paris, 1898.

FONTAINAS, A., *Verlaine-Rimbaud. Ce qu'on présume de leurs relations; ce qu'on sait*, Paris, 1931.

FONTAINE, A., *Verlaine, homme de lettres*, Paris, 1937.

LEPELLETIER, EDMOND, *Paul Verlaine*, Paris, 1907.

MONTEL, F., *Bibliographie de Paul Verlaine*, Paris, 1924.

MORICE, C., *Verlaine*, Paris, 1888.

MOUQUET, J., *Rimbaud raconté par Verlaine*, Paris, 1934.

NICOLSON, HAROLD, *Verlaine*, London, 1921.

PORCHÉ, F., *Verlaine tel qu'il fut*, Paris, 1933.

ROBERTS, C. E. B., *Paul Verlaine*, London, 1937.

RUCHON, F., *Verlaine. Documents iconographiques*, Paris, 1947.

SÉCHÉ, A. & BERTAUT, J., *Paul Verlaine*, Paris, 1910

UNDERWOOD, V. P., *Chronologie verlainienne*, Lille, 1938.

—— *Verlaine en Angleterre*, Paris, 1956.

VAN BEVER, A. & MONDA, M., *Bibliographie et iconographie de Verlaine*, Paris, 1926.

VERLAINE, MATHILDE, *Mémoires de ma vie*, Paris, 1935.

VIVY, M. LE FEBVE DE, *Les Verlaines*, Brussels, 1928.

BOOKS ON OR CONCERNING RIMBAUD

CARRÉ, J.-M., *La vie aventureuse de Rimbaud*, Paris, 1926.

DELAHAYE, E., *Rimbaud*, Paris, 1923. *Les Illuminations et Une Saison en Enfer de Rimbaud*, Paris, 1927.

ETIEMBLE, R., *Le Mythe de Rimbaud*, Paris, 1952, 1954.

GODCHOT, COLONEL, *Arthur Rimbaud 'ne varietur'*, Nice 1936-1937.

IZAMBARD, G., *Rimbaud tel que je l'ai connu*, Paris, 1946.

RIMBAUD, A., *Les Illuminations. Notice par P. Verlaine*, Paris, 1886.

—— *Œuvres complètes*. Ed. R. de Renéville et J. Mouquet, Paris, 1946.

—— Poèmes. *Les Illuminations. Une Saison en Enfer. Notice par P. Verlaine*, Paris, 1892.

—— *Poésies*, Ed. H. Bouillane de Lacoste, Paris, 1947. *Illuminations*, Ed. H. de Bouillane de Lacoste, Paris, 1949. *Une Saison en Enfer*, Paris, 1951.

—— *Poésies complètes. Avec une préface de P. Verlaine*, Paris, 1895.

RIMBAUD, ISABELLE, *Mon frère Arthur*, Paris, 1920.

RIMBAUD, I. & BERRICHON, P., *Rimbaud. Ebauches et correspondance*, Paris, 1937.

STARKIE, E., *Arthur Rimbaud*, London, 1938, 1947. *Rimbaud en Abyssinie*, Paris, 1938.

BIBLIOGRAPHY

BOOKS ON OR CONCERNING
THE VERLAINE CIRCLE

AICARD, JEAN, *La poésie de Jean Aicard*, Paris, 1909.

BANVILLE, THÉODORE DE, *Mes souvenirs*, Paris, 1882. *Nouveaux souvenirs*, Paris, 1890.

BAUDELAIRE, CHARLES, *Maître et disciple, Charles Baudelaire et Léon Cladel* by Judith Cladel, Paris, 1951. *Charles Baudelaire* by A. Séché and J. Bertaut, Paris, 1910. *Correspondance générale*, Paris 1917-1953.

BLÉMONT, ÉMILE, *Emile Blémont* by F. Clerget, Paris, 1906.

BLOY, LÉON, *Vie de Léon Bloy* by Bollery, Paris, 1938.

CALLIAS, HECTOR DE, *Le livre de la vie*, Paris, 1862.

CHABRIER, EMMANUEL, *Emmanuel Chabrier d'après ses lettres*, Ed. J. Desaymand, Paris, 1934.

CLADEL, LÉON, *La vie de Léon Cladel* by Judith Cladel, Paris, 1905.

COPPÉE, FRANÇOIS, Preface to *Poèmes de Paul Verlaine*, Paris, 1904. *François Coppée* by M. F. A. de Lescure, Paris, 1889. *Lettres à sa mère et à sa sœur, 1862-1908*, Paris, 1914. *Souvenirs d'un Parisien*, Paris, 1910. *La vie et l'œuvre de François Coppée* by L. le Meur, Paris, 1932. *Toute une jeunesse*, Paris, 1911.

CORBIÈRE, TRISTAN, *Tristan Corbière* by R. Martineau, Paris, 1925. *Tristan Corbière. Un essai par Jean Rousselot*, Paris, 1951.

D'ALQ, LOUISE D', *Causeries familières*, Paris, 1882-4.

DESBORDES-VALMORE, MARCELINE, *Le vie douloureuse de Marceline Desbordes-Valmore* by L. Descaves, Paris, 1911.

DIERX, LÉON, *Léon Dierx* by E. Noulet, Paris, 1925.

FANTIN-LATOUR, I., *Fantin-Latour: sa vie et ses amitiés* by Adolphe Jullien, Paris, 1909. *Fantin-Latour* by G. Kahn, Paris, 1927.

FÉNÉON, FELIX, *Œuvres de Felix Fénéon*. Introd. by Jean Paulhan, Paris, 1948.

FORAIN, JEAN, *En écoutant Forain* by L. Vaillat, Paris, 1931.

FRANCE, ANATOLE, *Le vie et les opinions d'Anatole France* by Anatole Thibault, Paris, 1925. *Les carnets intimes d'Anatole France*, Ed. L. Carias, Paris, 1946. *Anatole France* by Edwin P. Dargan, London, 1937. *La vie littéraire*, Paris, n.d.

GILL, ANDRÉ, *André Gill, sa vie* by A. Lods, Paris, 1887.

GLATIGNY, ALBERT, *Lettres d'A. Glatigny à Théodore de Banville*, Paris, 1923. *Albert Glatigny: La vie—l'homme—le poète* by J. Reymond, Paris, 1936.

GONCOURT BROTHERS, *The Goncourt Journals, 1851-1870*, London, 1937.

GOURMONT, RÉMY DE, *Promenades littéraires*, Paris, 1909.

BIBLIOGRAPHY

HEREDIA, J. M. DE, *The technique of the French Alexandrine: A study of the works of J. M. de Heredia* by H. P. Thième, London, 1898. *José-Maria de Heredia* by Miodrag Ibrovac, Paris, 1923.

HUGO, VICTOR, *Olympio* by André Maurois, Paris, 1954.

HUYSMANS, J.-K., *Souvenirs*, Paris, 1924.

KAHN, GUSTAVE, *Silhouettes littéraires*, Paris, 1925. *Les origines du symbolisme*, Paris, 1936.

LAFORGUE, JULES, *Jules Laforgue et ses poésies* by Léon Guichard, Paris, 1950. *Jules Laforgue and the ironic inheritance* by Warren Ramsay, London, 1953.

LECONTE DE LISLE, CHARLES, *Leconte de Lisle* by Irving Brown, New York, 1929. *Leconte de Lisle* by P. C. J. Bourget, Paris, 1886. *Leconte de Lisle and his contemporaries* by Irving Putter, New York, 1951. *Leconte de Lisle intime* by Jean Dormis, Paris, 1895. *Un Demi-siècle littéraire. Leconte de Lisle et ses amis* by F. Calmettes, Paris, 1902.

LEMERRE, A., *Le livre du bibliophile*, Paris, 1874.

MAETERLINCK, M., *Life and writings of Maurice Maeterlinck* by Jethro Bithell, London, 1913. *Bulles bleues*, Monaco, 1948.

MALLARMÉ, STÉPHANE, *Mallarmé* by Wallace Fowlie, London, 1953. *L'Amitié de Verlaine et Mallarmé* by H. Mondor, Paris, 1939. *Vie de Mallarmé* by H. Mondor, Paris, 1946. *Autobiographie*, Paris, 1924. *Stéphane Mallarmé 1842-1898. Poèmes et lettres*, Paris, 1948. *Les Miens*, Brussels, 1892. *Correspondance inédite de Stéphane Mallarmé*, Geneva, 1949. *Mallarmé par un des siens* by E. Dujardin, Paris, 1936. *Divagations*, Paris, 1897. *Verlaine, professeur à Rethel*, Paris, 1897.

MÉNARD, LOUIS, *Louis Ménard et son œuvre* by P. Berthelot, Paris, 1902.

MENDÈS, CATULLE, *Le mouvement poétique française de 1867-1900*, Paris, 1903. *La légende du Parnasse contemporain*, Brussels, 1884. *La maison de la vieille*, Paris, 1914.

MÉRAT, ALBERT, *Œuvres choisies, 1863-1904*, Paris, 1906. *Vers le soir. Impressions et souvenirs*, Paris, 1900.

MERRILL, STUART, *Stuart Merrill* by Marjorie L. Henry, London, 1927.

MORÉAS, JEAN, *Jean Moréas* by R. Niklaus, Paris, 1936. *Adieu à Moréas* by A. M. Barrès, Paris, 1910.

NOUVEAU, GERMAIN, *La vie étrange d'Humilis*, by Léon Verane, Paris, 1929. *Valentines.* Preface by Ernest Delahaye, Paris, 1921. *Œuvres poétiques*, Paris, 1953. *Poésies d'Humilis et vers inédits*, Paris, 1924. *Germain Nouveau et Rimbaud* by Jean Richepin, Paris, 1927.

RÉGAMEY, F., *Verlaine dessinateur*, Paris, 1896.

RETTÉ, ADOLPHE, *Le Symbolisme. Anecdotes et souvenirs*, Paris, 1903. *Adolphe Retté* by W. K. Cornell, London, 1942.

BIBLIOGRAPHY

RICARD, L.-X. DE, *Ciel, rue et foyer*, Paris, 1866. *Mémoires d'une déclassée.* Paris, 1903. *Petites mémoires d'un Parnassien*, Paris, 1898-1900. *Anatole France et le Parnasse contemporain*, Paris, 1902.

RICHEPIN, JEAN, *Mes paradis*, Paris, 1894. *Recueil de morceaux choisis*, Paris, 1912. *Souvenirs*, La Revue de France 1920-1930.

ROTHENSTEIN, WILLIAM, *Men and memories*, London, 1931-9. *Paul Verlaine: Three Portraits*, London, 1931-9.

SILVESTRE, PAUL ARMAND, *Portraits et souvenirs 1886-1891*, Paris, 1891.

SIVRY, CHARLES DE, *Souvenirs et regrets*, Paris, 1901.

SUARÈS, ANDRÉ, *Cité, nef de Paris*, Paris, 1934. *André Suarès et Paul Claudel: Correspondance*, Paris, 1951.

SULLY PRUDHOMME, *The technique of the French Alexandrine. A study of the works of Sully Prudhomme* by H. P. Thième, London, 1898. *Sully Prudhomme et sa pensée* by P. Flottes, Paris, 1930. *Journal intime. Lettres—pensées*, Paris, 1922.

SYMONS, ARTHUR, *Collected Works*, London, 1924.

VALADE, LÉON, *Léon Valade. Conférence, etc.*, by Jules Truffier, Paris, 1904. *Œuvres*, Paris, 1887.

VALÉRY, PAUL, *Villon et Verlaine*, Paris, 1937.

VANIER, LÉON, *Examen du manifeste*, Paris, 1889. *Les premières armes du symbolisme*, Paris, 1889.

VIÉLÉ-GRIFFIN, FRANCIS, *Son œuvre* by J. de Cours, Paris, 1930.

VILLIERS DE L'ISLE-ADAM, AUGUSTE, *Villiers de l'Isle-Adam* by R. Y. M. du Pontavice de Heussey, London, 1894. *Villiers de l'Isle-Adam* by F. Clerget, Paris, 1921. *Villiers de l'Isle-Adam* by M. Daireaux, Paris, 1936. *Faces et profils. Souvenirs de Villiers de l'Isle-Adam, J. Laforgue etc.*, by H. de Régnier, Paris, 1931.

ZILCKEN, PHILIPPE, *Paul Verlaine*, Paris, 1897. *Souvenirs*, Paris, 1900. *Au jardin du passé*, The Hague, 1930.

OTHER WORKS CONSULTED

ADAM, MME, *Chez les passants*, Paris, 1890. *Mes sentiments et mes idées avant 1870*, Paris, 1905.

Autour du Symbolisme, Lille, 1955.

BÉDIER, C. M. J. & HAZARD, P., *Histoire de la littérature française illustré*, Paris, 1923-4.

BERGERAT, A. E., *Souvenirs d'un enfant de Paris*, Paris, 1911-13.

BERSAUCOURT, A. DE, *Au temps des Parnassiens: Nina de Villard et ses amis*, Paris, 1925.

BINGHAM, D., *Recollections of Paris*, London, 1898.

BONNIÈRES, R. DE, *Mémoires d'aujourd'hui*, Paris, 1883-8.

BOURGET, P. C. J., *Quelques témoignages*, Paris, 1928-33.

BIBLIOGRAPHY

CAREL, A., *Histoire anecdotique des contemporains*, Paris, 1885.

CASSAGNE, A., *La théorie de l'art pour l'art chez les derniers romantiques et chez les premiers parnassiens*, Paris, 1906.

DAUDET, ALPHONSE, *Alphonse Daudet* by Léon Daudet, Paris, 1898.

DEMONT-BRENTON, V., *Maisons que j'ai connues*, Paris, 1927. *Nos amis artistes*, Paris, 1928.

DUFOY, P., *Chez Nina de Villard*, Paris, 1927.

ELLIS, HAVELOCK, *From Rousseau to Proust*, London, 1936.

ELTON, OLIVER, *Frederick York Powell*, London, 1906.

FORD, F. M., *Return to yesterday*, London, 1931.

FOUCHER, PAUL HENRI, *Les coulisses du passé*, Paris, 1873.

GOSSE, E. W., *Collected Essays: French profiles*, London, 1912.

GRIERSON, J. FRANCIS, *Parisian portraits*, London, 1911.

HARRIS, FRANK, *Contemporary portraits*, London, 1925.

HOUSSAYE, ARSÈNE, *Mes confessions*, Paris, 1885.

HURET, JULES, *Enquête sur l'évolution littéraire*, Paris, 1901.

JADART, HENRI, *Souvenirs*, Paris, 1899.

JEZIERSKI, LOUIS, *La bataille des Sept Jours*, Paris, 1892.

LE GALLIENNE, RICHARD, *The Romantic Nineties*, London, 1901.

LELEUX, CHARLES, *Quand nous étions jeunes . . .* , Paris, 1930. *Mémorial du Collège Notre-Dame de Rethel*, Paris, 1933.

MAY, JAMES L., *John Lane and the Nineties*, London, 1936.

MARTINO, PIERRE, *Parnasse et symbolisme*, Paris, 1925.

MOORE, G., *Impressions and opinions*, London, 1891.

MORICE, CHARLES, *Quelques maîtres modernes*, Paris, 1921.

O'SHAUGHNESSY, A., *Songs of a worker*, London, 1881.

RAYNAUD, ERNEST, *La bohème sous le second empire*, Paris, 1930. *La mêlée symboliste*, Paris, 1918. *Souvenirs de police au temps de Ravachol*, Paris, 1923.

RÉGNIER, H. DE, *De mon temps*, Paris, 1933.

RENARD, JULES, *Journal*, Paris, 1901.

SAINTE-BEUVE, *Correspondance*, Paris, 1877.

SOURIAU, M., *Histoire du Parnasse*, Paris, 1929.

TAILHADE, LAURENT, *Quelques fantômes de jadis*, Paris, 1920.

THEURIET, ANDRÉ, *Souvenirs des vertes saisons*, Paris, 1903.

VERHAEREN, ÉMILE, *Impressions*, Paris, 1928.

WILSON, EDMUND, *Axel's Castle*, New York, 1931.

ZOLA, ÉMILE, *Documents littéraires*, Paris, 1894.

INDEX

INDEX

Istace, M., 184
Izambard, Georges, 145-7, 150, 258, 284

Kahn, Gustave, 282, 283, 285, 295, 296, 300, 302, 311, 354, 355
Krantz, Eugénie, 332-6, 338-44, 346-51

Lafenestre, Georges, 46
La Fontaine, 209, 331
Lamartine, 88
Lancret, 102
Landry, M., 26, 27, 38, 39
Lane, John, 327, 328, 330, 331
Langlois, Fernand, 323, 324
Lecocq, 81
Leconte de Lisle, 36, 41, 50, 62-4, 73-8, 80, 82, 85, 86, 88-94, 103, 108, 110, 111, 122, 123, 131, 132, 146, 150, 160, 161, 163, 182, 216, 233, 234, 260, 264, 280, 292, 299, 301, 303, 314, 325
Lemaître, Jules, 302
Lemerre, Alphonse, 90-3, 97, 101, 102, 111, 124, 131, 155, 162, 215, 234, 263, 305, 308, 309
Leopold of Hohenzollern, 125-7
Lepelletier, Edmond, 29-31, 34, 35, 37, 38, 40, 45, 48, 64, 65, 85, 92, 109-11, 121, 128, 131, 138-40, 156, 159, 160, 183, 184, 186-9, 191, 216, 217, 219, 222, 224, 228, 232, 244, 247, 249, 260, 262, 280-3, 292, 298, 309, 321, 347, 350, 352, 355
Létinois, Lucien, 252-64, 266-70, 272, 275, 277, 285, 304, 337, 340
Létinois, M., 253-5, 257, 259, 261-3, 270
Létinois, Mme, 254-7, 259, 261-3, 270
Levi, Eliphas, 86
Lily the Vouzinoise, 274, 288, 306
London, Theodore, 330
Louis Napoleon, 21, 22, 24, 33, 34, 38, 49, 65, 66, 101, 125, 126, 128, 130, 131
Louis Philippe, 14, 19, 21, 75
Louis XVIII, 14
Louise, the maid, 138, 139

MacMahon, Marshal, 127, 138, 142
Maeterlinck, 317-20
Malherbe, 355
Mallarmé, 70, 71, 86, 99, 104, 110, 132, 158, 168, 233, 249, 260, 264, 279, 280, 282, 286, 299-301, 306, 308, 316, 317, 322, 350, 354, 355
Mallarmé, Mlle, 300
Mallarmé, Mme, 300
Manet, 66, 85, 92, 322
Manning, Cardinal, 244
Manoury, Marquise de, 124
Matuszewicz, M., 200, 206
Maupassant, 258
Mauté, M., 115, 117, 118, 120, 122, 124, 132, 133, 138, 141, 152, 157, 165, 167, 173, 187, 216, 218, 244, 251-3, 268, 271, 277, 281, 292
Mauté, Mme, 112, 115, 118, 132-4, 138, 141, 153, 154, 165, 178, 251, 271, 277
Ménard, Louis, 52, 73-5, 77, 131
Mendelssohn, 186
Mendès, Catulle, 36, 50, 52-64, 66, 68-78, 80, 82, 84, 86-95, 97, 99, 111, 131, 215, 216, 233, 262, 264, 278, 294, 302, 305, 308-10, 350, 352, 354, 355
Mendès, Judith (Gautier), 91, 131, 233
Mérat, Albert, 46-8, 50, 59, 85, 91, 110, 121, 132, 152, 158-60, 163, 184, 233, 263-5, 278
Michel, Louise, 130, 137, 140
Milton, 229
Mince, Georges, 319, 320
Moncomble, Elisa, 18-20, 24-7, 41, 43, 97, 106, 107, 109, 267, 268
Moncomble, Victor, 26, 27
Montesquiou, Robert de, 308, 311, 348, 350

INDEX

INDEX

INDEX

Printed in Great Britain
by T. and A. CONSTABLE LTD., Hopetoun Street,
Printers to the University of Edinburgh